BLADE

OF THE IMMORTAL

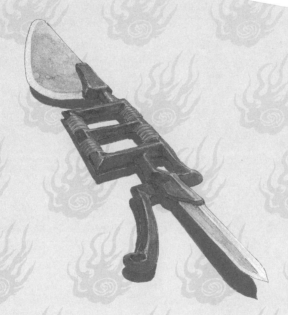

Raining Chaos

publisher
Mike Richardson

editor
Philip R. Simon

assistant editor
Everett Patterson

collection designer
Kat Larson

digital production
Ryan Jorgensen

Dedicated to Toren Smith.

Special thanks to Michael Gombos,
Annie Gullion, Dana Lewis, and Rich Powers.

Dark Horse Manga
A division of Dark Horse Comics, Inc.
10956 SE Main Street
Milwaukie, OR 97222

DarkHorse.com

To find a comics shop in your area, call the
Comic Shop Locator Service toll-free at 1-888-266-4226.

First edition: January 2014
ISBN 978-1-61655-321-0

1 3 5 7 9 10 8 6 4 2

Printed in the United States of America

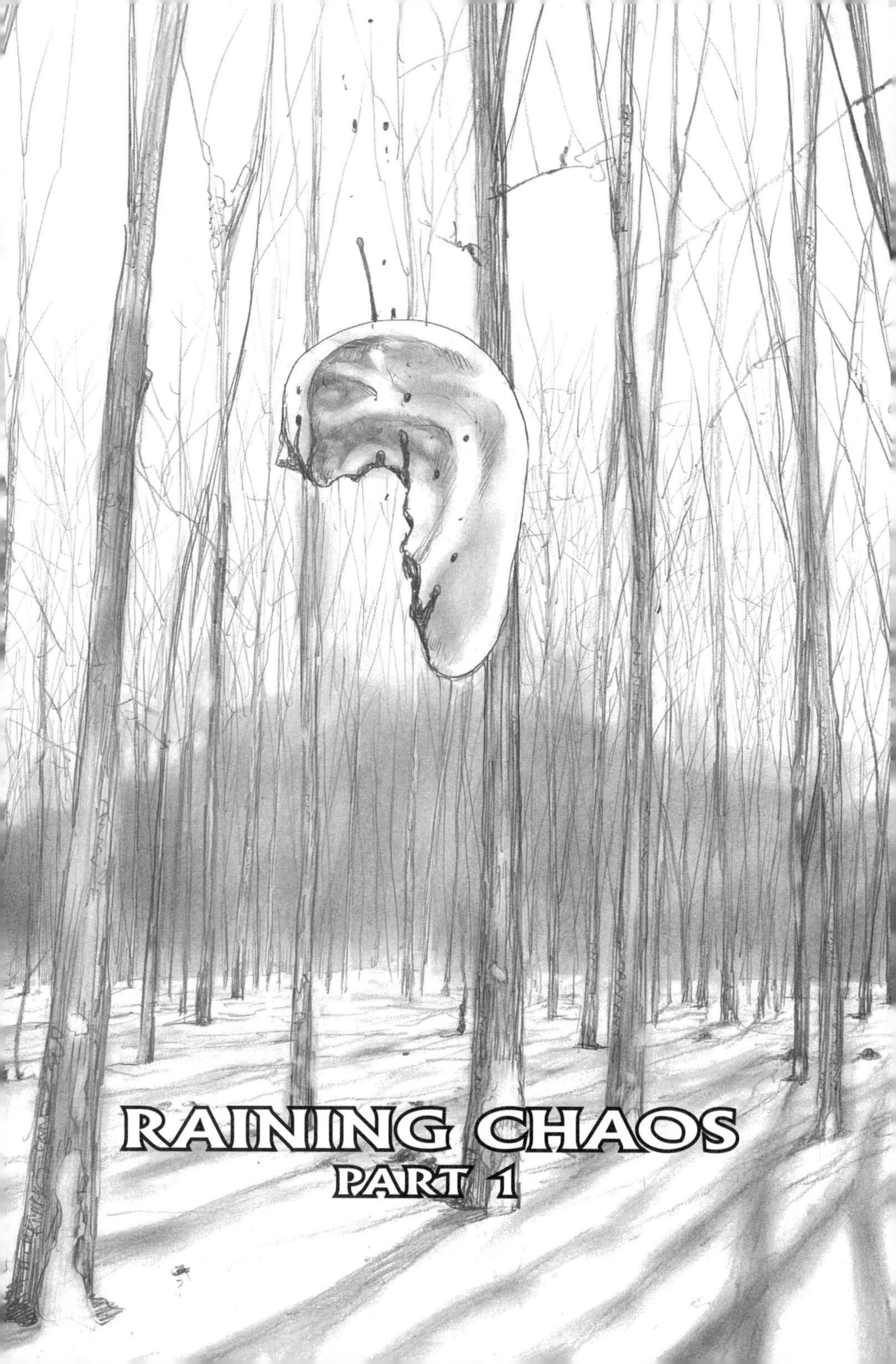
RAINING CHAOS
PART 1

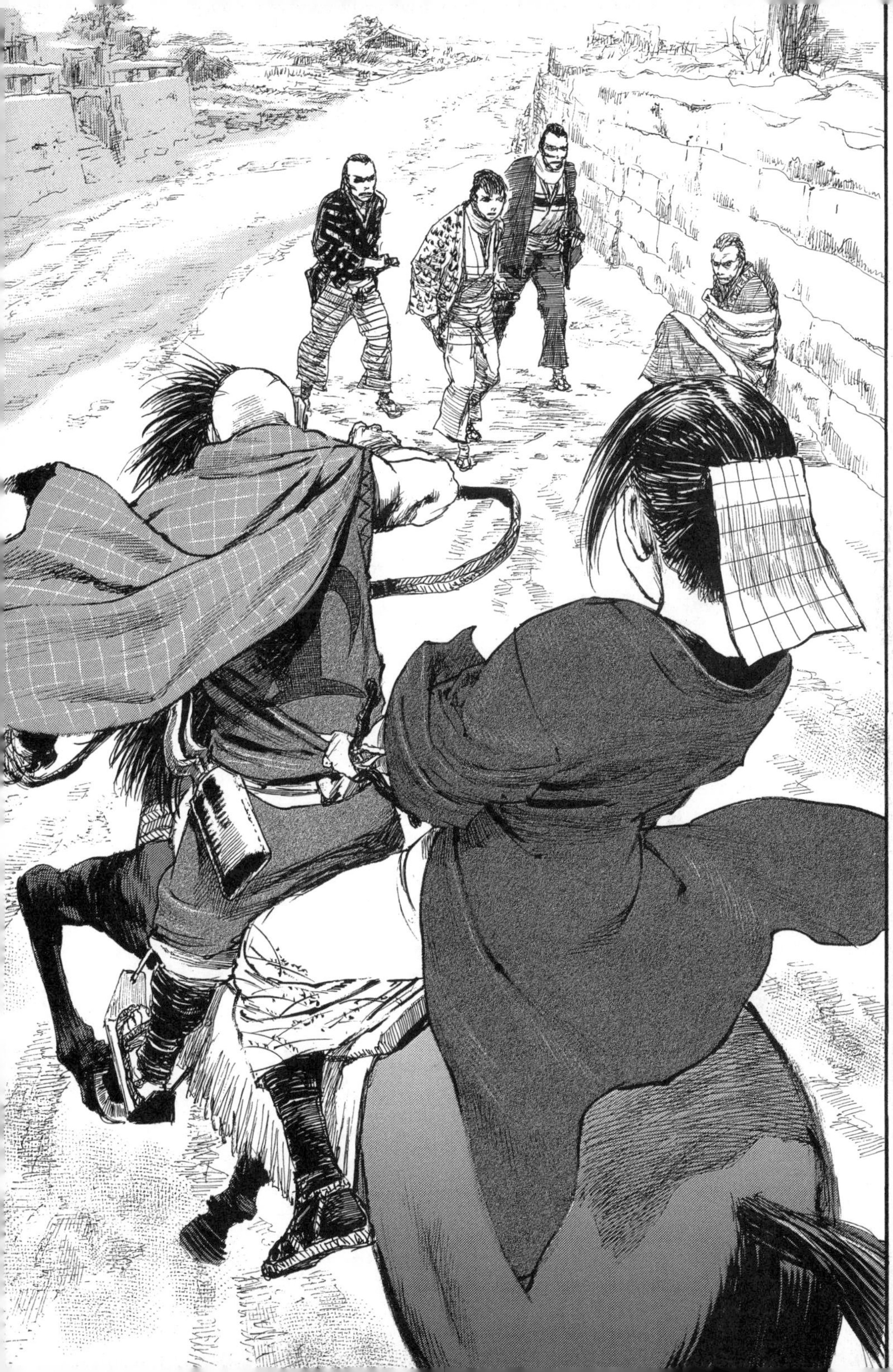

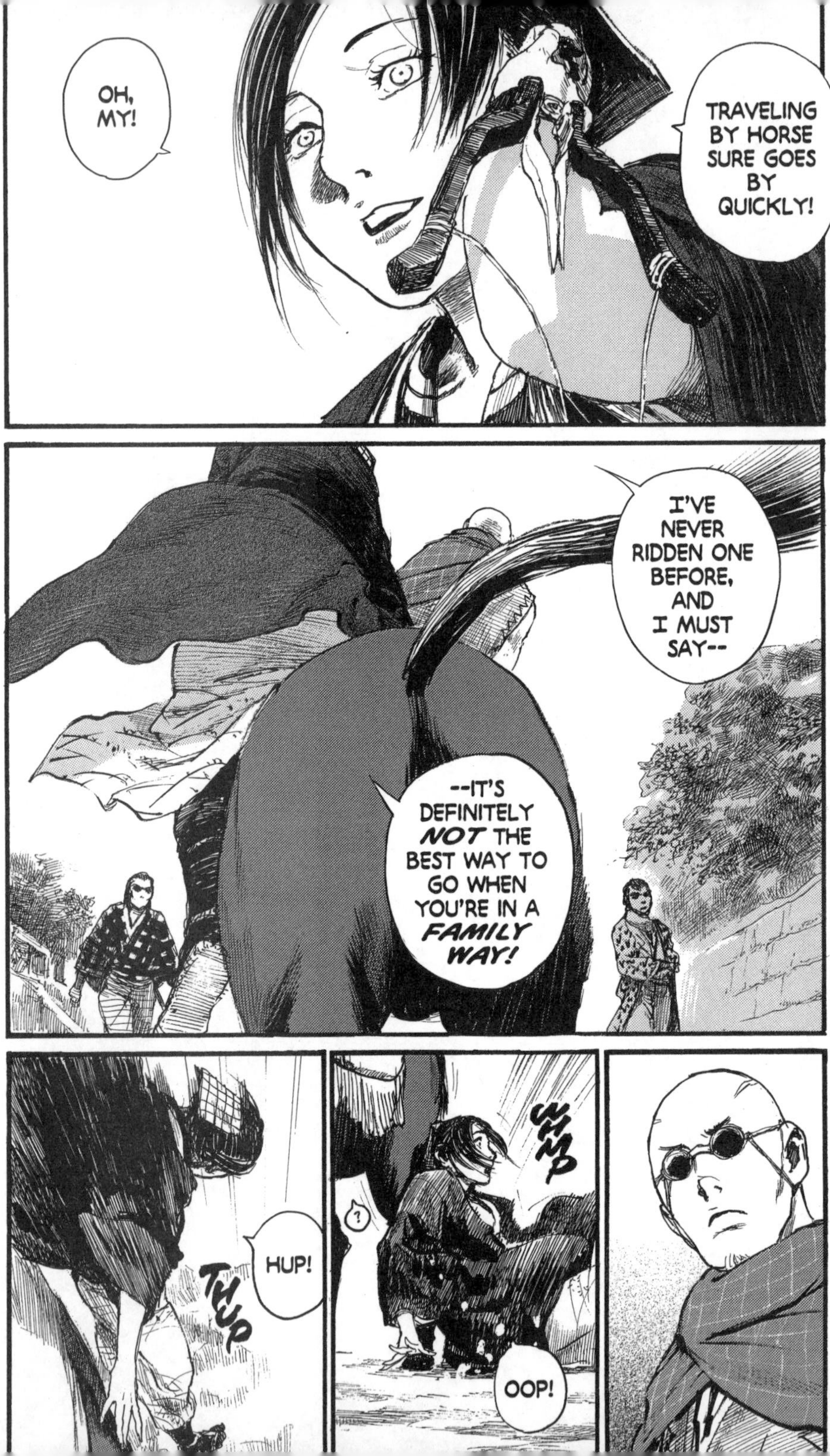
OH, MY!
TRAVELING BY HORSE SURE GOES BY QUICKLY!
I'VE NEVER RIDDEN ONE BEFORE, AND I MUST SAY--
--IT'S DEFINITELY NOT THE BEST WAY TO GO WHEN YOU'RE IN A FAMILY WAY!
HUP!
THUP
WHMP
?
OOP!

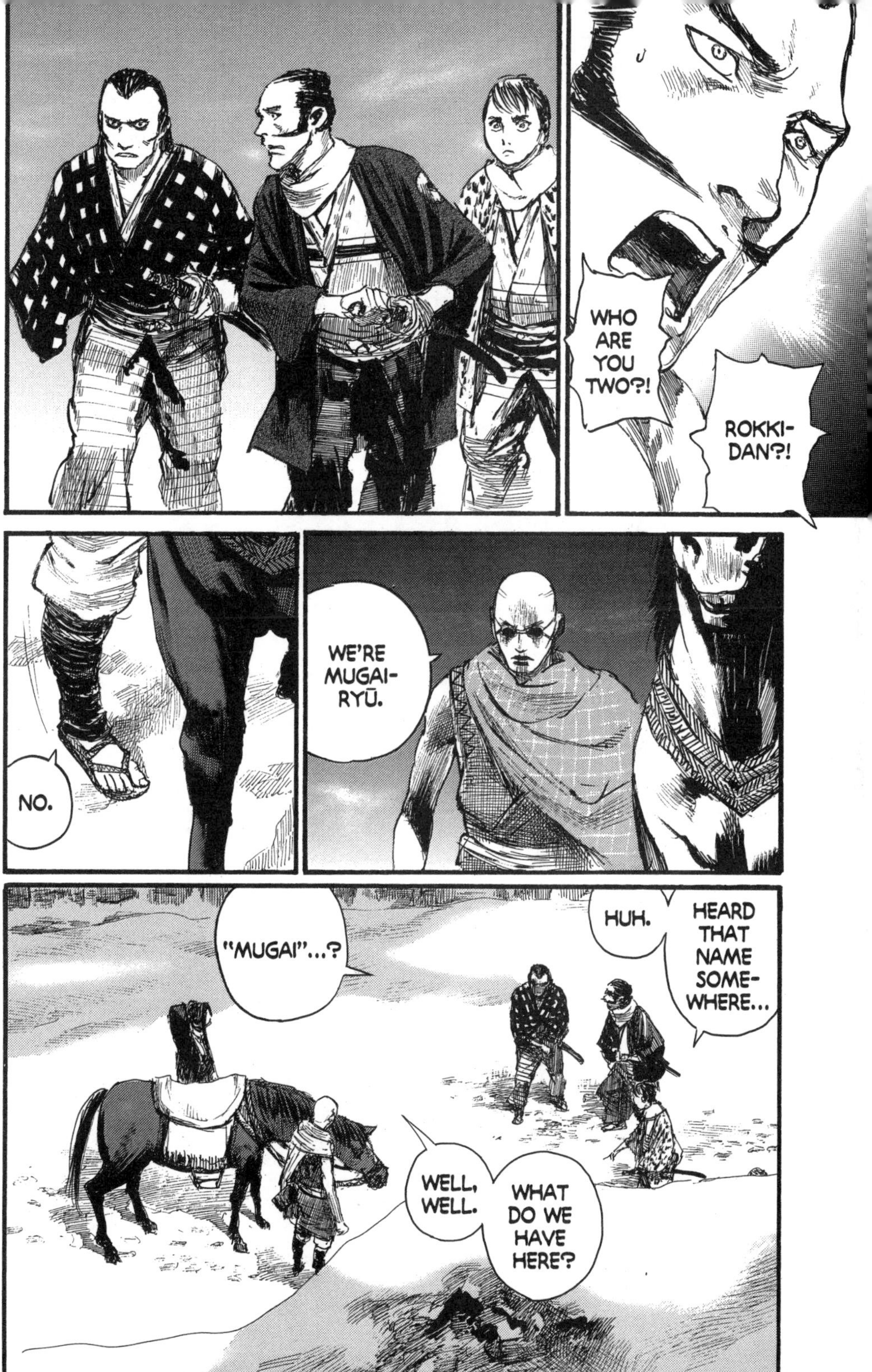
WHO ARE YOU TWO?!
ROKKI-DAN?!
NO.
WE'RE MUGAI-RYŪ.
"MUGAI"...?
HUH.
HEARD THAT NAME SOMEWHERE...
WELL, WELL.
WHAT DO WE HAVE HERE?

YOU THINK THIS PATHETIC BUNCH ARE WITH THE ITTŌ-RYŪ?

WELL, I GUESS THEY HAVE BECOME A THING OF THE PAST.

HEH. I DON'T REMEMBER THEM BEING *THIS* WELL MANNERED AND STILL.

SEE, MY IMAGE OF THE ITTŌ-RYŪ WAS MORE... *RUSTIC*, Y'KNOW?

HYAKU...

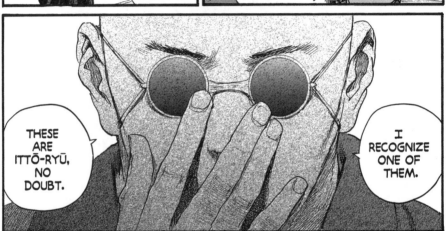

THESE ARE ITTŌ-RYŪ, NO DOUBT.

I RECOGNIZE ONE OF THEM.

YEAH...?

?

AH!

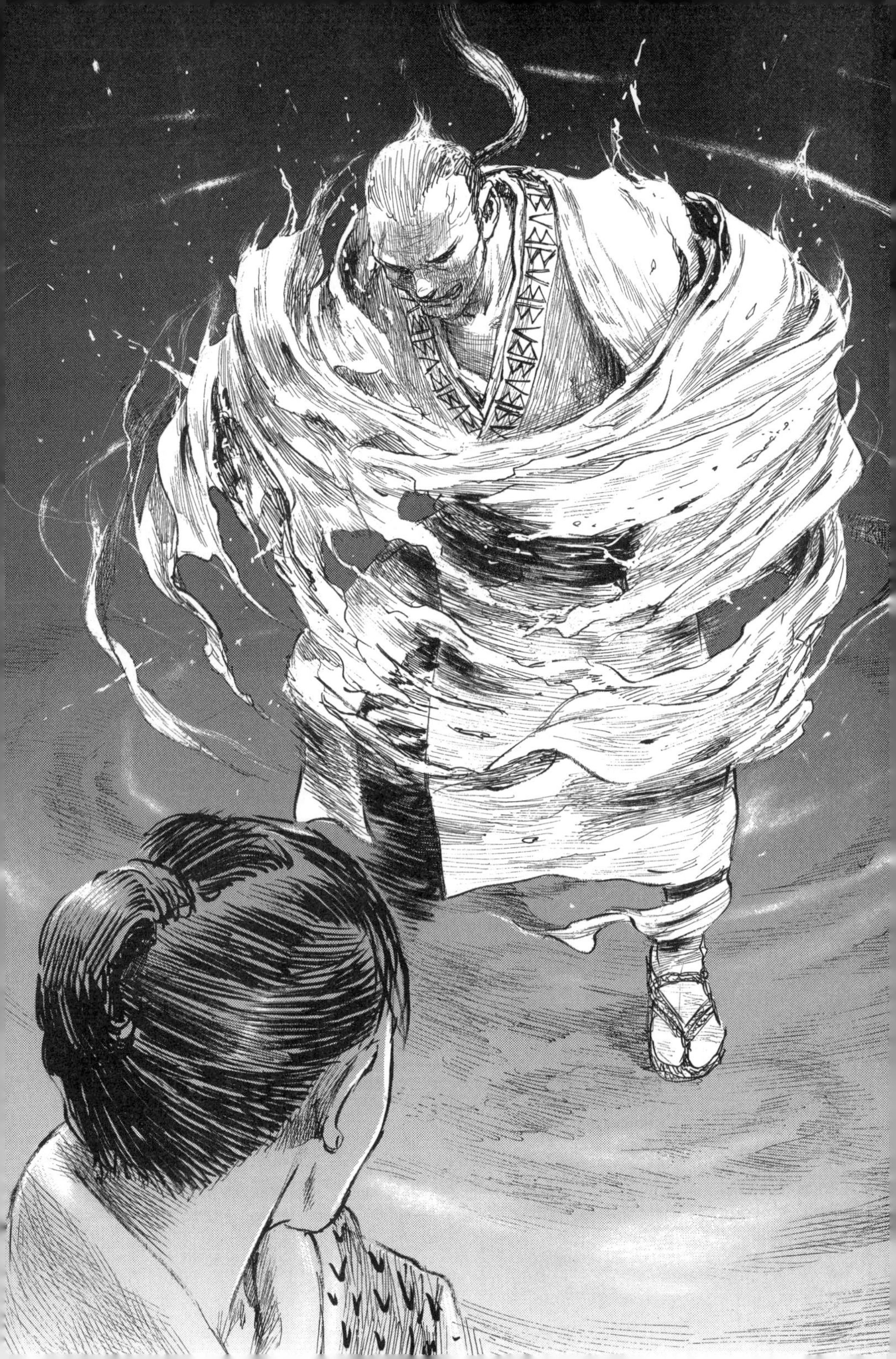

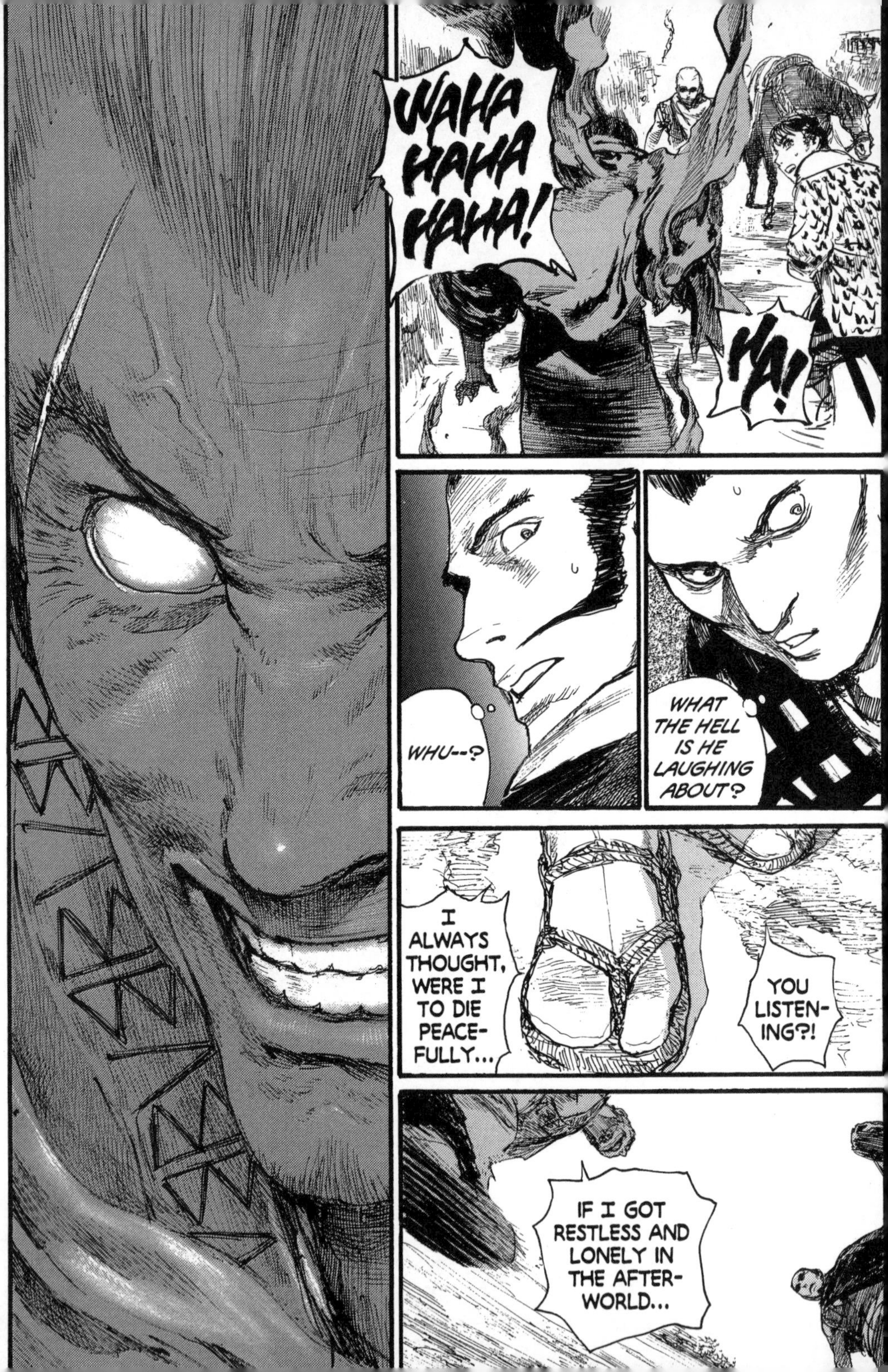
WAHA HAHA HAHA!
YA!
WHAT THE HELL IS HE LAUGHING ABOUT?
WHU--?
YOU LISTENING?!
I ALWAYS THOUGHT, WERE I TO DIE PEACEFULLY...
IF I GOT RESTLESS AND LONELY IN THE AFTERWORLD...

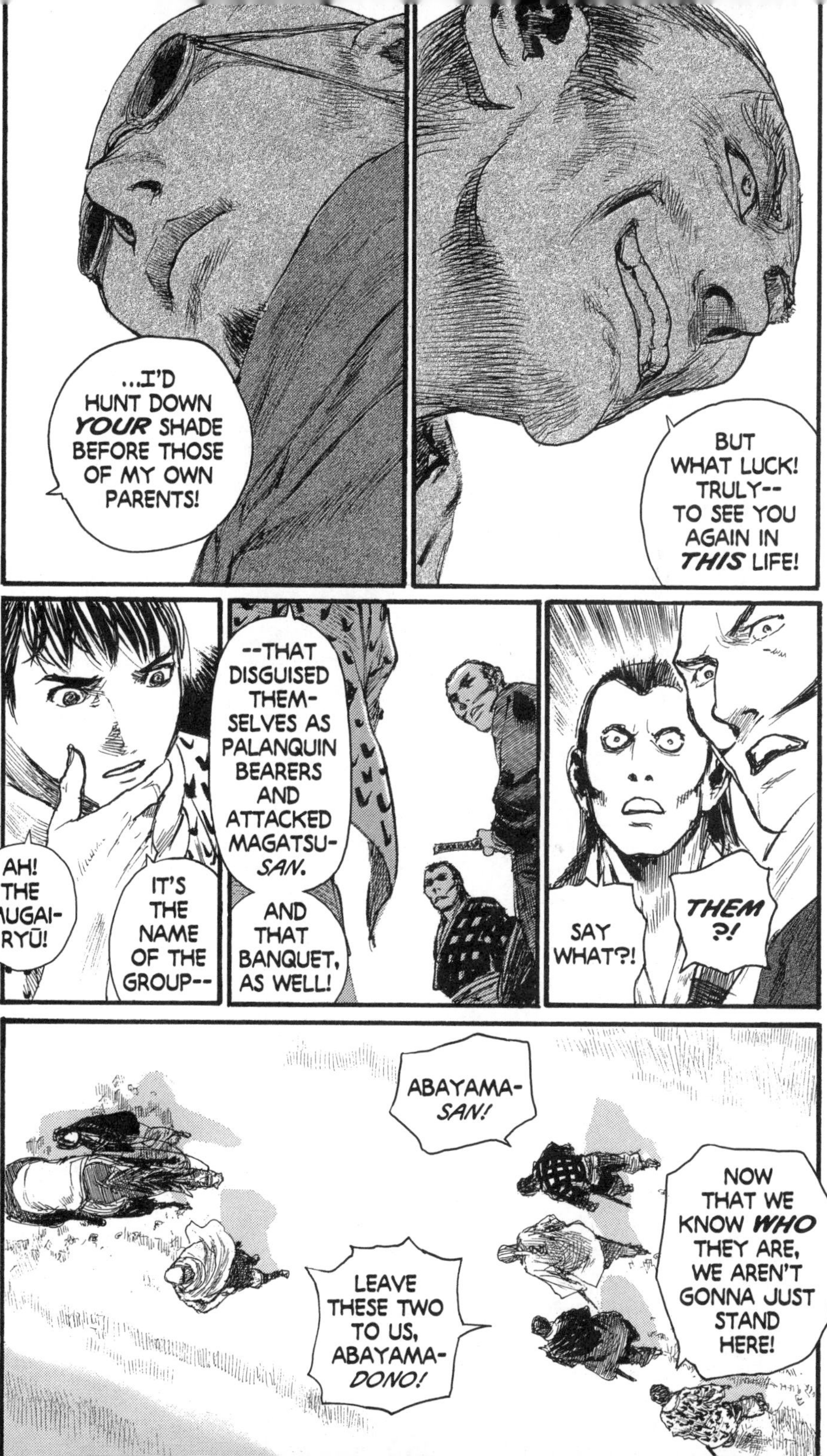
...I'D HUNT DOWN *YOUR* SHADE BEFORE THOSE OF MY OWN PARENTS!
BUT WHAT LUCK! TRULY-- TO SEE YOU AGAIN IN *THIS* LIFE!
AH! THE MUGAI-RYŪ!
IT'S THE NAME OF THE GROUP--
--THAT DISGUISED THEM-SELVES AS PALANQUIN BEARERS AND ATTACKED MAGATSU-*SAN*.
AND THAT BANQUET, AS WELL!
SAY WHAT?!
THEM ?!
ABAYAMA-*SAN!*
NOW THAT WE KNOW *WHO* THEY ARE, WE AREN'T GONNA JUST STAND HERE!
LEAVE THESE TWO TO US, ABAYAMA-*DONO!*

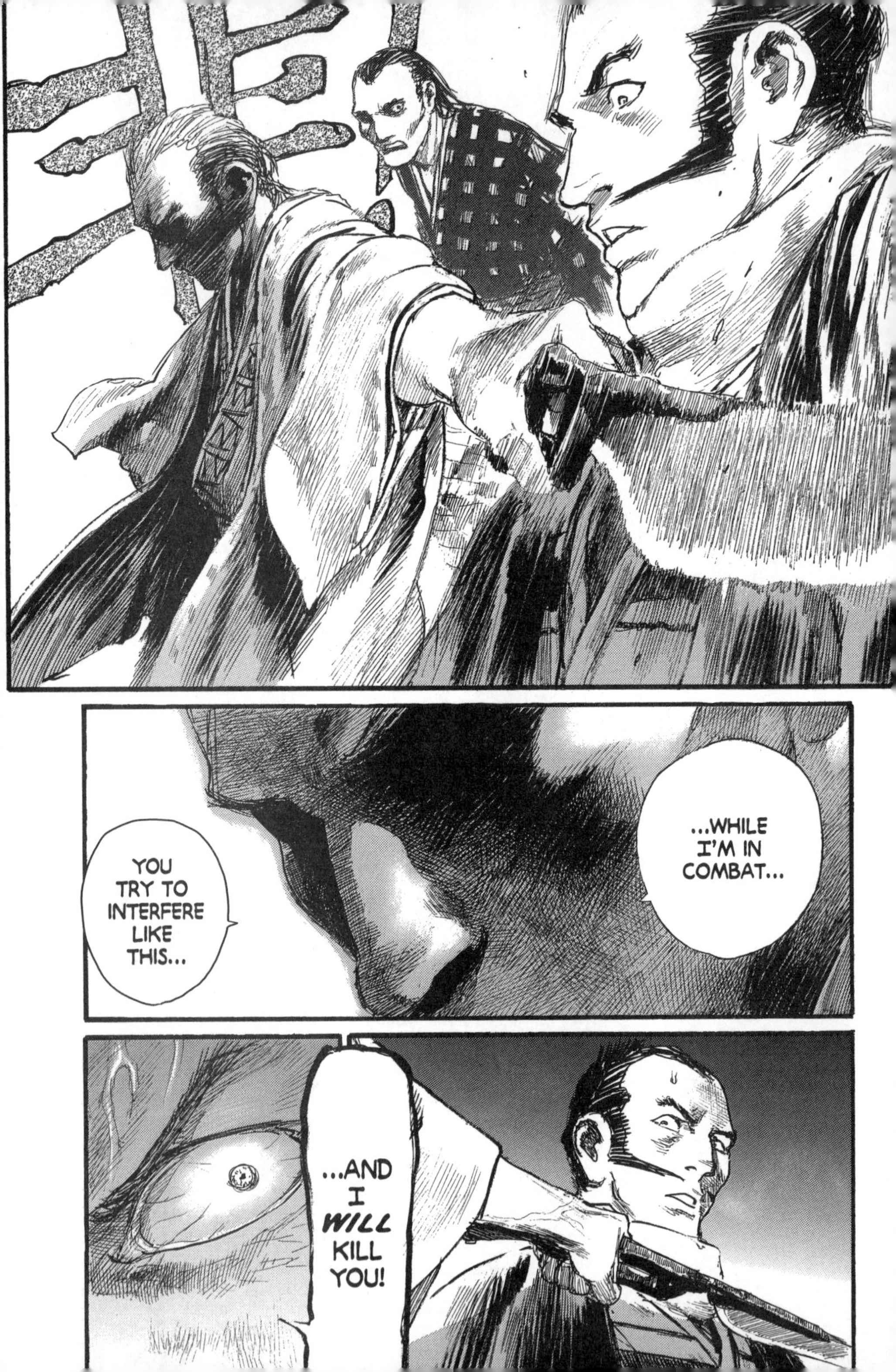
...WHILE I'M IN COMBAT...
YOU TRY TO INTERFERE LIKE THIS...
...AND I *WILL* KILL YOU!

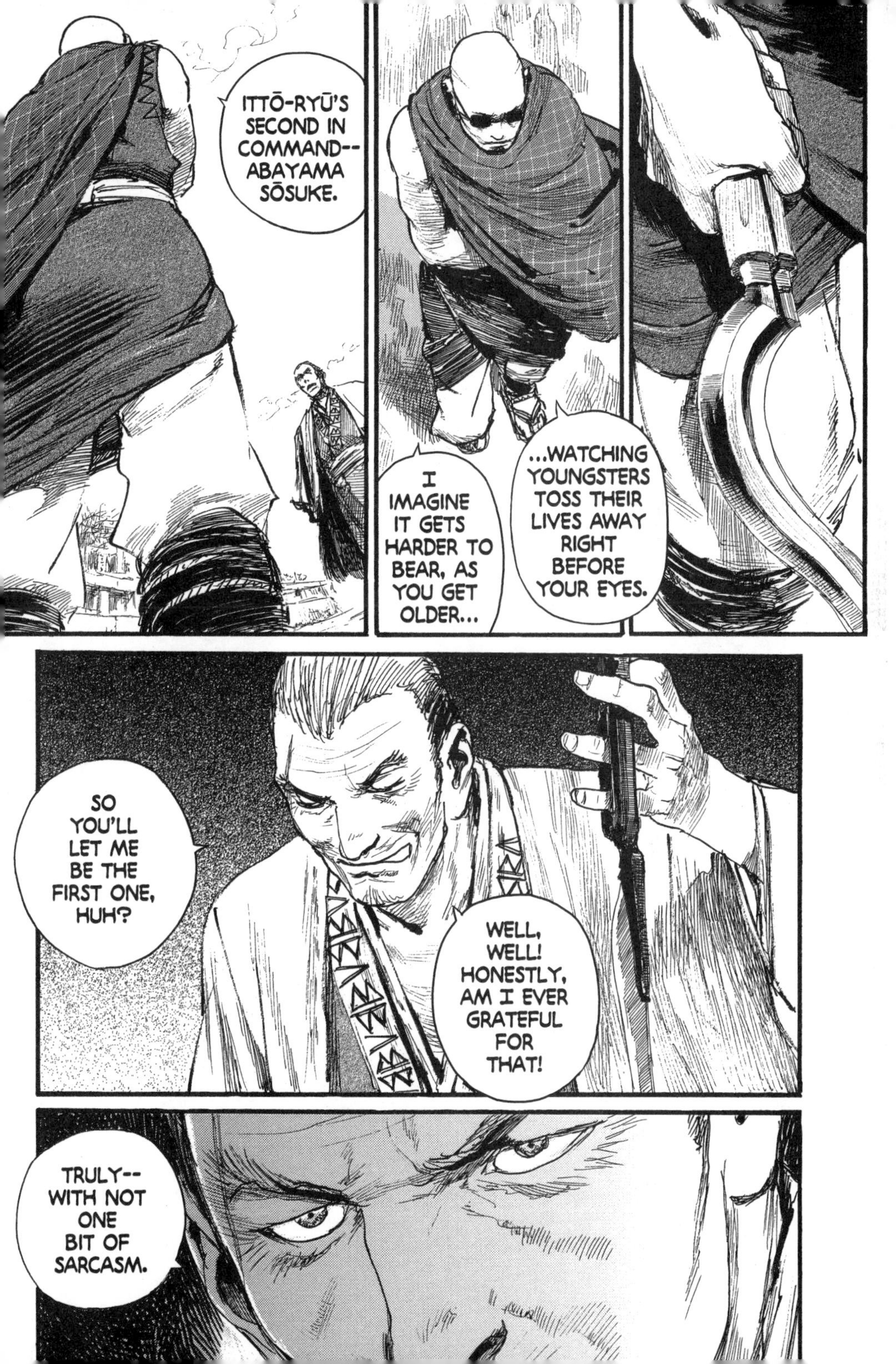
ITTŌ-RYŪ'S SECOND IN COMMAND-- ABAYAMA SŌSUKE.
I IMAGINE IT GETS HARDER TO BEAR, AS YOU GET OLDER...
...WATCHING YOUNGSTERS TOSS THEIR LIVES AWAY RIGHT BEFORE YOUR EYES.
SO YOU'LL LET ME BE THE FIRST ONE, HUH?
WELL, WELL! HONESTLY, AM I EVER GRATEFUL FOR THAT!
TRULY-- WITH NOT ONE BIT OF SARCASM.

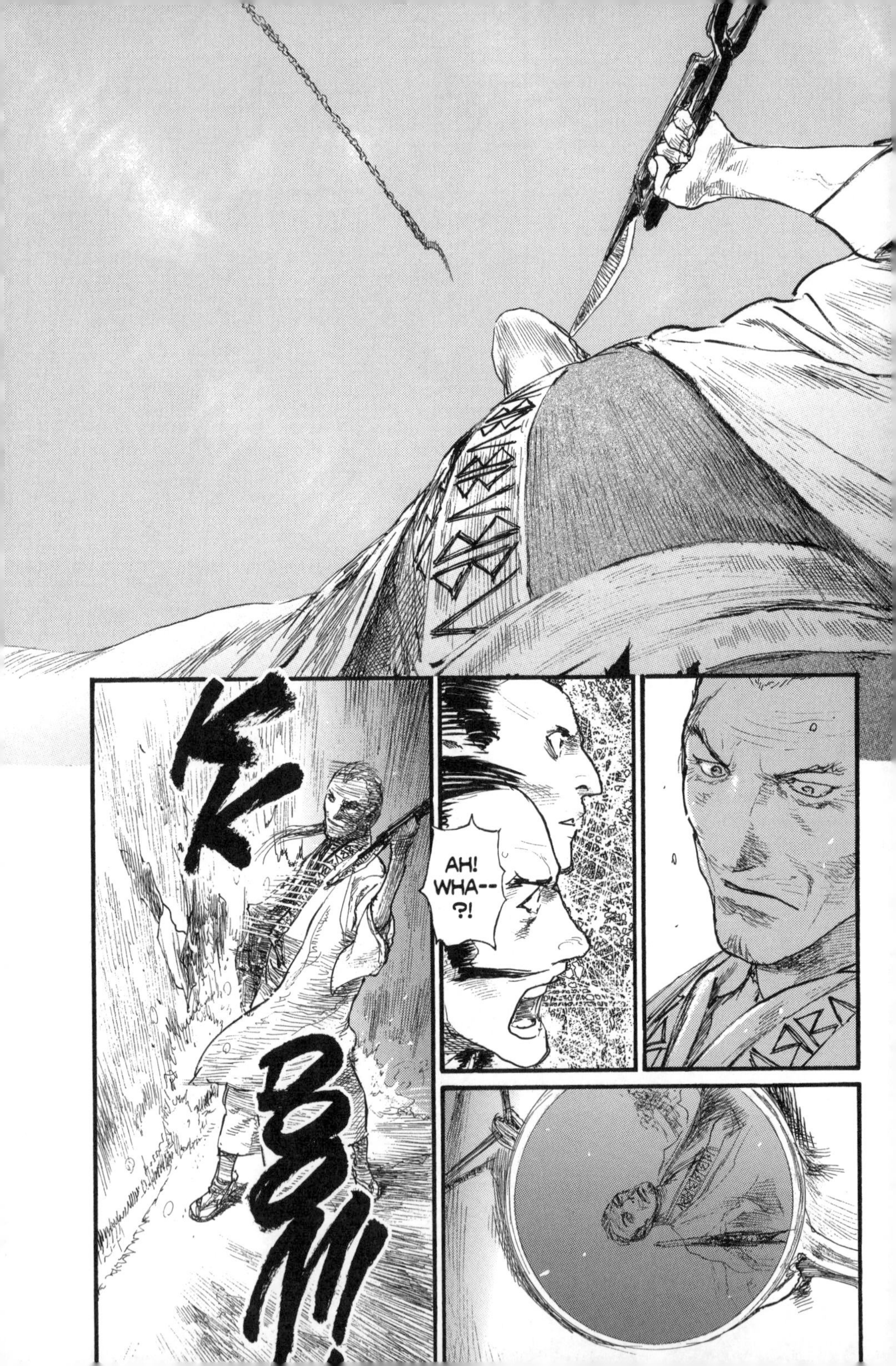
AH! WHA-- ?!
KA-BOOM!

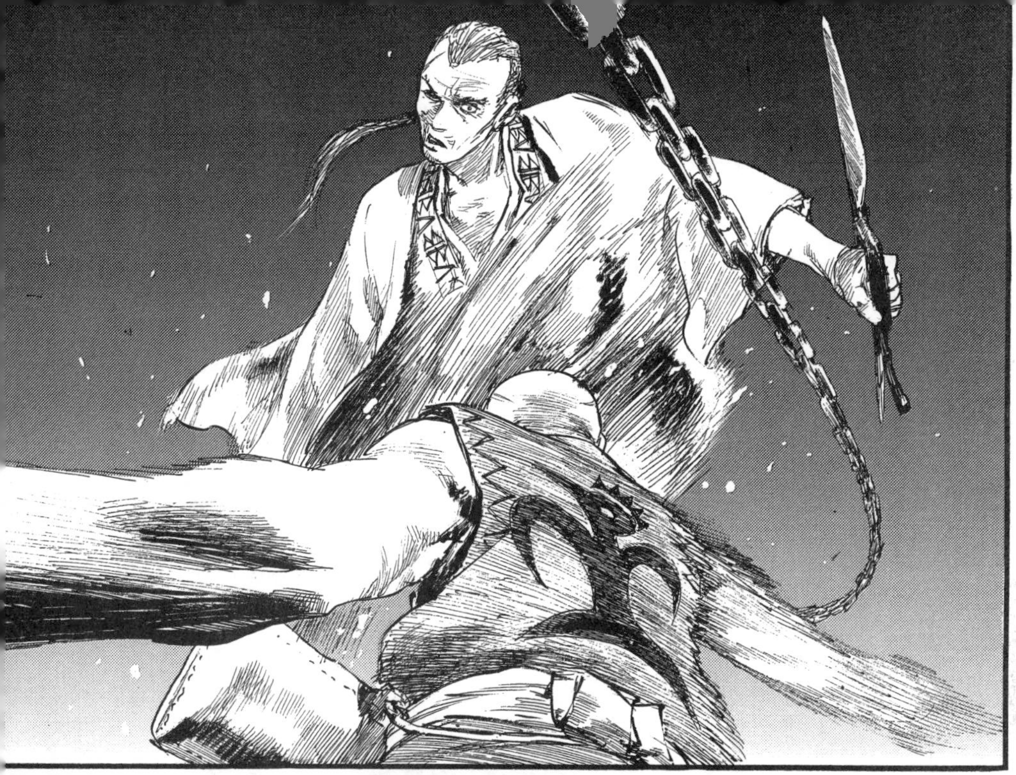
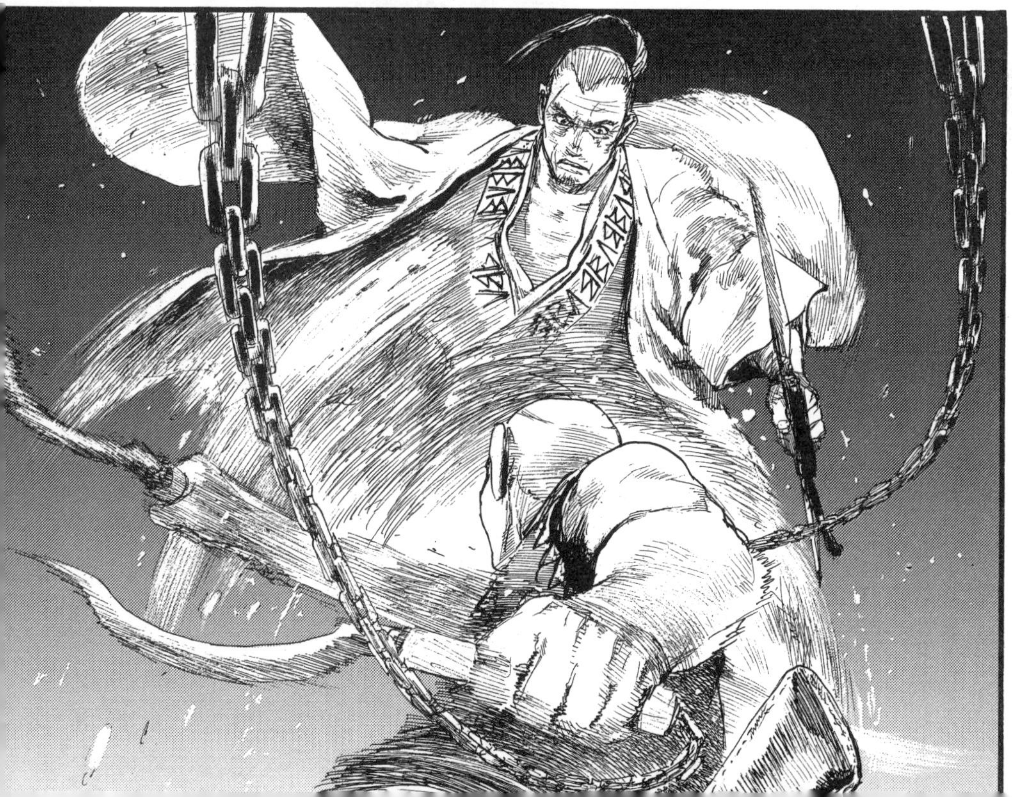

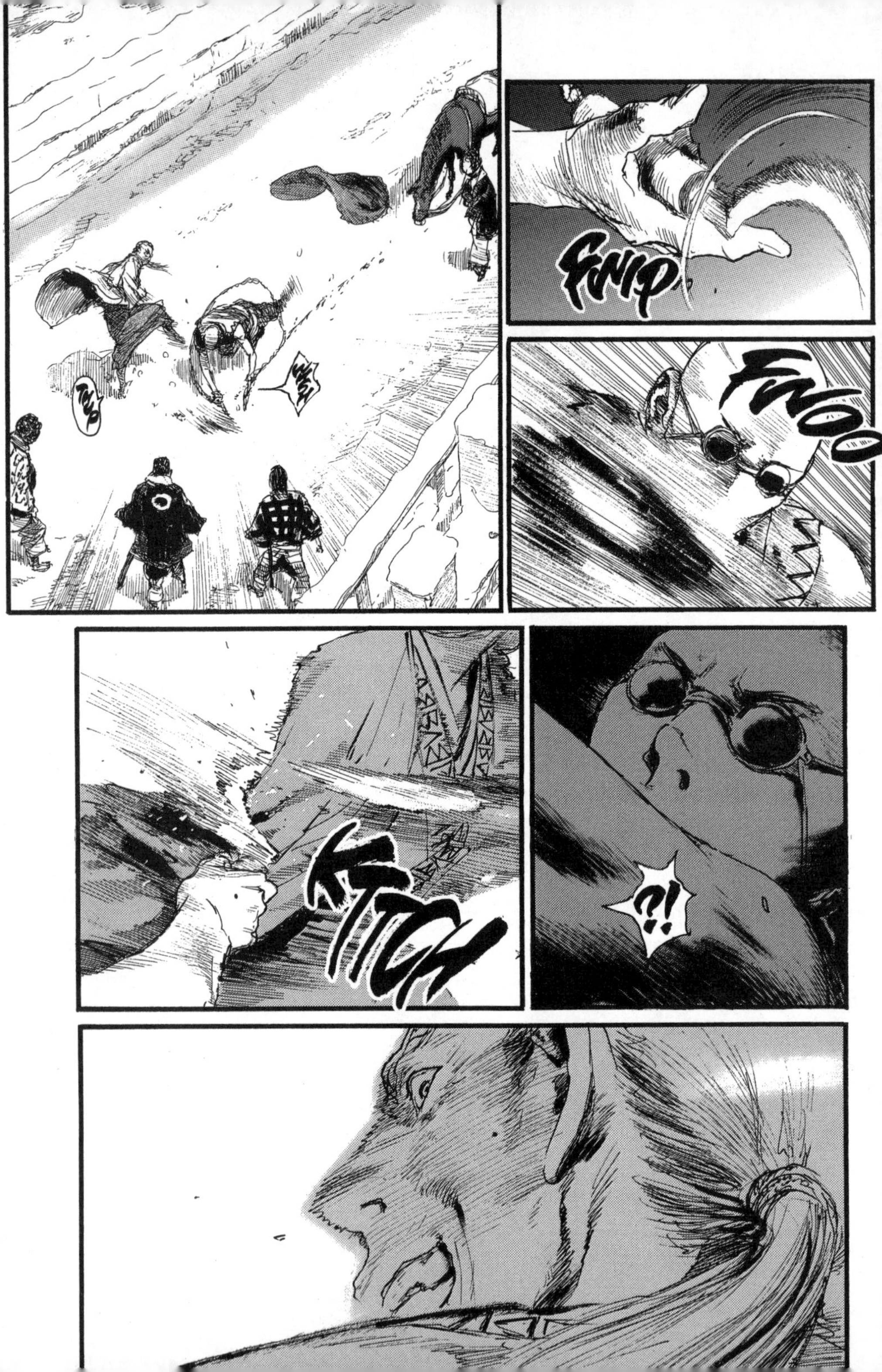
FSNIP
FWOO
THUP
?!
KTTCH

DANNNG!

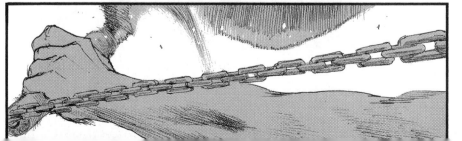

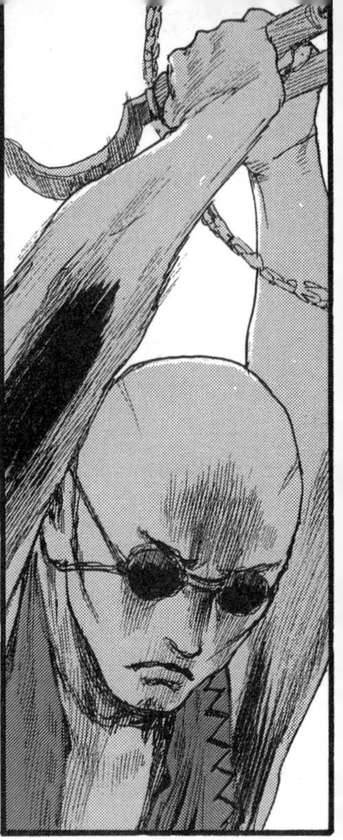
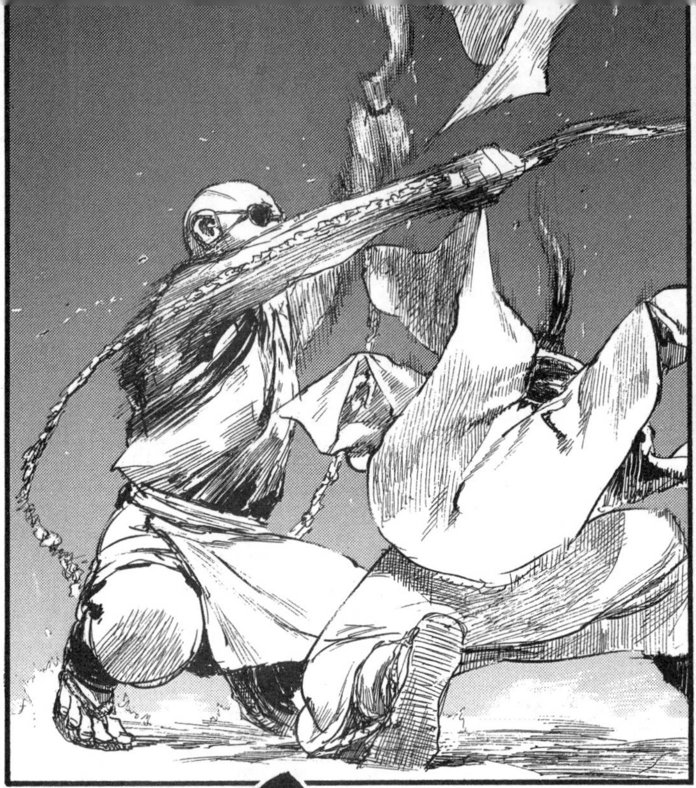
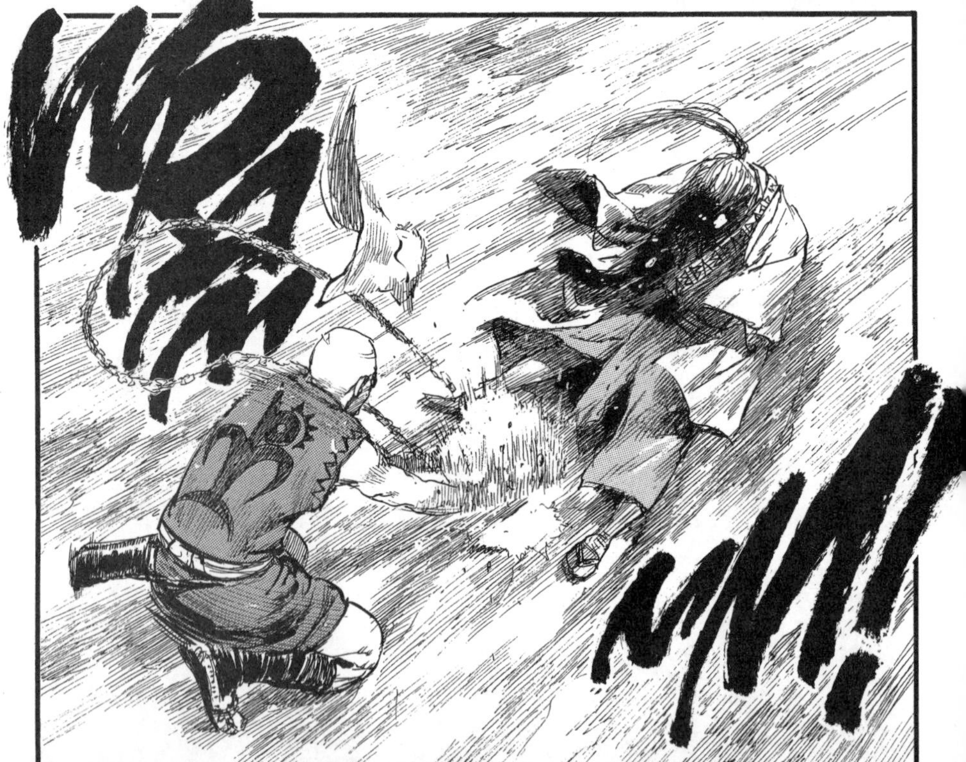

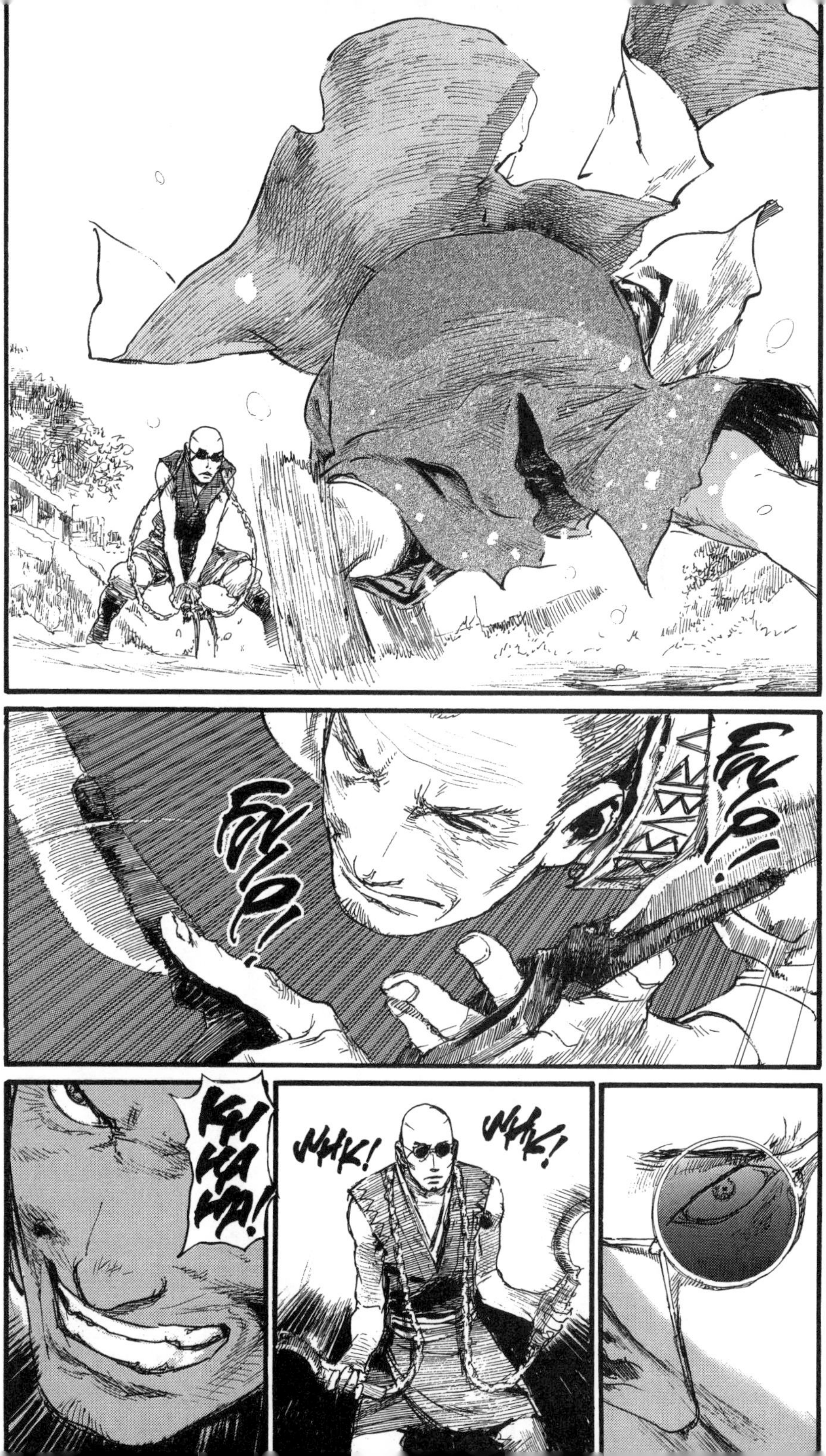
FWP!
FWP!
UNK!
UNK!
KH HA HA!

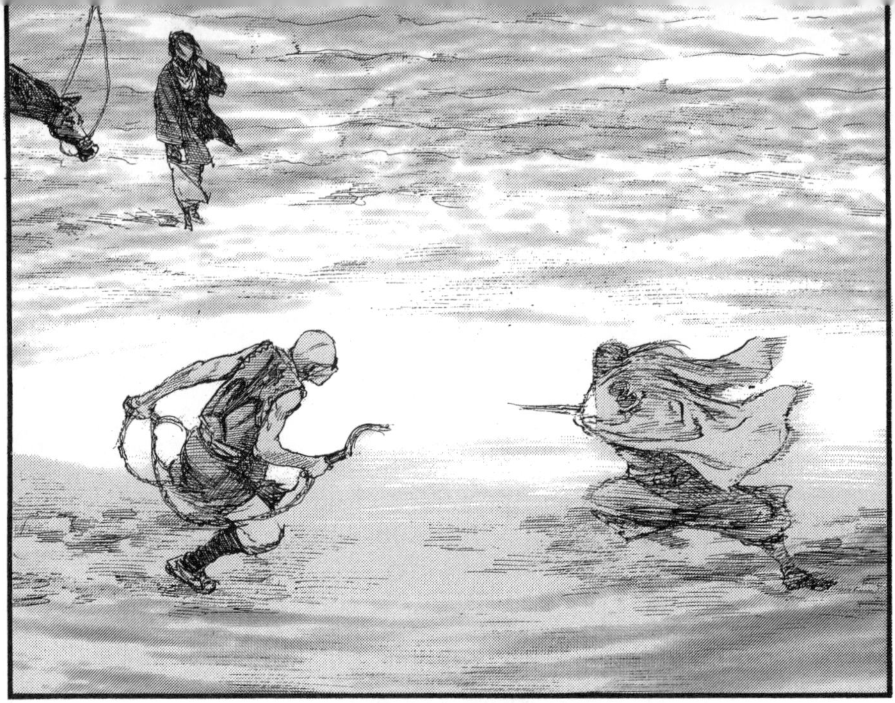
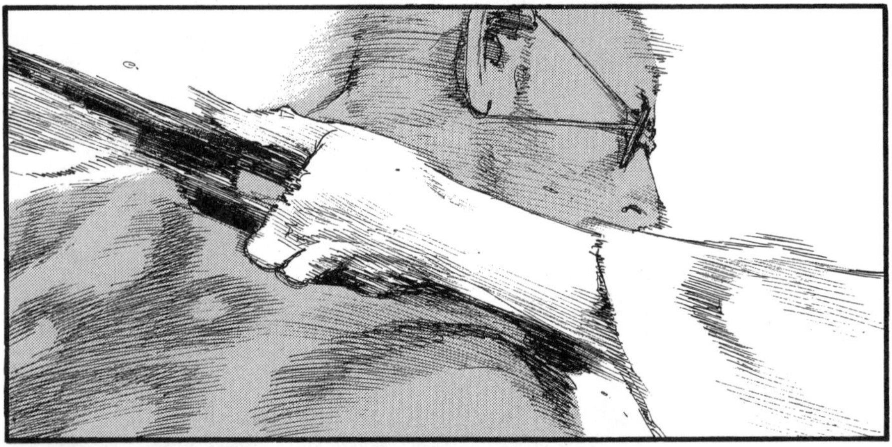
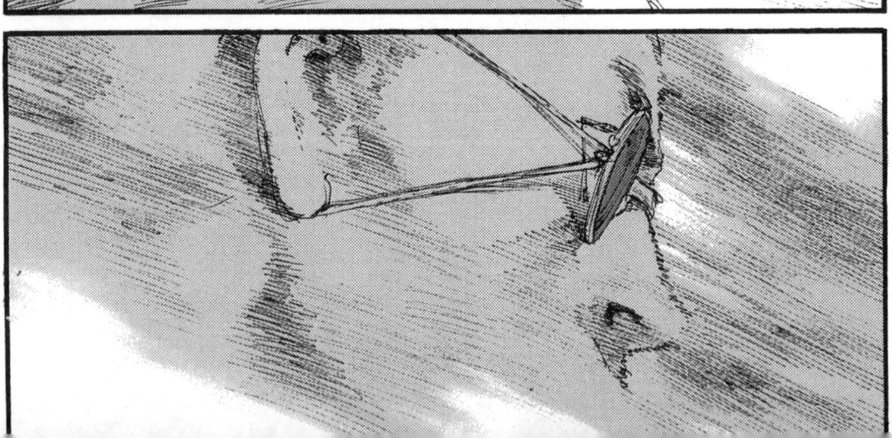

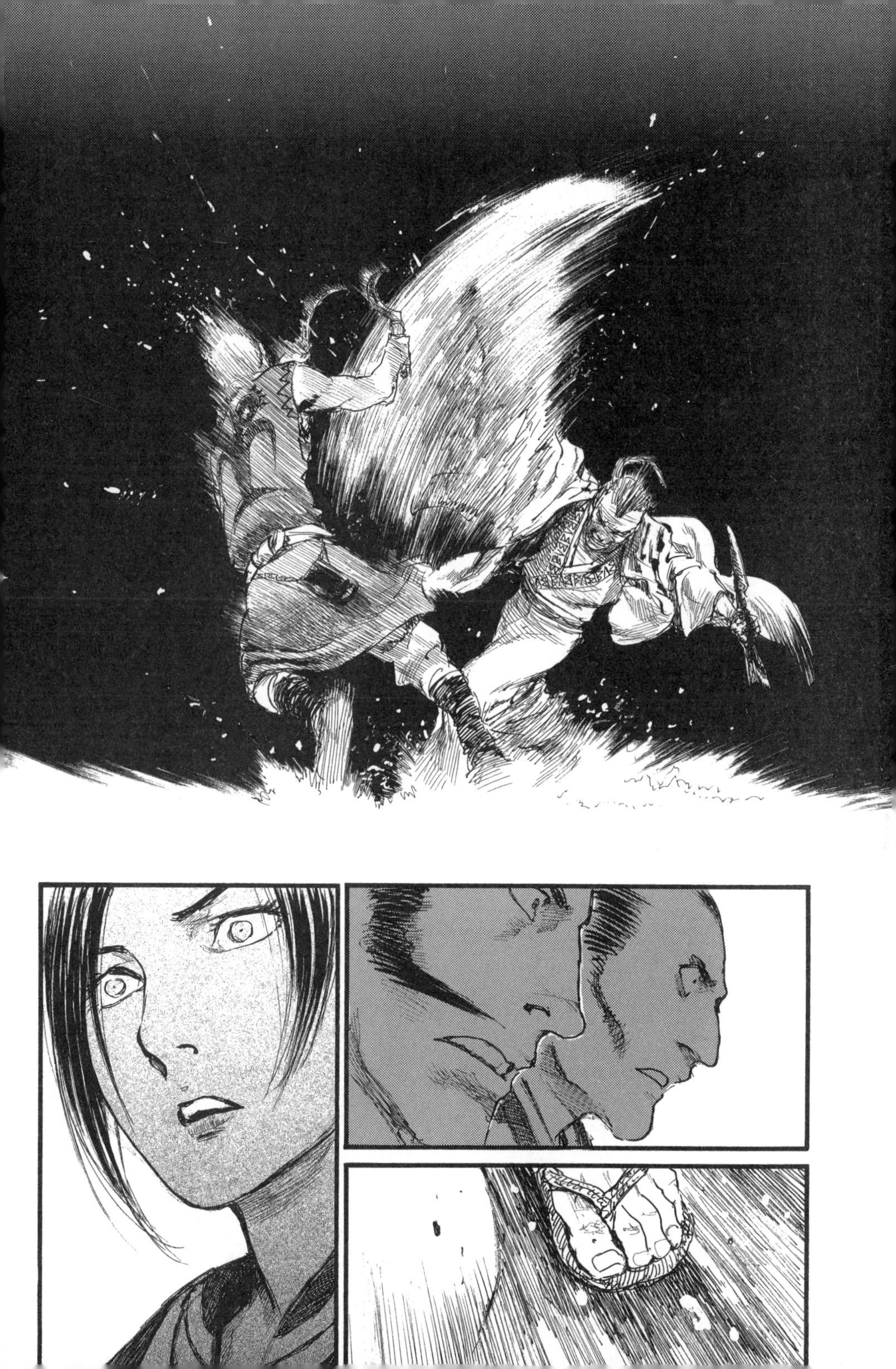

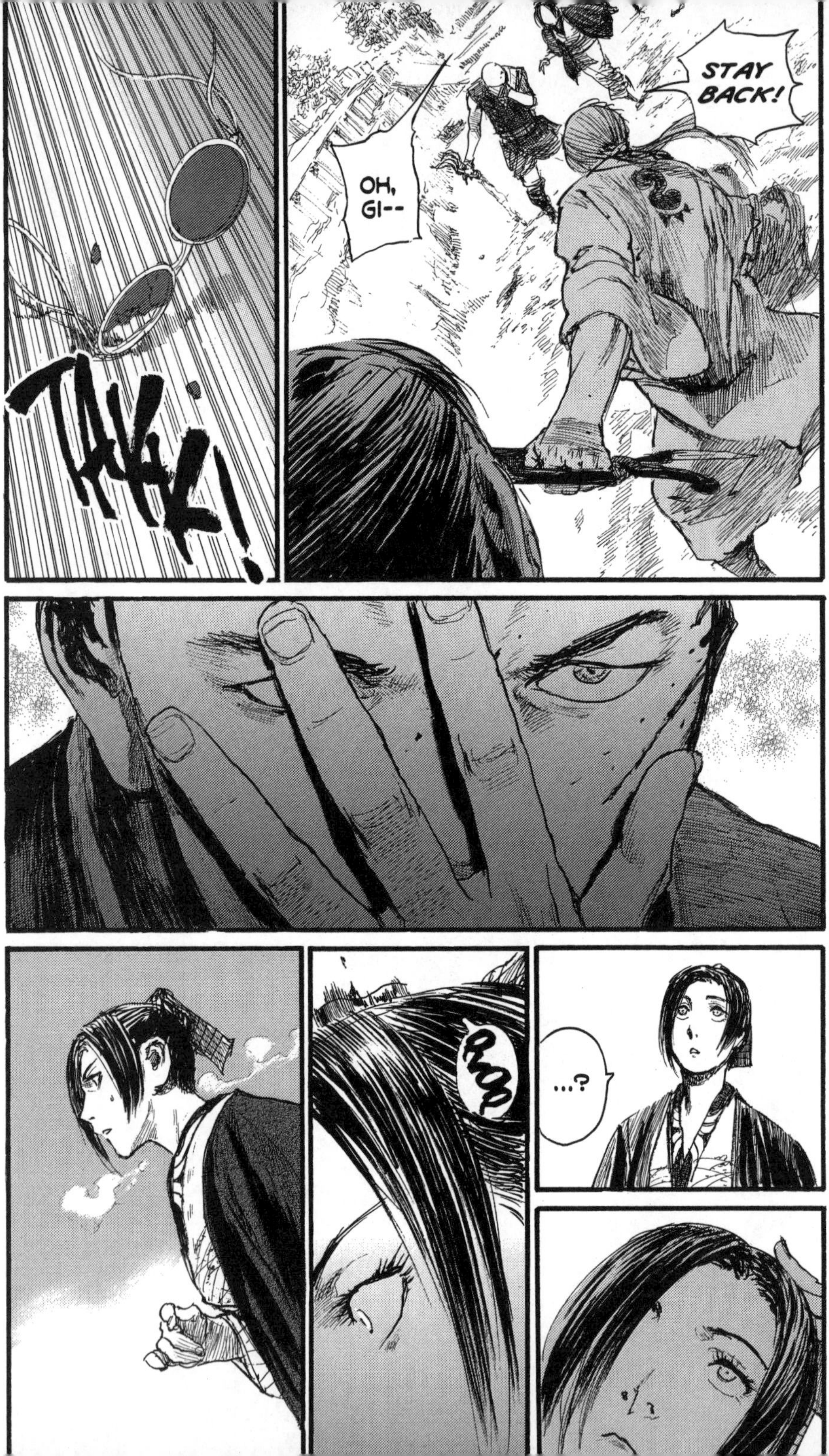
STAY BACK!
OH, GI--
TAKK!
...?

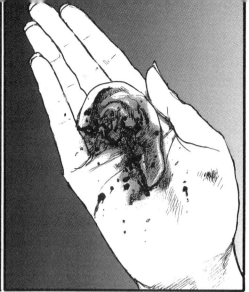

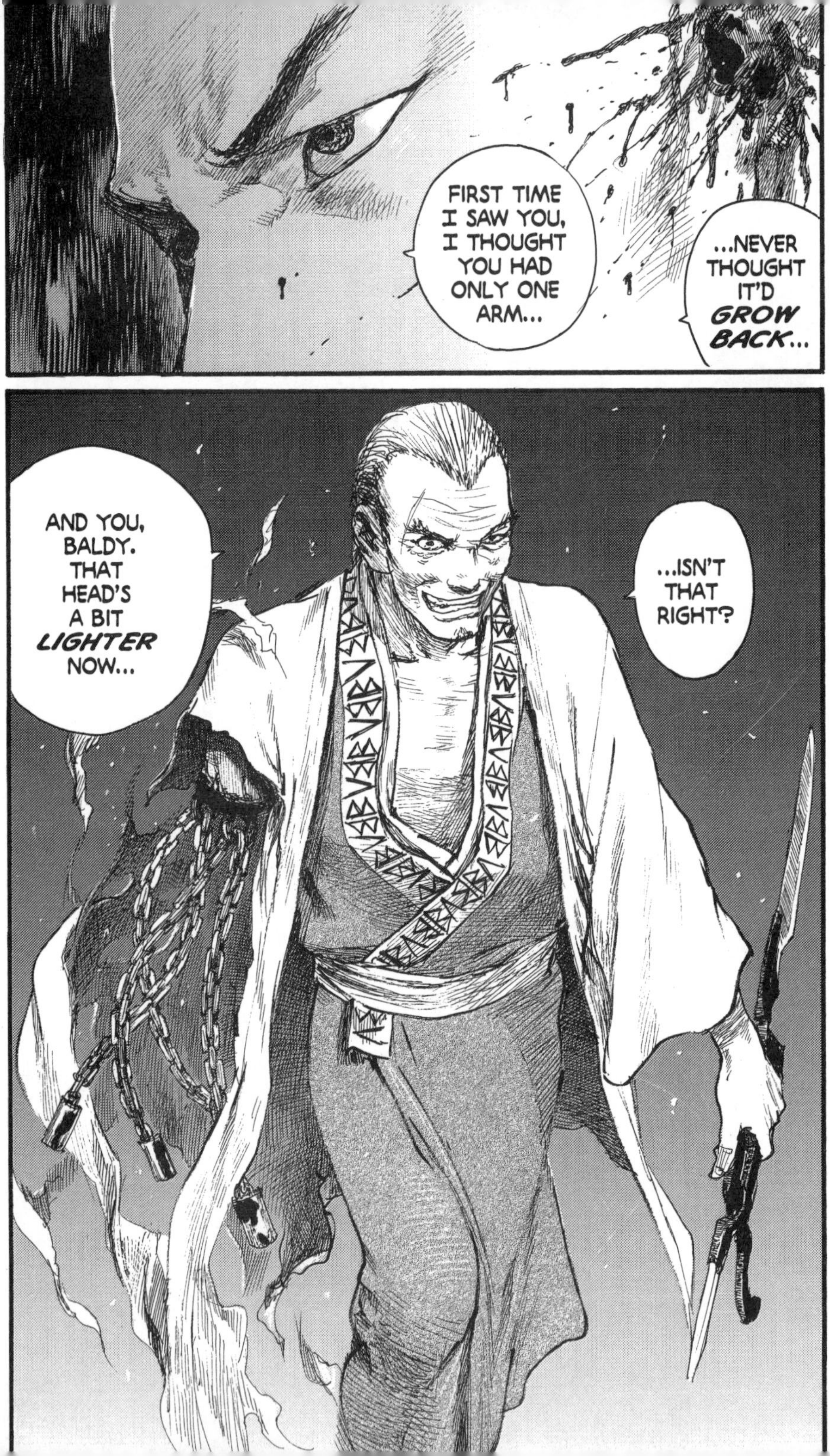
FIRST TIME I SAW YOU, I THOUGHT YOU HAD ONLY ONE ARM...
...NEVER THOUGHT IT'D GROW BACK...
AND YOU, BALDY. THAT HEAD'S A BIT LIGHTER NOW...
...ISN'T THAT RIGHT?

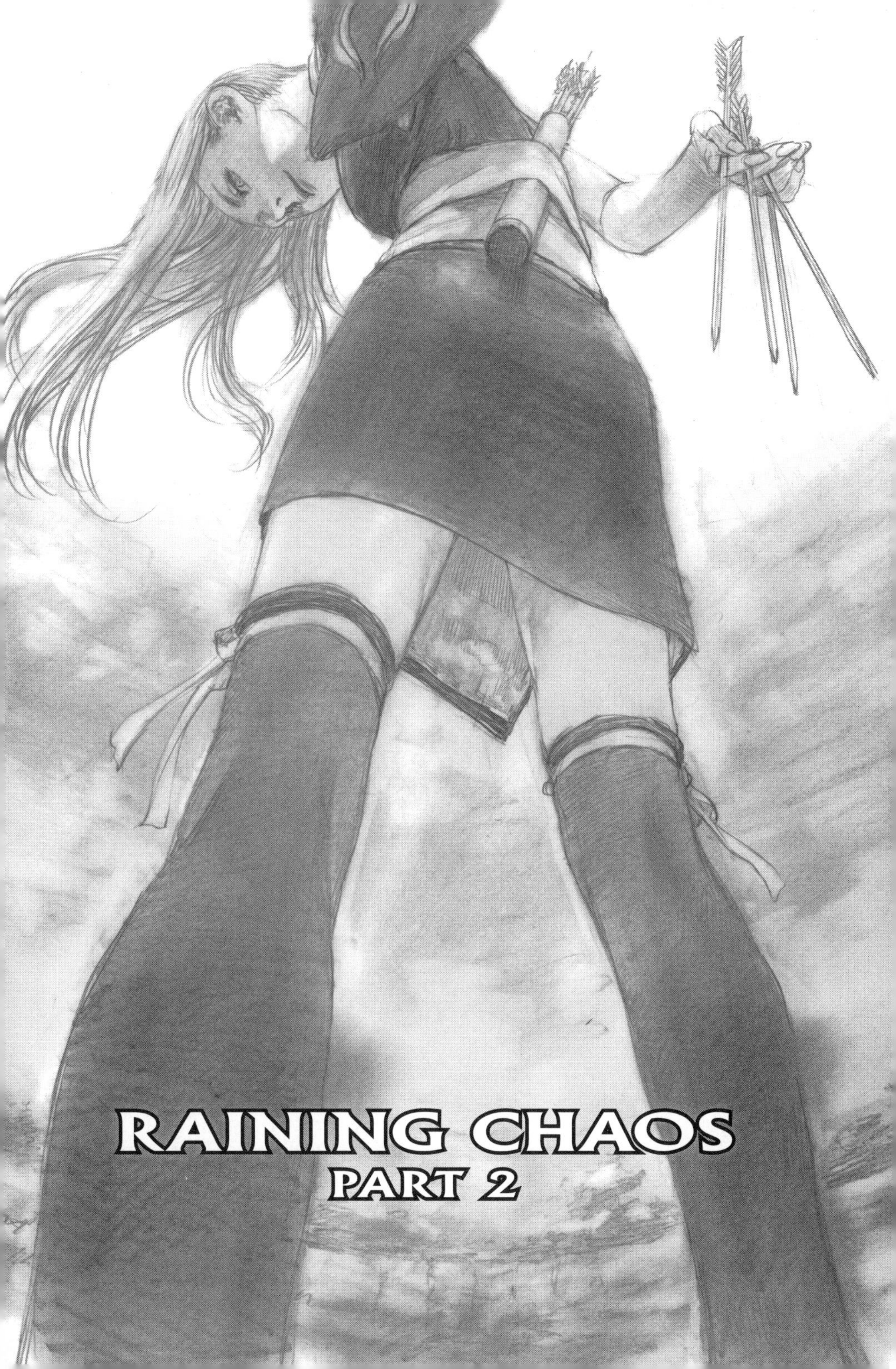
RAINING CHAOS
PART 2

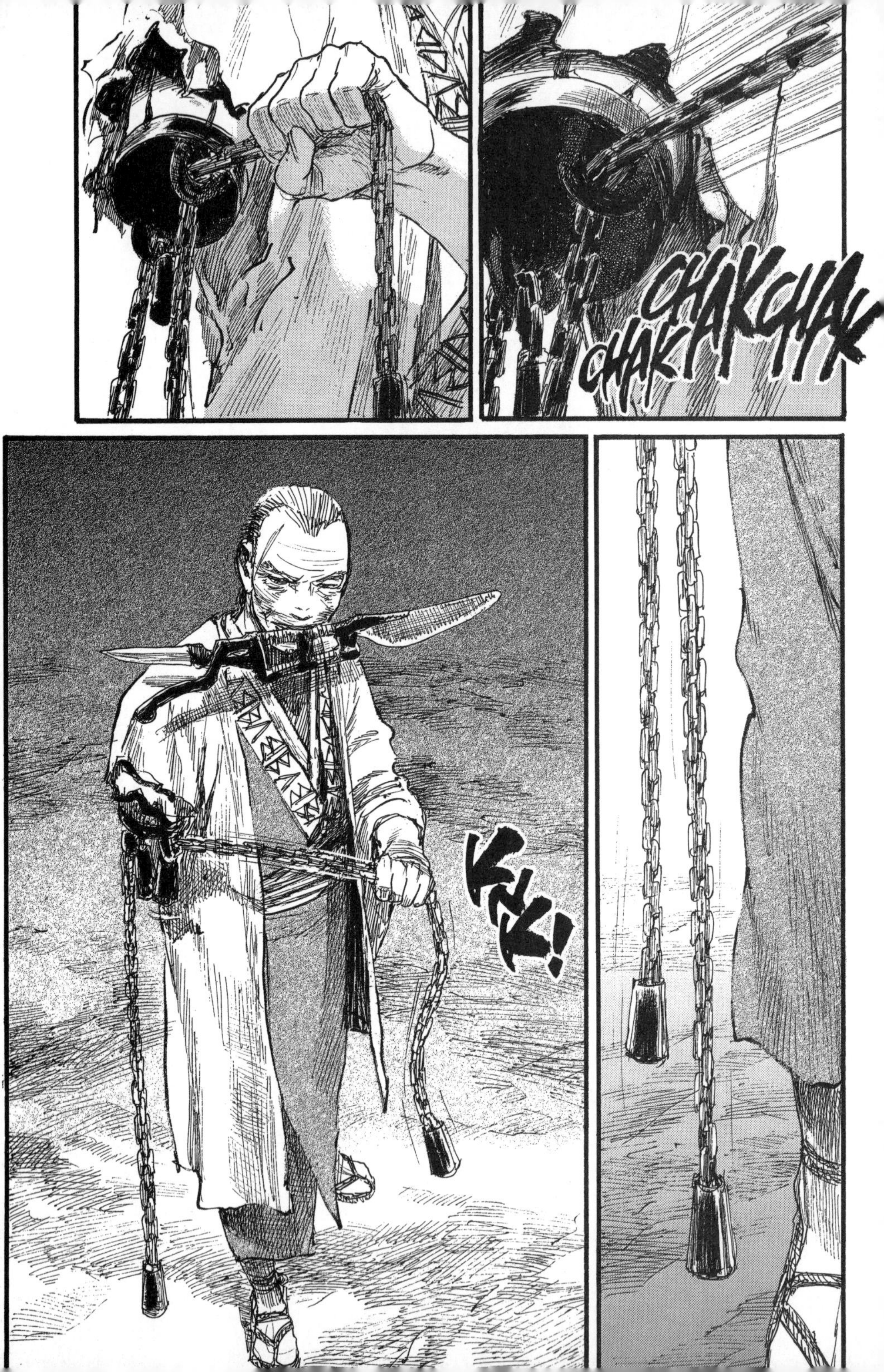
CHAKCHAK
CHAKCHAK
KYK!

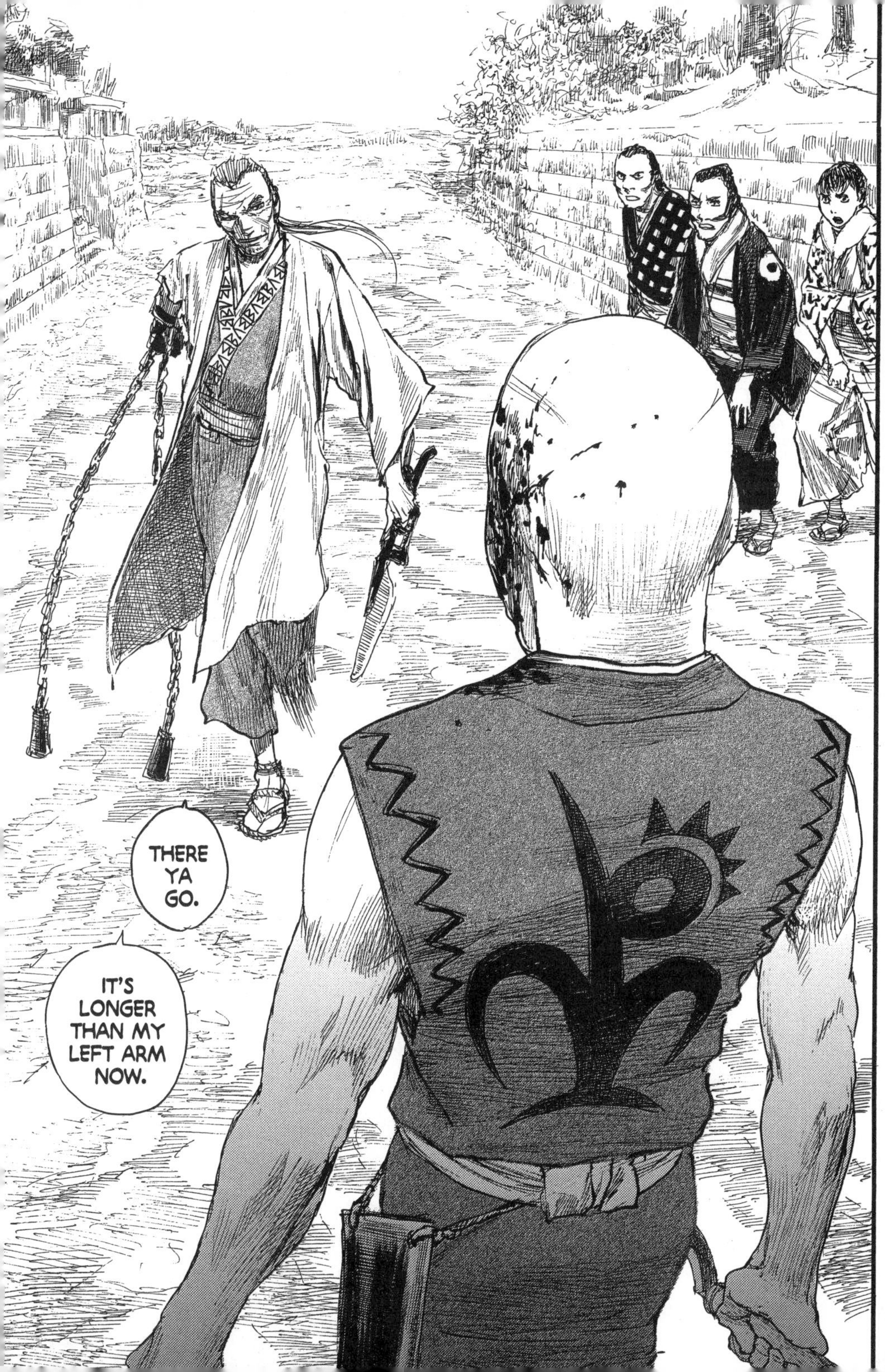
THERE YA GO.
IT'S LONGER THAN MY LEFT ARM NOW.

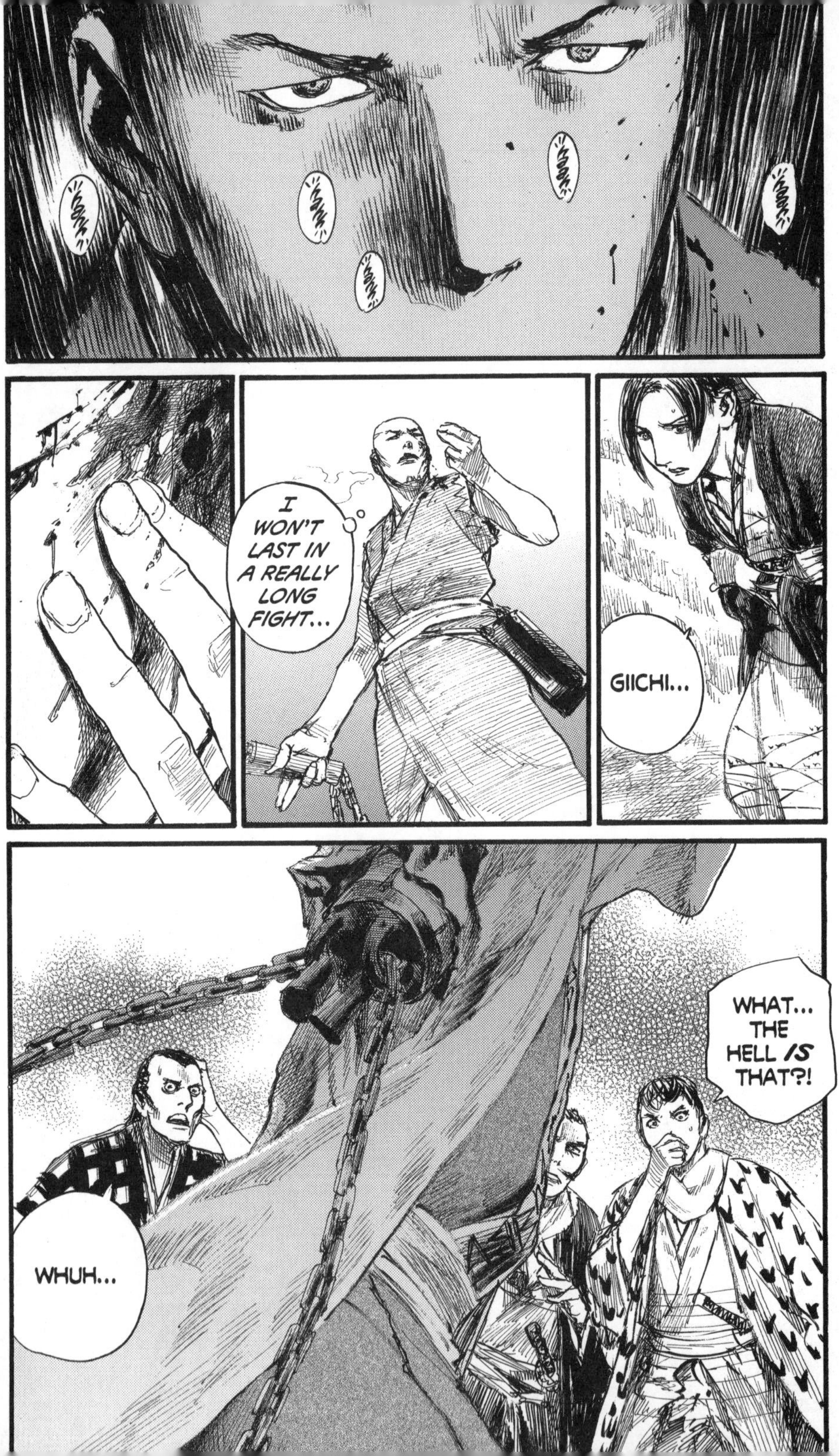
GIICHI...
I WON'T LAST IN A REALLY LONG FIGHT...
WHAT... THE HELL *IS* THAT?!
WHUH...

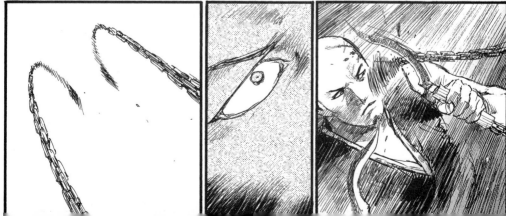

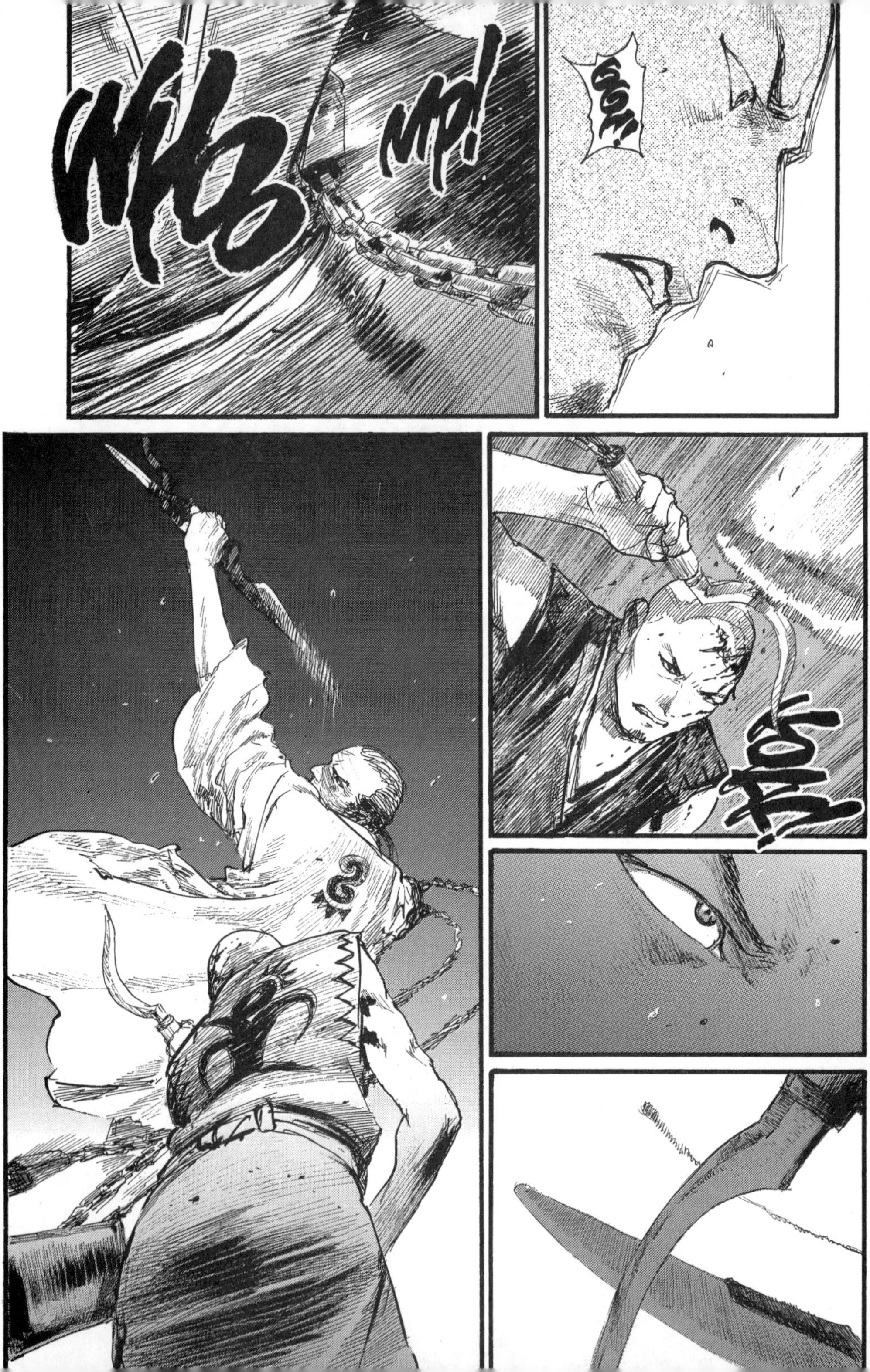
WHOOMP!

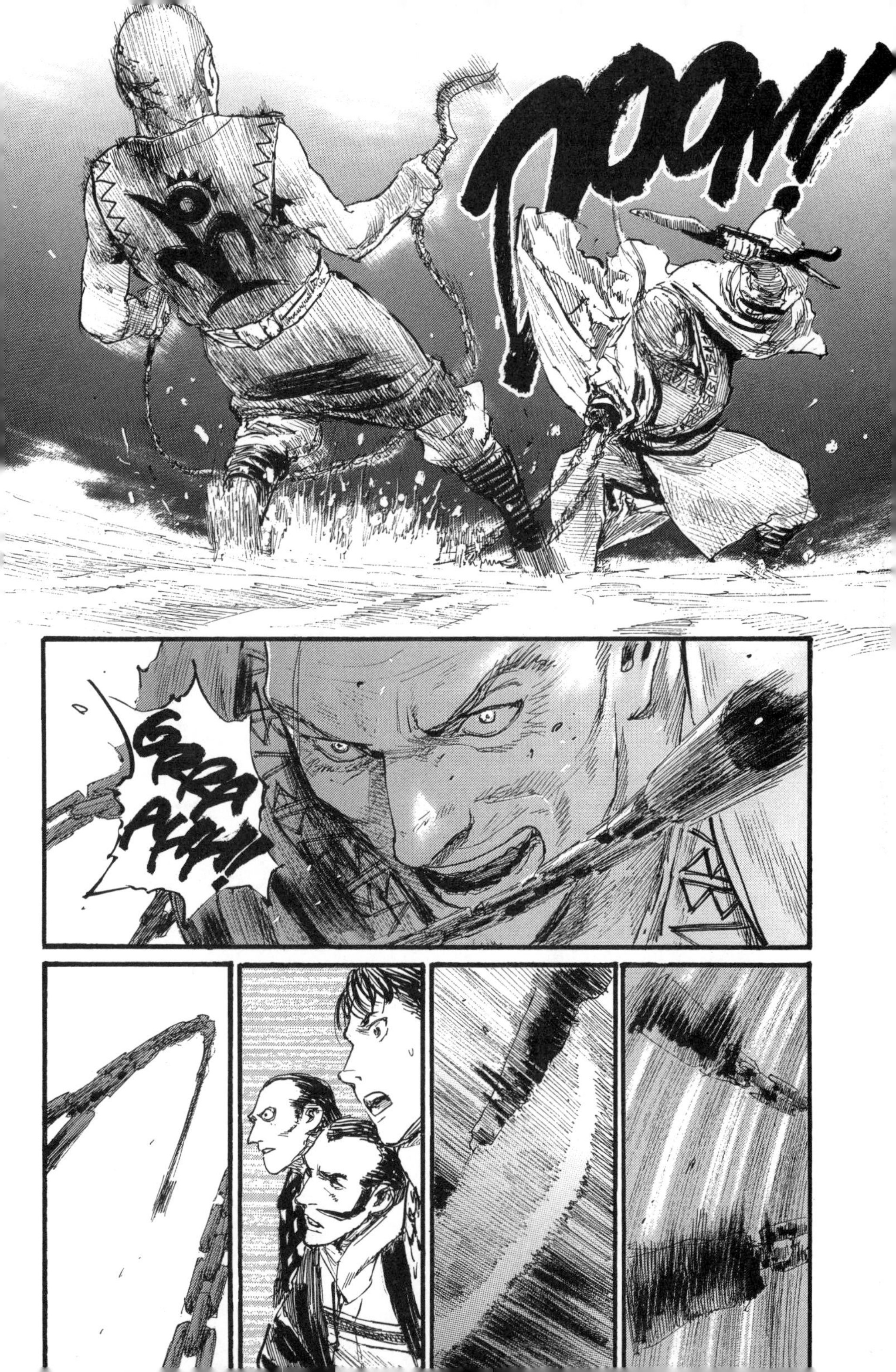
DOOM!!
GRRRAAHH!!

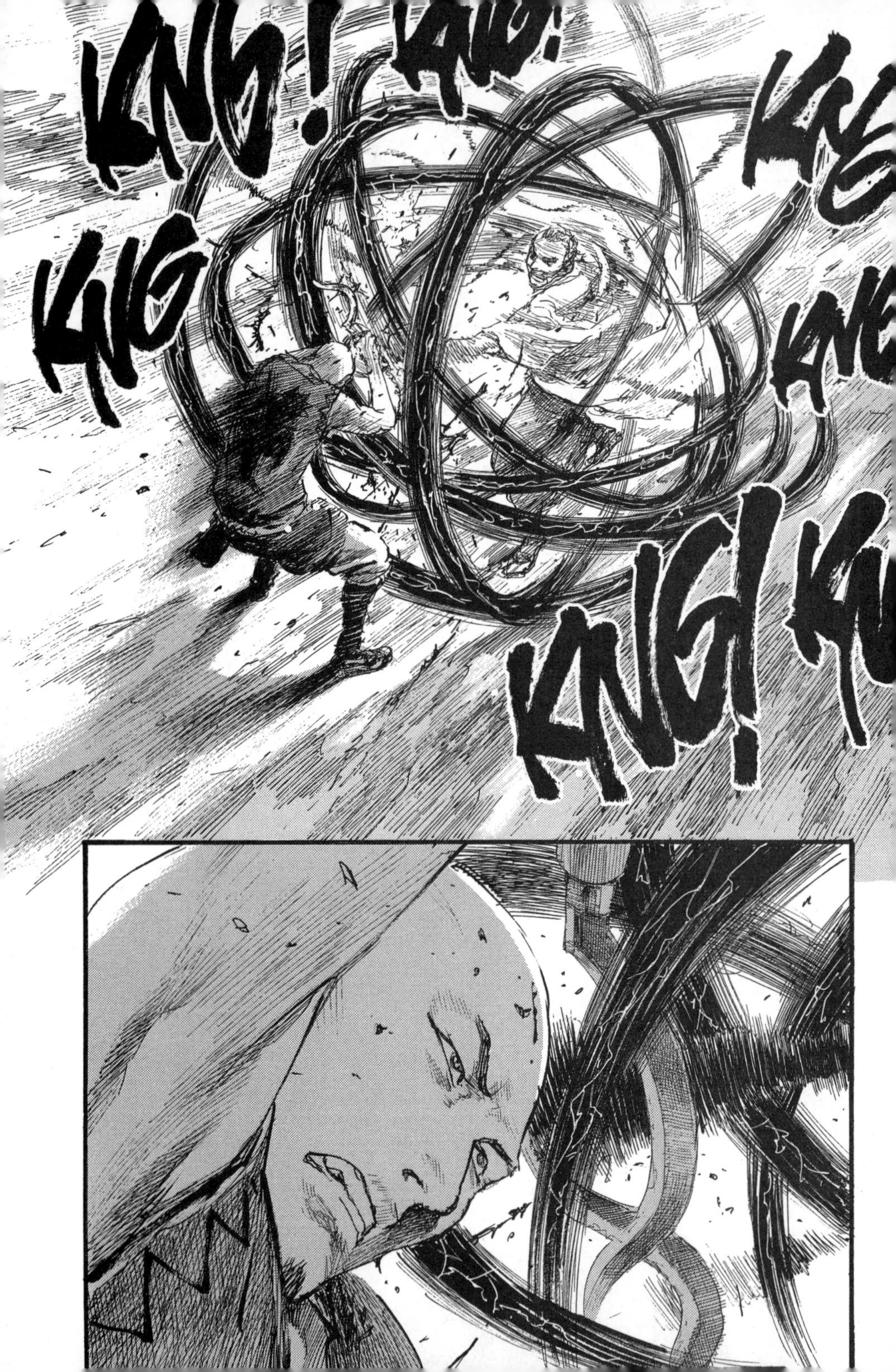
KANG! KANG!
KANG
KANG!

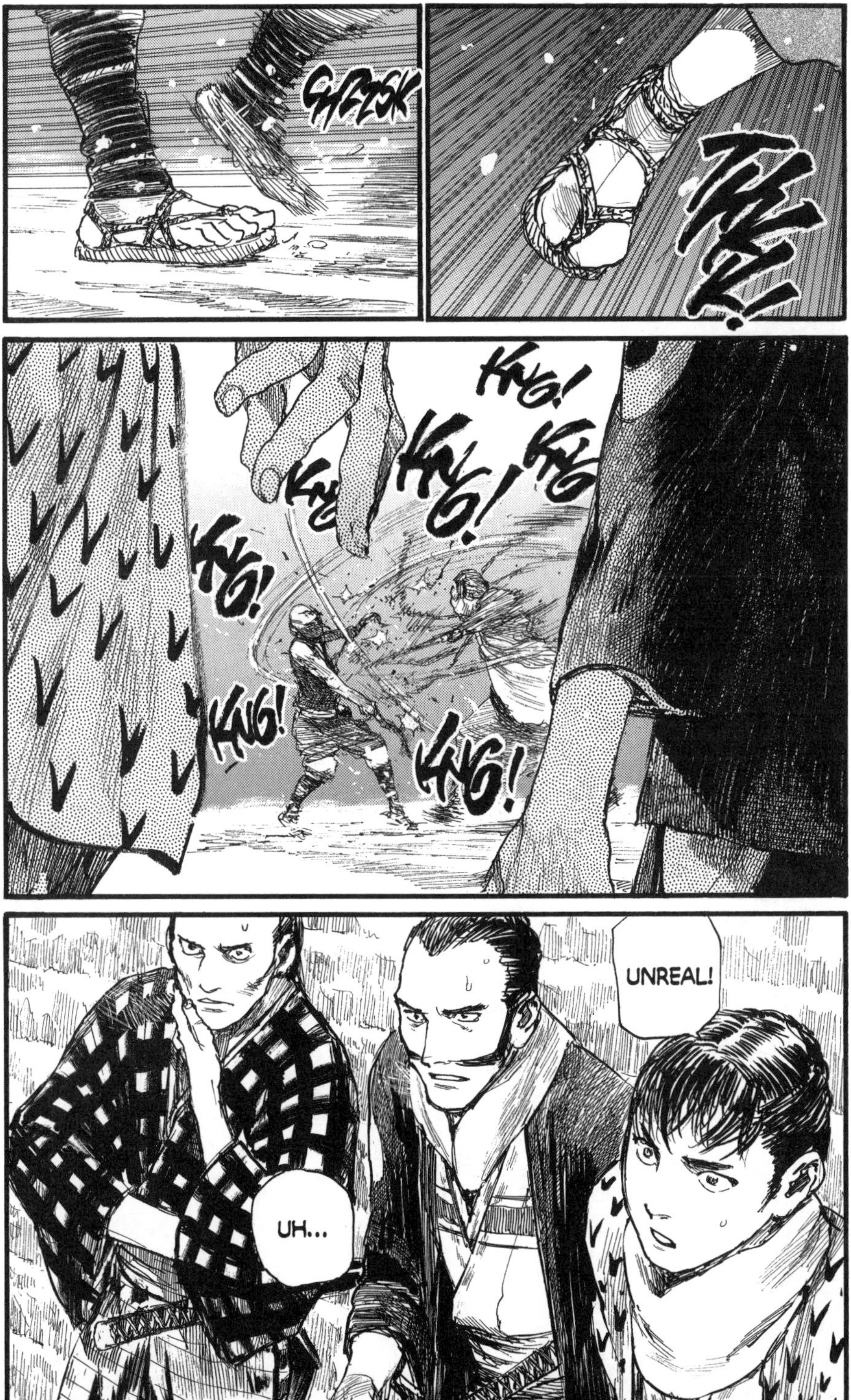
THUK!
SHRSK
KNG!
KNG!
KNG!
KNG!
KNG!
KNG!
KNG!
UNREAL!
UH...

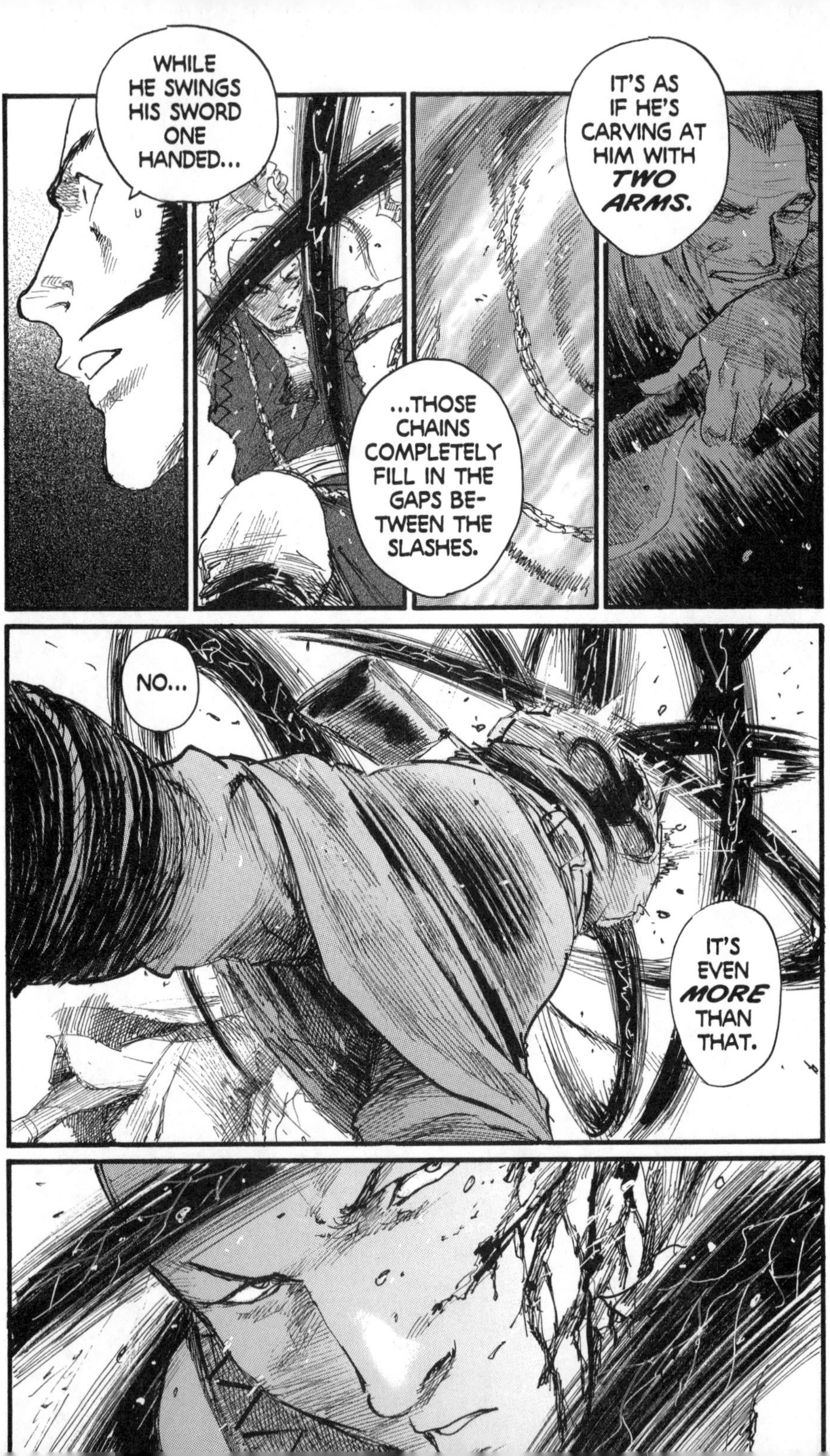
WHILE HE SWINGS HIS SWORD ONE HANDED...
...THOSE CHAINS COMPLETELY FILL IN THE GAPS BE- TWEEN THE SLASHES.
IT'S AS IF HE'S CARVING AT HIM WITH *TWO ARMS.*
NO...
IT'S EVEN *MORE* THAN THAT.

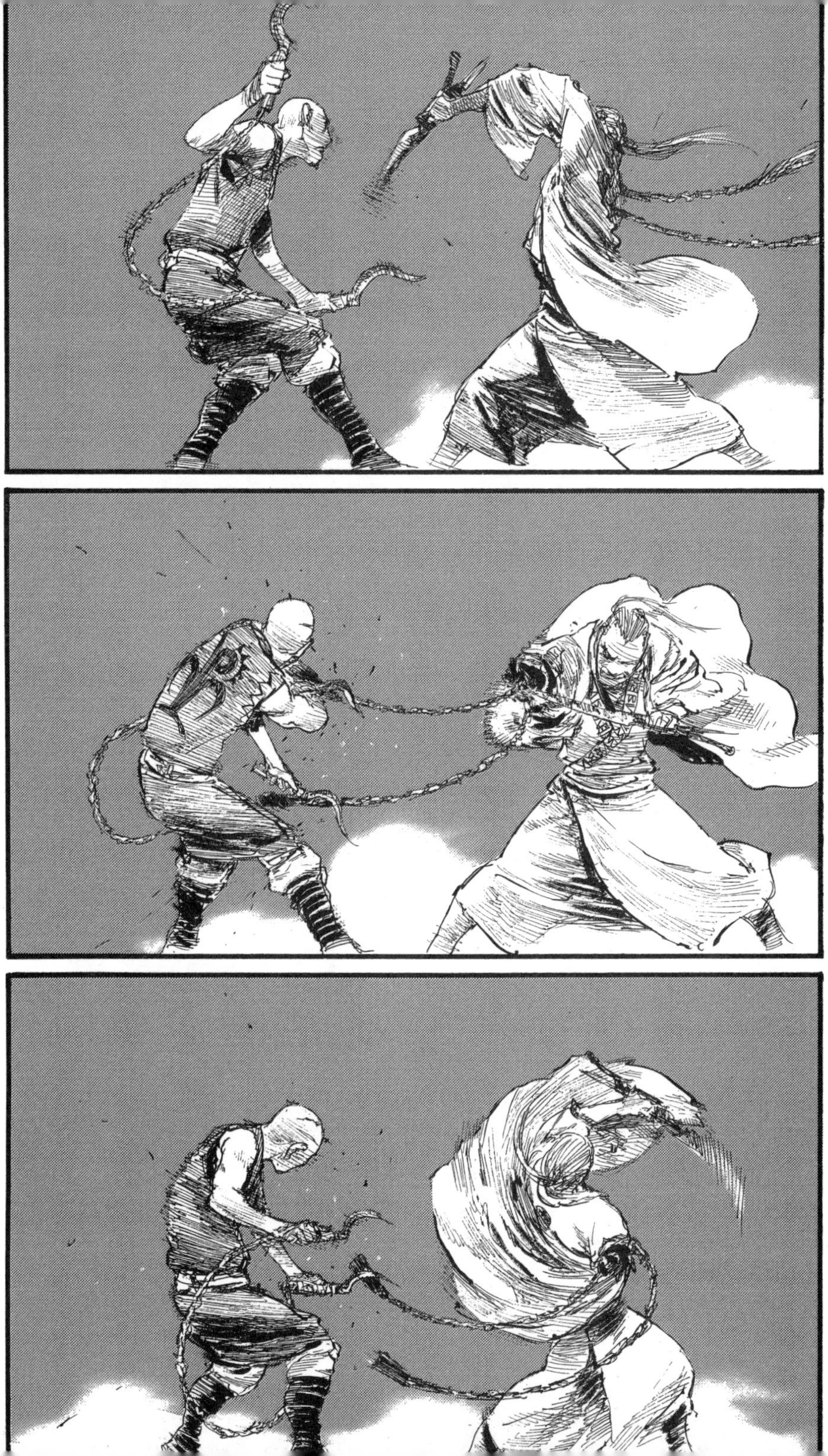

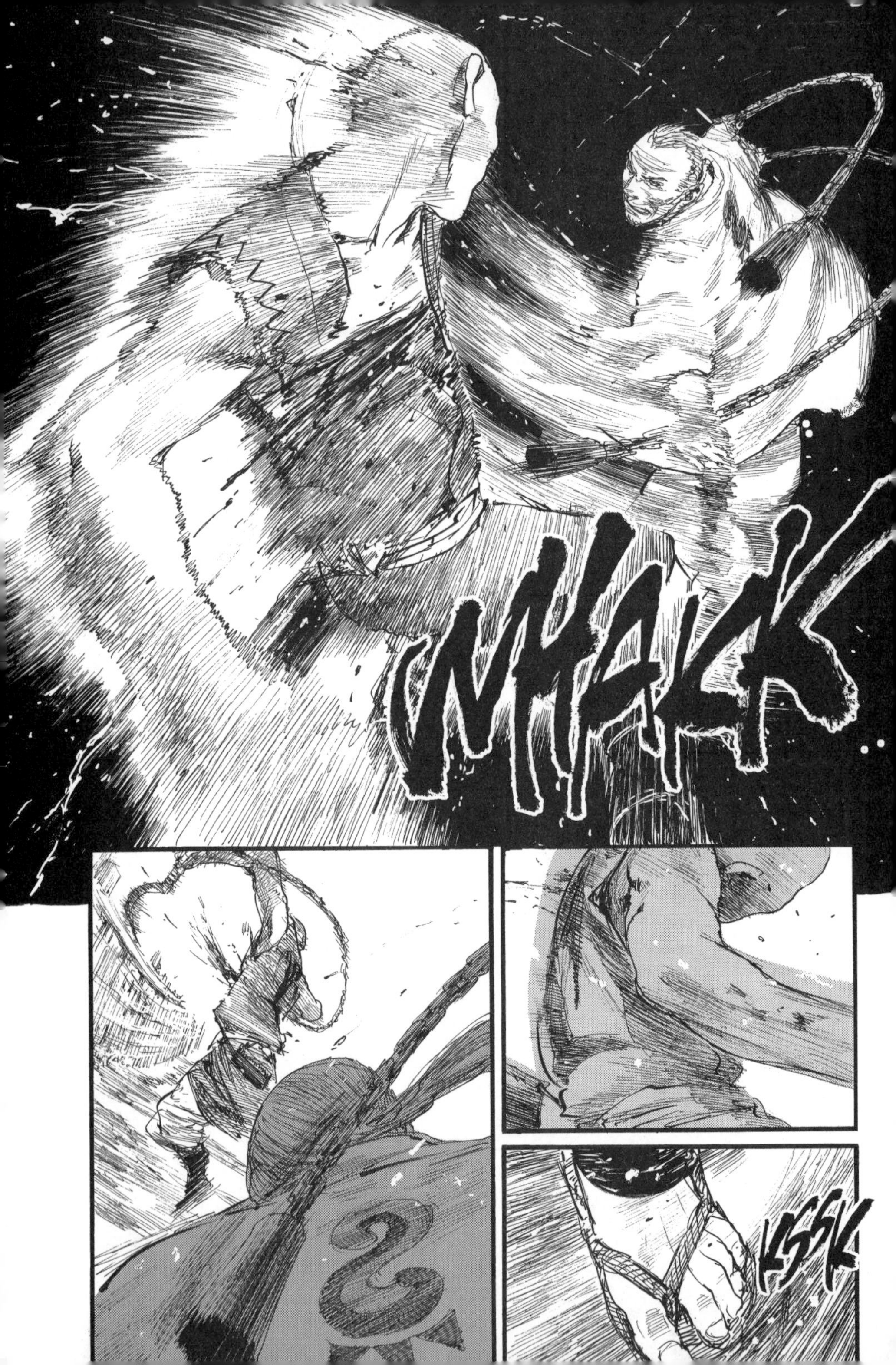
WHAK
KSSK

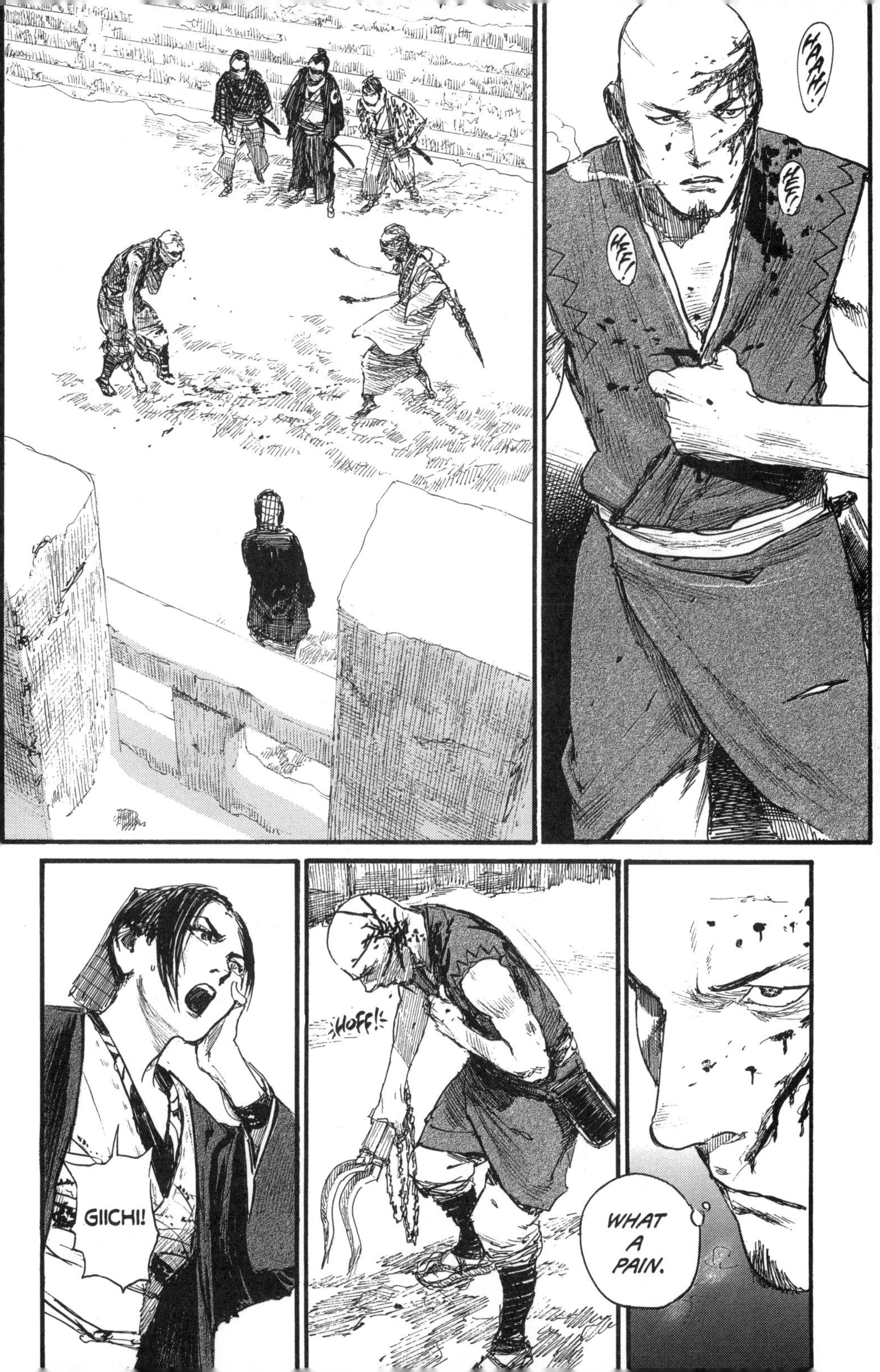
HAAH!
HEF!
HEF!
WHAT A PAIN.
HOFF!
GIICHI!

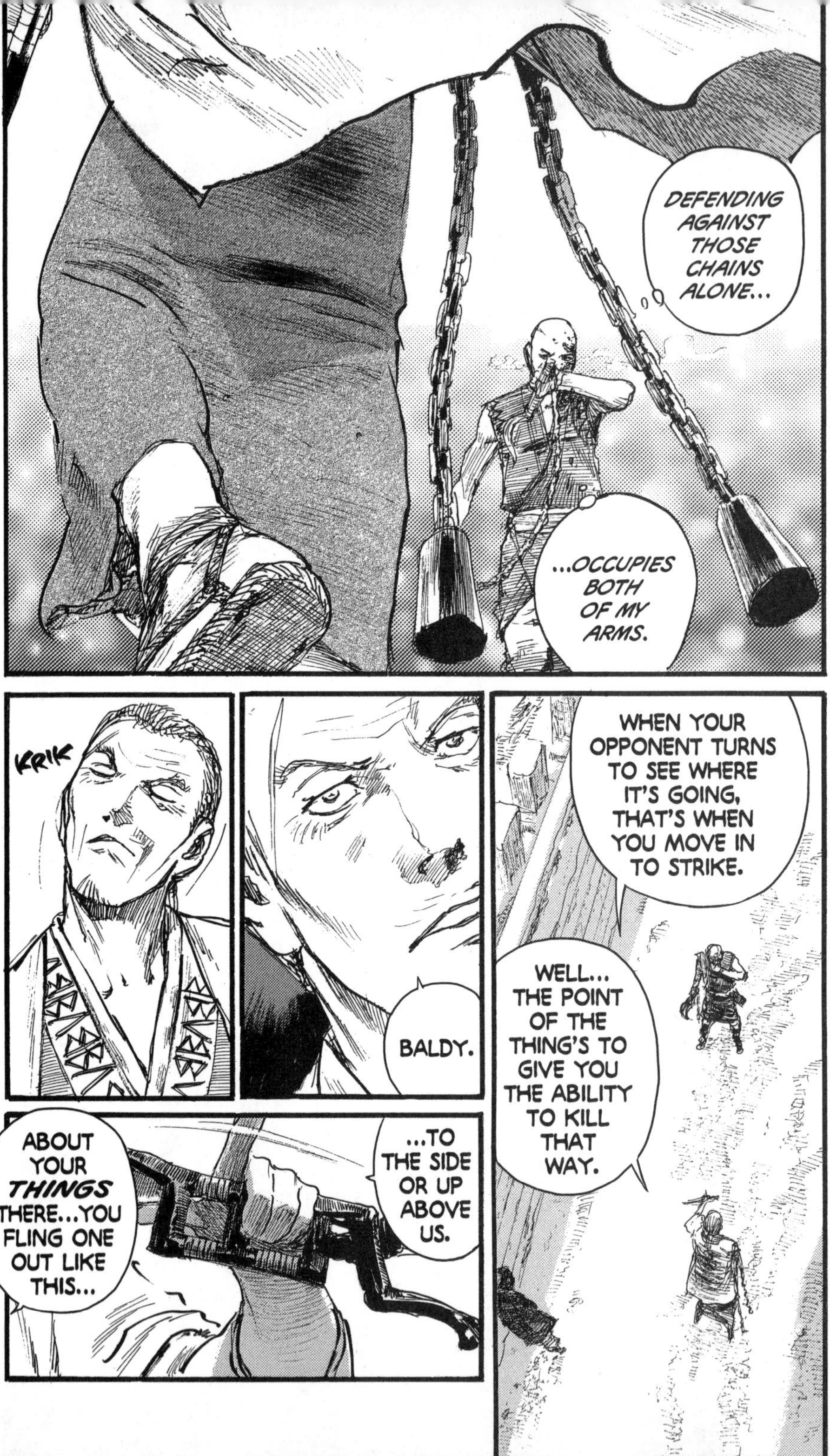
DEFENDING AGAINST THOSE CHAINS ALONE...
...OCCUPIES BOTH OF MY ARMS.
KRIK
BALDY.
ABOUT YOUR *THINGS* THERE...YOU FLING ONE OUT LIKE THIS...
...TO THE SIDE OR UP ABOVE US.
WHEN YOUR OPPONENT TURNS TO SEE WHERE IT'S GOING, THAT'S WHEN YOU MOVE IN TO STRIKE.
WELL... THE POINT OF THE THING'S TO GIVE YOU THE ABILITY TO KILL THAT WAY.

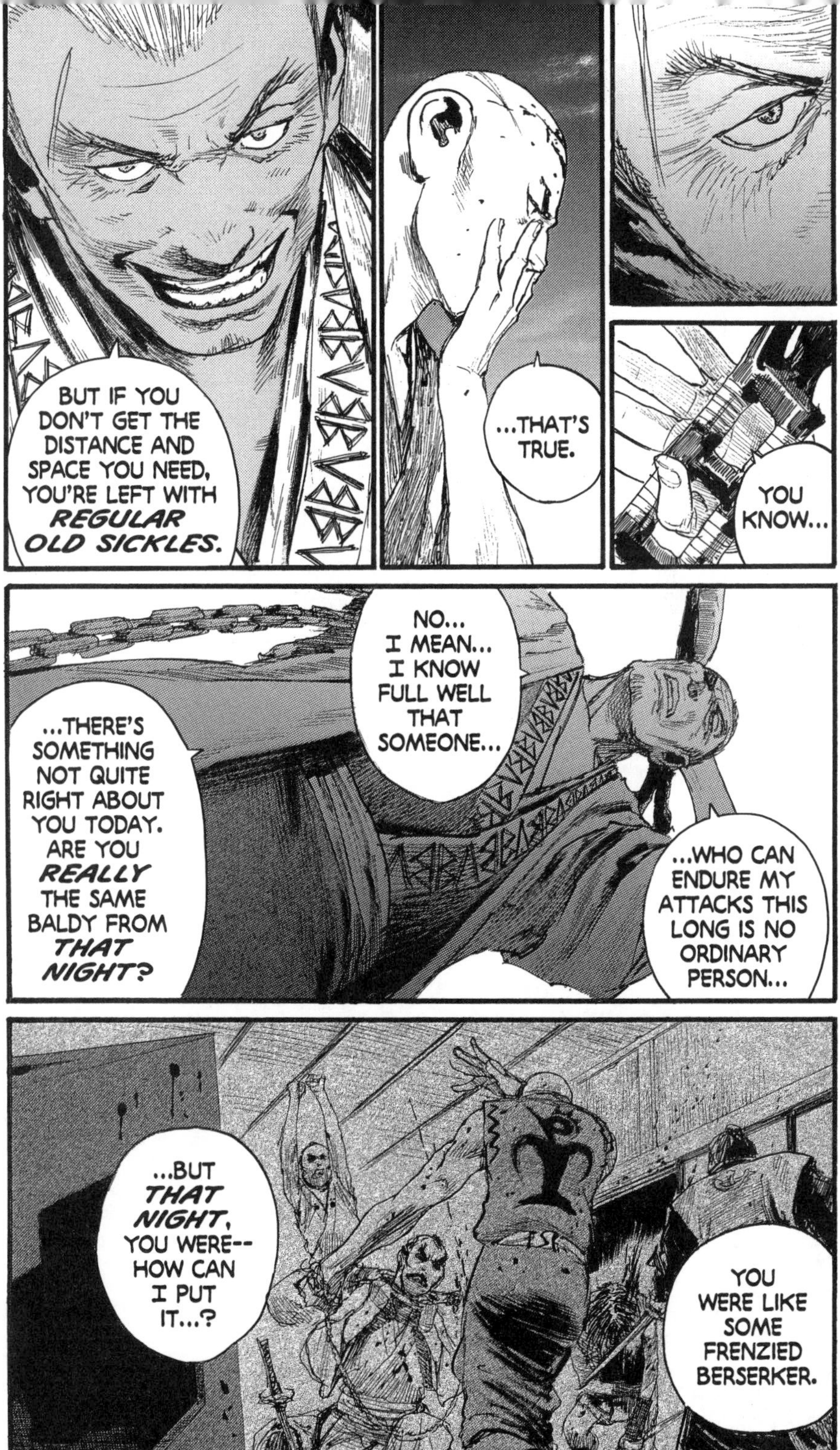
BUT IF YOU DON'T GET THE DISTANCE AND SPACE YOU NEED, YOU'RE LEFT WITH *REGULAR OLD SICKLES.*
...THAT'S TRUE.
YOU KNOW...
...THERE'S SOMETHING NOT QUITE RIGHT ABOUT YOU TODAY. ARE YOU *REALLY* THE SAME BALDY FROM *THAT NIGHT?*
NO... I MEAN... I KNOW FULL WELL THAT SOMEONE...
...WHO CAN ENDURE MY ATTACKS THIS LONG IS NO ORDINARY PERSON...
...BUT *THAT NIGHT*, YOU WERE-- HOW CAN I PUT IT...?
YOU WERE LIKE SOME FRENZIED BERSERKER.

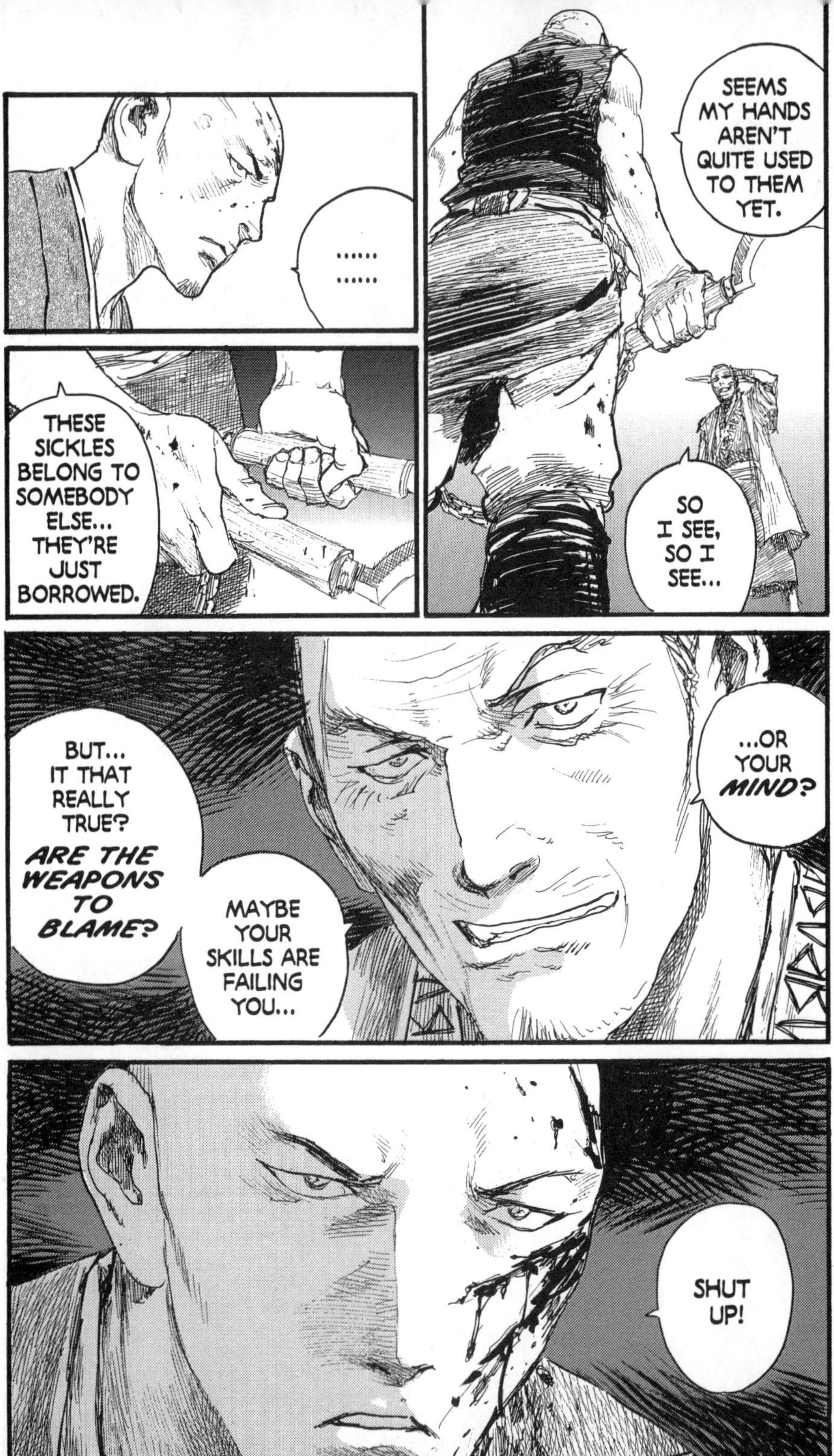
......
......
THESE SICKLES BELONG TO SOMEBODY ELSE... THEY'RE JUST BORROWED.
SEEMS MY HANDS AREN'T QUITE USED TO THEM YET.
SO I SEE, SO I SEE...
BUT... IT THAT REALLY TRUE? ARE THE WEAPONS TO BLAME?
MAYBE YOUR SKILLS ARE FAILING YOU...
...OR YOUR MIND?
SHUT UP!

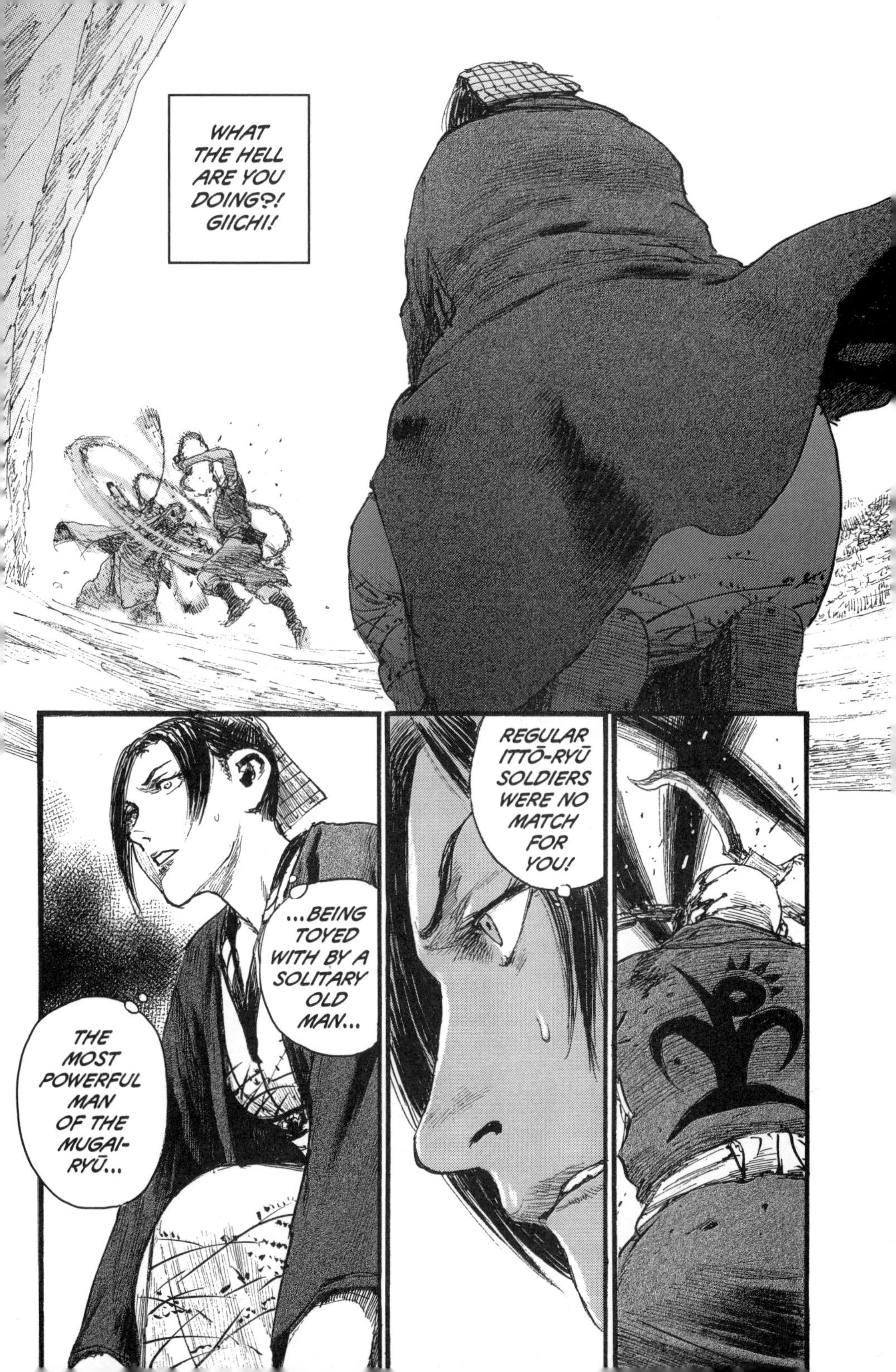
WHAT THE HELL ARE YOU DOING?! GIICHI!
REGULAR ITTŌ-RYŪ SOLDIERS WERE NO MATCH FOR YOU!
THE MOST POWERFUL MAN OF THE MUGAI-RYŪ...
...BEING TOYED WITH BY A SOLITARY OLD MAN...

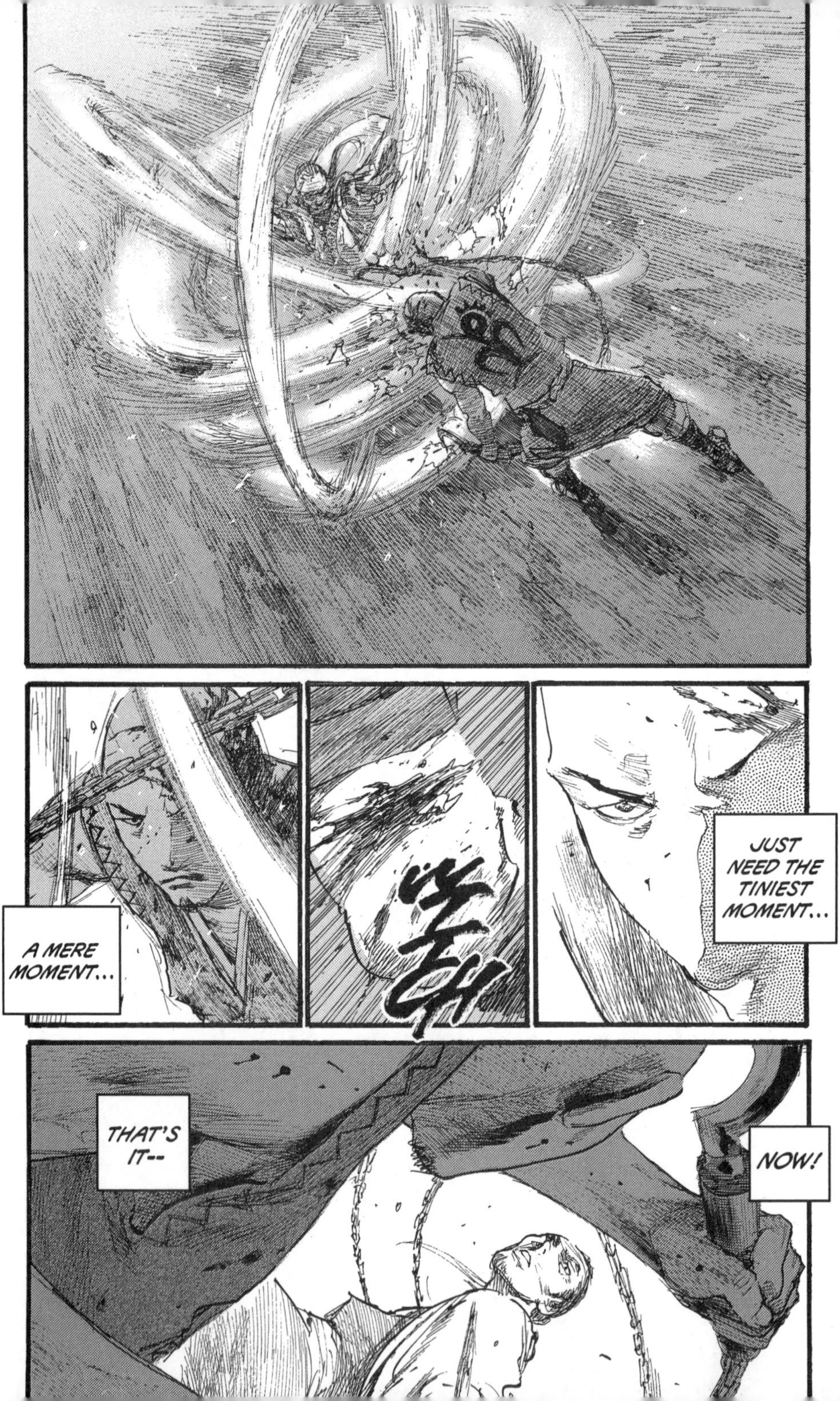
JUST NEED THE TINIEST MOMENT...
A MERE MOMENT...
THAT'S IT--
NOW!

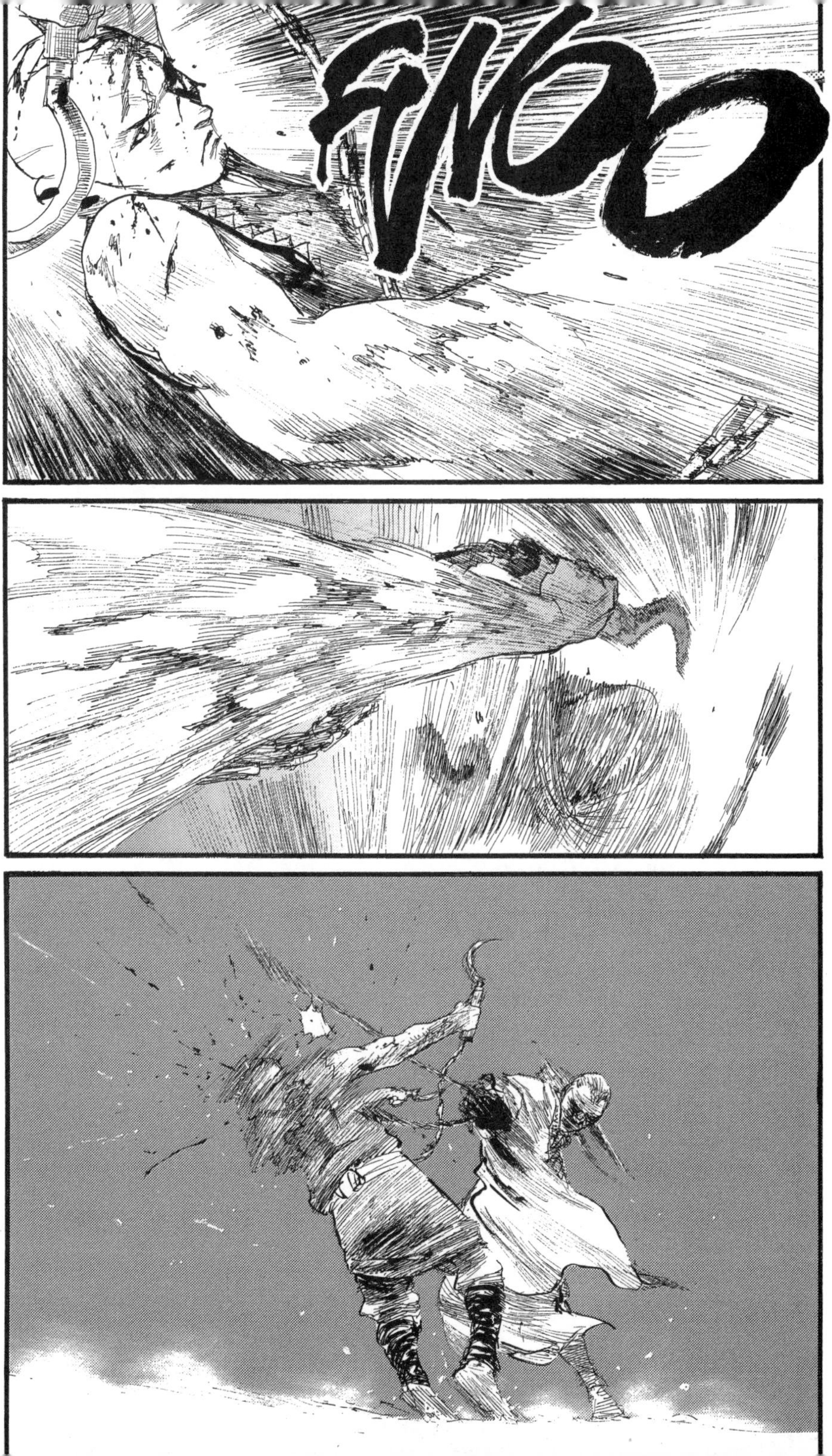
FWOO

THEY'RE GOING SO FAST! I CAN'T EVEN FOLLOW WHAT'S HAPPENING.

......
......

WATCHING THEM FROM THE SIDELINES LIKE THIS, IT'S QUITE CLEAR THAT THIS OPPONENT IS A FIGHTER OF CONSIDERABLE SKILL.

BUT EVEN SO, DOES HE HAVE ANY HOPE AT ALL...

...AGAINST WEAPONS LIKE THOSE?!

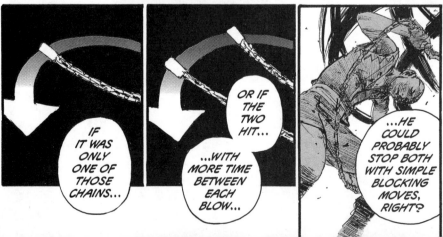

IF IT WAS ONLY ONE OF THOSE CHAINS...

OR IF THE TWO HIT...

...WITH MORE TIME BETWEEN EACH BLOW...

...HE COULD PROBABLY STOP BOTH WITH SIMPLE BLOCKING MOVES, RIGHT?

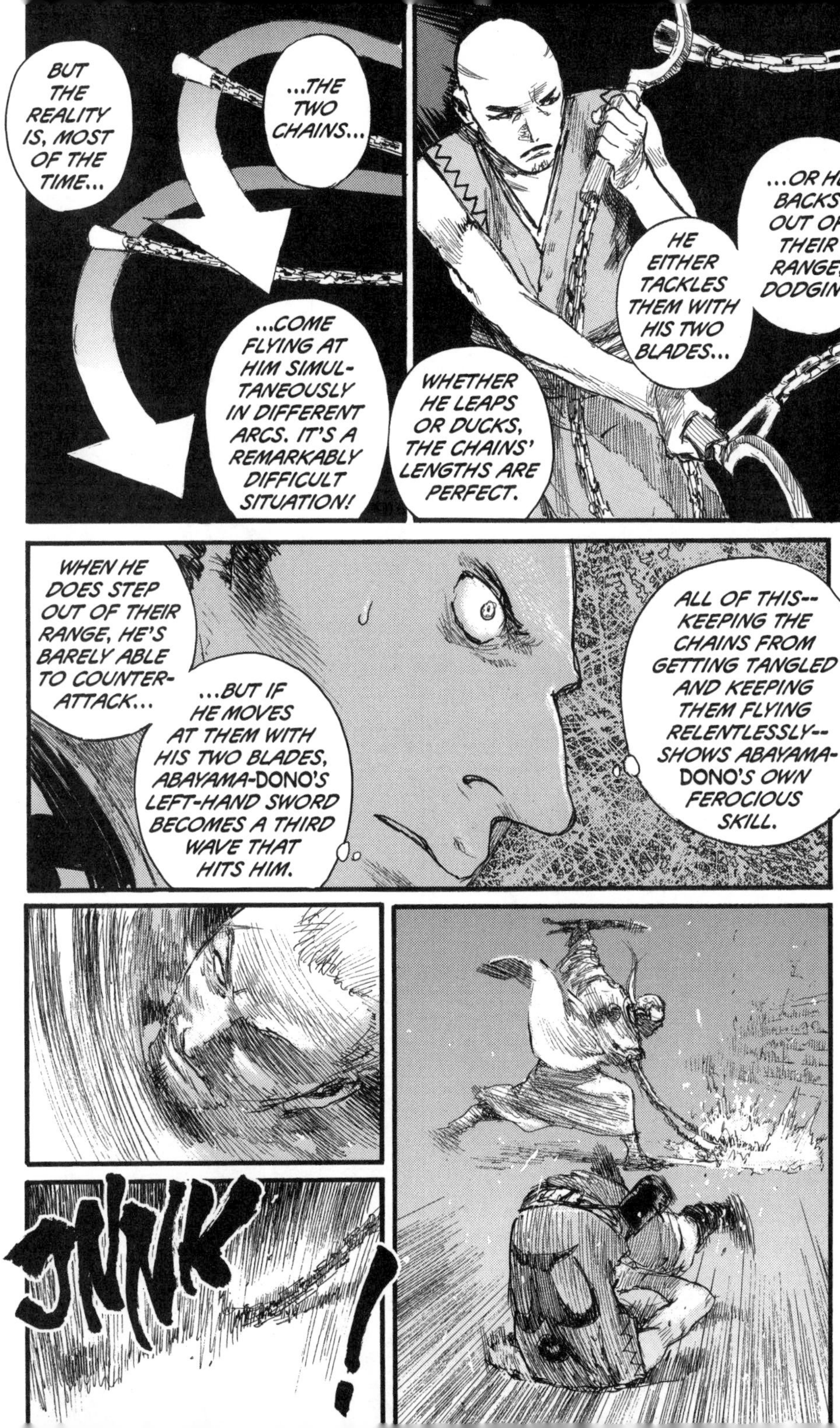
BUT THE REALITY IS, MOST OF THE TIME...
...THE TWO CHAINS...
...COME FLYING AT HIM SIMUL-TANEOUSLY IN DIFFERENT ARCS. IT'S A REMARKABLY DIFFICULT SITUATION!
WHETHER HE LEAPS OR DUCKS, THE CHAINS' LENGTHS ARE PERFECT.
HE EITHER TACKLES THEM WITH HIS TWO BLADES...
...OR HE BACKS OUT OF THEIR RANGE, DODGING.
WHEN HE DOES STEP OUT OF THEIR RANGE, HE'S BARELY ABLE TO COUNTER-ATTACK...
...BUT IF HE MOVES AT THEM WITH HIS TWO BLADES, ABAYAMA-DONO'S LEFT-HAND SWORD BECOMES A THIRD WAVE THAT HITS HIM.
ALL OF THIS--KEEPING THE CHAINS FROM GETTING TANGLED AND KEEPING THEM FLYING RELENTLESSLY--SHOWS ABAYAMA-DONO'S OWN FEROCIOUS SKILL.
JINK!

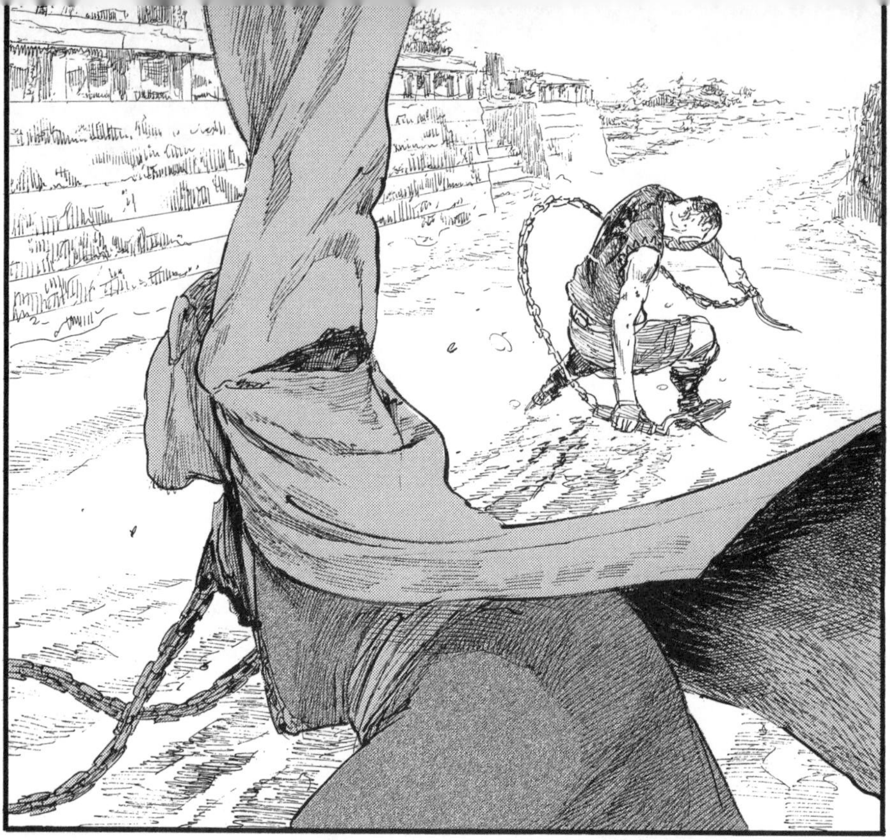
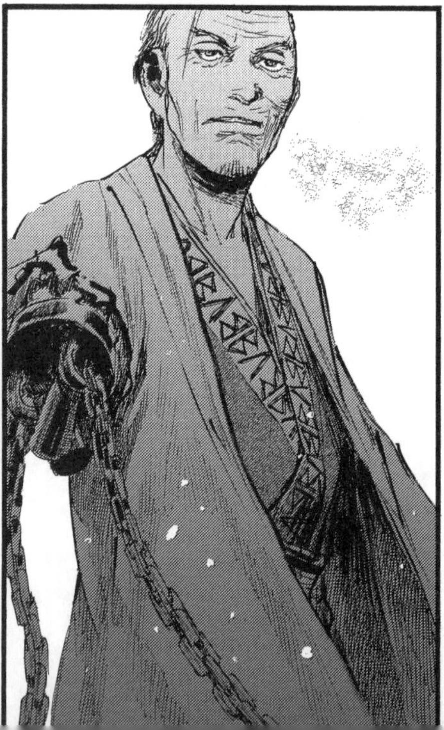
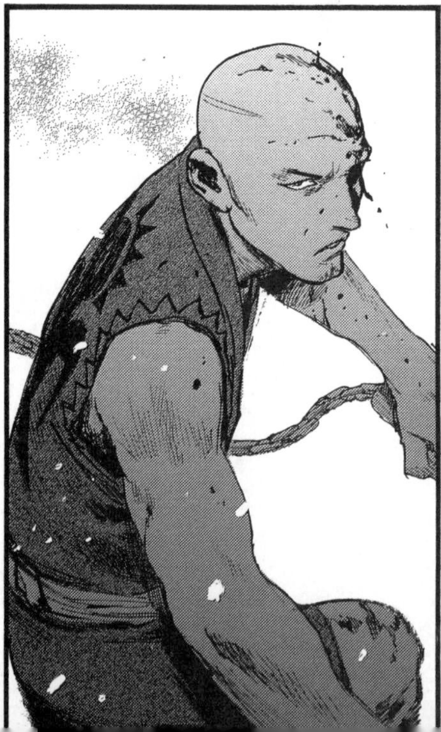

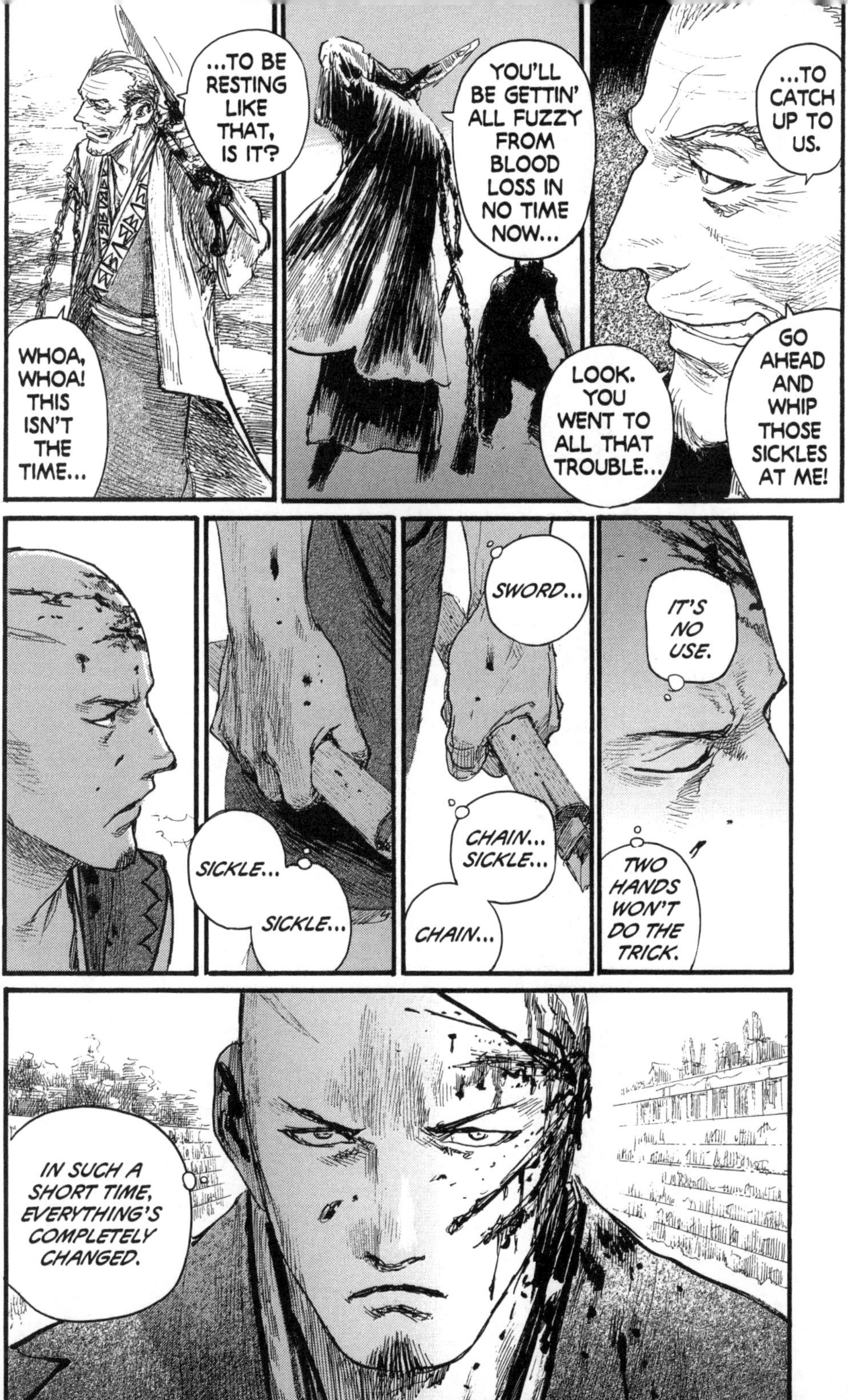
WHOA, WHOA! THIS ISN'T THE TIME...
...TO BE RESTING LIKE THAT, IS IT?
YOU'LL BE GETTIN' ALL FUZZY FROM BLOOD LOSS IN NO TIME NOW...
LOOK. YOU WENT TO ALL THAT TROUBLE...
...TO CATCH UP TO US.
GO AHEAD AND WHIP THOSE SICKLES AT ME!
SICKLE...
SICKLE...
SWORD...
CHAIN... SICKLE...
CHAIN...
IT'S NO USE.
TWO HANDS WON'T DO THE TRICK.
IN SUCH A SHORT TIME, EVERYTHING'S COMPLETELY CHANGED.

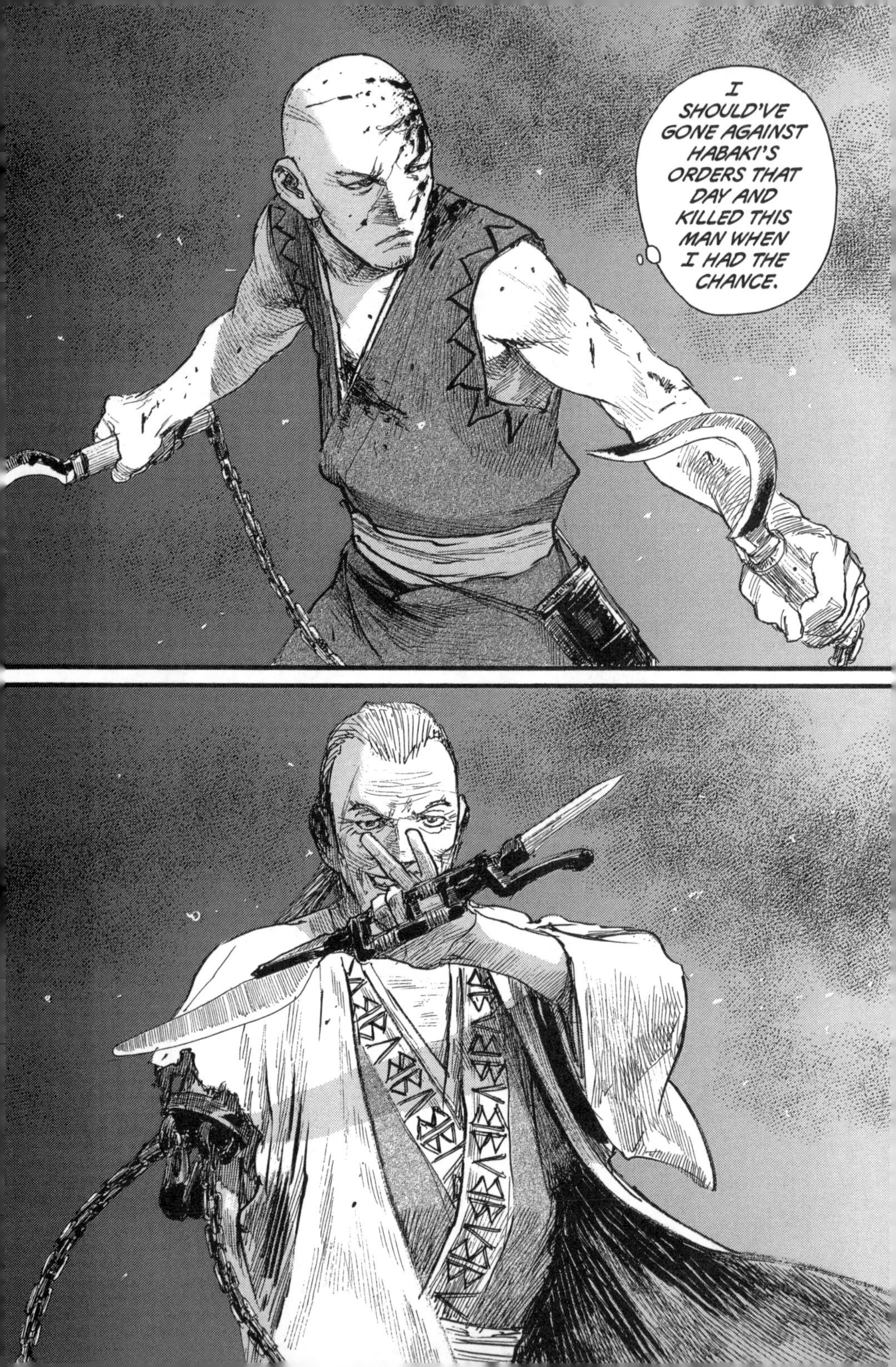
I SHOULD'VE GONE AGAINST HABAKI'S ORDERS THAT DAY AND KILLED THIS MAN WHEN I HAD THE CHANCE.

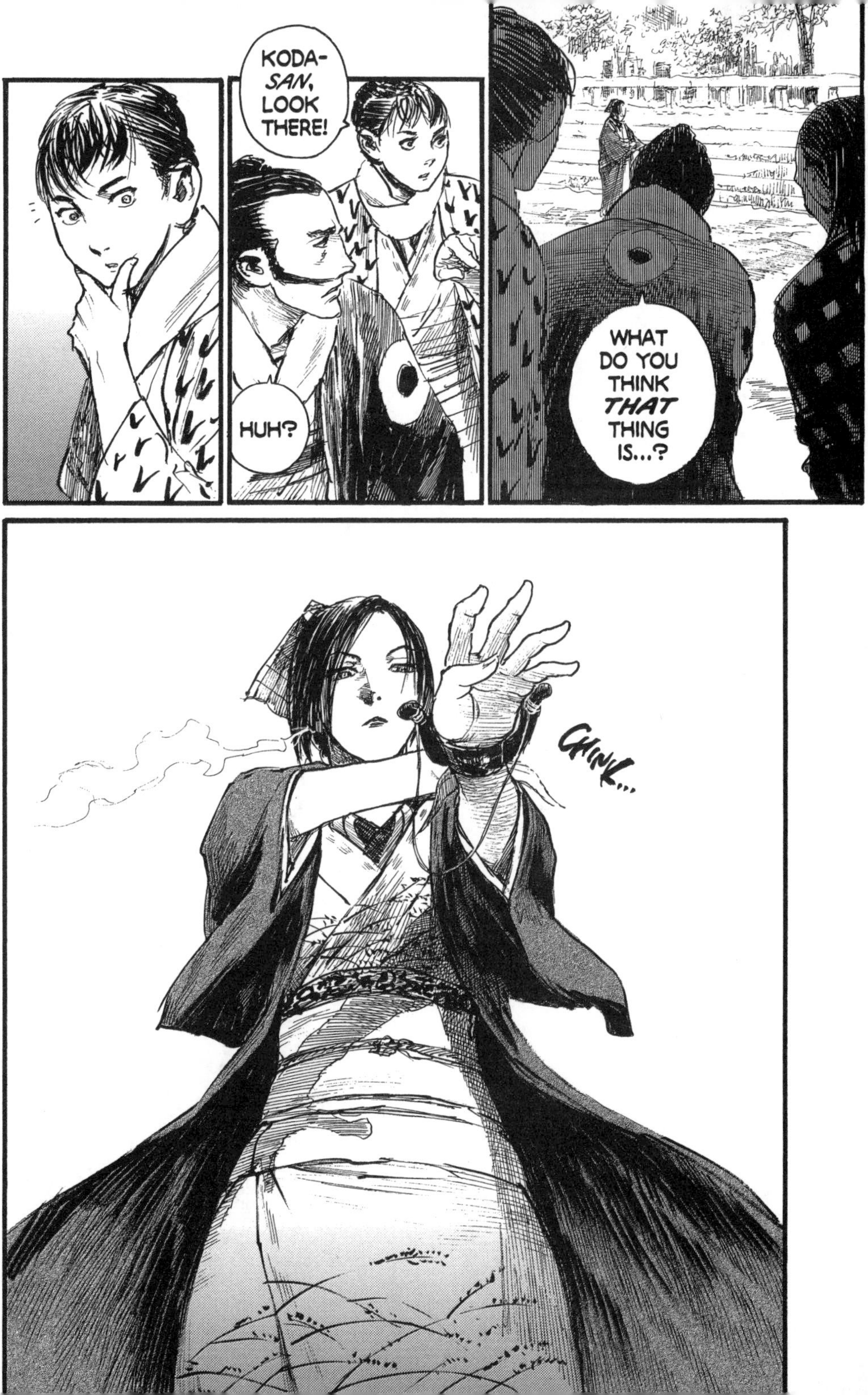
WHAT DO YOU THINK *THAT* THING IS...?
KODA-*SAN*, LOOK THERE!
HUH?
CHINK...

TUUU!

CHKK!

KCHK!

KRKKRRRK

WHA--?!

WHAT *IS* THAT? A BOW?!

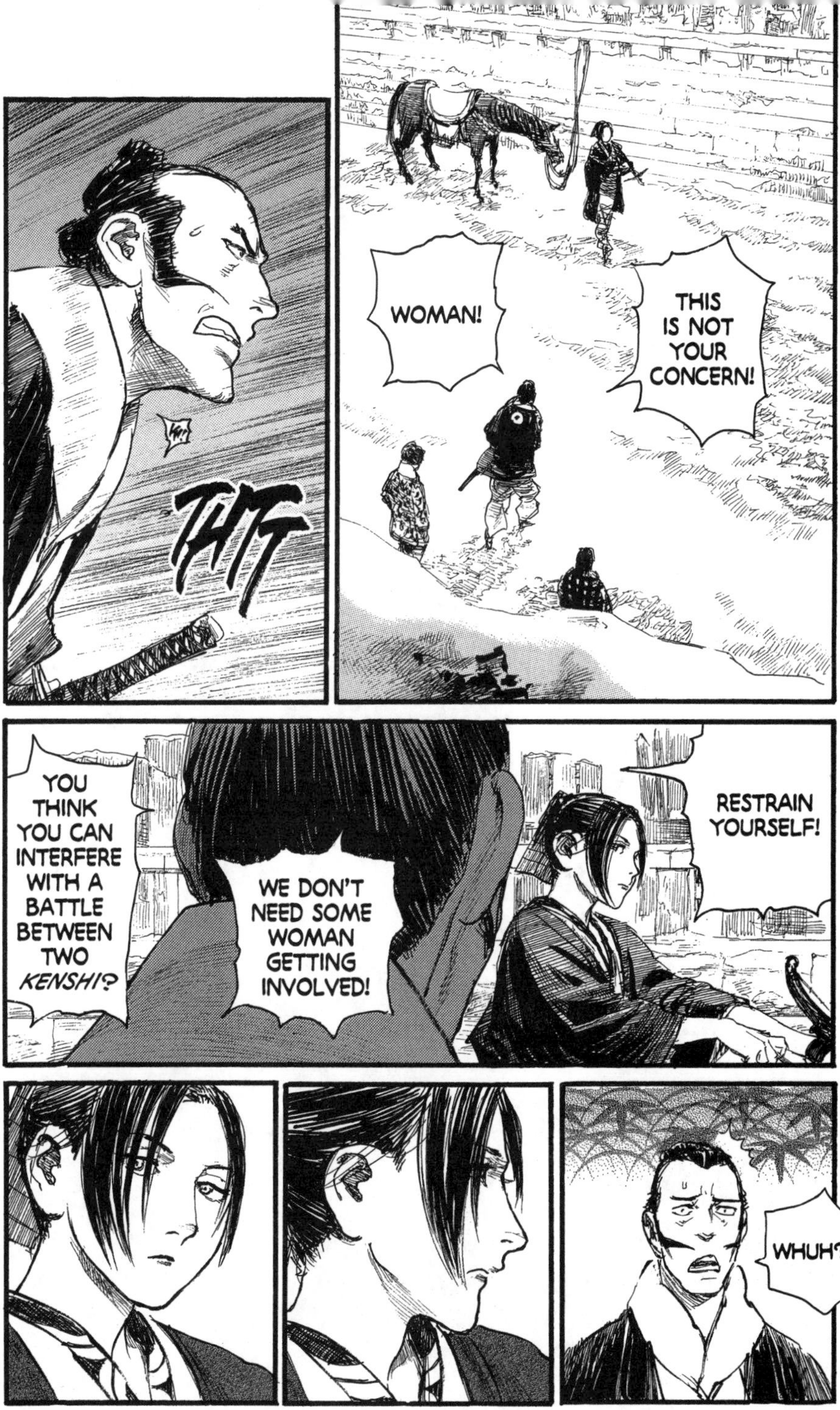
WOMAN!
THIS IS NOT YOUR CONCERN!
THTT
RESTRAIN YOURSELF!
WE DON'T NEED SOME WOMAN GETTING INVOLVED!
YOU THINK YOU CAN INTERFERE WITH A BATTLE BETWEEN TWO *KENSHI*?
WHUH?

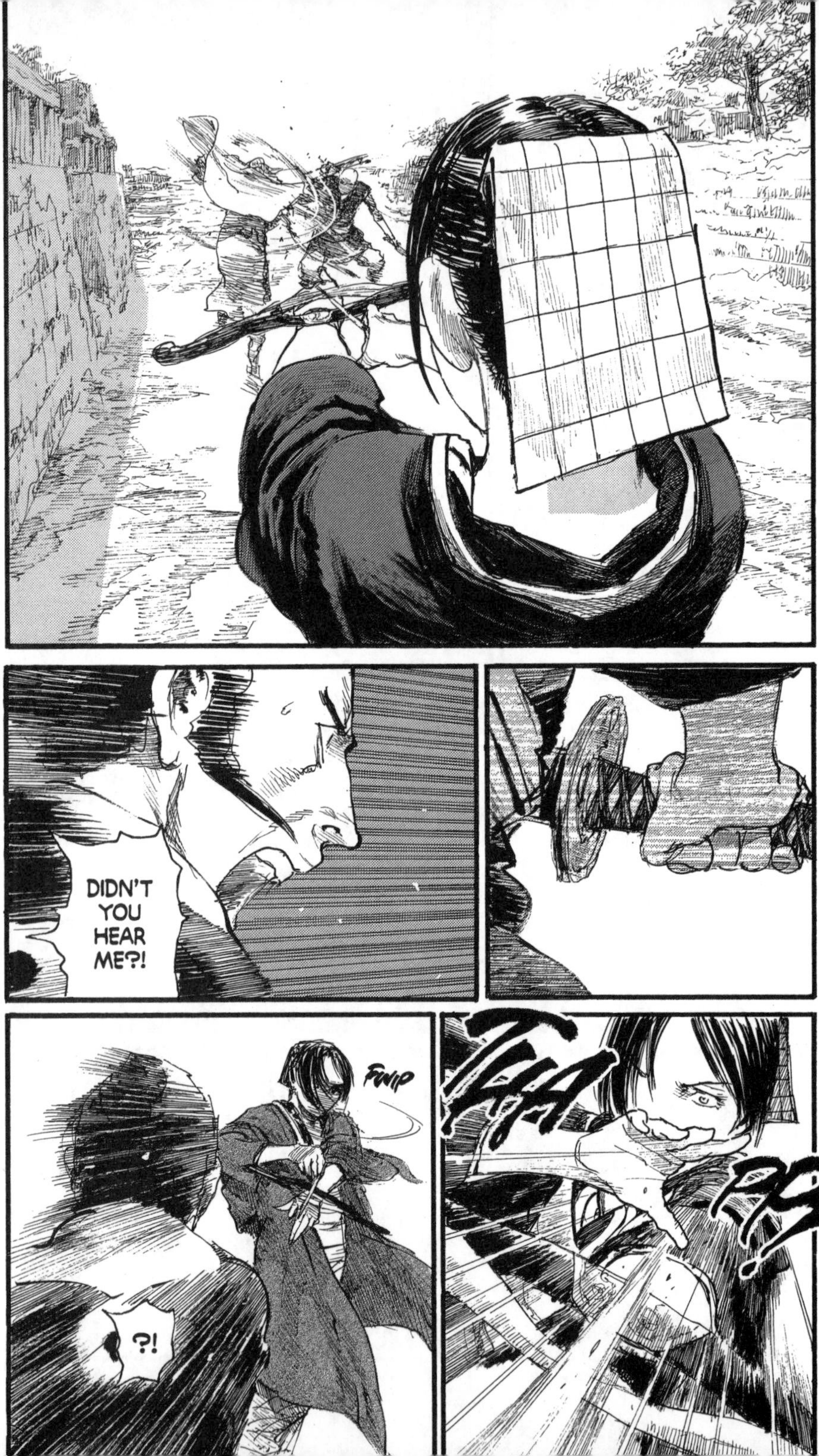
DIDN'T YOU HEAR ME?!
FWIP
?!

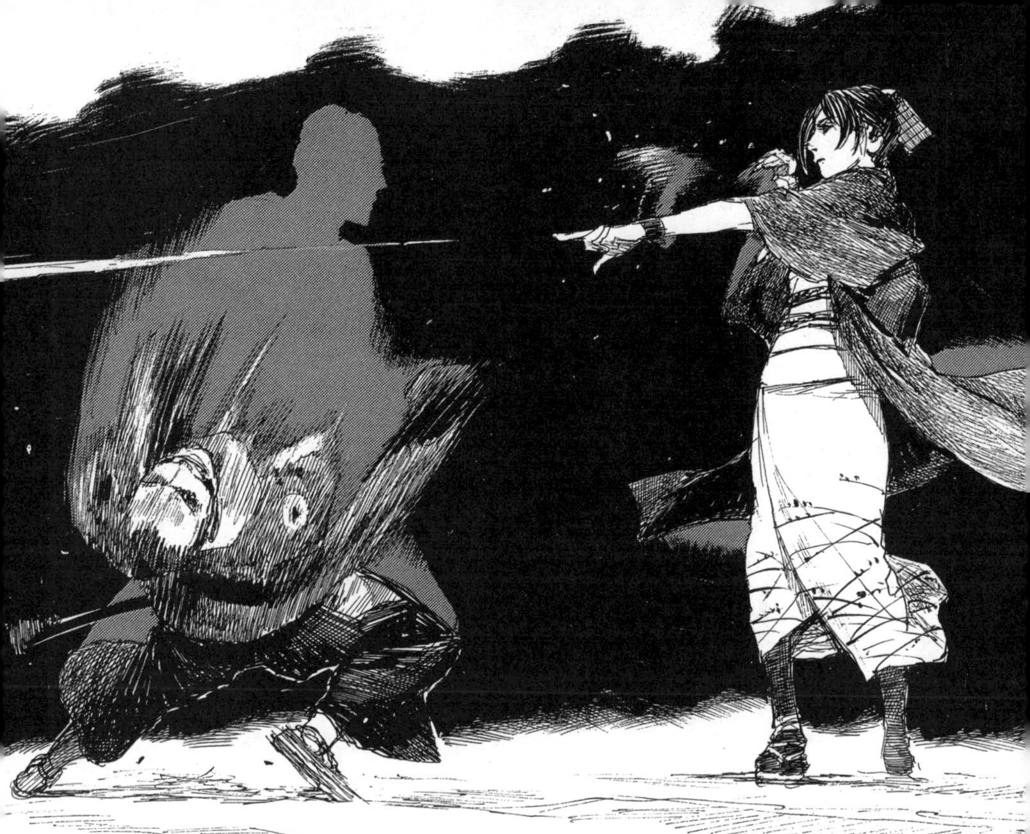

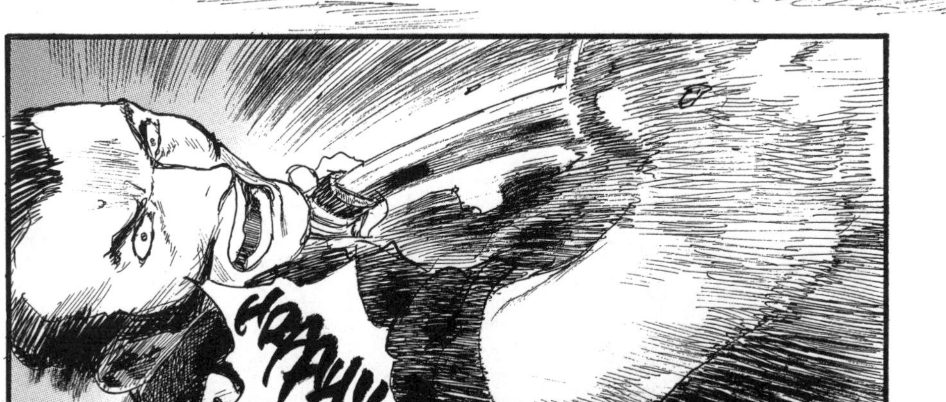
GWAAH!!

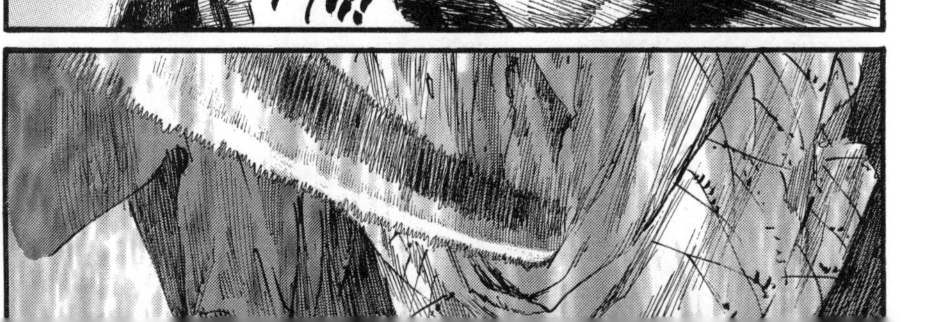

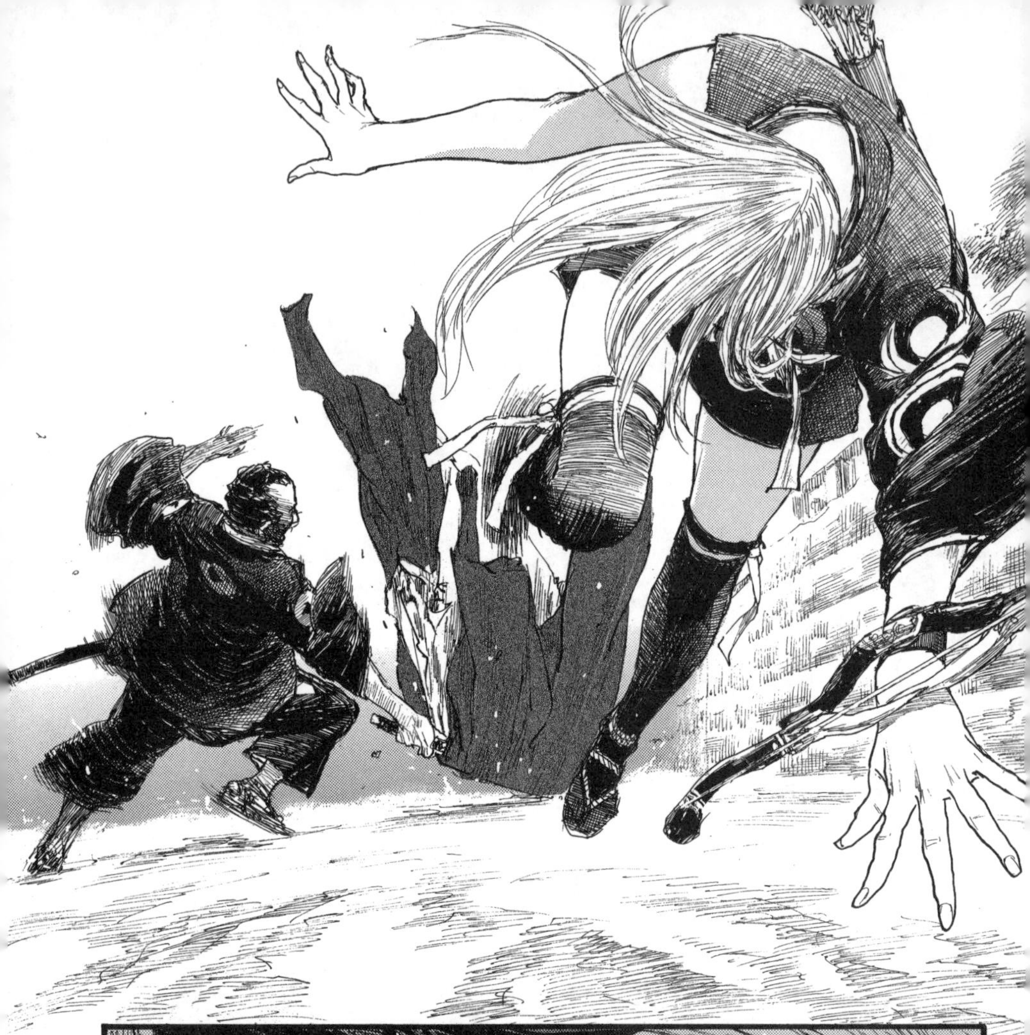
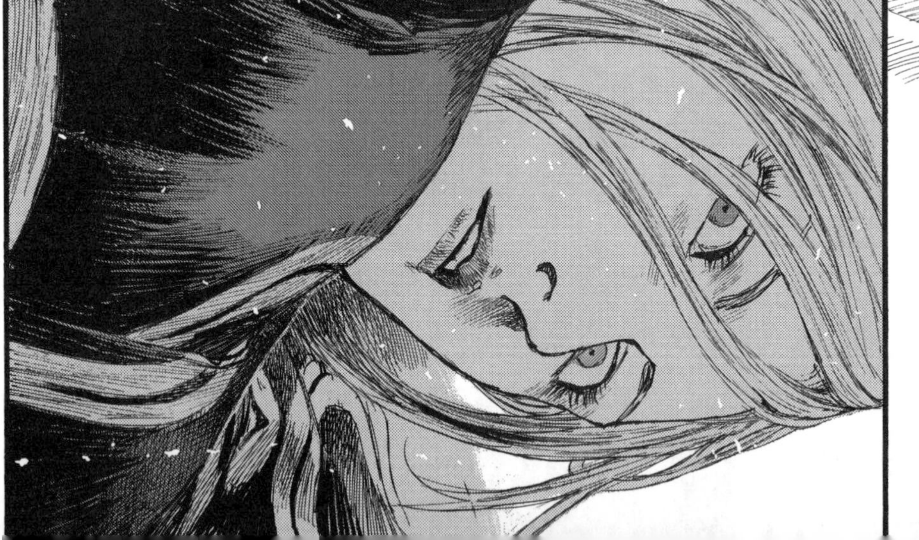

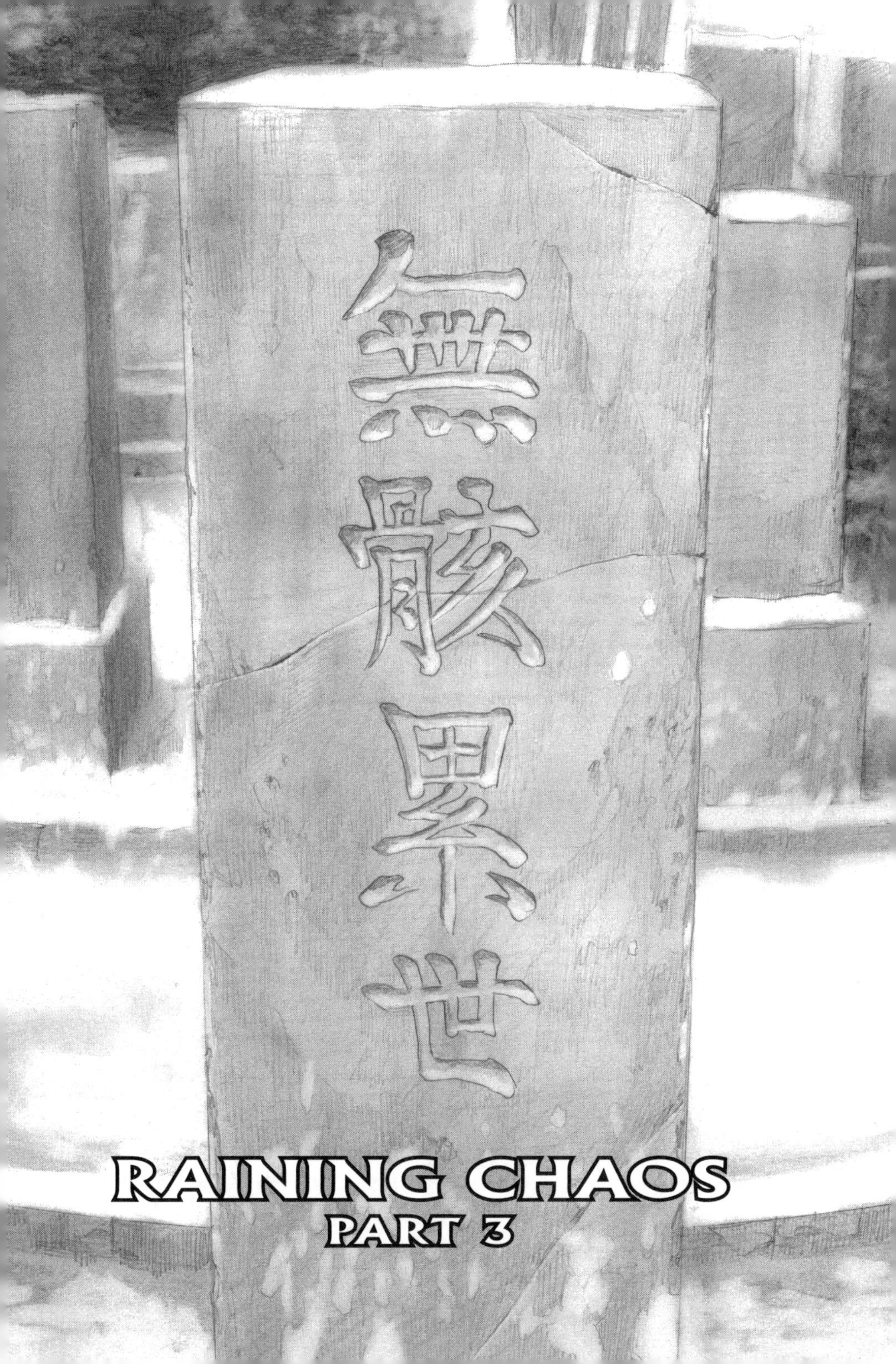
無骸果世

RAINING CHAOS
PART 3

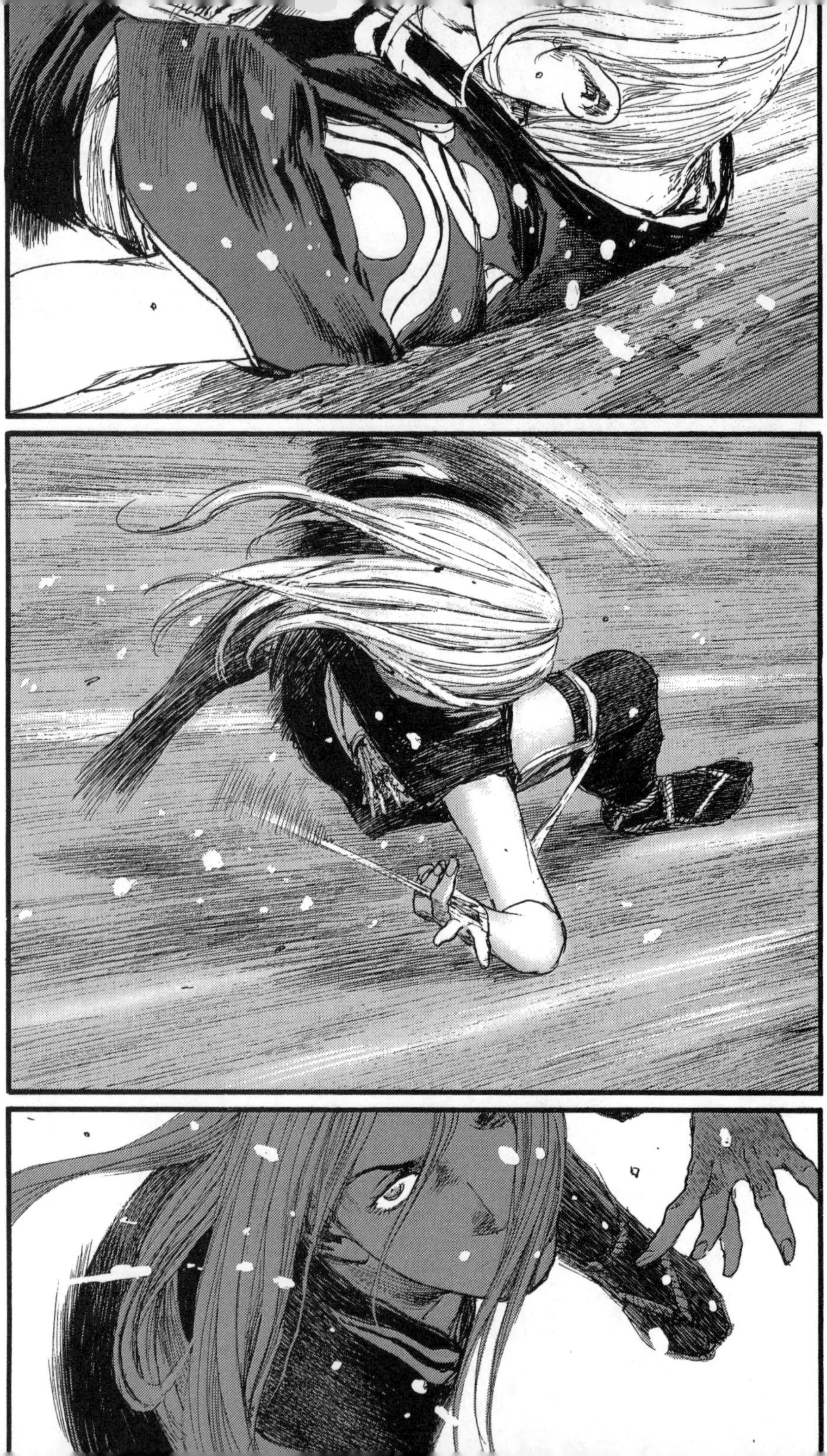

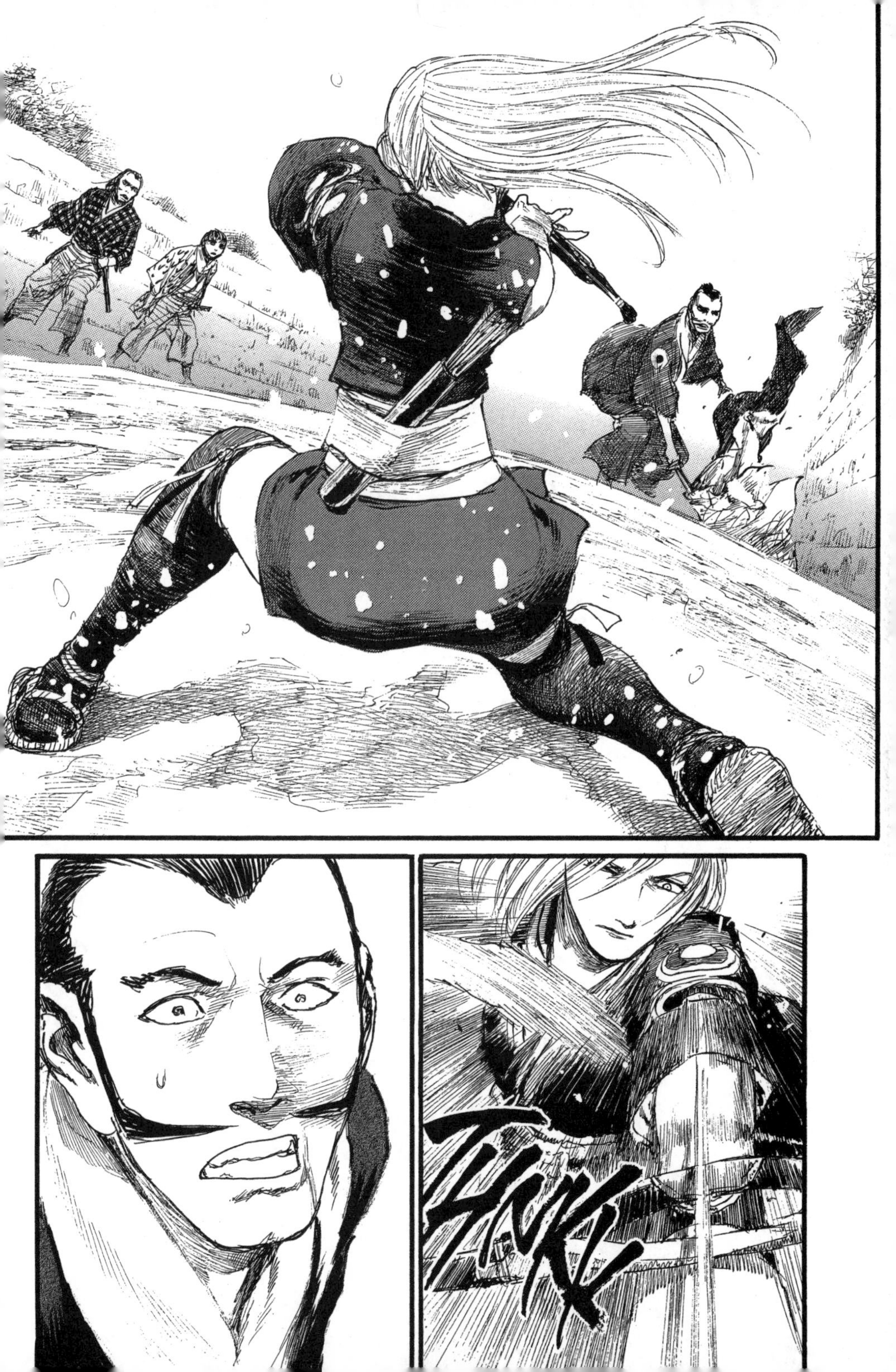

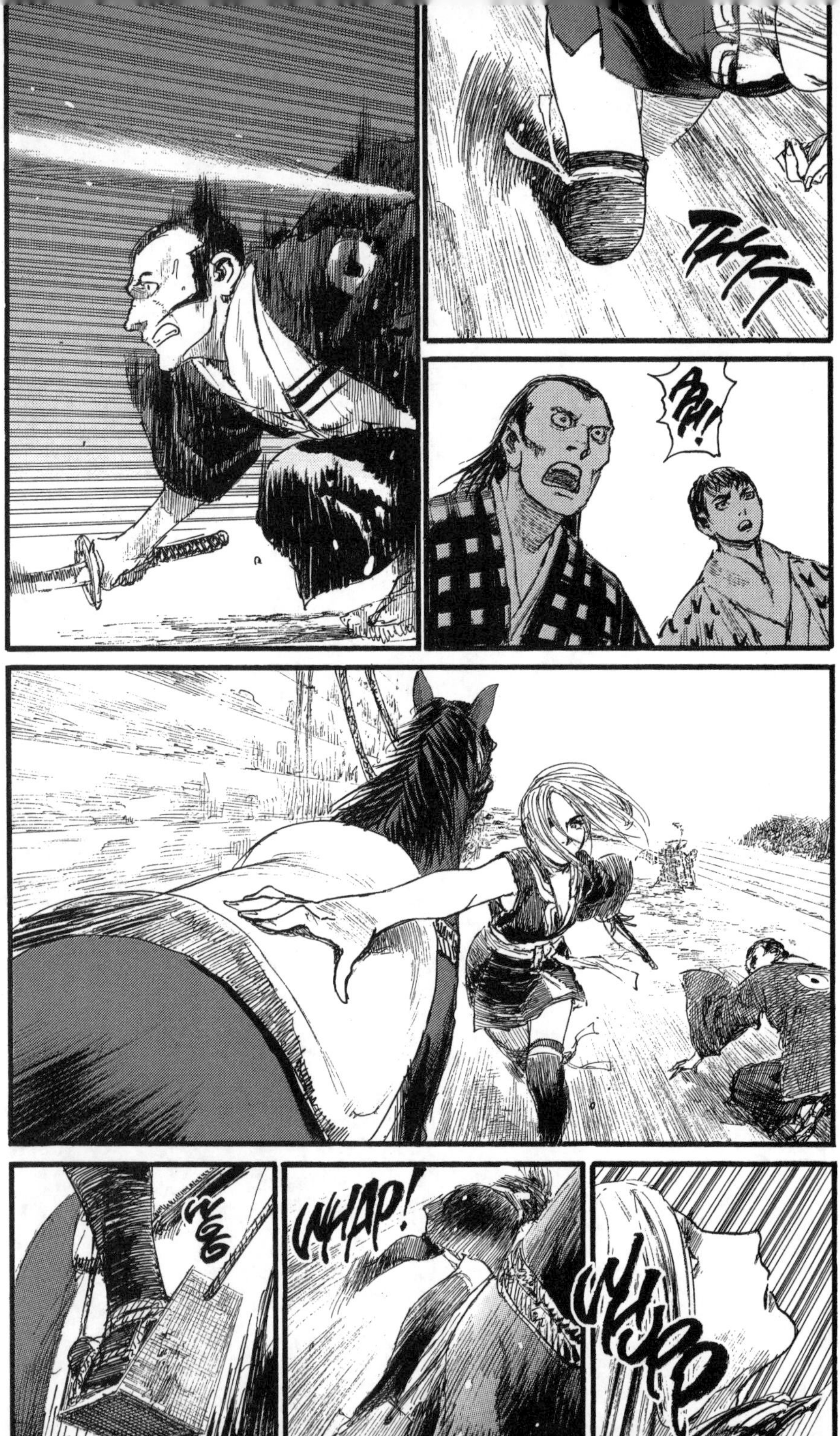
AH!
WHAP!

DODUMP

YOW...
OW...

...
...

SHIT!

COOL IT, KODA!

DON'T LOSE YOUR HEAD!

YOU'LL BECOME AN EASY TARGET!

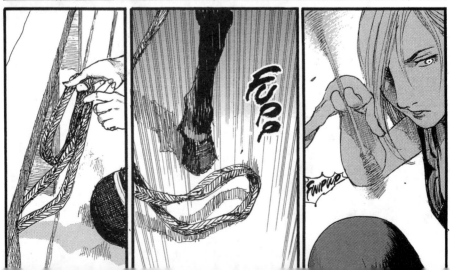

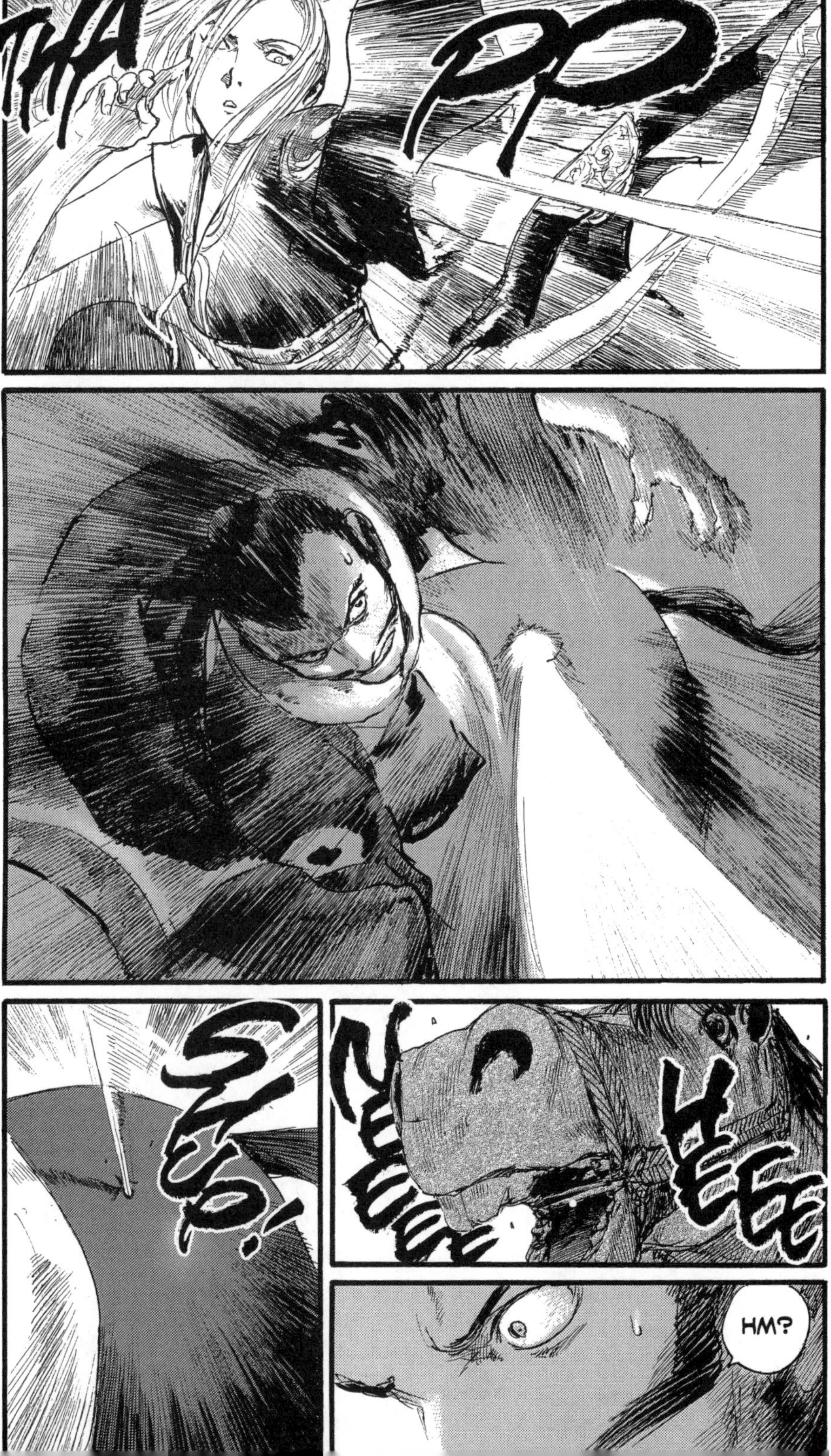
THAPP
HEEE
NEEEEE
HM?
SHUP!

KAK!!

KODA!

KODA-
DONO!

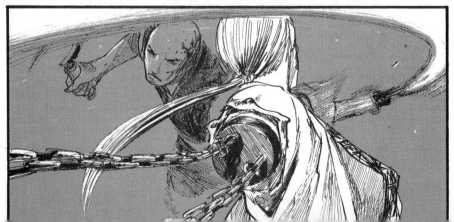

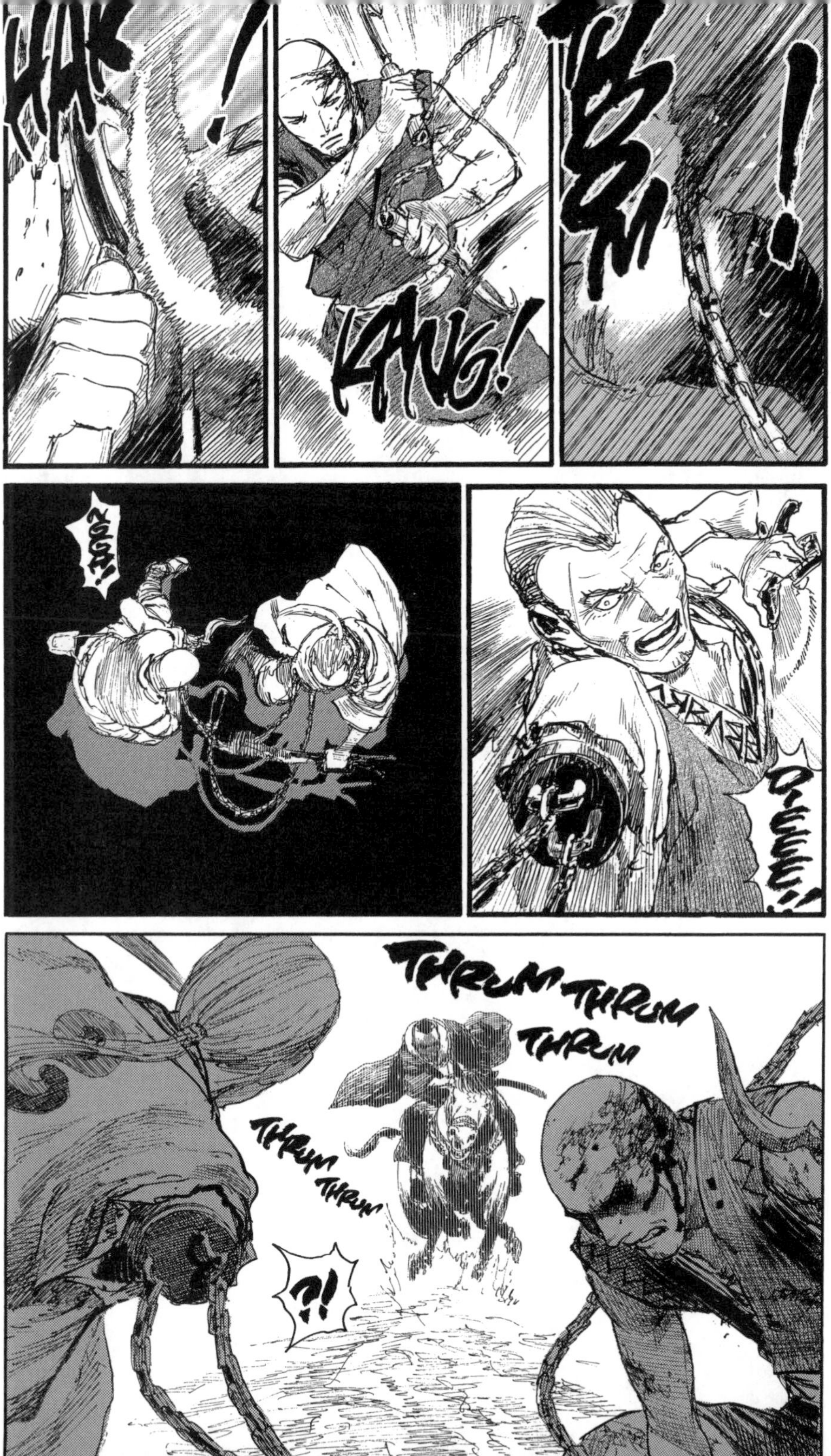
KANG!
NGGH!
THRUM THRUM
THRUM
THRUM THRUM
?!

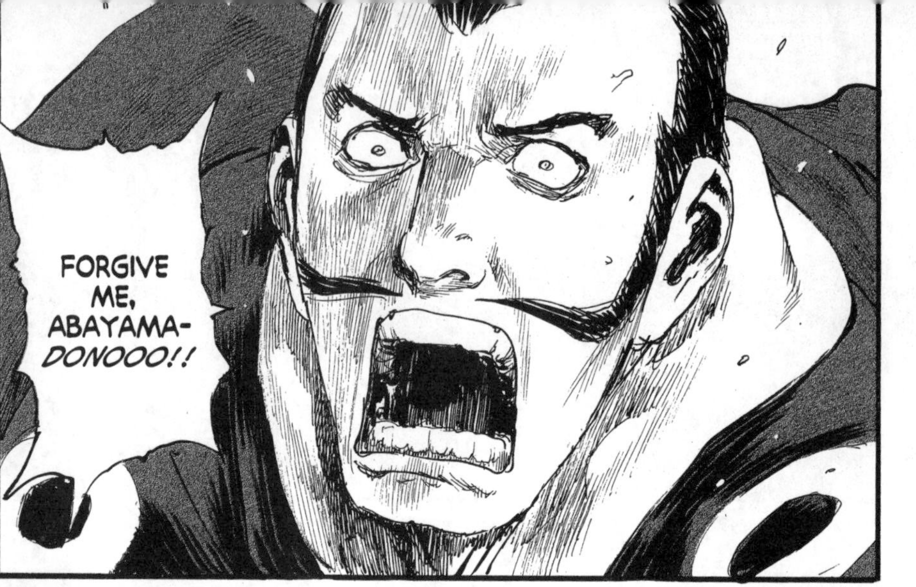
FORGIVE ME, ABAYAMA-DONOOO!!

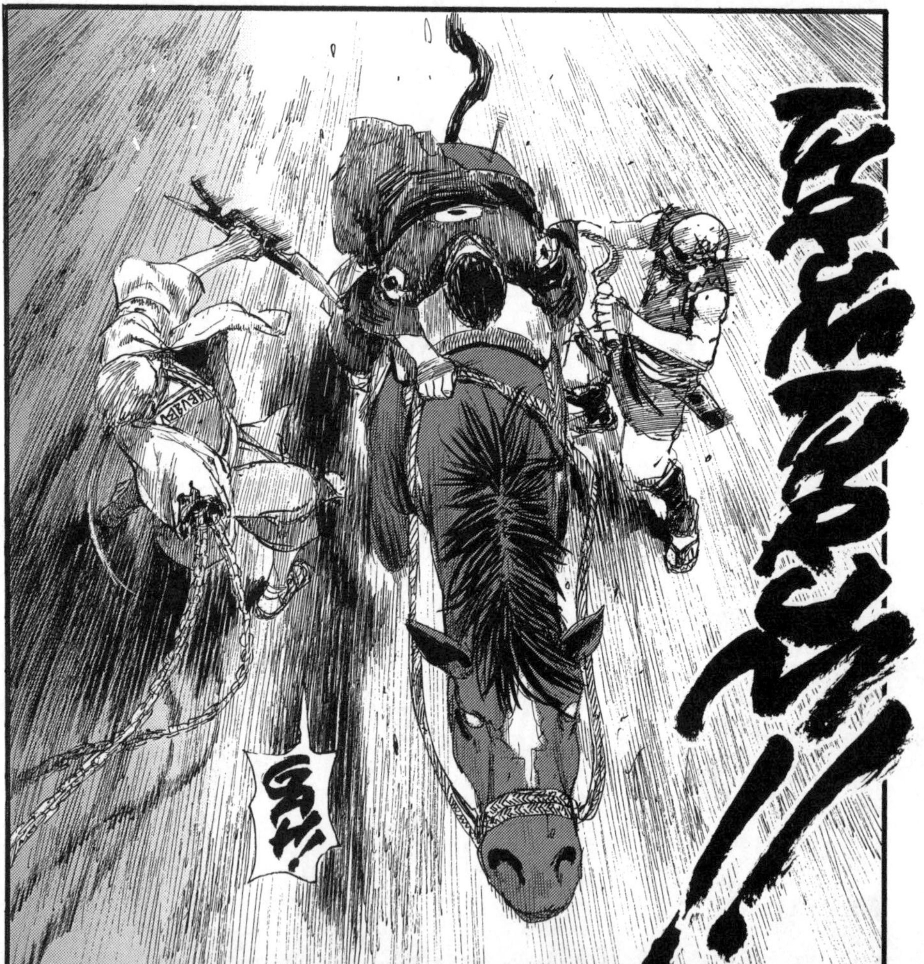

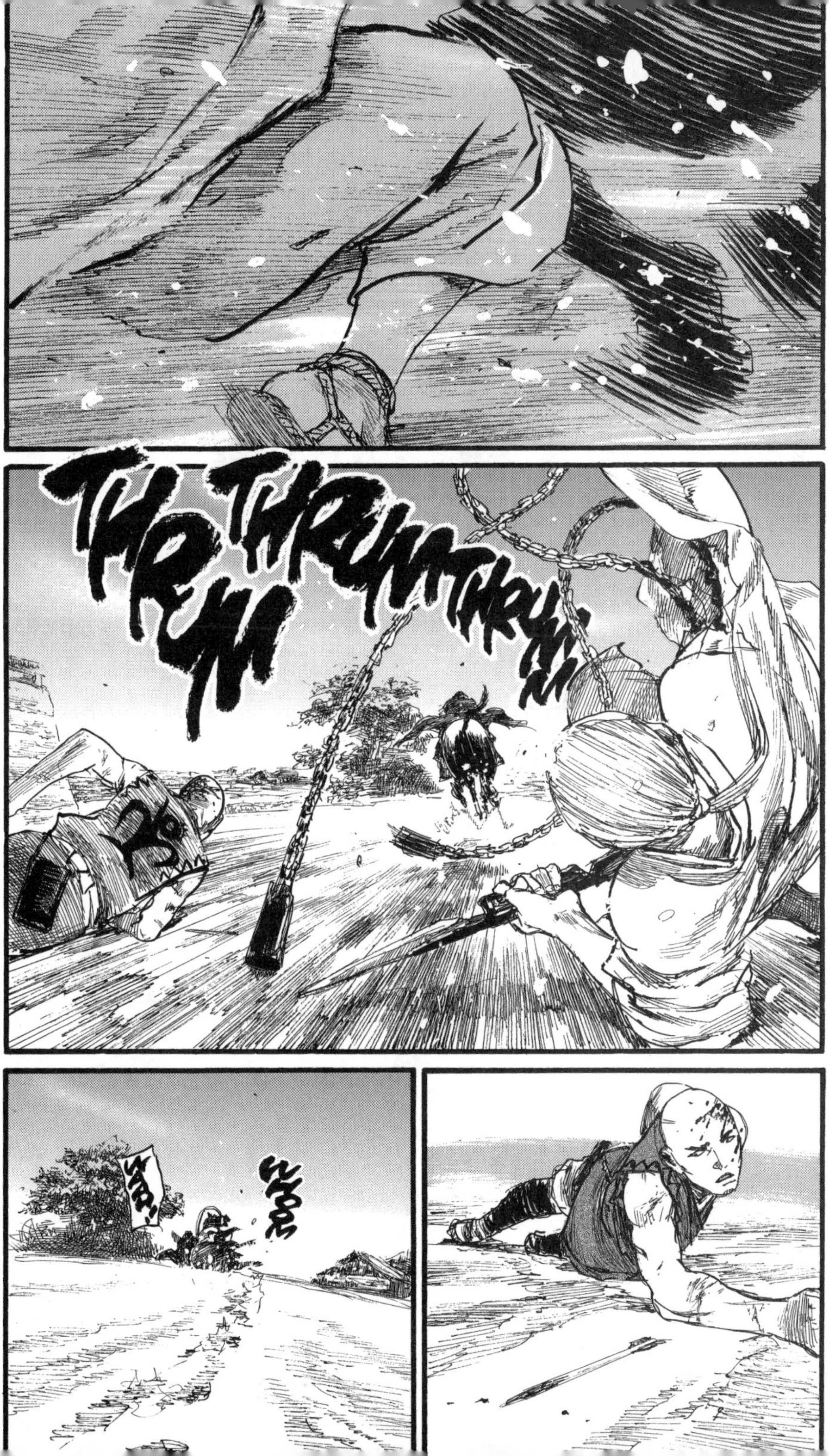
THRUM
THRUMTHRUM

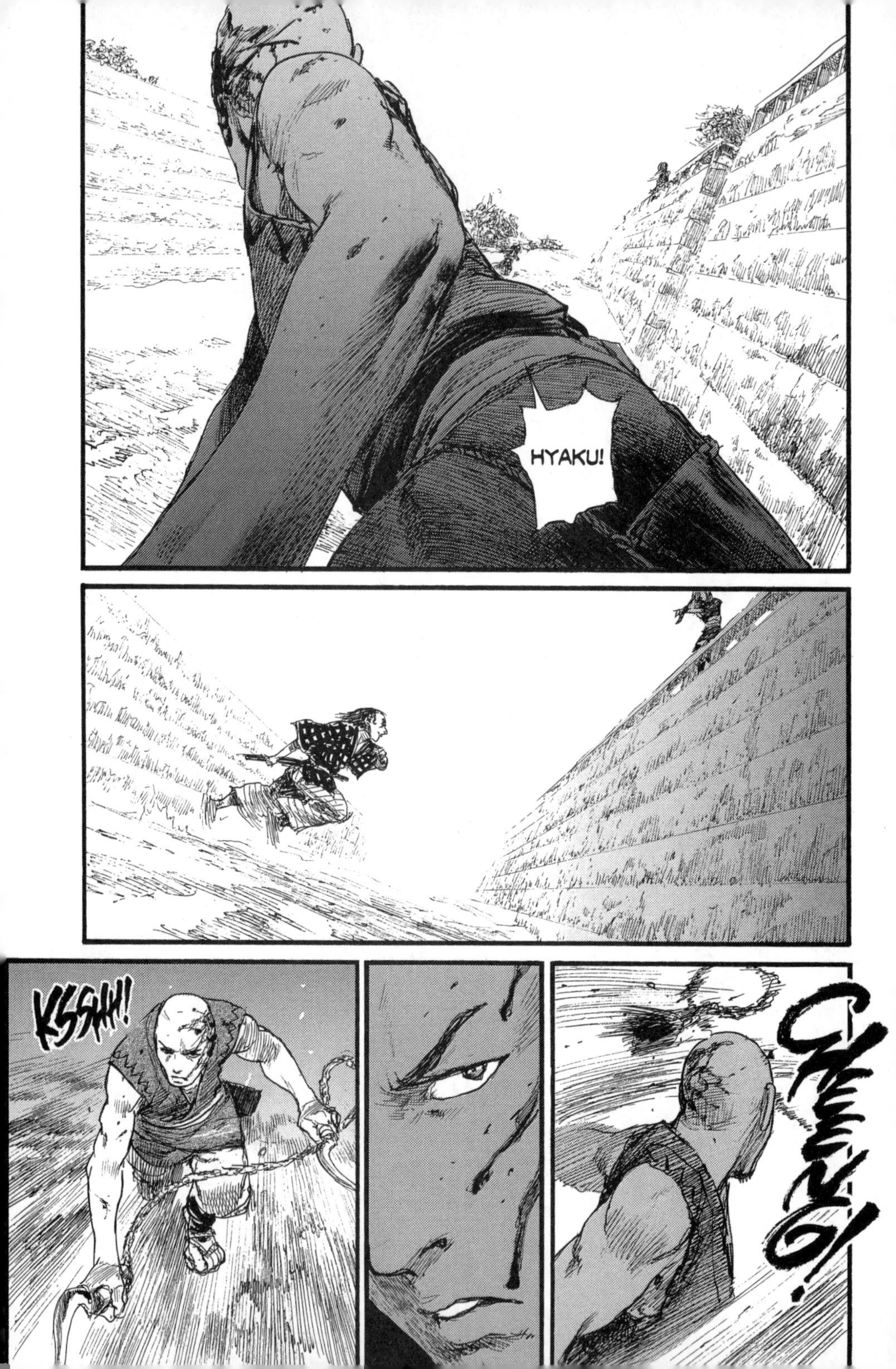
HYAKU!
CHUNG!
KSSAH!

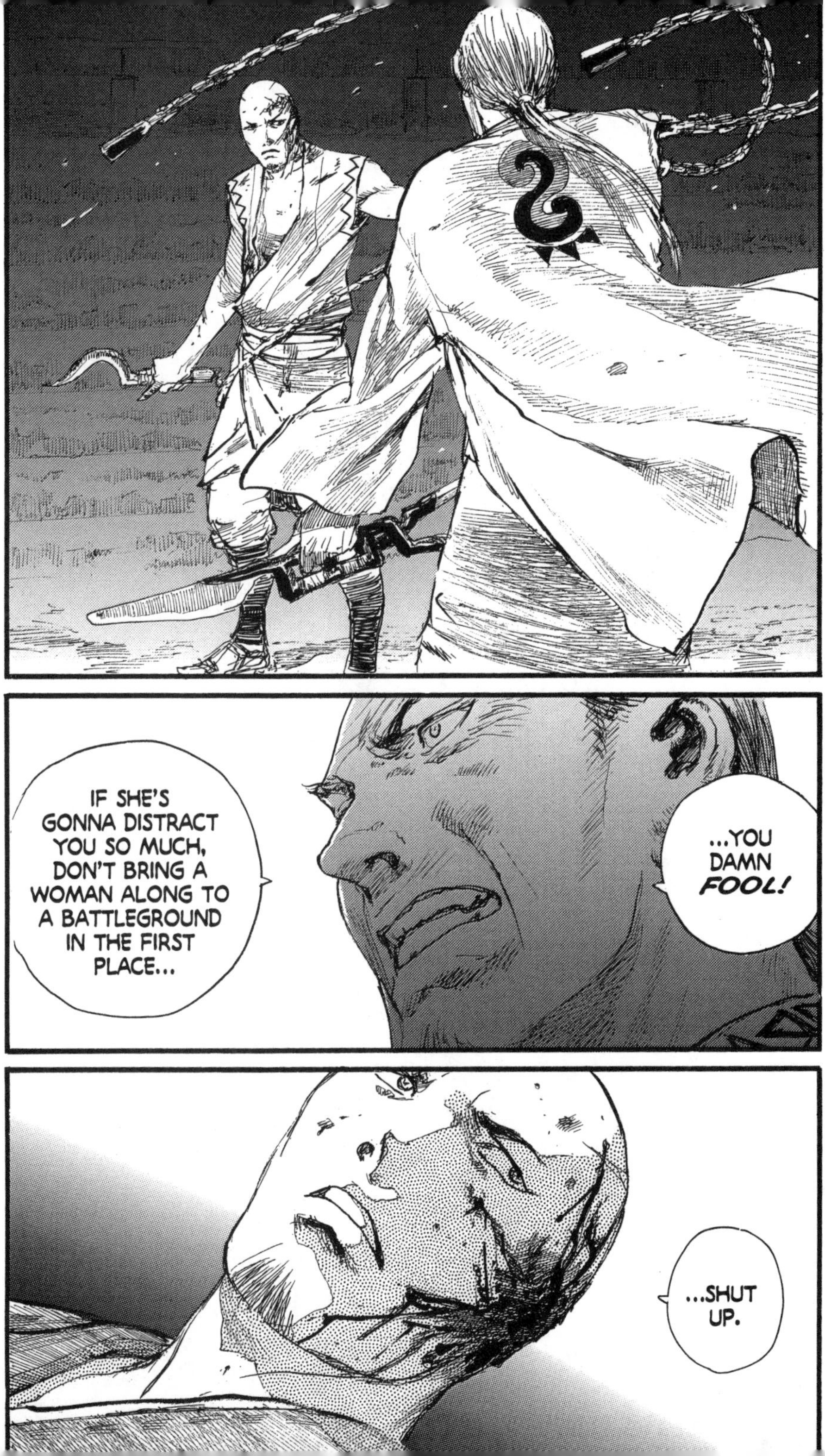
...YOU DAMN FOOL!
IF SHE'S GONNA DISTRACT YOU SO MUCH, DON'T BRING A WOMAN ALONG TO A BATTLEGROUND IN THE FIRST PLACE...
...SHUT UP.

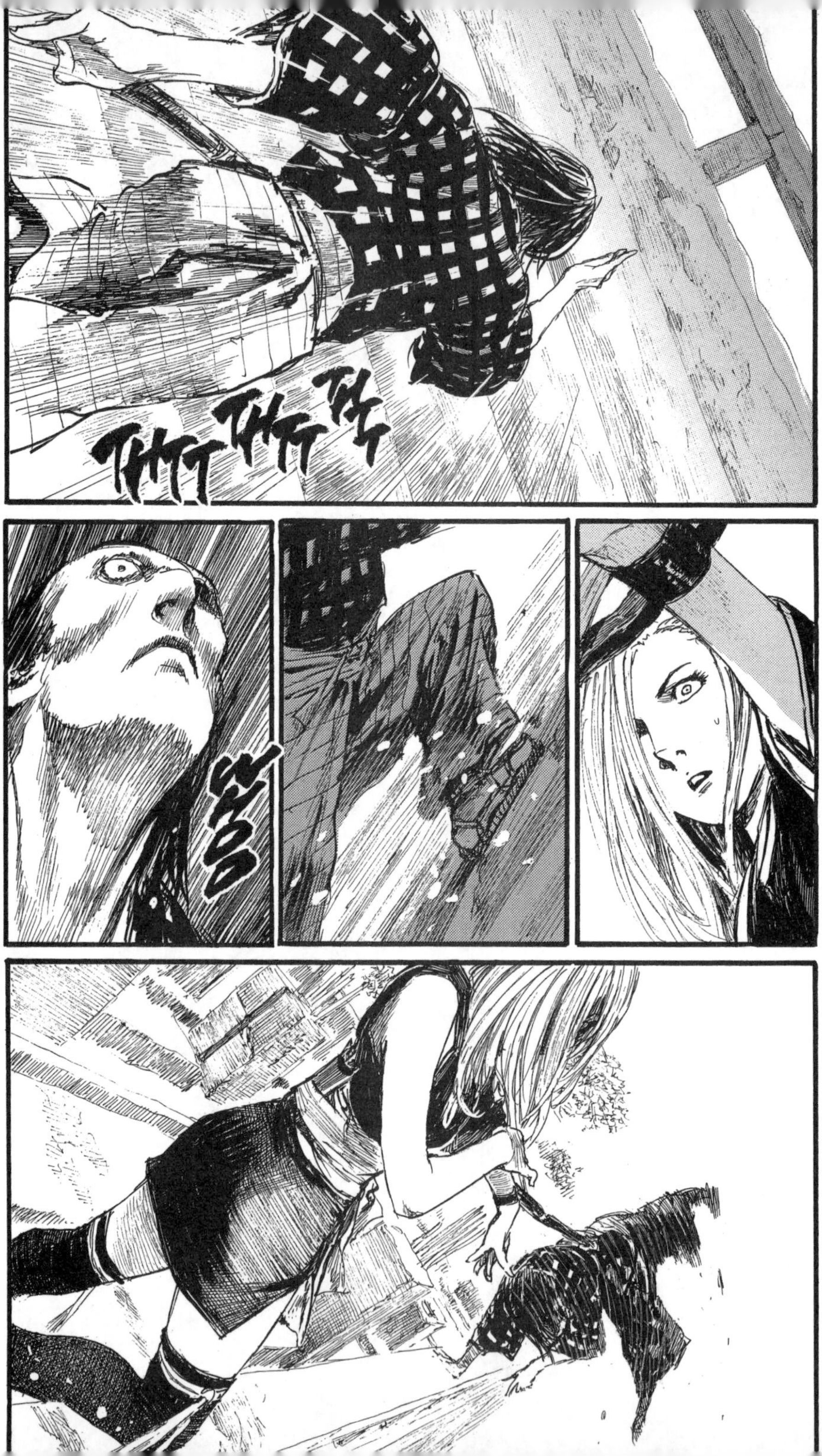
THTT THTT THT

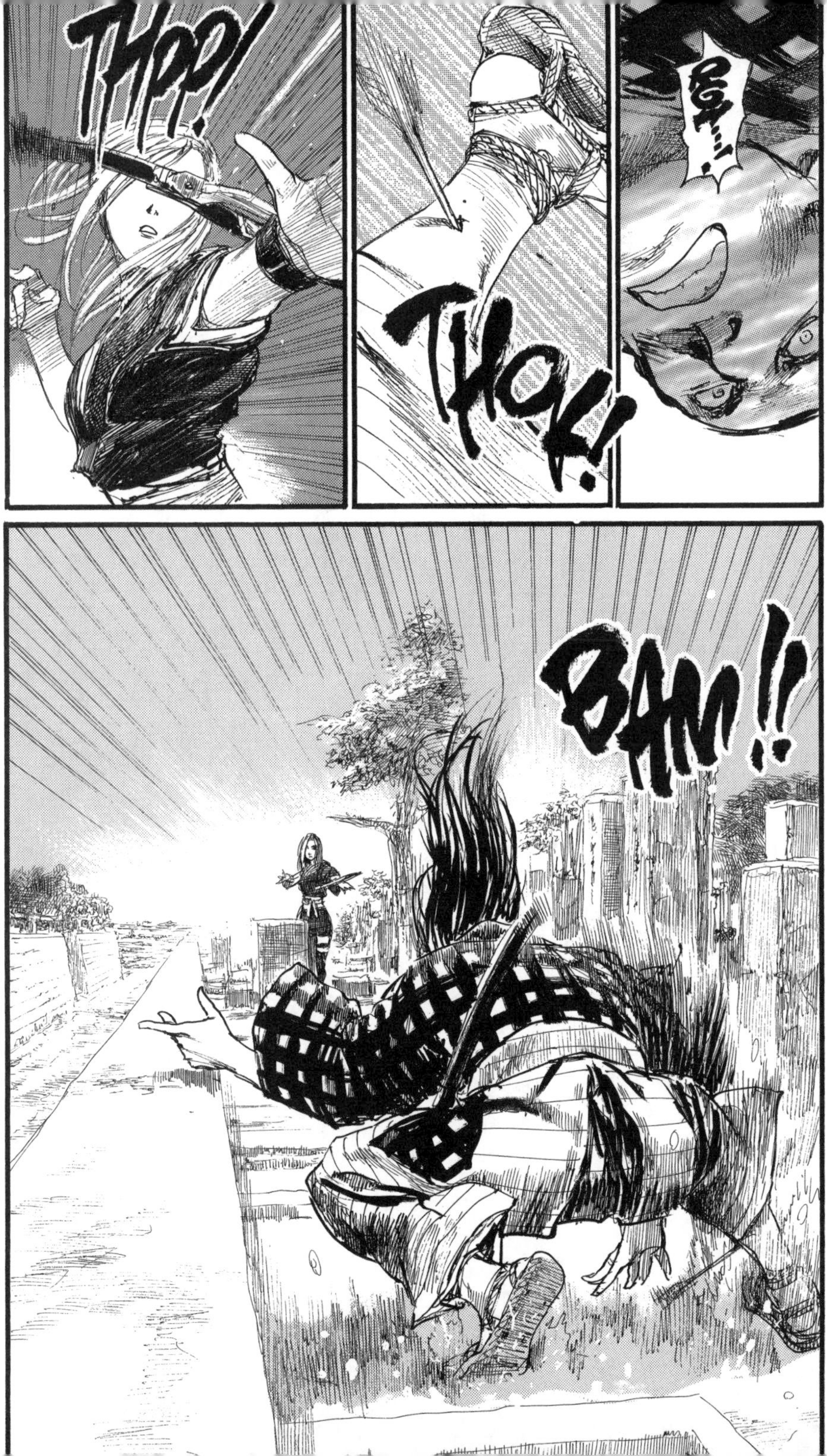
THPP!
THOK!
RGH...!
BAM!!

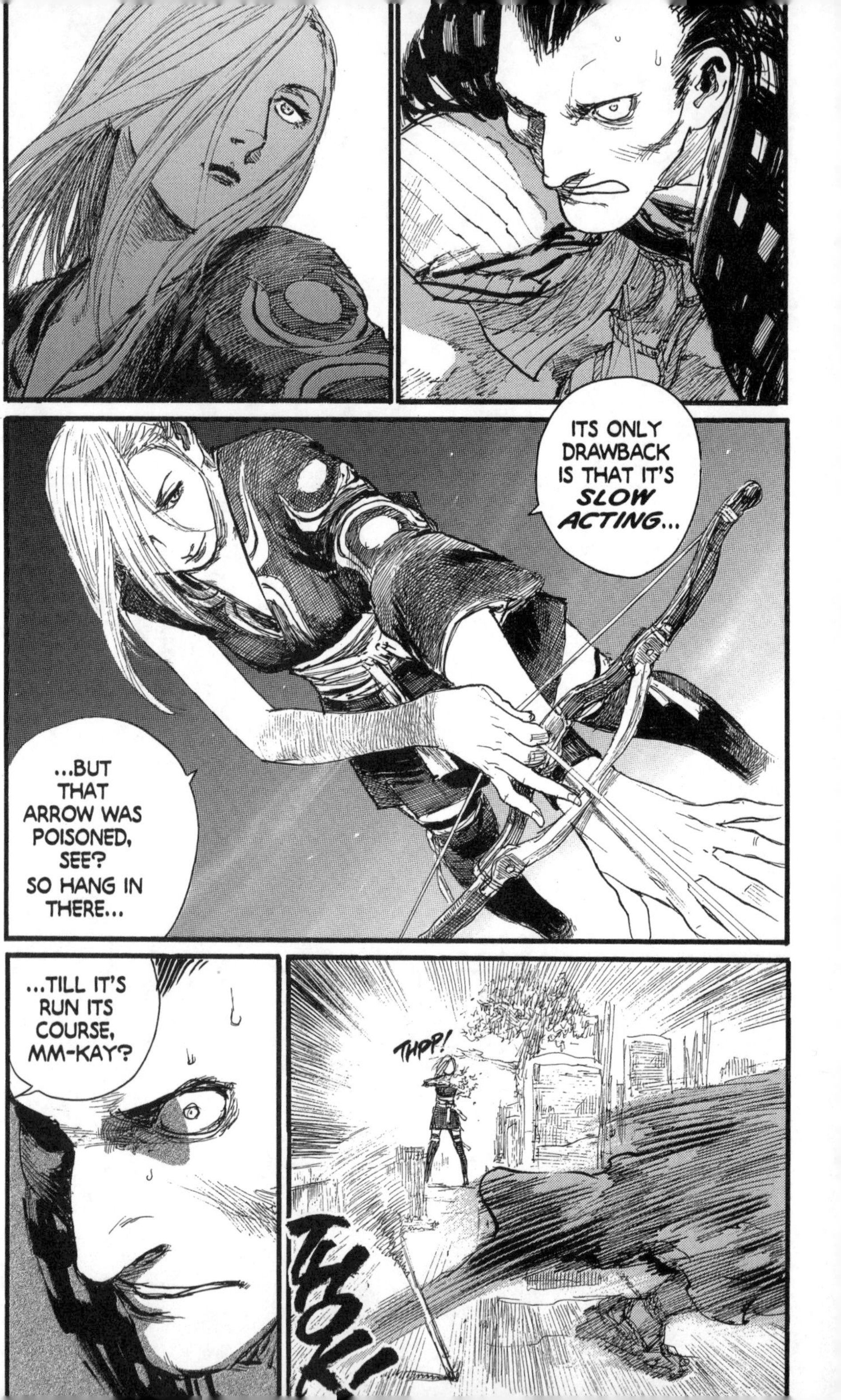
ITS ONLY DRAWBACK IS THAT IT'S SLOW ACTING...
...BUT THAT ARROW WAS POISONED, SEE? SO HANG IN THERE...
...TILL IT'S RUN ITS COURSE, MM-KAY?
THPP!
THOK!

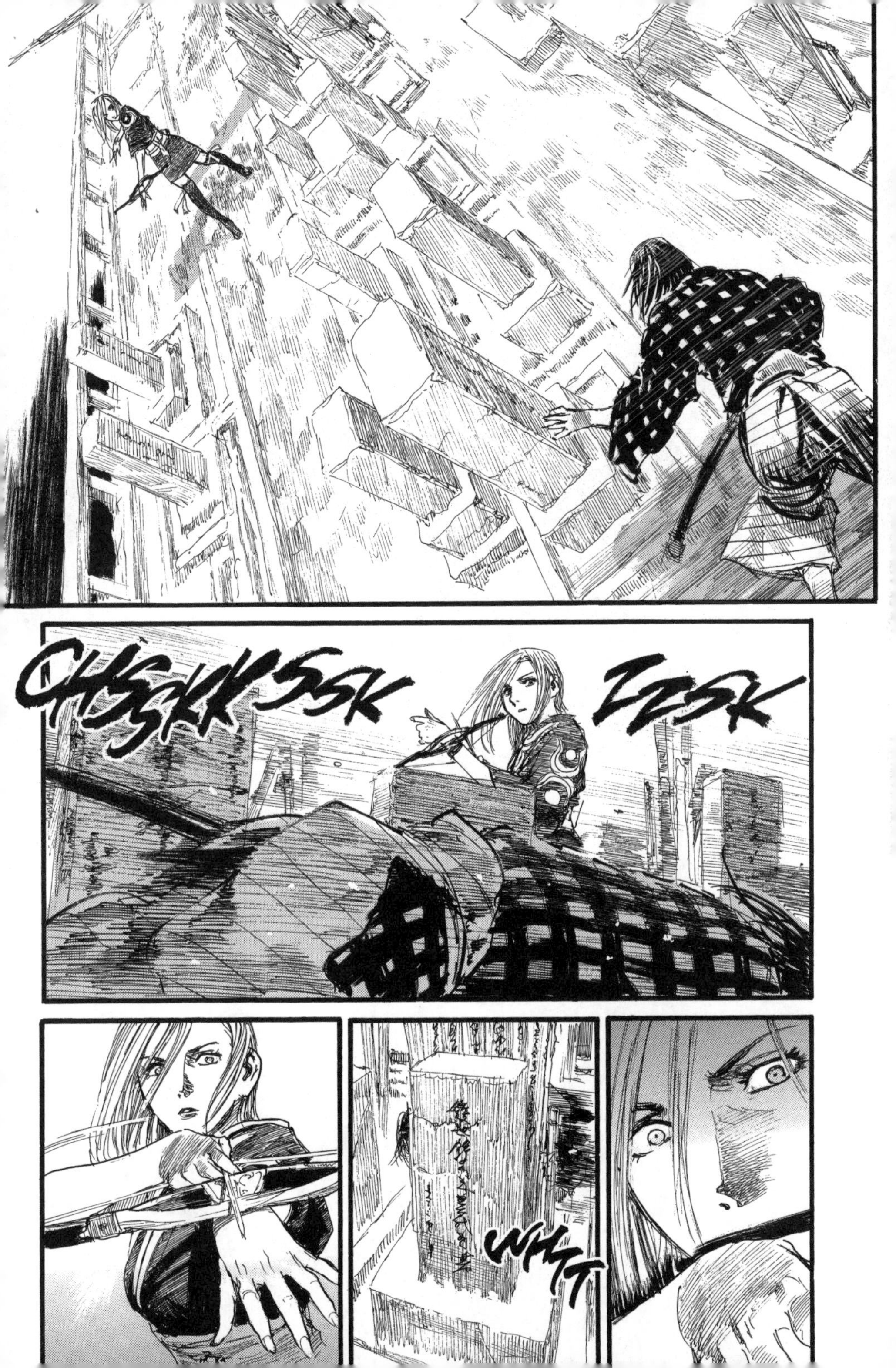
ZZSK
CHSKK SSK
WHTT

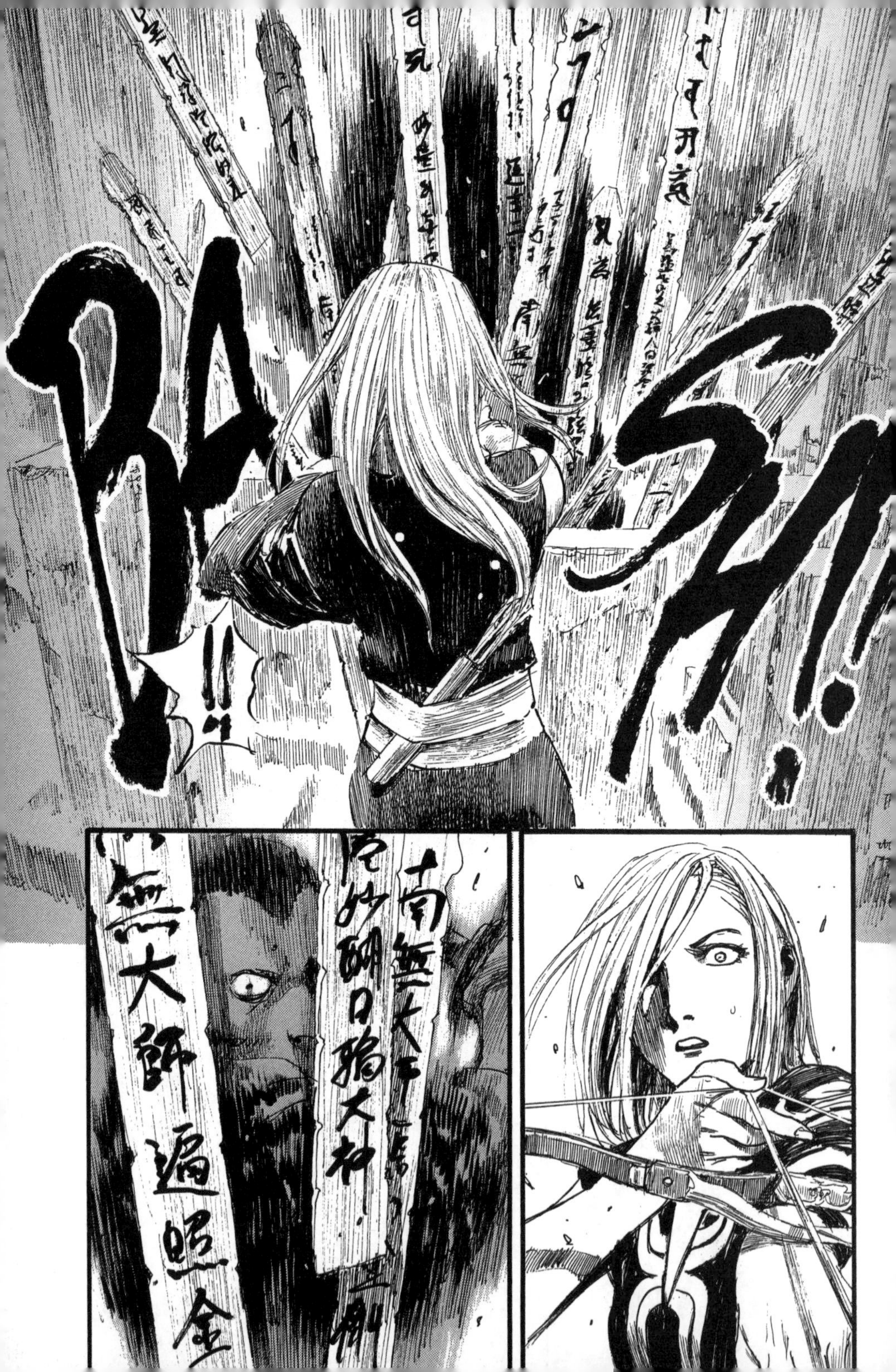
BASH!!
!!
無大師遍照金

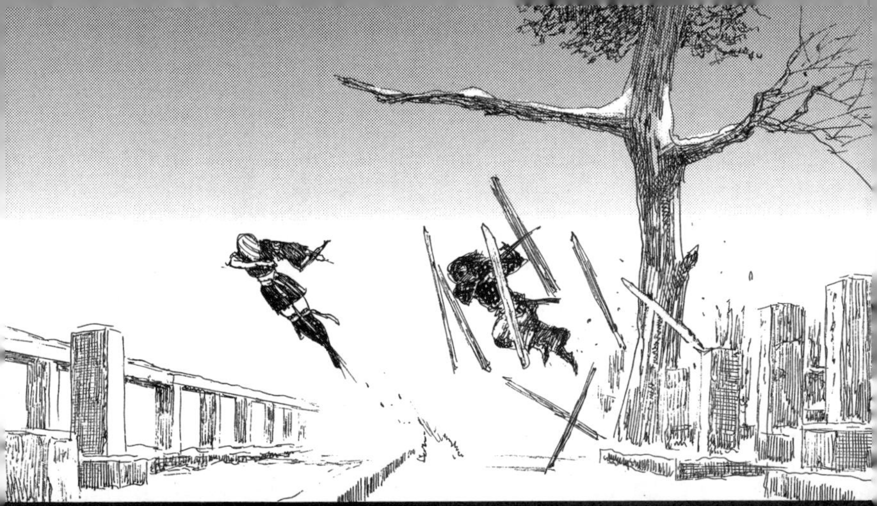
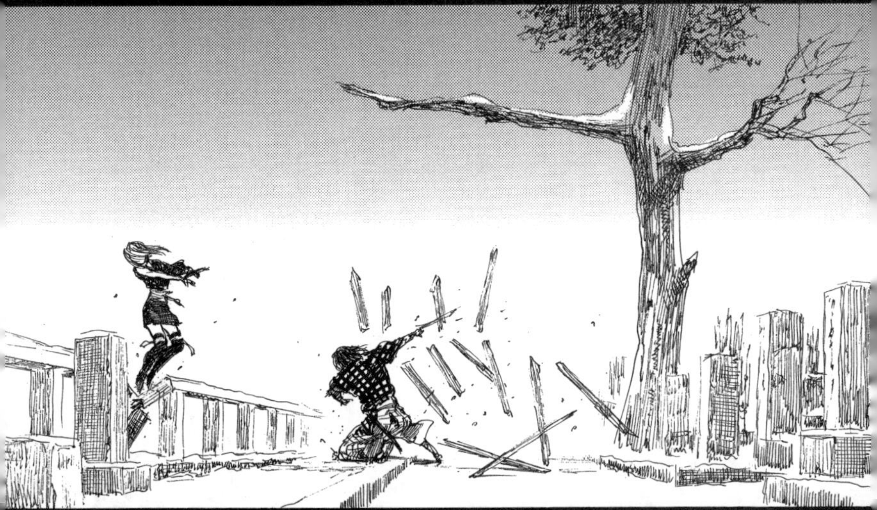
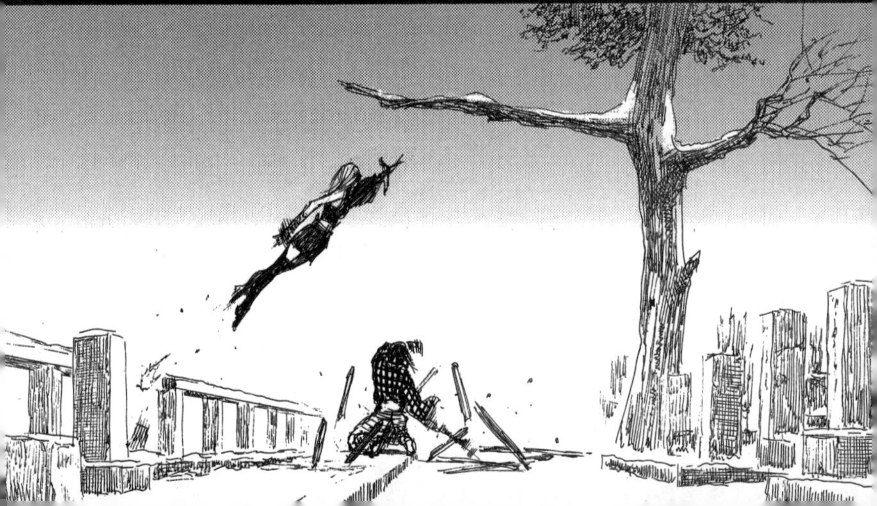

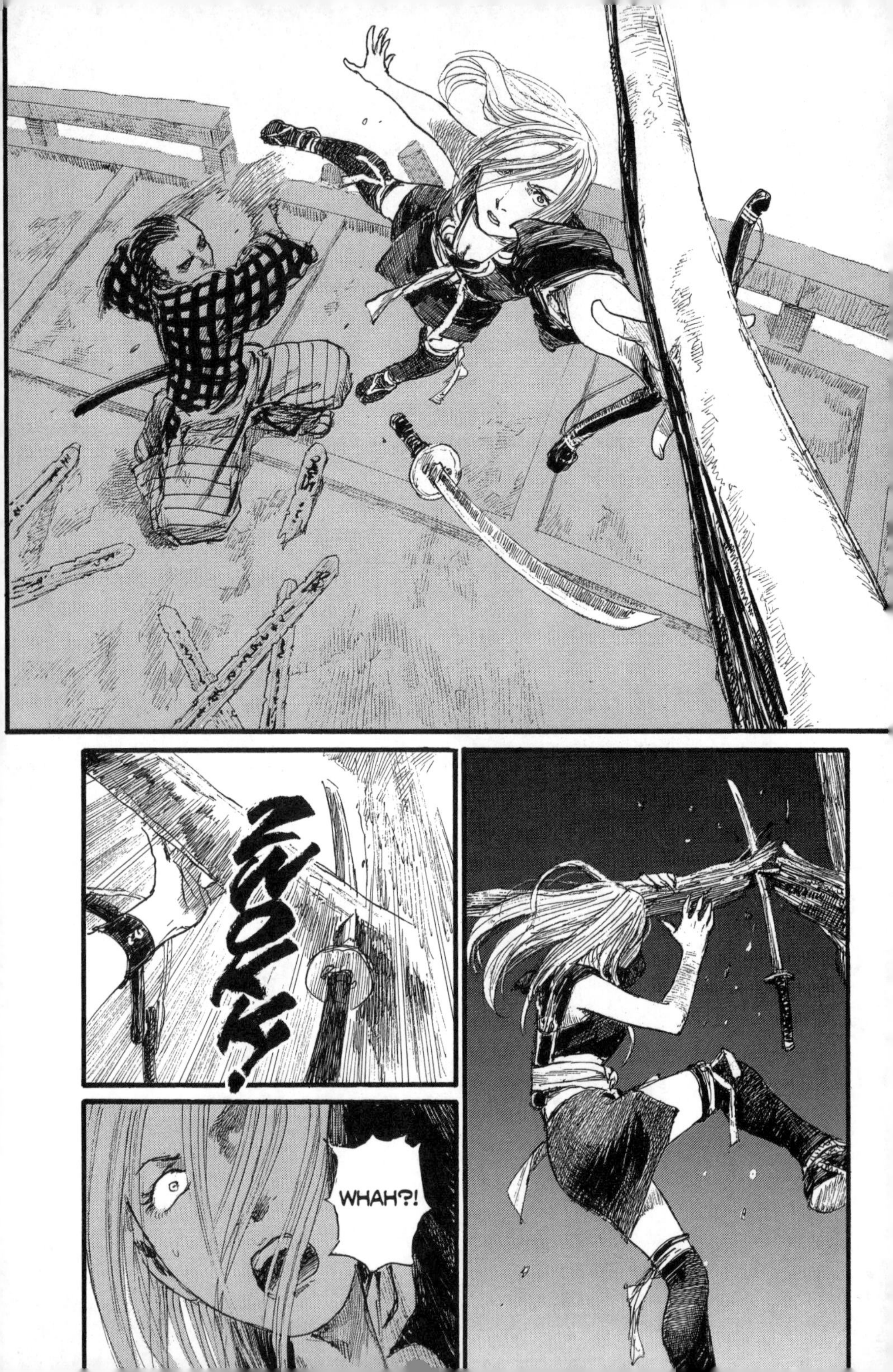
ZWOK!
WHAH?!

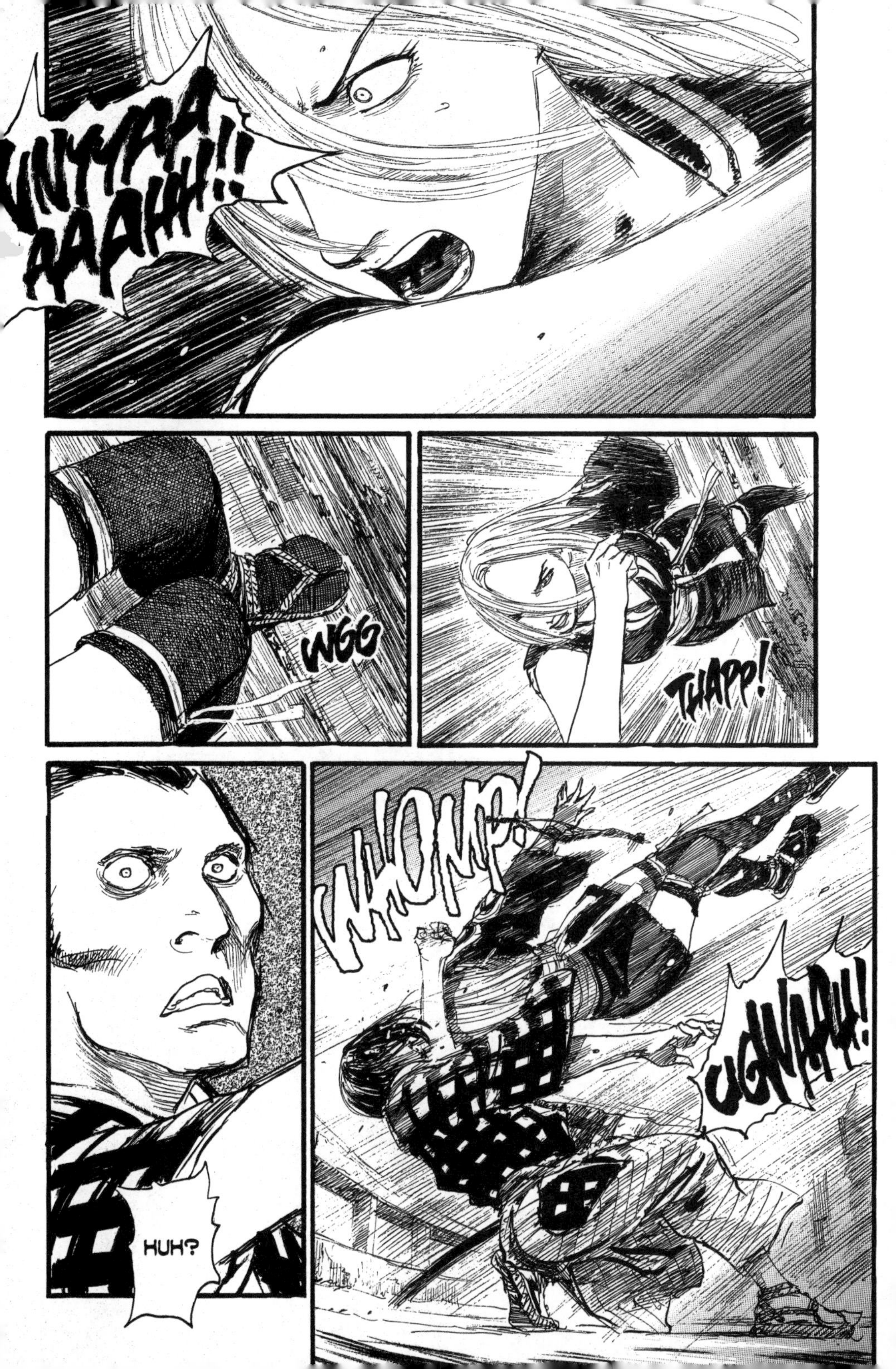
UNYAAA AAAHH!!
THAPP!
WIGG
WHOMP!
UGWAAH!
HUH?

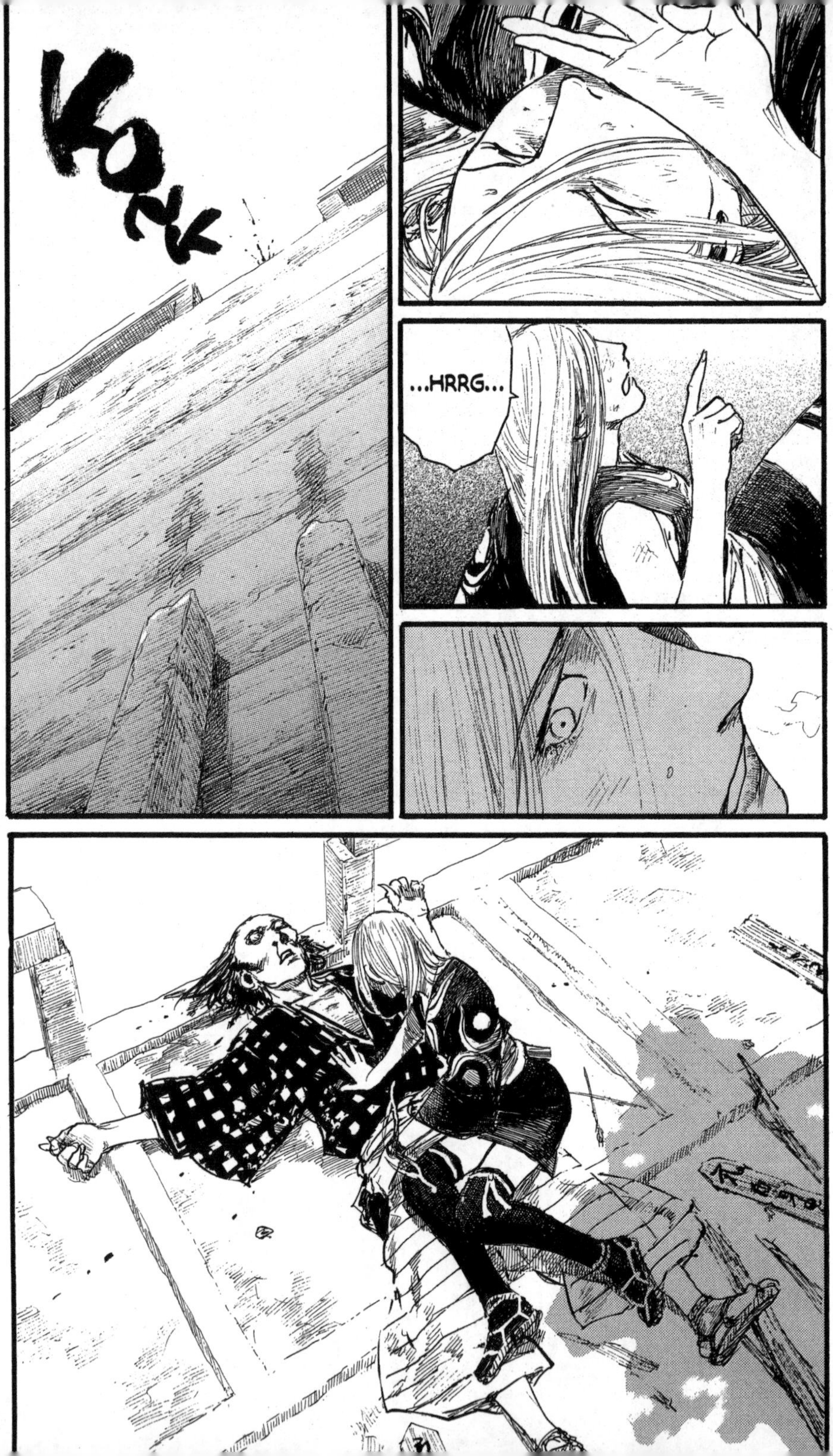
KONK
...HRRG...

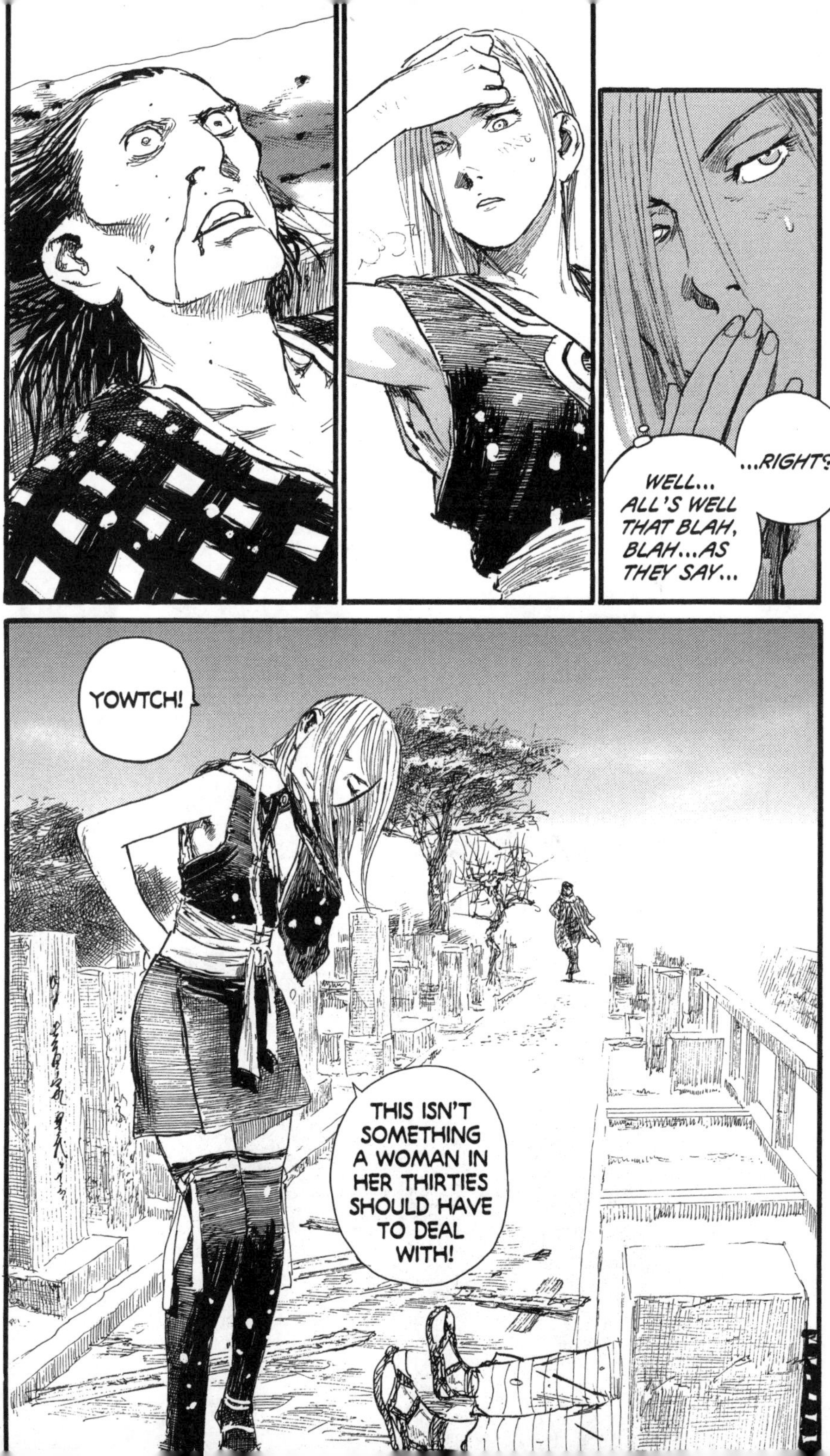
WELL... ALL'S WELL THAT BLAH, BLAH...AS THEY SAY...
...RIGHT?
YOWTCH!
THIS ISN'T SOMETHING A WOMAN IN HER THIRTIES SHOULD HAVE TO DEAL WITH!

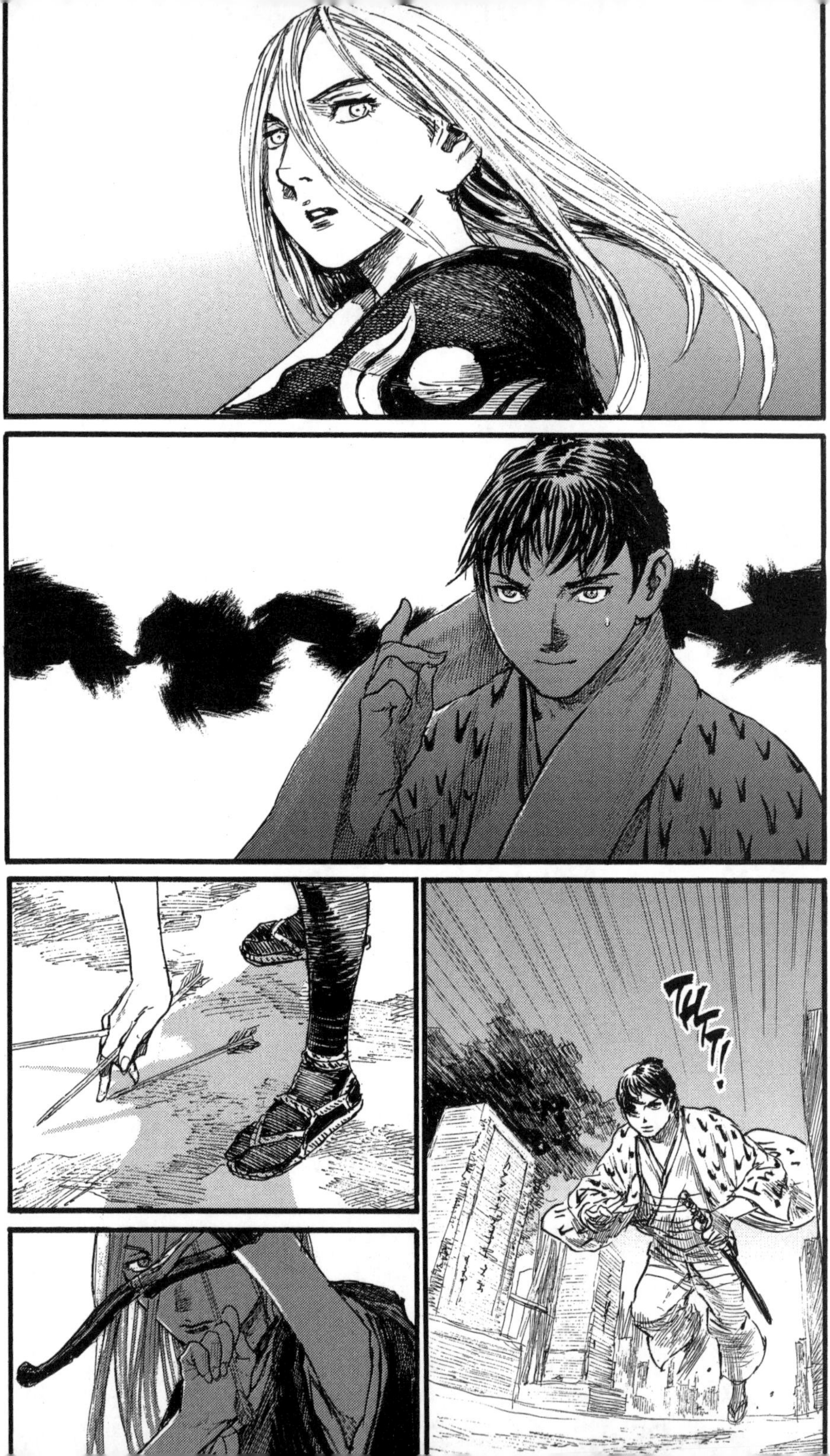
THKT!

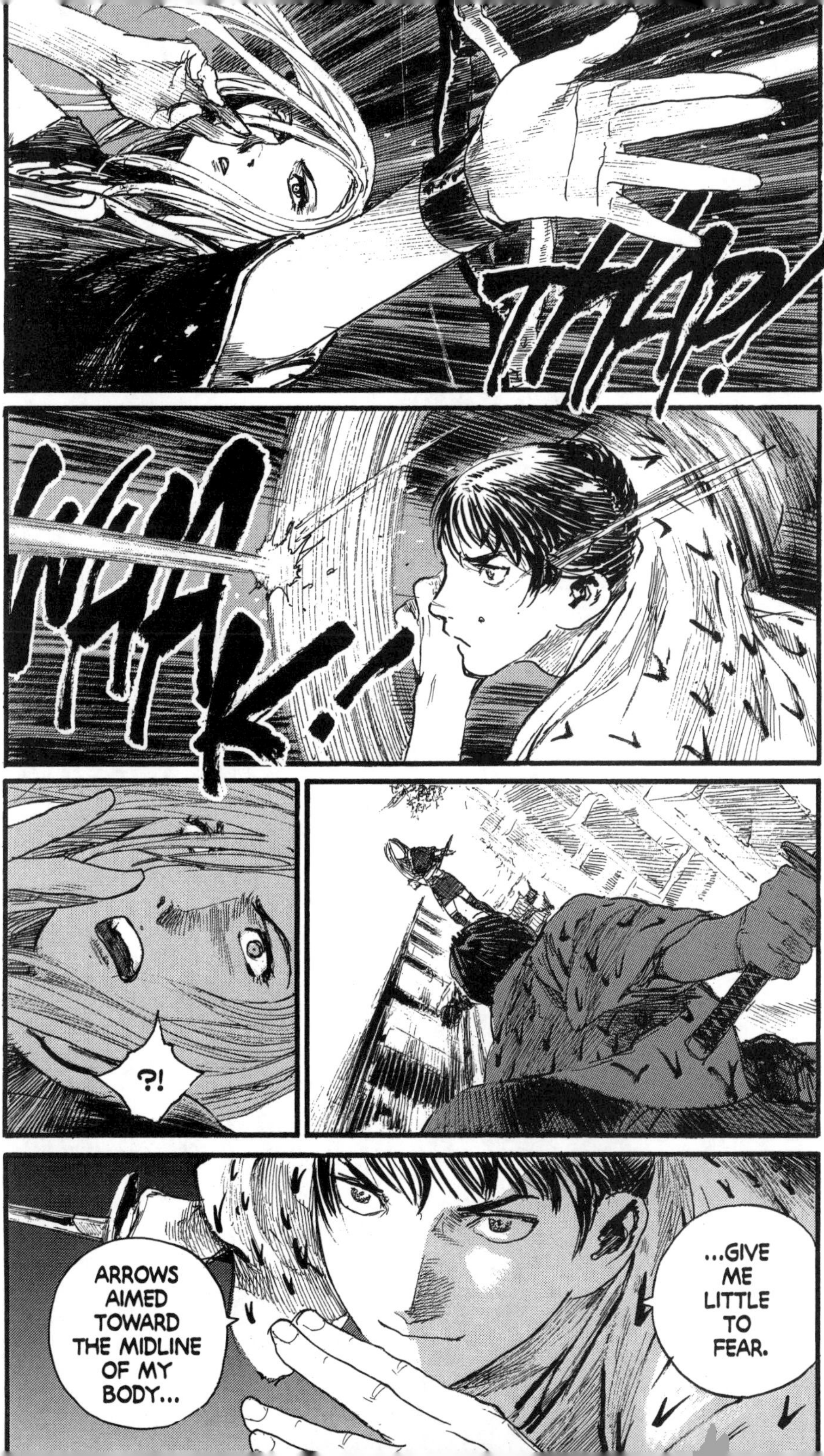
THHAP!
WHAK!
?!
ARROWS AIMED TOWARD THE MIDLINE OF MY BODY...
...GIVE ME LITTLE TO FEAR.

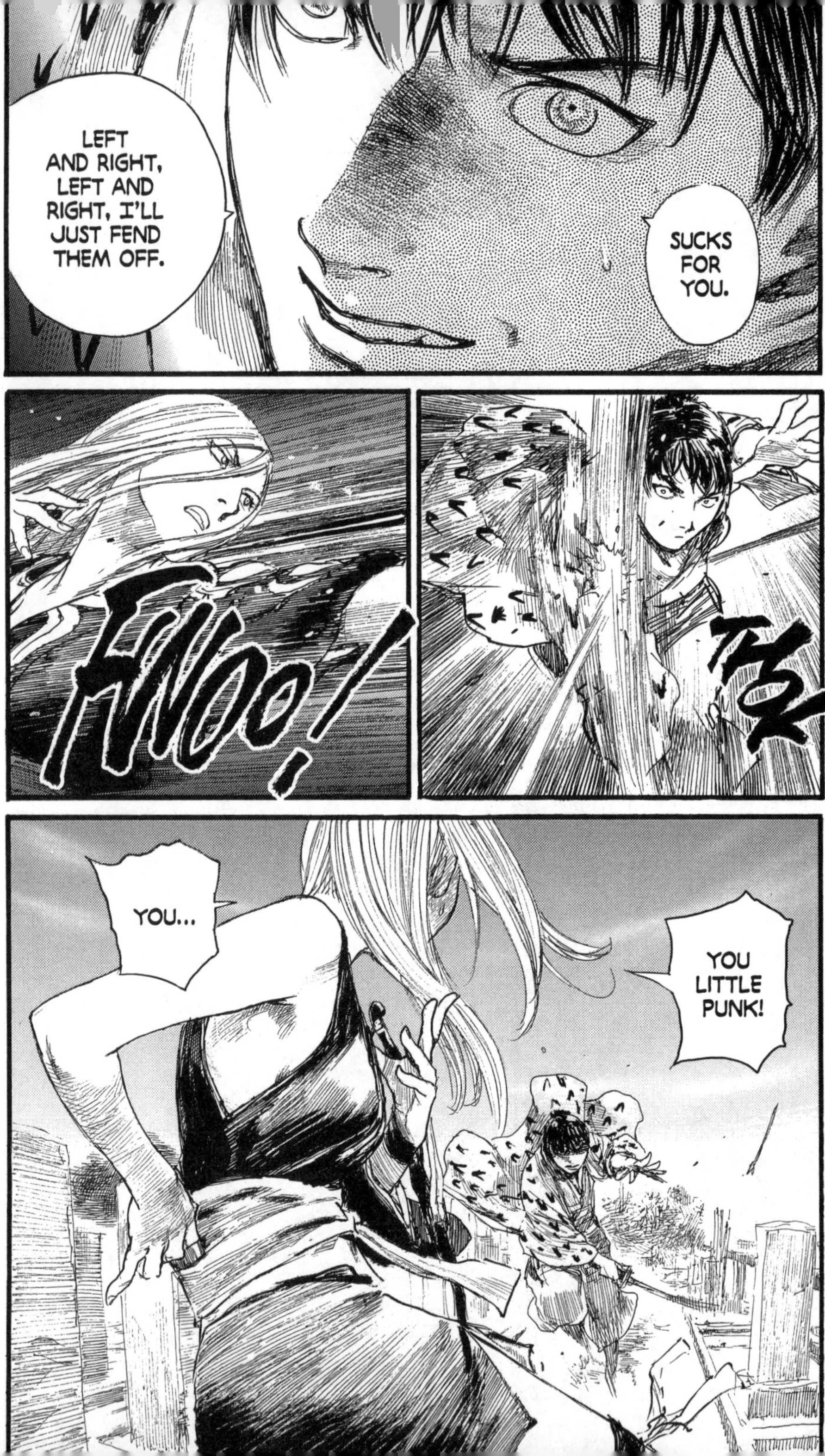
LEFT AND RIGHT, LEFT AND RIGHT, I'LL JUST FEND THEM OFF.
SUCKS FOR YOU.
FWOO!
TSK
YOU...
YOU LITTLE PUNK!

WHPP!

KHOW!

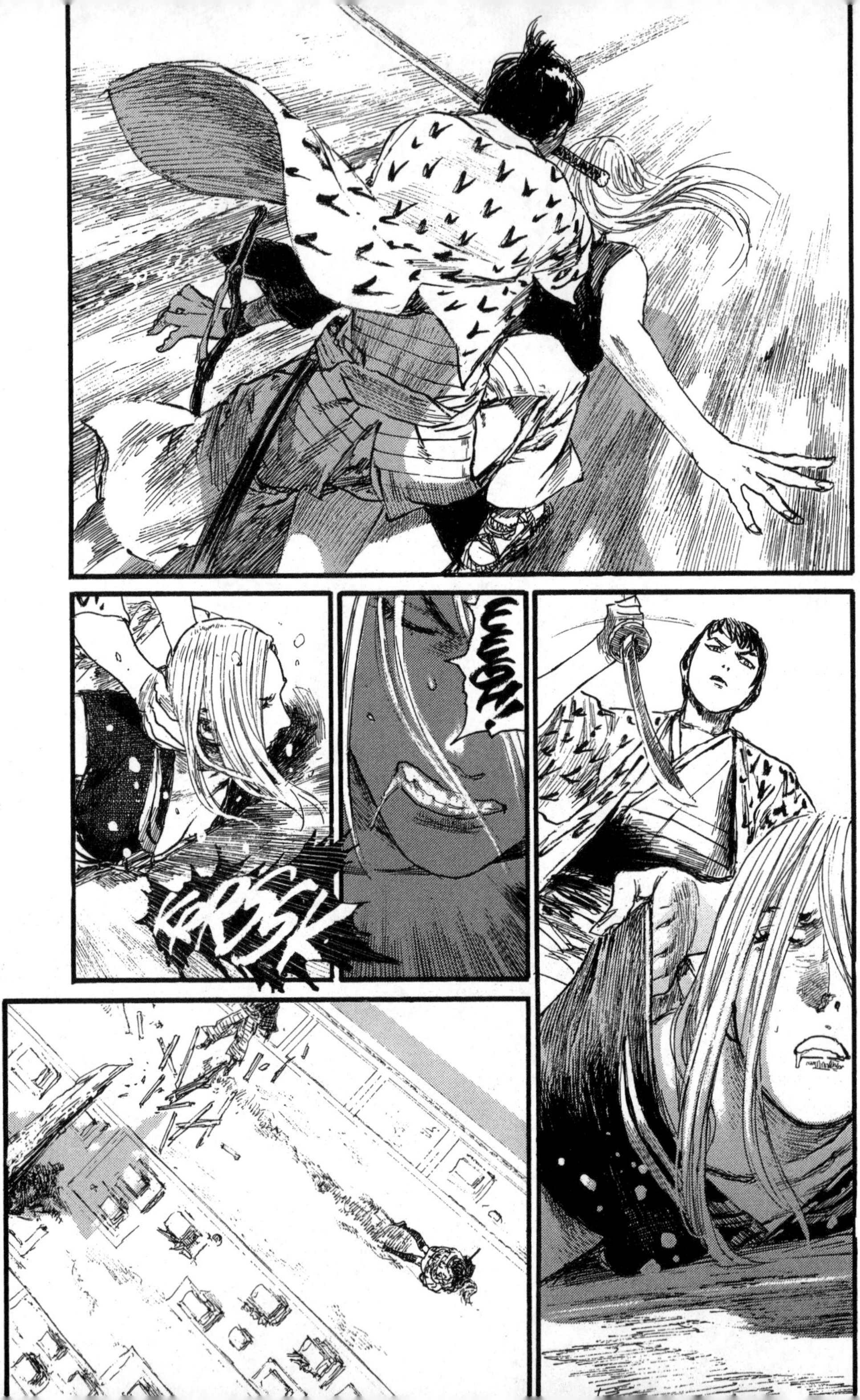
WWOH!
KROSK

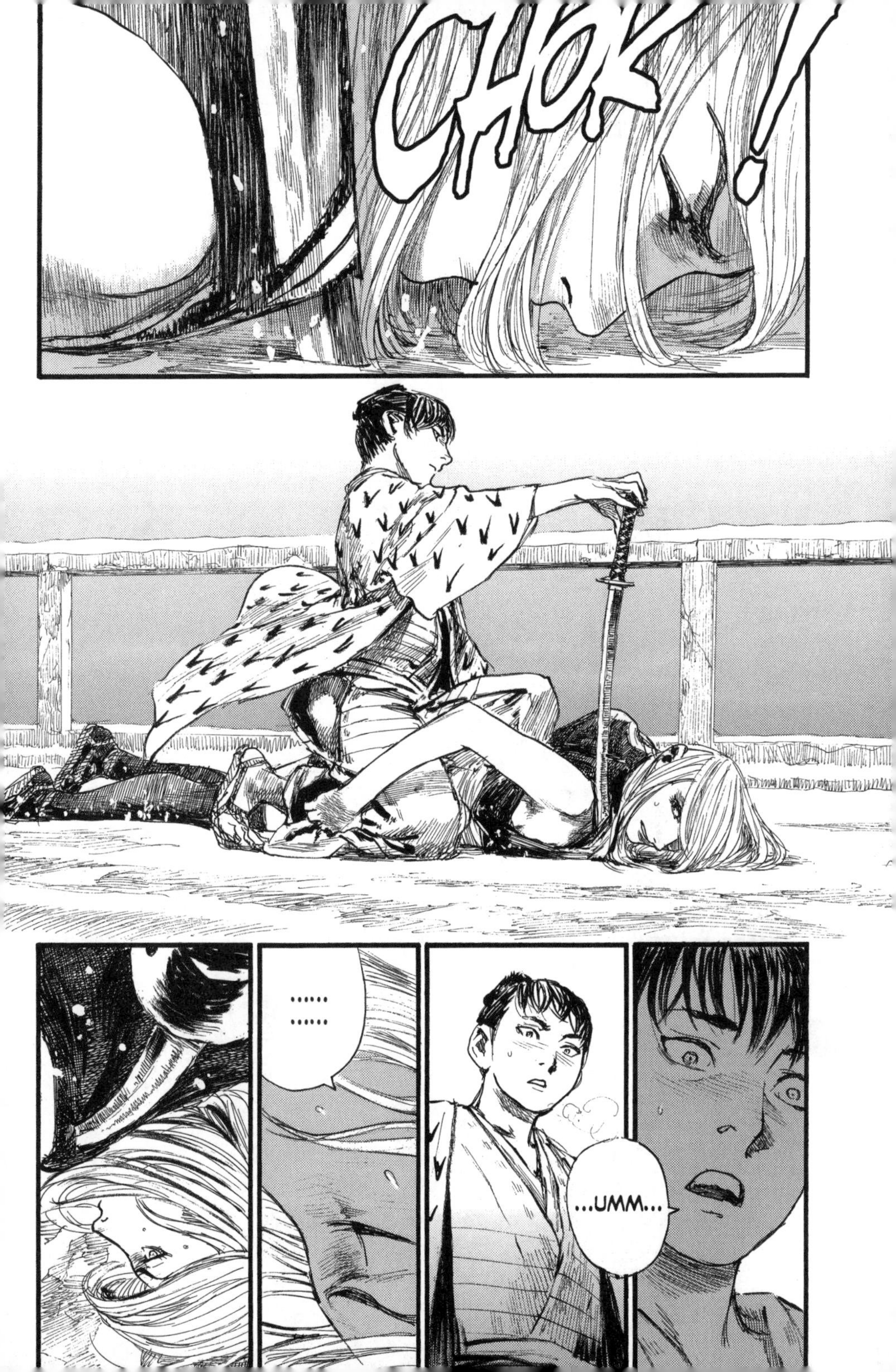
CHOK!
...UMM...
......
......

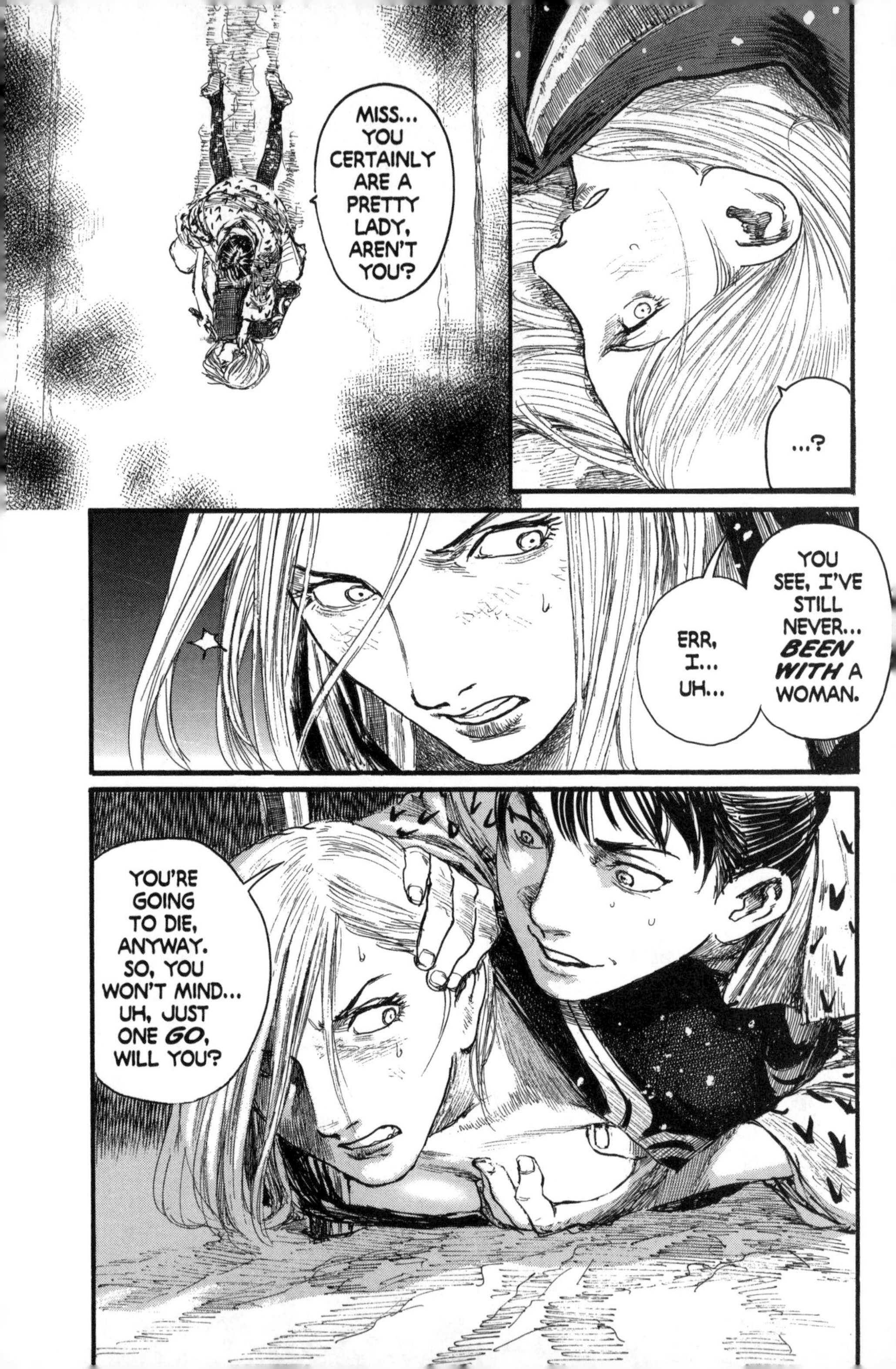
...?
MISS... YOU CERTAINLY ARE A PRETTY LADY, AREN'T YOU?
ERR, I... UH...
YOU SEE, I'VE STILL NEVER... *BEEN WITH* A WOMAN.
YOU'RE GOING TO DIE, ANYWAY. SO, YOU WON'T MIND... UH, JUST ONE *GO*, WILL YOU?

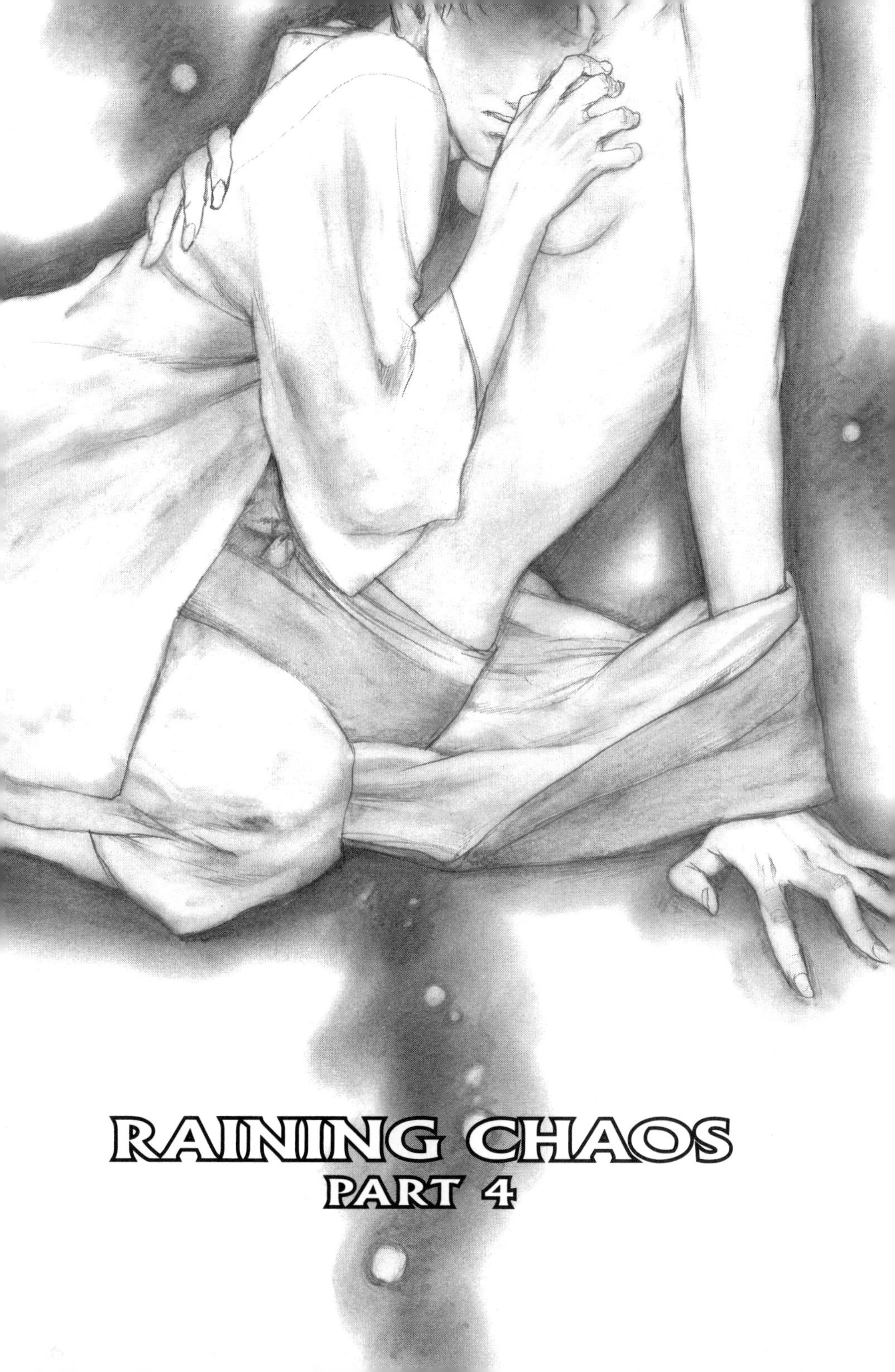

RAINING CHAOS
PART 4

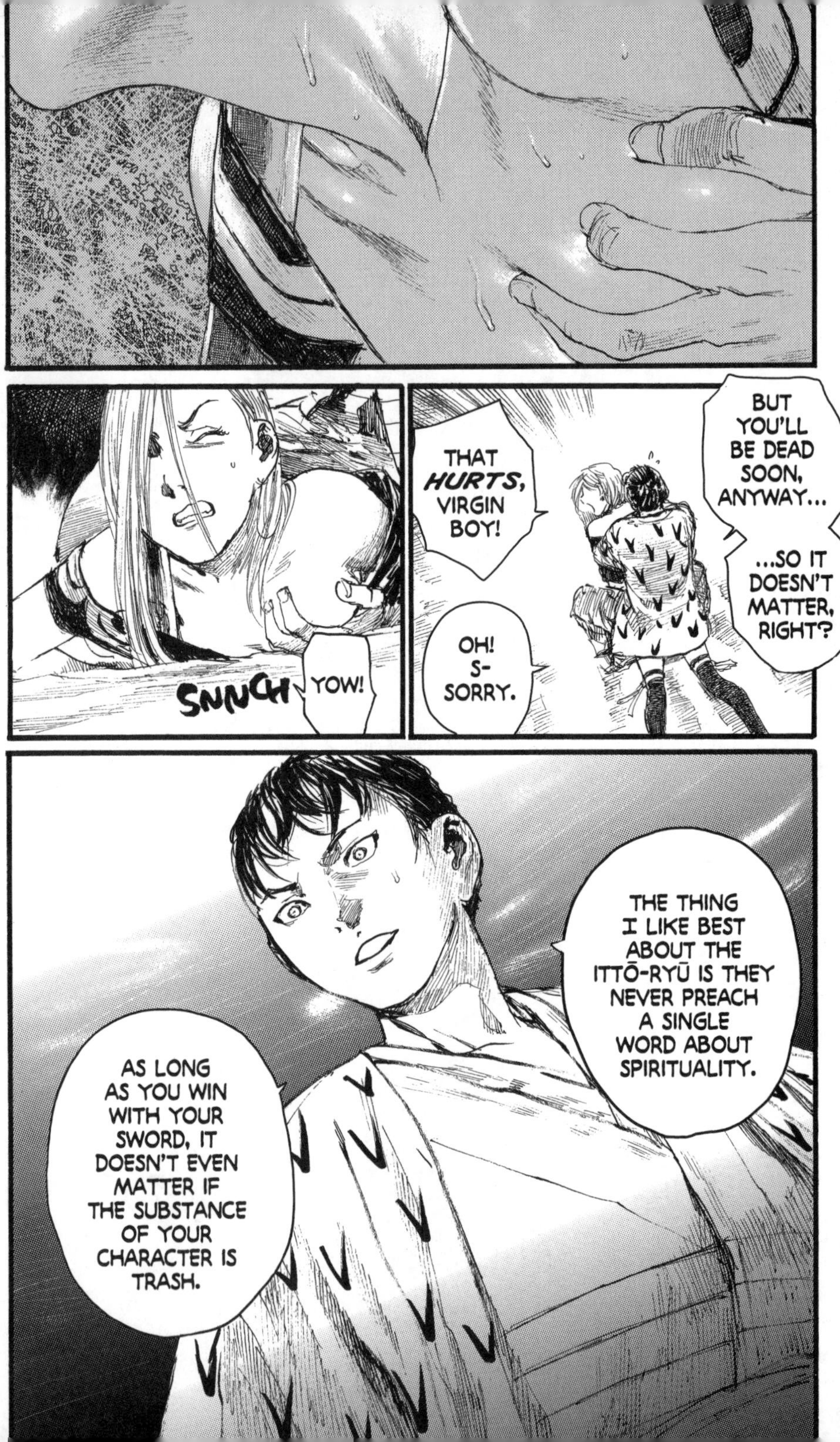
BUT YOU'LL BE DEAD SOON, ANYWAY...
...SO IT DOESN'T MATTER, RIGHT?
THAT *HURTS*, VIRGIN BOY!
OH! S-SORRY.
SNNCH
YOW!
THE THING I LIKE BEST ABOUT THE ITTŌ-RYŪ IS THEY NEVER PREACH A SINGLE WORD ABOUT SPIRITUALITY.
AS LONG AS YOU WIN WITH YOUR SWORD, IT DOESN'T EVEN MATTER IF THE SUBSTANCE OF YOUR CHARACTER IS TRASH.

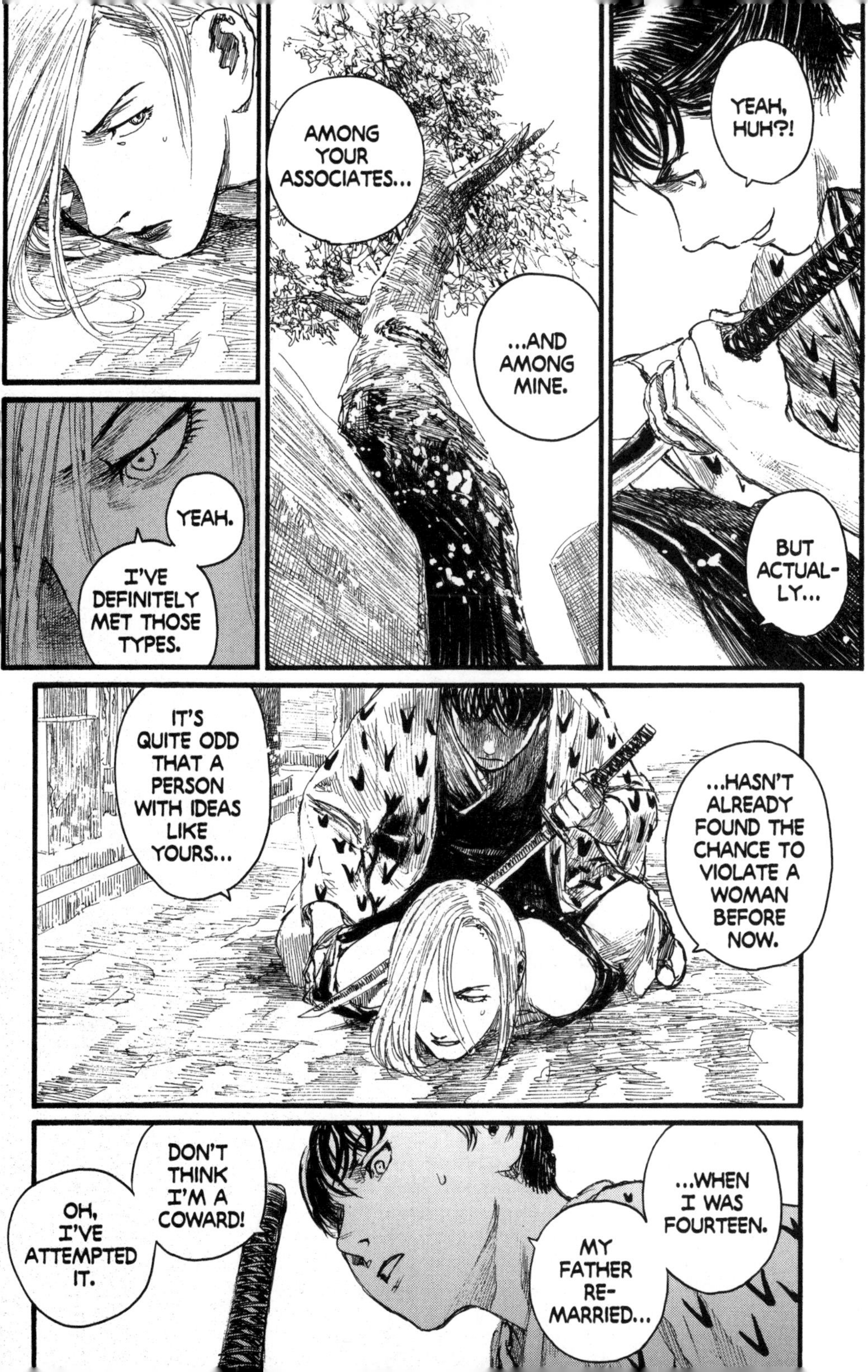
YEAH.
I'VE DEFINITELY MET THOSE TYPES.
AMONG YOUR ASSOCIATES...
...AND AMONG MINE.
YEAH, HUH?!
BUT ACTUAL-LY...
IT'S QUITE ODD THAT A PERSON WITH IDEAS LIKE YOURS...
...HASN'T ALREADY FOUND THE CHANCE TO VIOLATE A WOMAN BEFORE NOW.
OH, I'VE ATTEMPTED IT.
DON'T THINK I'M A COWARD!
MY FATHER RE-MARRIED...
...WHEN I WAS FOURTEEN.

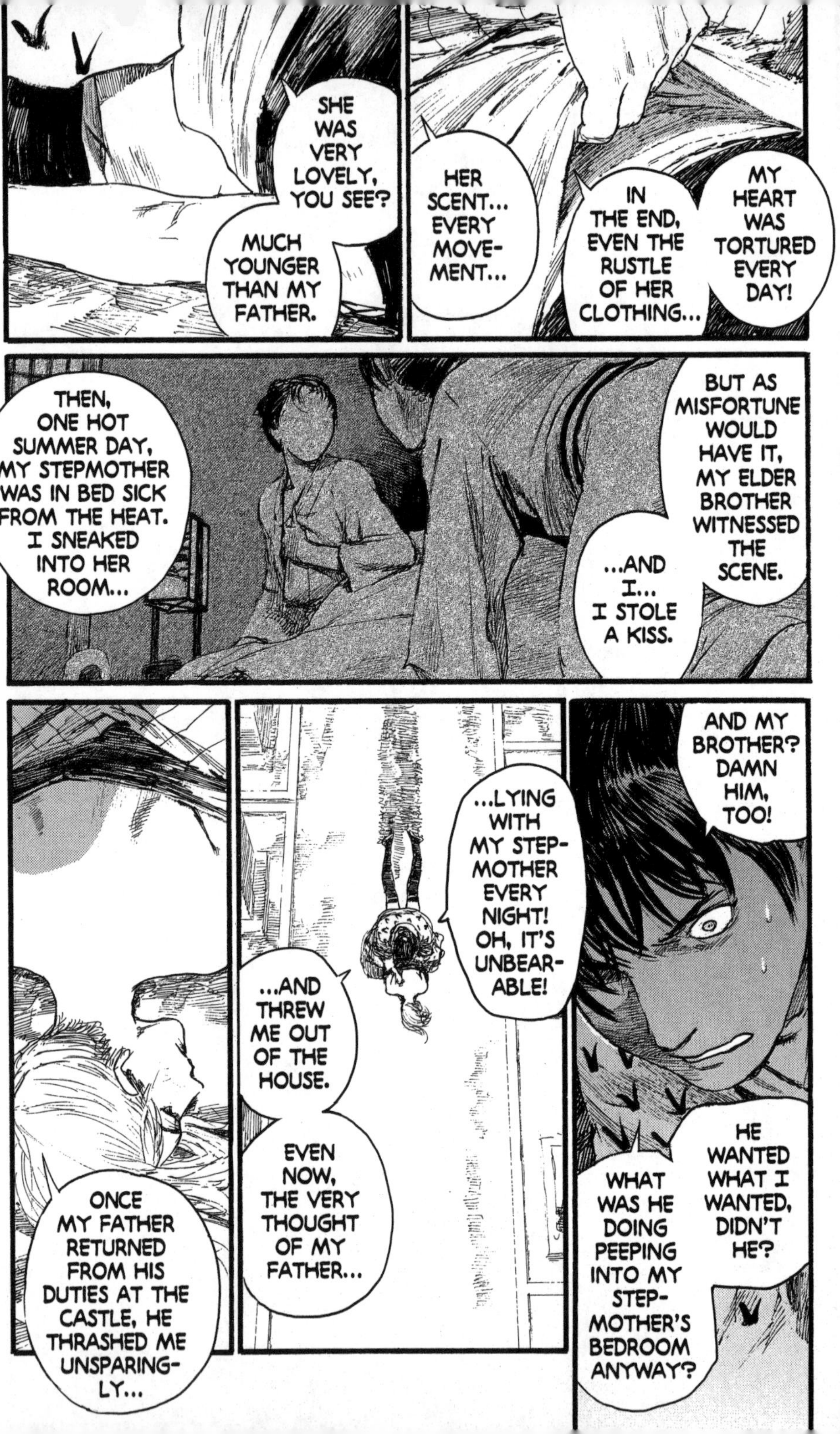
SHE WAS VERY LOVELY, YOU SEE?
MUCH YOUNGER THAN MY FATHER.
HER SCENT... EVERY MOVE-MENT...
IN THE END, EVEN THE RUSTLE OF HER CLOTHING...
MY HEART WAS TORTURED EVERY DAY!
THEN, ONE HOT SUMMER DAY, MY STEPMOTHER WAS IN BED SICK FROM THE HEAT. I SNEAKED INTO HER ROOM...
...AND I... I STOLE A KISS.
BUT AS MISFORTUNE WOULD HAVE IT, MY ELDER BROTHER WITNESSED THE SCENE.
ONCE MY FATHER RETURNED FROM HIS DUTIES AT THE CASTLE, HE THRASHED ME UNSPARING-LY...
...AND THREW ME OUT OF THE HOUSE.
EVEN NOW, THE VERY THOUGHT OF MY FATHER...
...LYING WITH MY STEP-MOTHER EVERY NIGHT! OH, IT'S UNBEAR-ABLE!
AND MY BROTHER? DAMN HIM, TOO!
WHAT WAS HE DOING PEEPING INTO MY STEP-MOTHER'S BEDROOM ANYWAY?
HE WANTED WHAT I WANTED, DIDN'T HE?

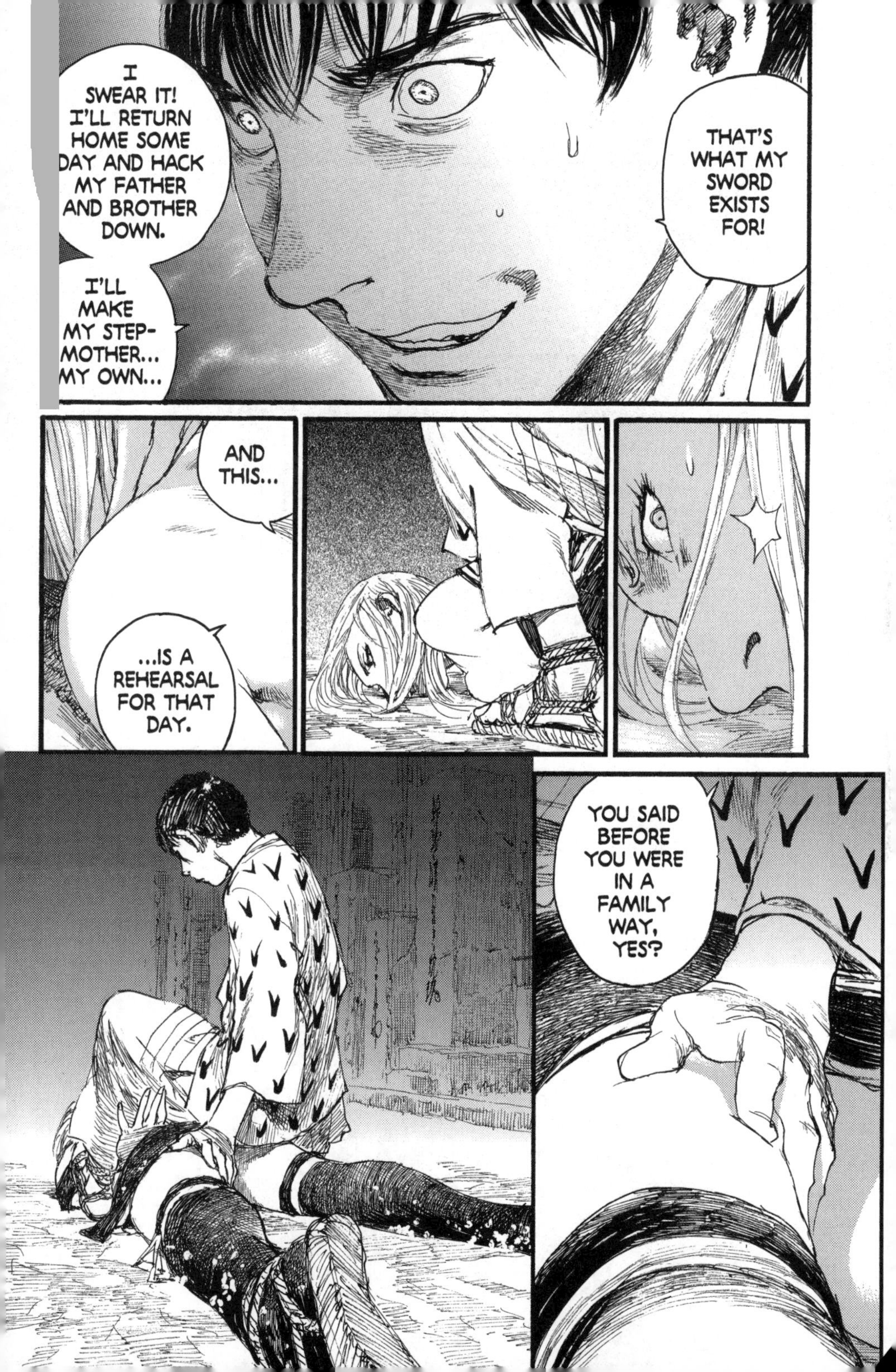
I SWEAR IT! I'LL RETURN HOME SOME DAY AND HACK MY FATHER AND BROTHER DOWN.
I'LL MAKE MY STEP-MOTHER... MY OWN...
THAT'S WHAT MY SWORD EXISTS FOR!
AND THIS...
...IS A REHEARSAL FOR THAT DAY.
YOU SAID BEFORE YOU WERE IN A FAMILY WAY, YES?

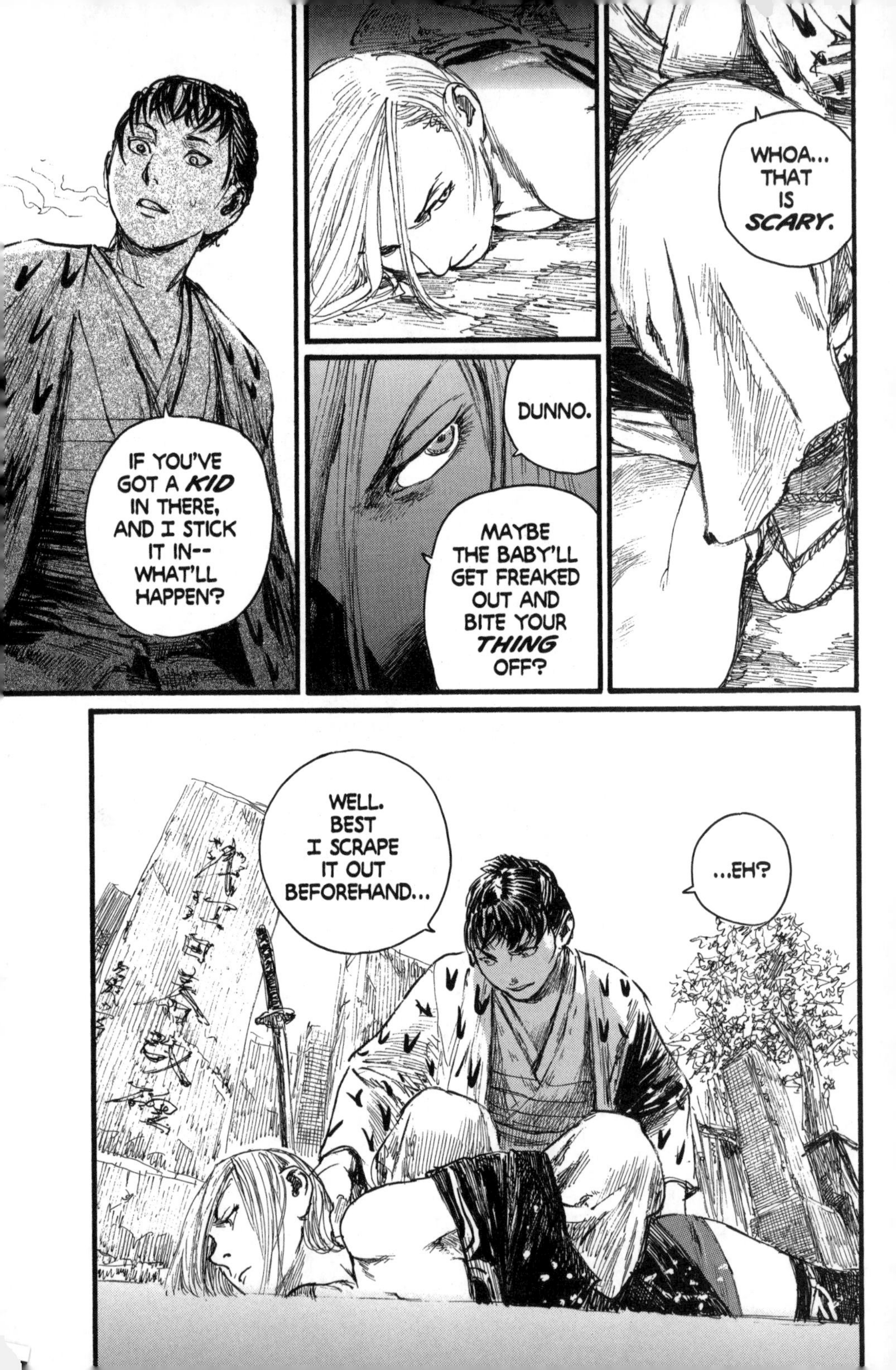
IF YOU'VE GOT A KID IN THERE, AND I STICK IT IN-- WHAT'LL HAPPEN?
DUNNO.
MAYBE THE BABY'LL GET FREAKED OUT AND BITE YOUR THING OFF?
WHOA... THAT IS SCARY.
WELL. BEST I SCRAPE IT OUT BEFOREHAND...
...EH?

HRRR!

THMP

THMP

HRR!

AH!

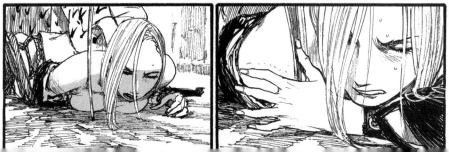

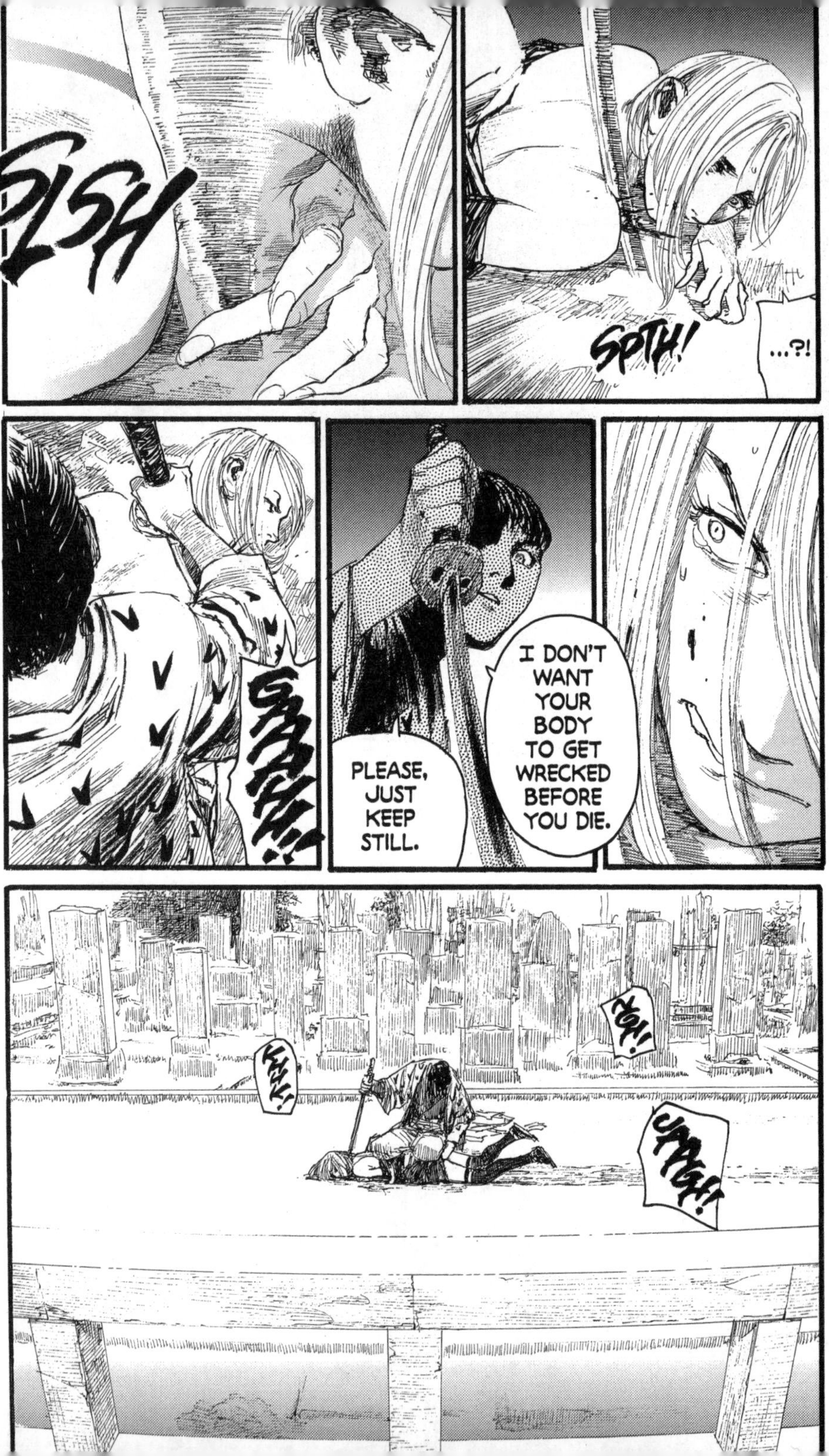
SPTH!
...?!
SISH
I DON'T WANT YOUR BODY TO GET WRECKED BEFORE YOU DIE.
PLEASE, JUST KEEP STILL.

AH! THIS IS THE WORST!

I PROMISED I WOULDN'T GET INVOLVED IN THE BATTLE. I FORCED HIM TO BRING ME ALONG...

...AND LOOK HOW BAD I FUCKED IT ALL UP!

THE CHILD IN MY BELLY...

...WAS MADE IN A SIMILARLY EVIL SITUATION.

A BASTARD.

UNWANTED, UNNEEDED...

...BUT STILL...

...HOW FUCKING IRRITATING!

OW!

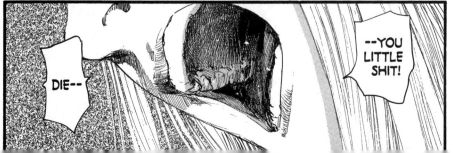

DIE--

--YOU LITTLE SHIT!

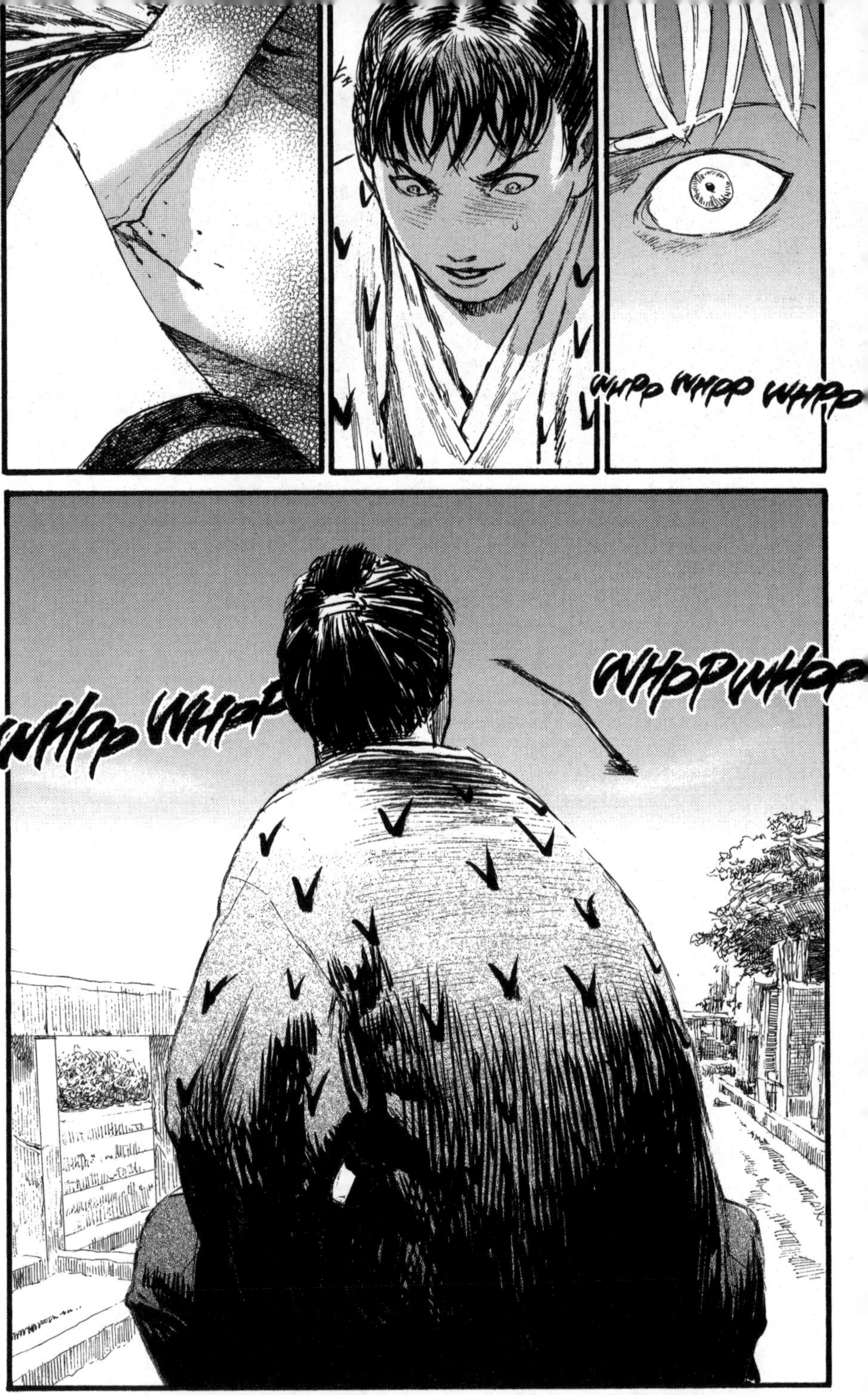
WHPP WHPP WHPP
WHPP WHPP
WHPP WHPP

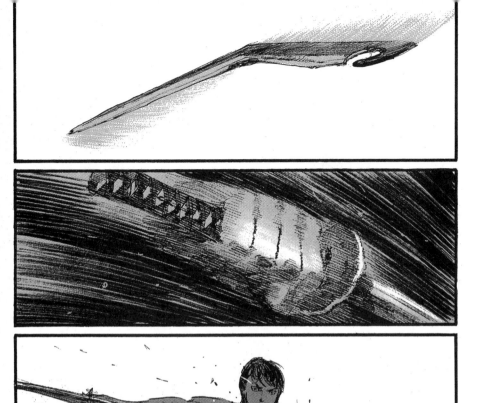

TIN NG!

KAK!

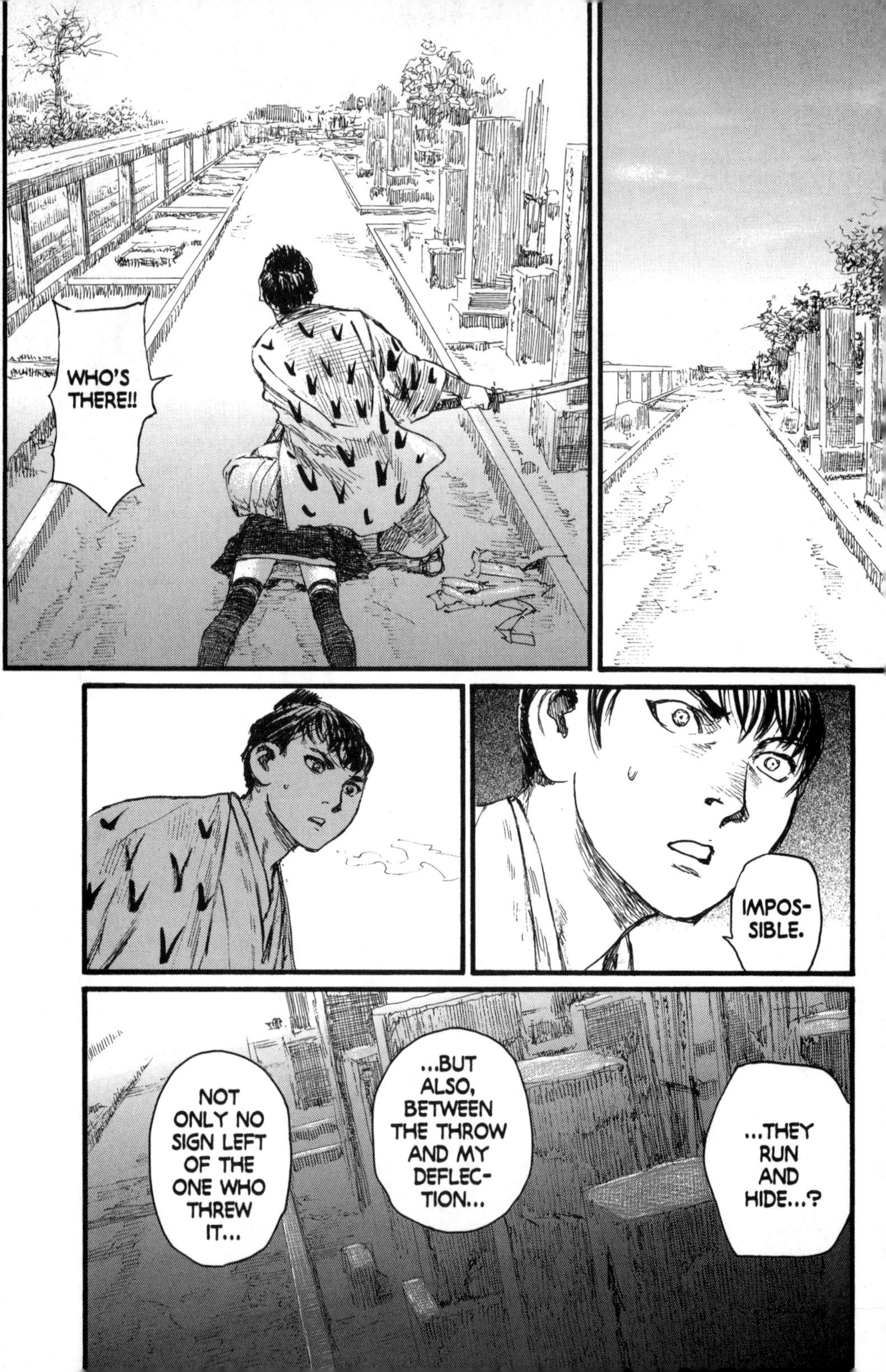
WHO'S THERE!!
IMPOS-SIBLE.
NOT ONLY NO SIGN LEFT OF THE ONE WHO THREW IT...
...BUT ALSO, BETWEEN THE THROW AND MY DEFLEC-TION...
...THEY RUN AND HIDE...?

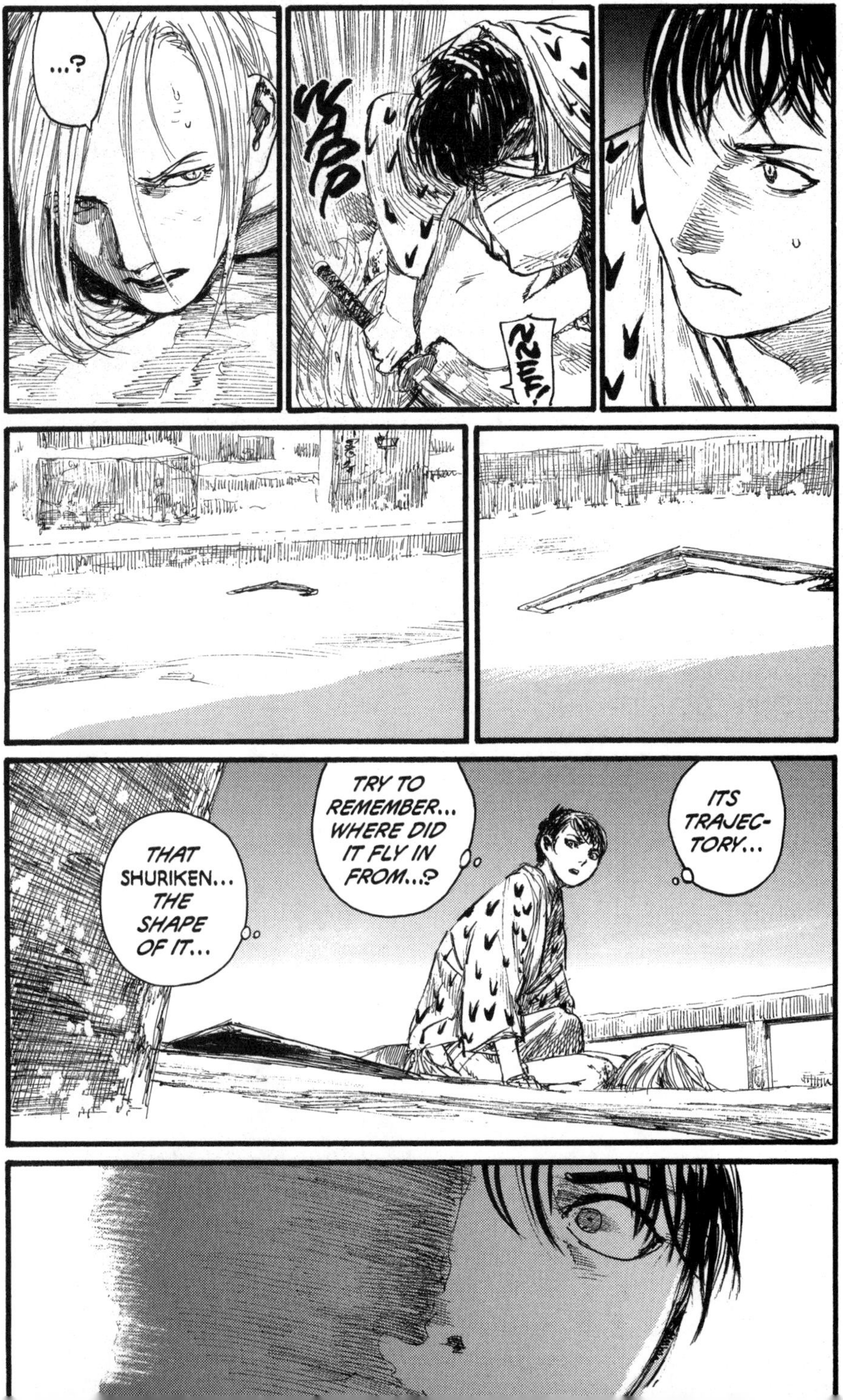
NNEF!
...?
ITS TRAJECTORY...
TRY TO REMEMBER... WHERE DID IT FLY IN FROM...?
THAT SHURIKEN... THE SHAPE OF IT...

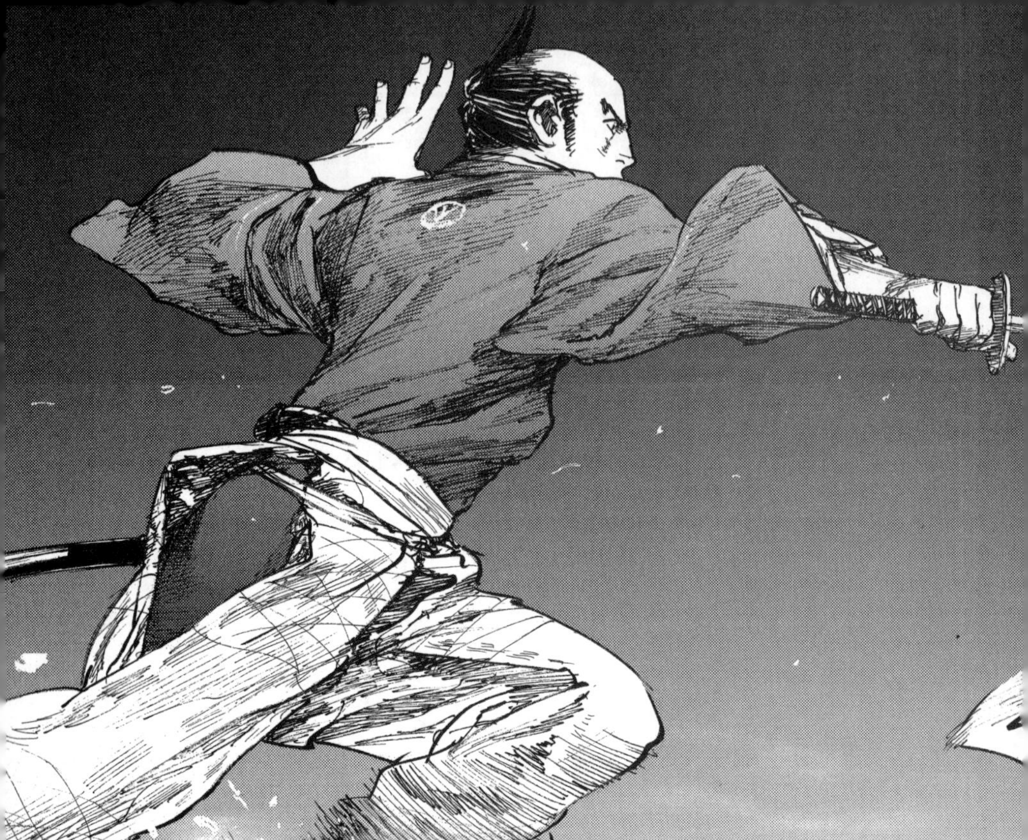
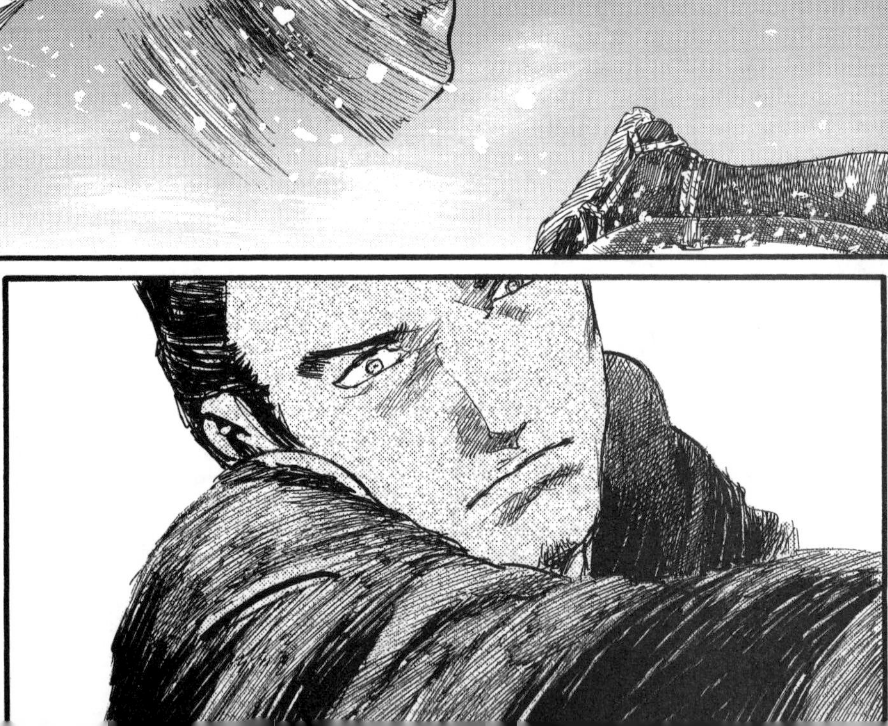

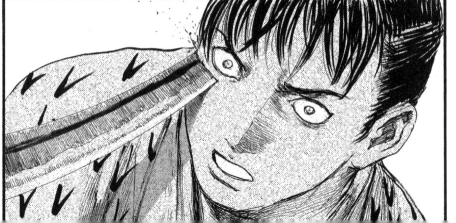

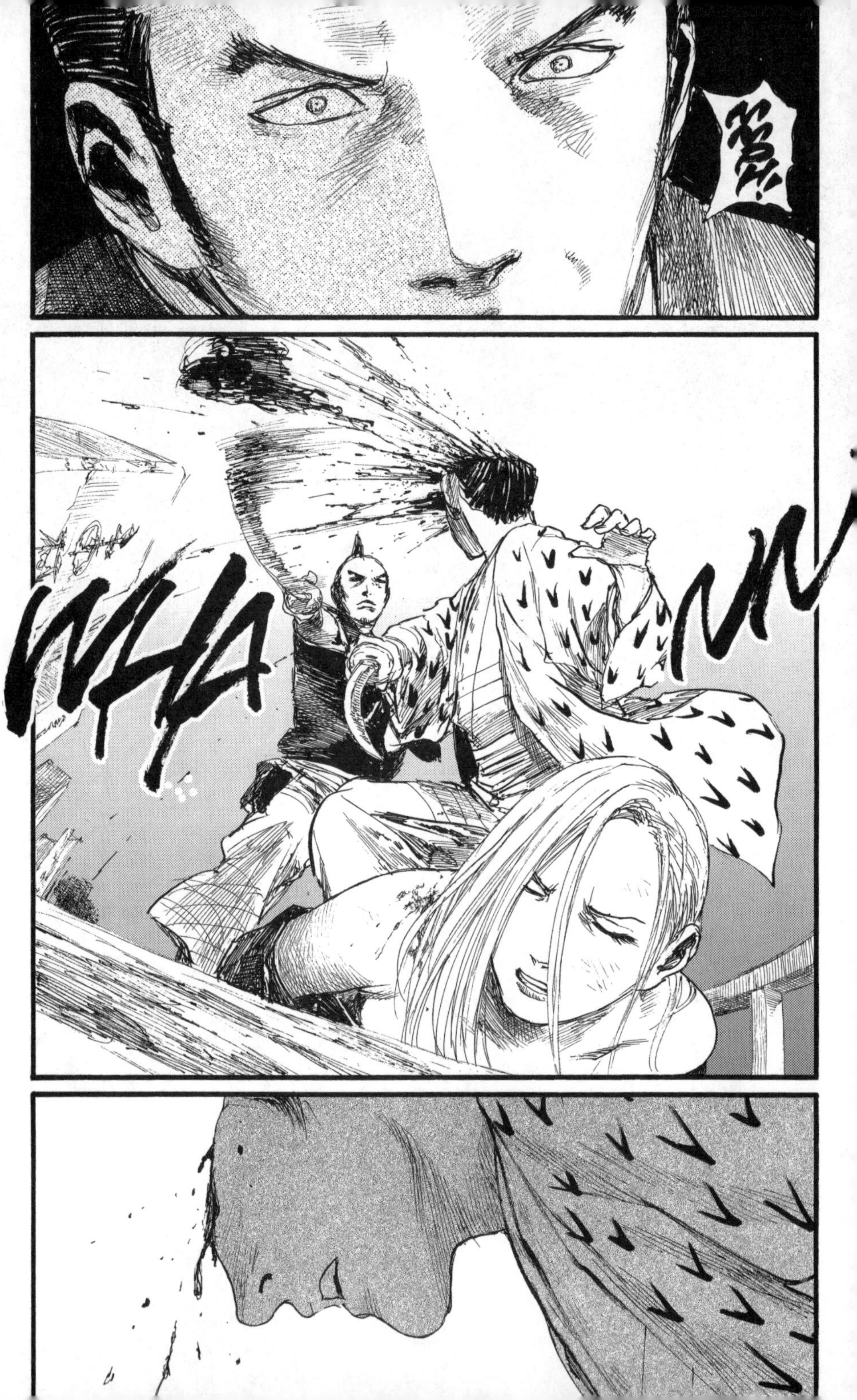
WHAM

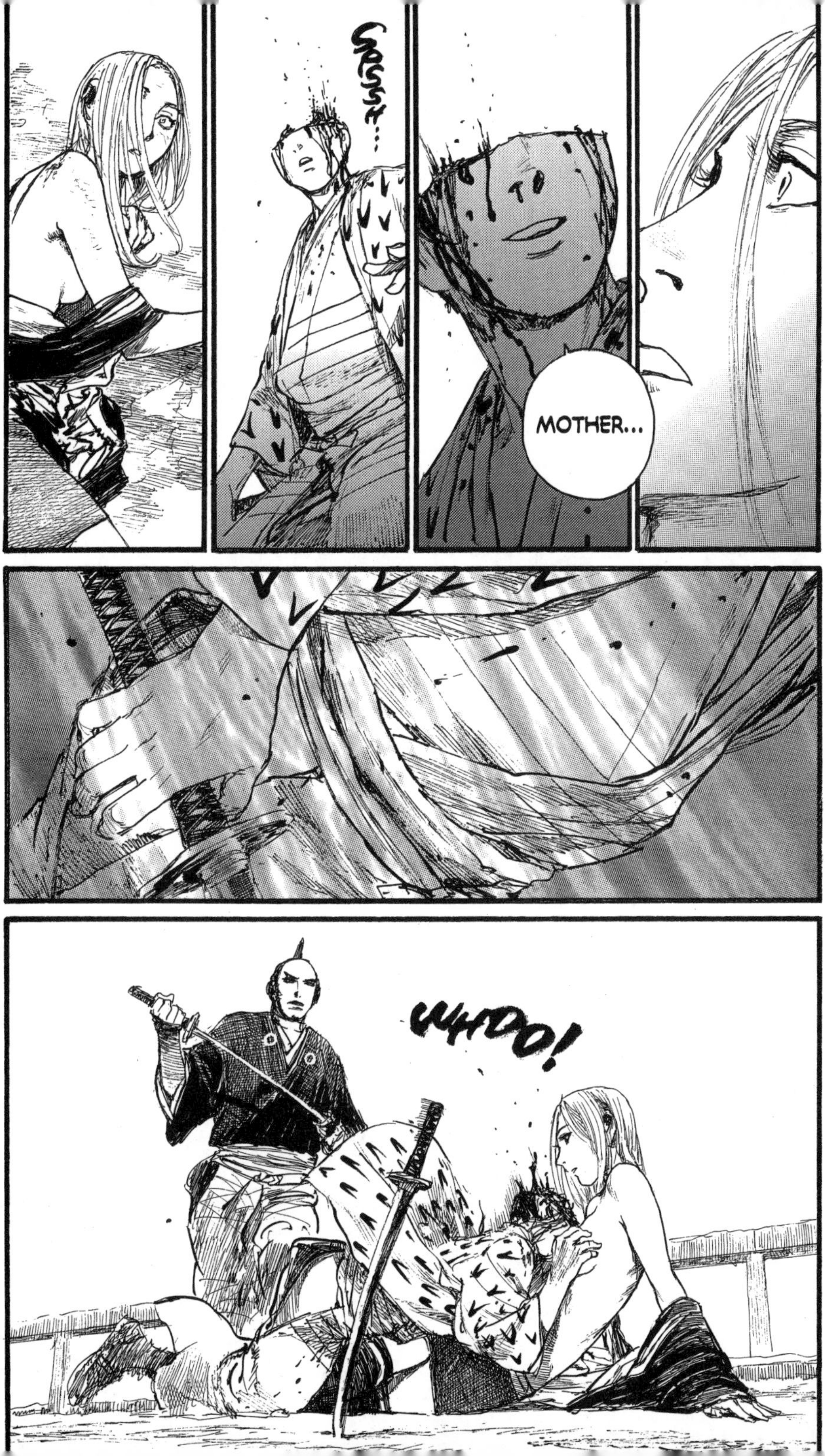
MOTHER...
GRSSSH...
WHOO!

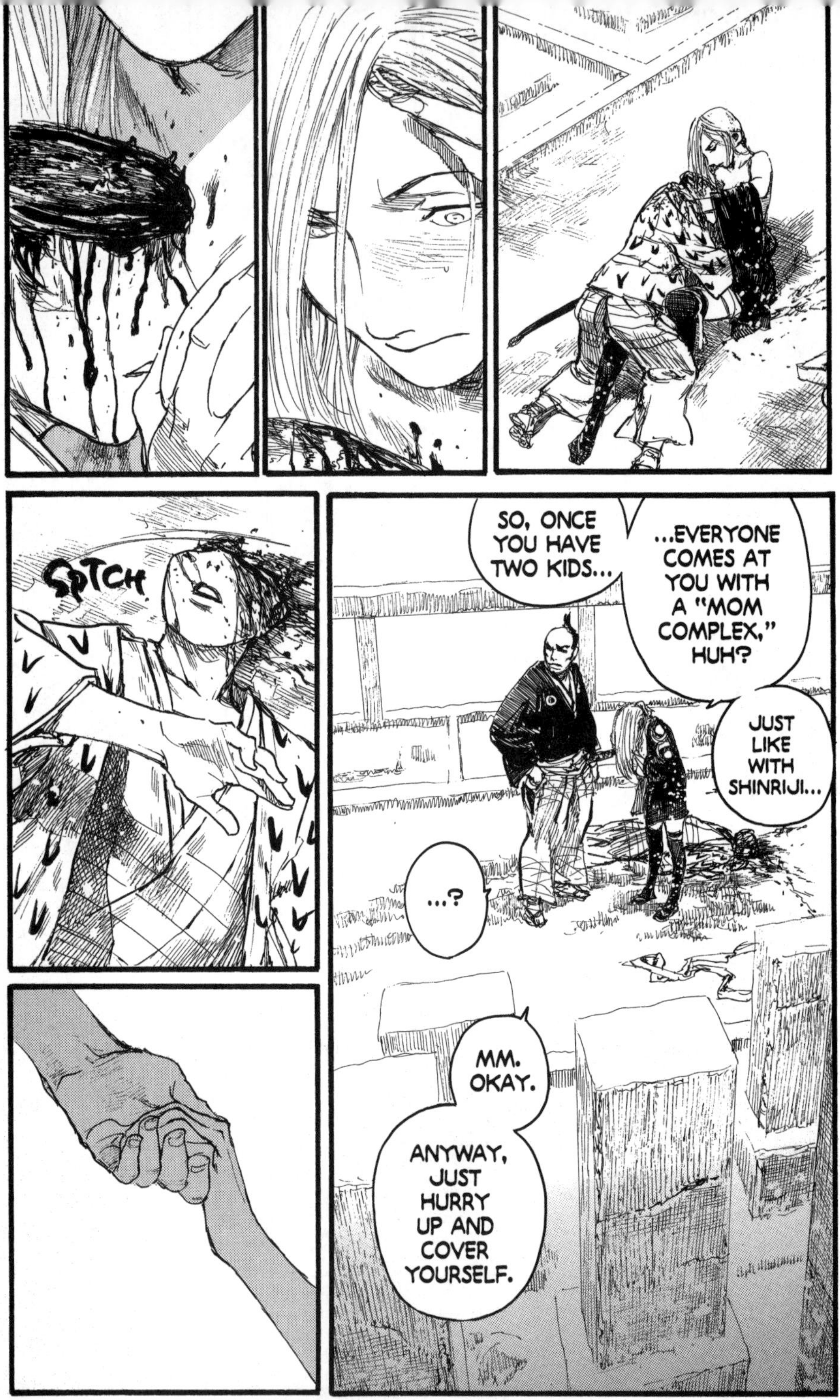
SO, ONCE YOU HAVE TWO KIDS...
...EVERYONE COMES AT YOU WITH A "MOM COMPLEX," HUH?
JUST LIKE WITH SHINRIJI...
...?
MM. OKAY.
ANYWAY, JUST HURRY UP AND COVER YOURSELF.
SPTCH

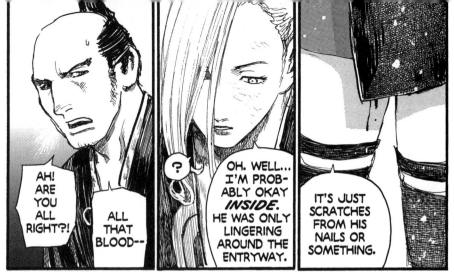

AH! ARE YOU ALL RIGHT?!

ALL THAT BLOOD--

OH. WELL... I'M PROBABLY OKAY *INSIDE.* HE WAS ONLY LINGERING AROUND THE ENTRYWAY.

IT'S JUST SCRATCHES FROM HIS NAILS OR SOMETHING.

ARIUSU!!

YATOIN!!

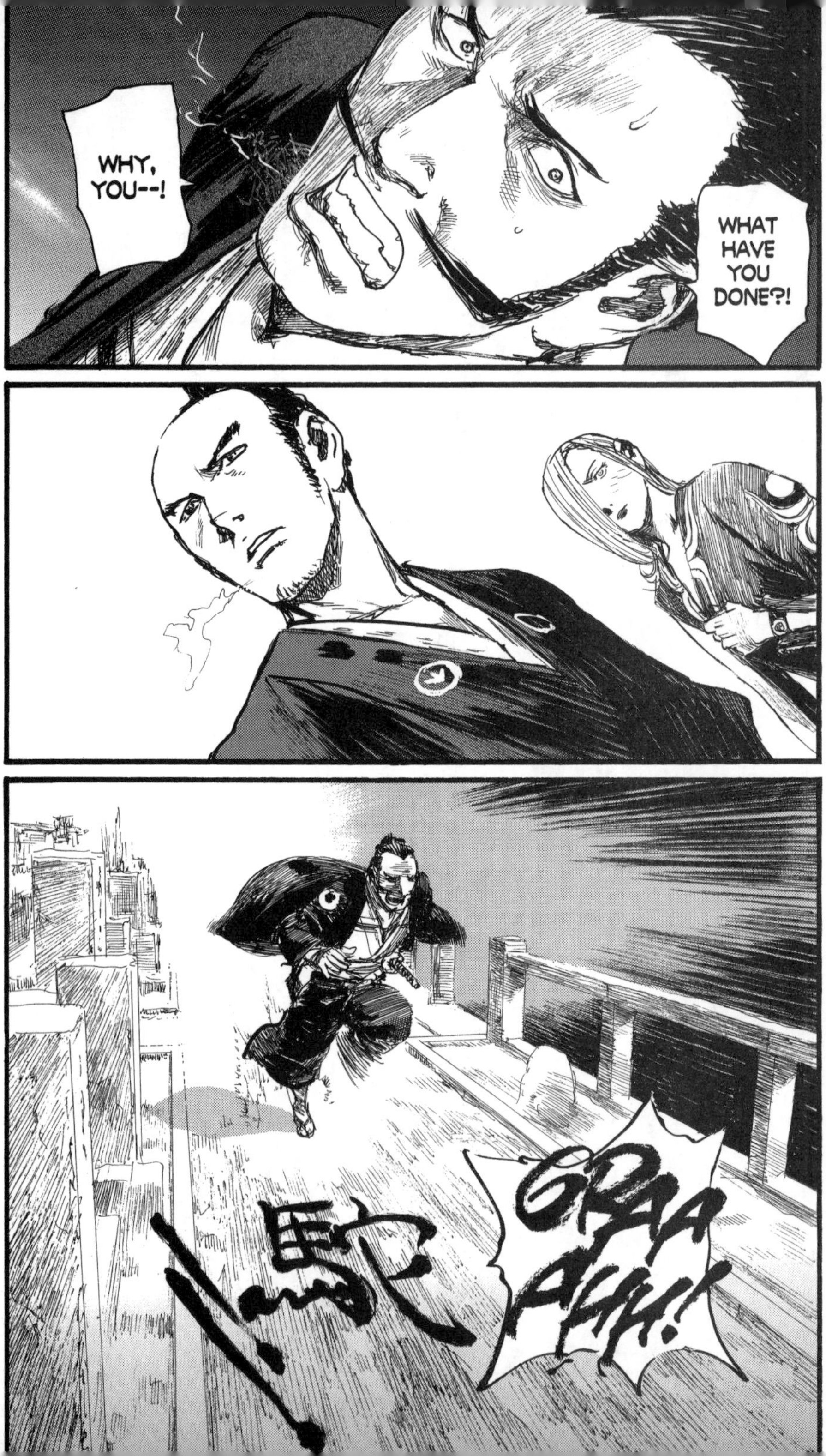
WHAT HAVE YOU DONE?!
WHY, YOU--!
GRAA AHH!
駆

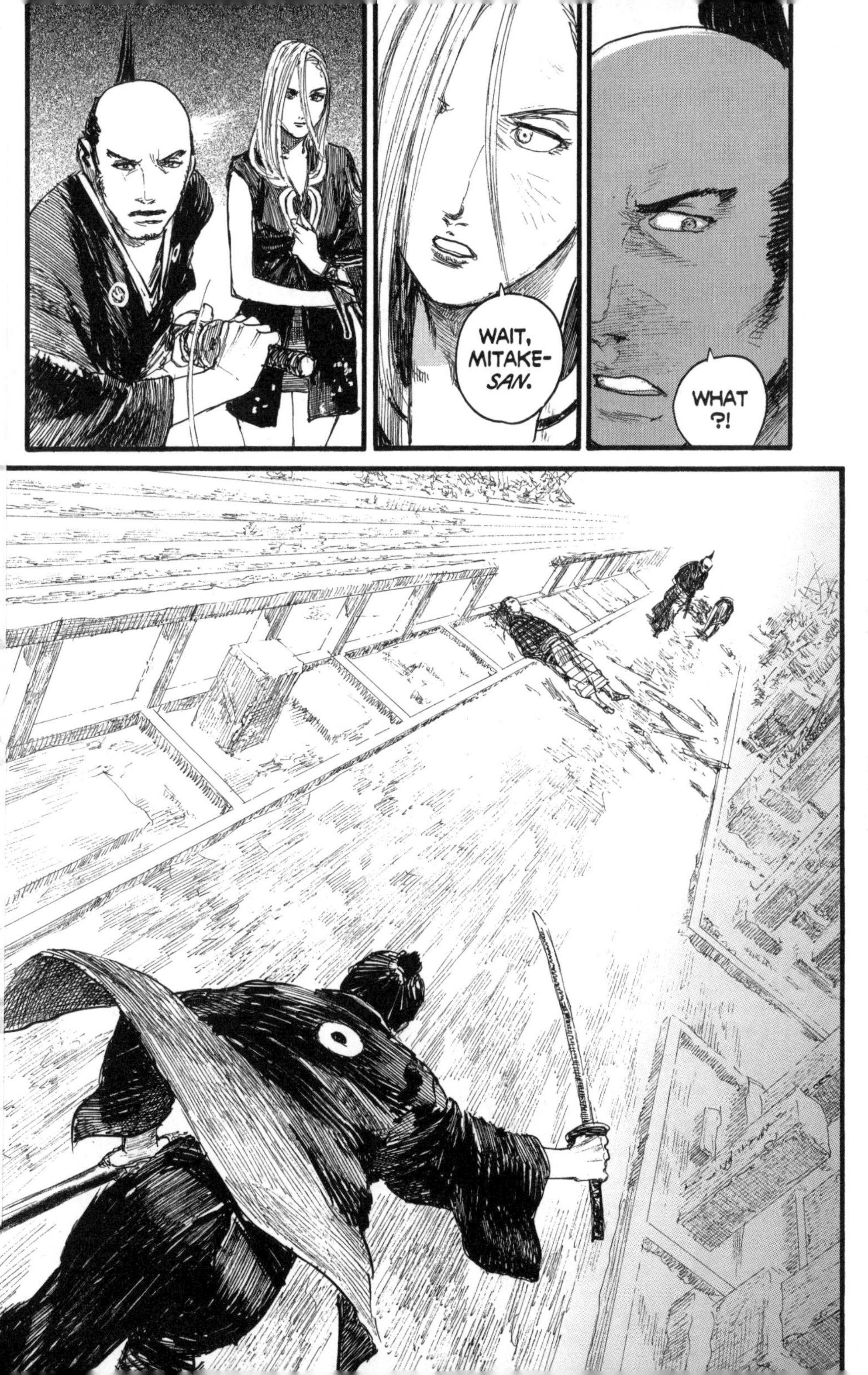
WAIT, MITAKE-*SAN*.
WHAT ?!

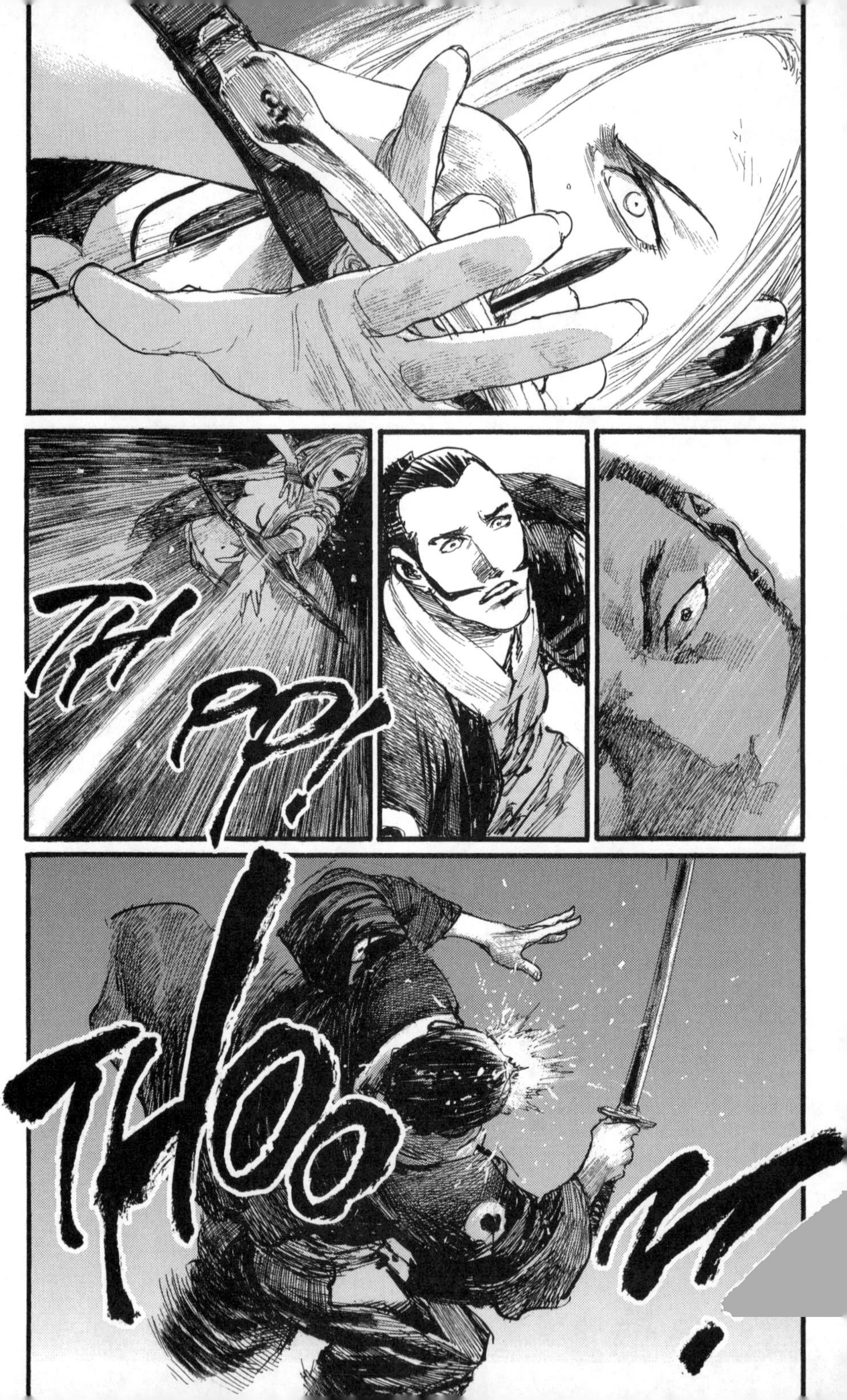
THOP!
THOOM!

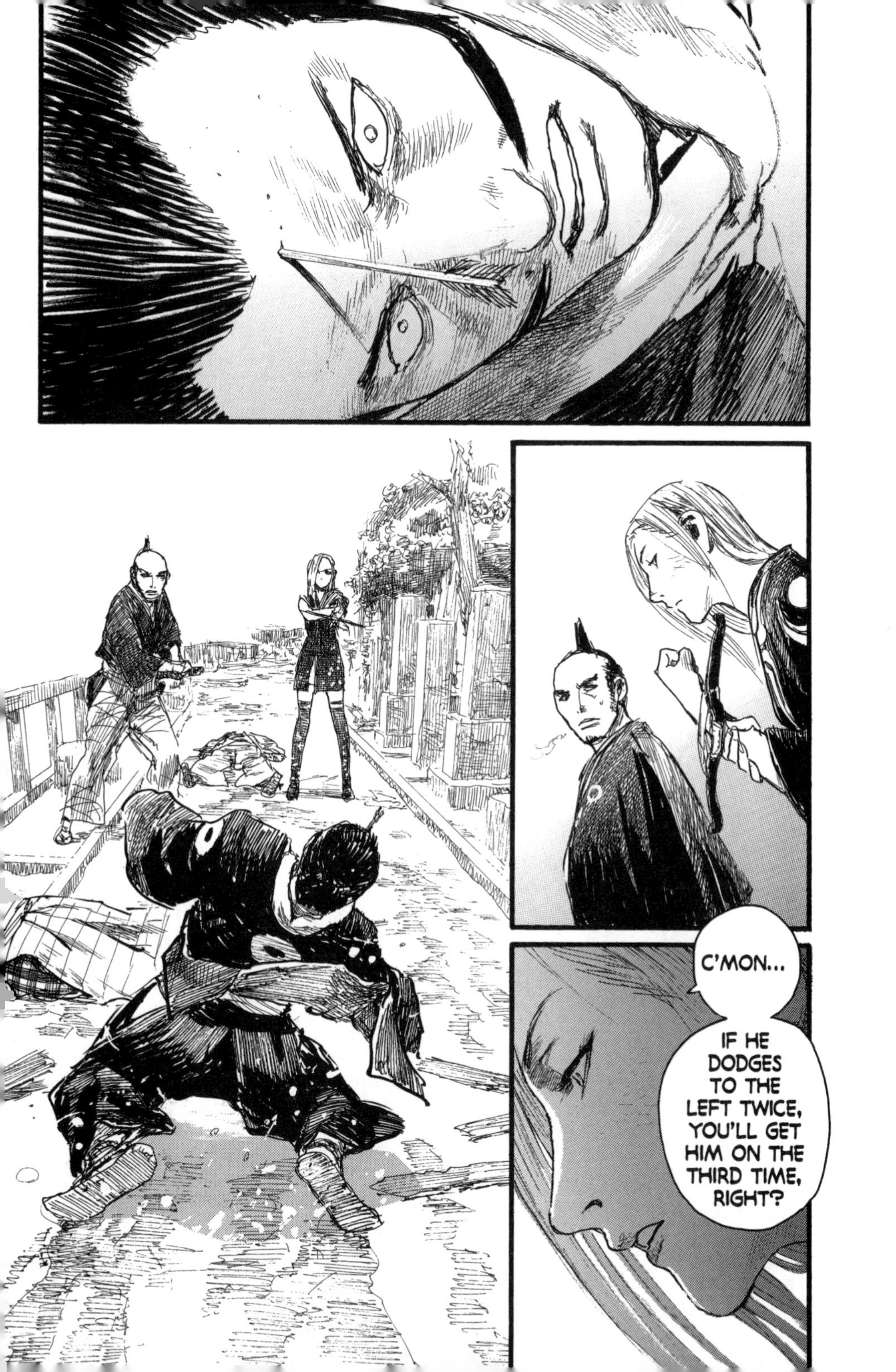
C'MON...
IF HE DODGES TO THE LEFT TWICE, YOU'LL GET HIM ON THE THIRD TIME, RIGHT?

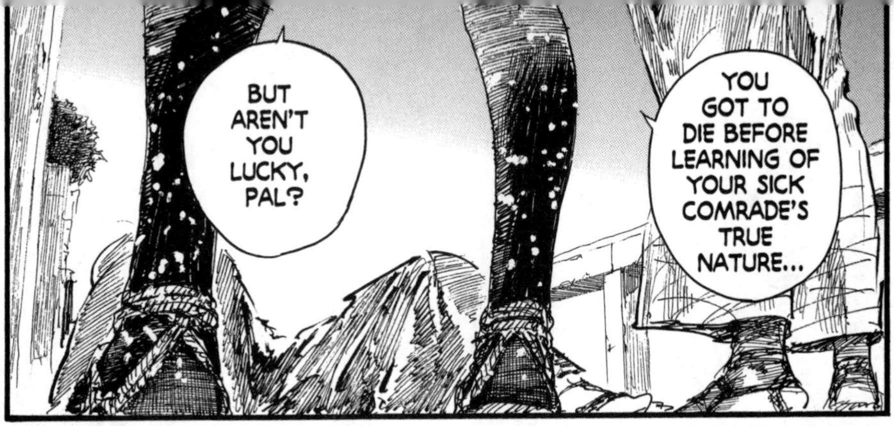
BUT AREN'T YOU LUCKY, PAL?
YOU GOT TO DIE BEFORE LEARNING OF YOUR SICK COMRADE'S TRUE NATURE...
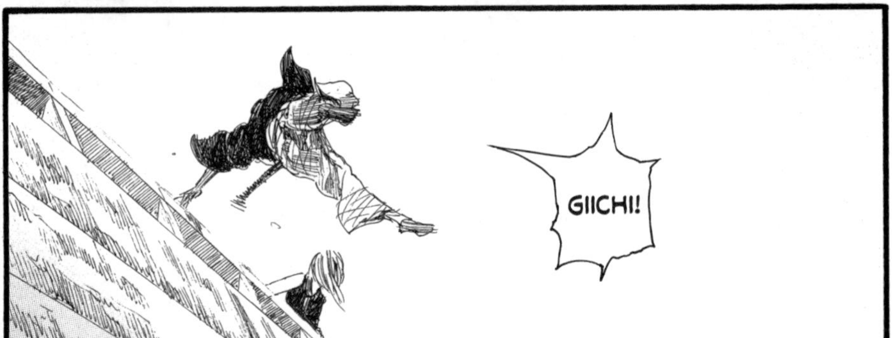
GIICHI!
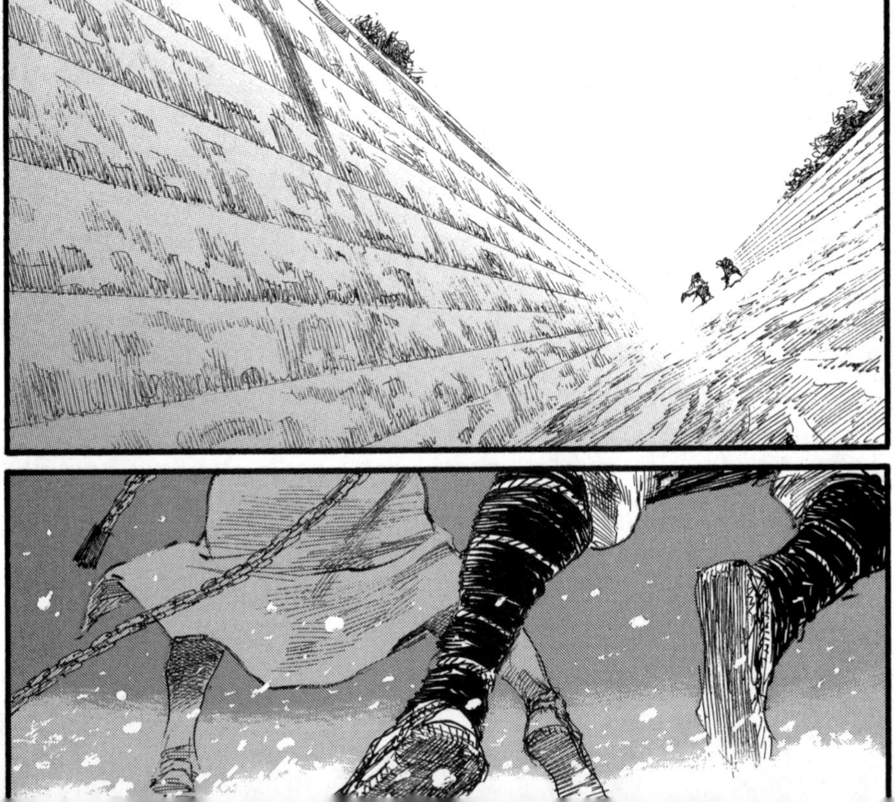

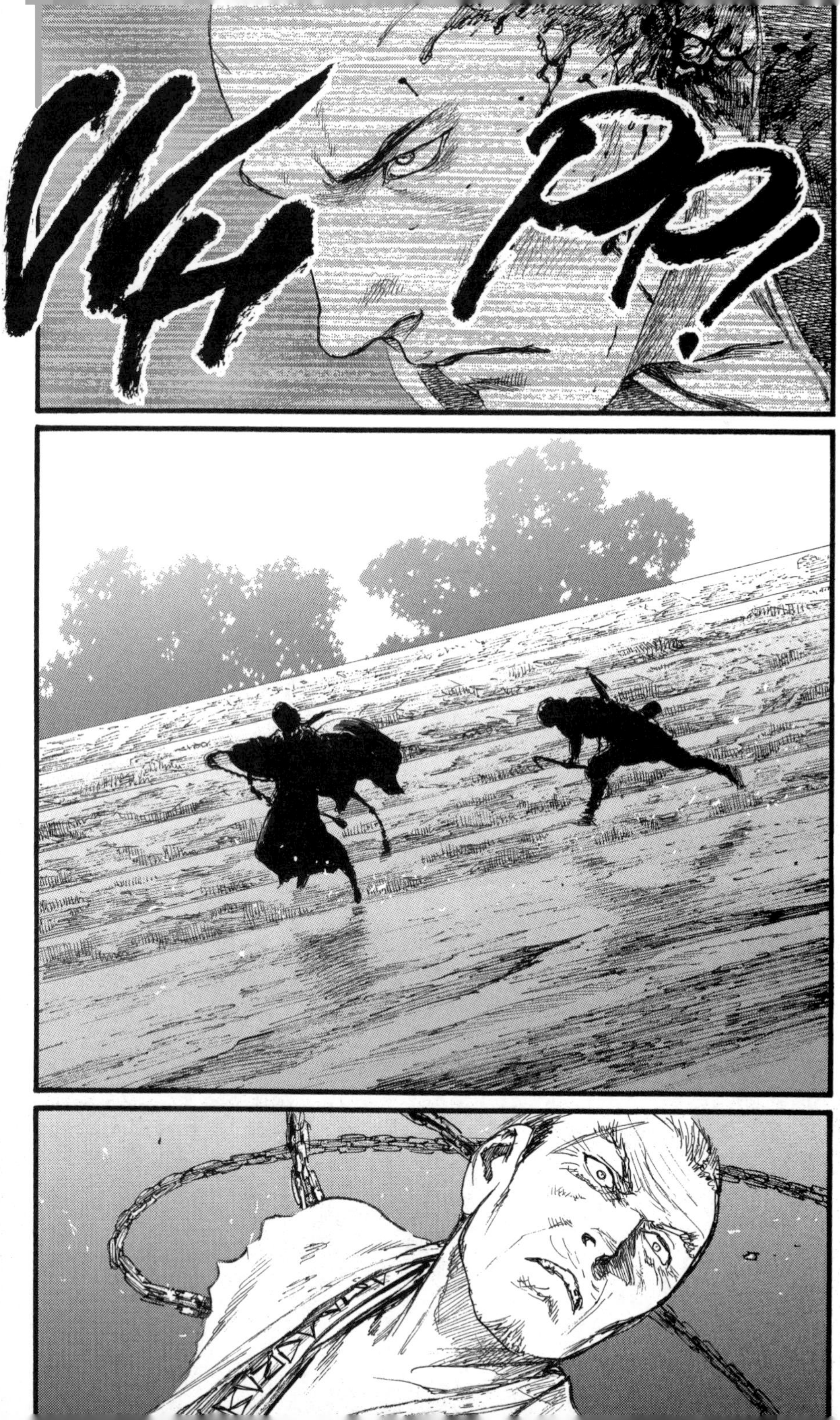
CHAP?!

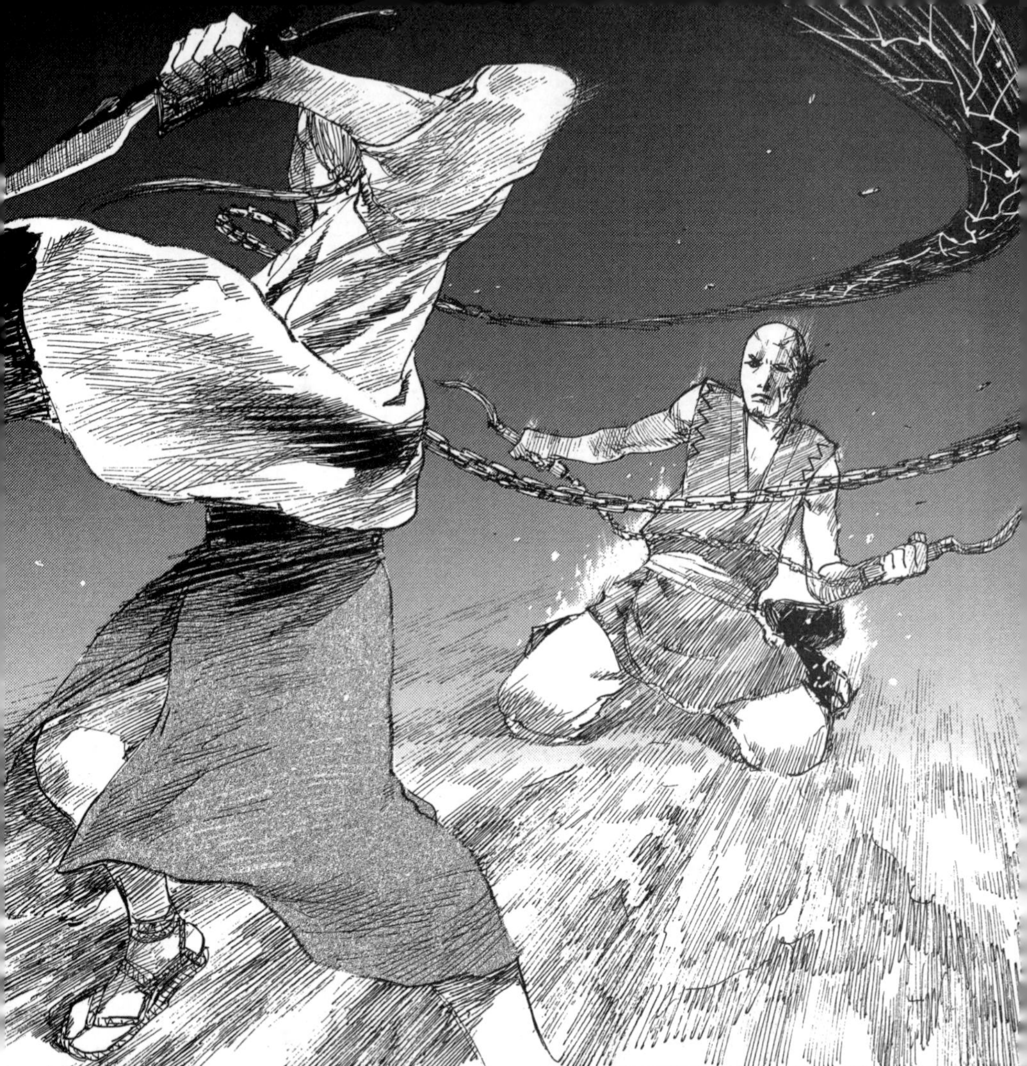
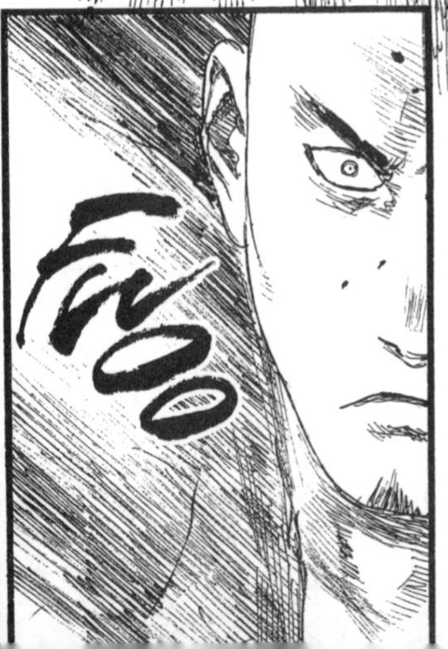
FWOO
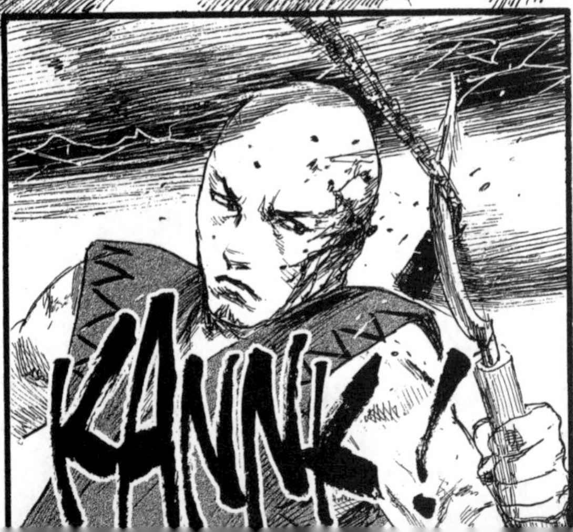
KANNK!

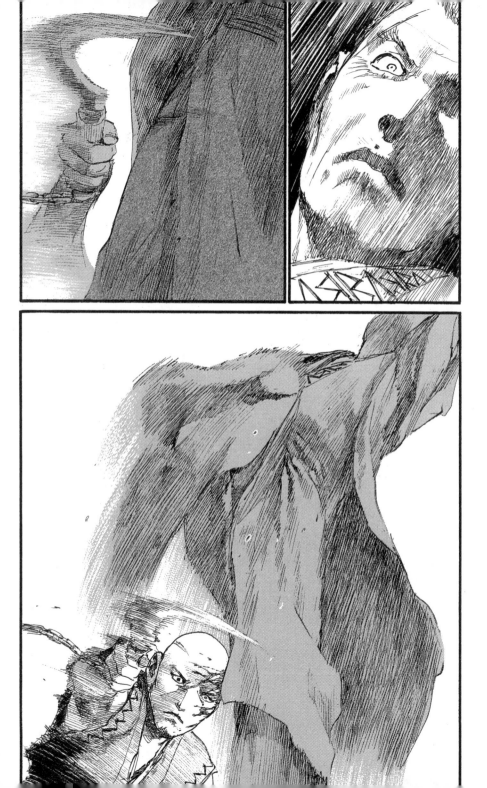

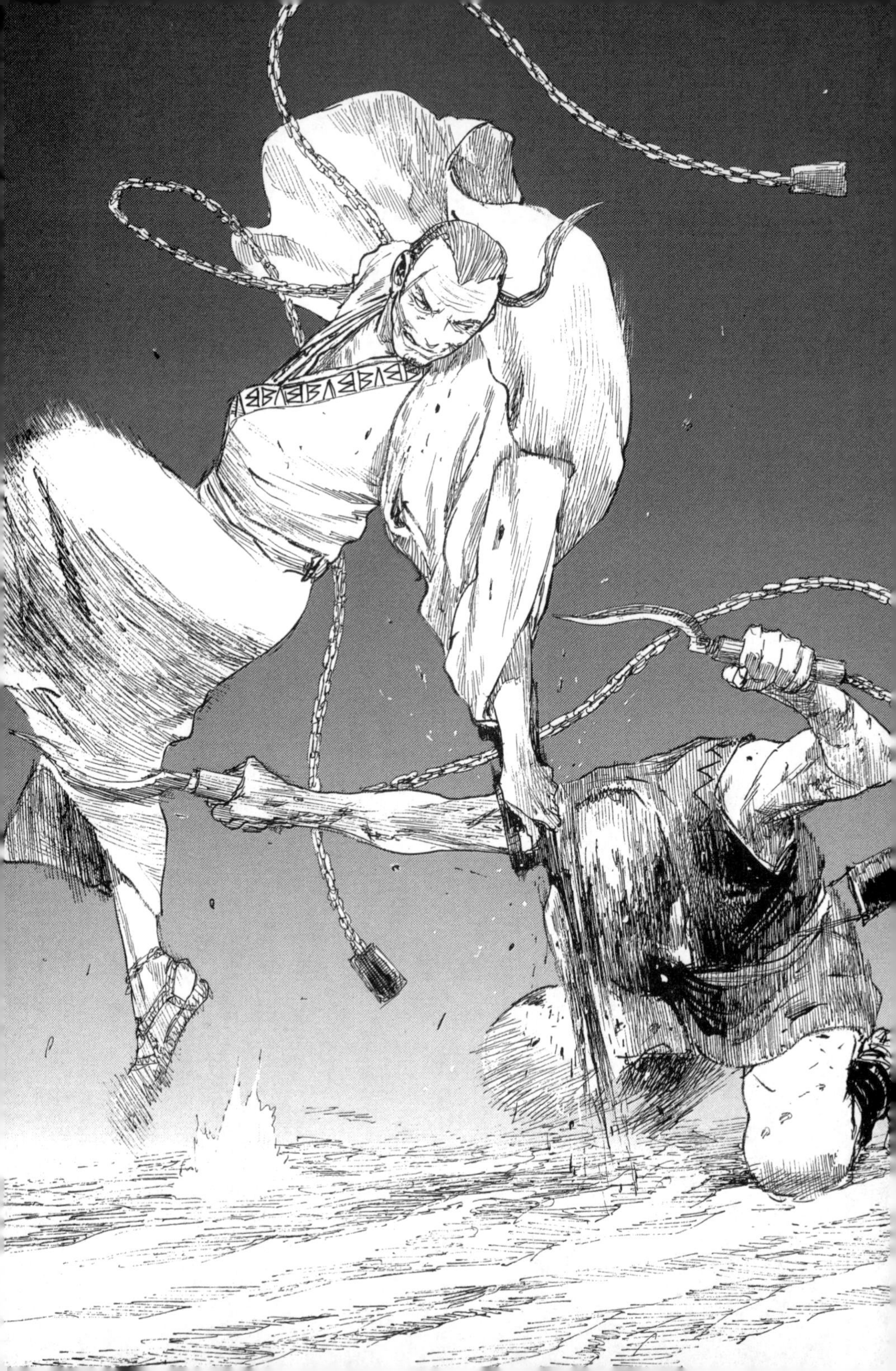

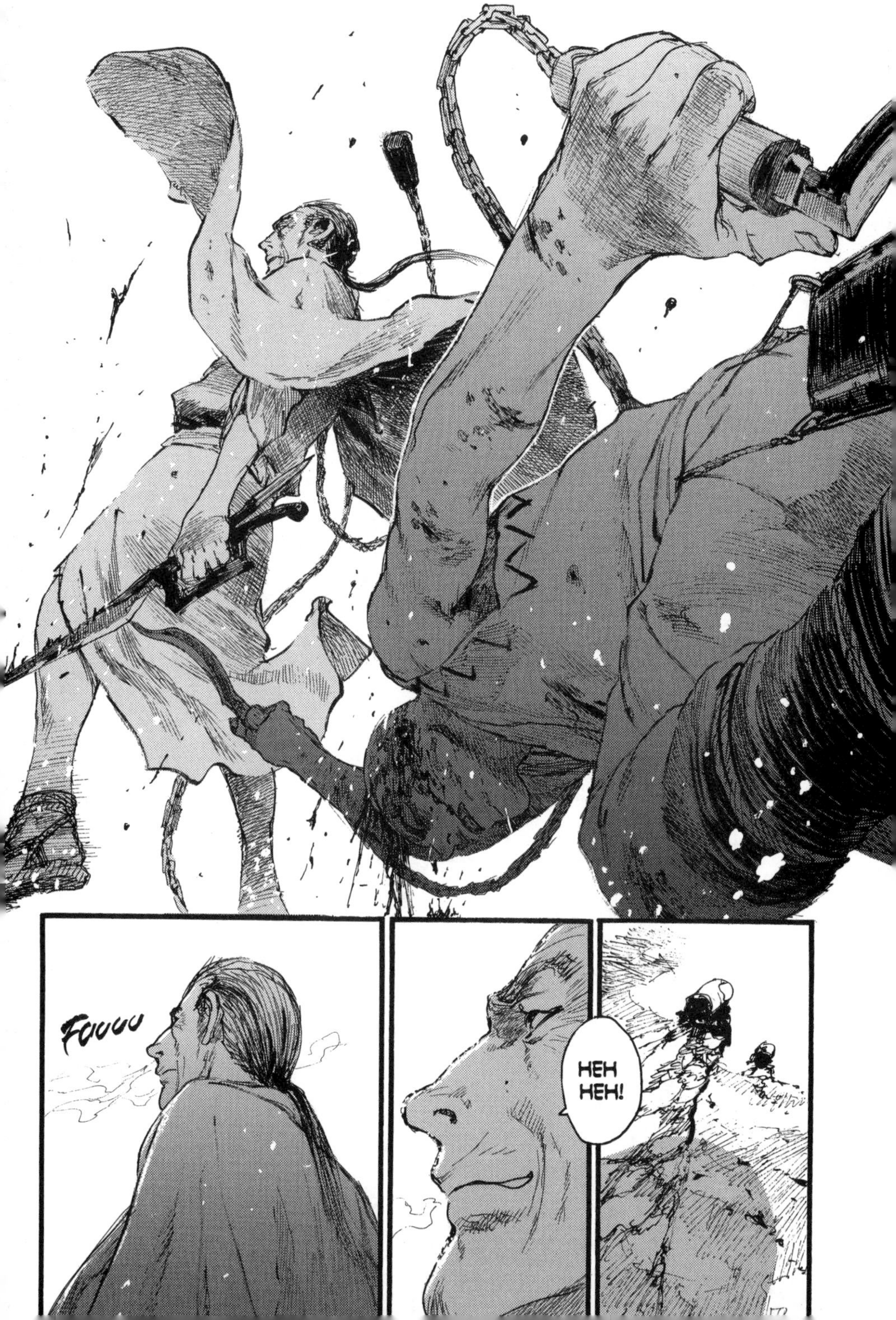
HEH HEH!
Fuuuu

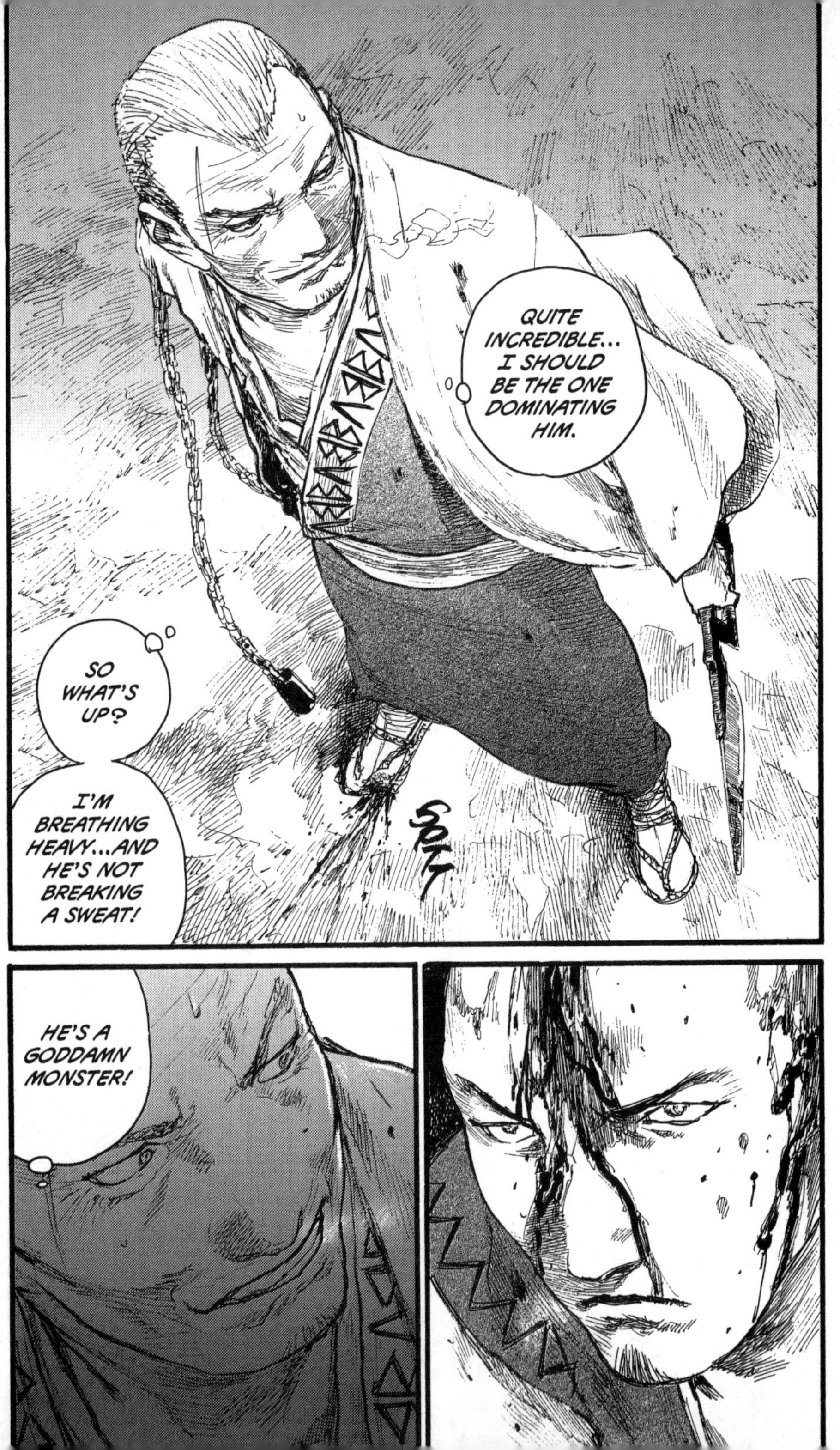
QUITE INCREDIBLE... I SHOULD BE THE ONE DOMINATING HIM.
SO WHAT'S UP?
I'M BREATHING HEAVY...AND HE'S NOT BREAKING A SWEAT!
HE'S A GODDAMN MONSTER!

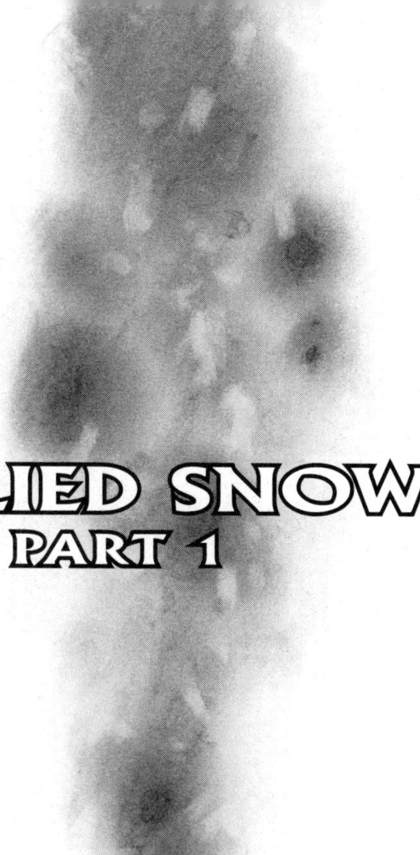

SULLIED SNOW
PART 1

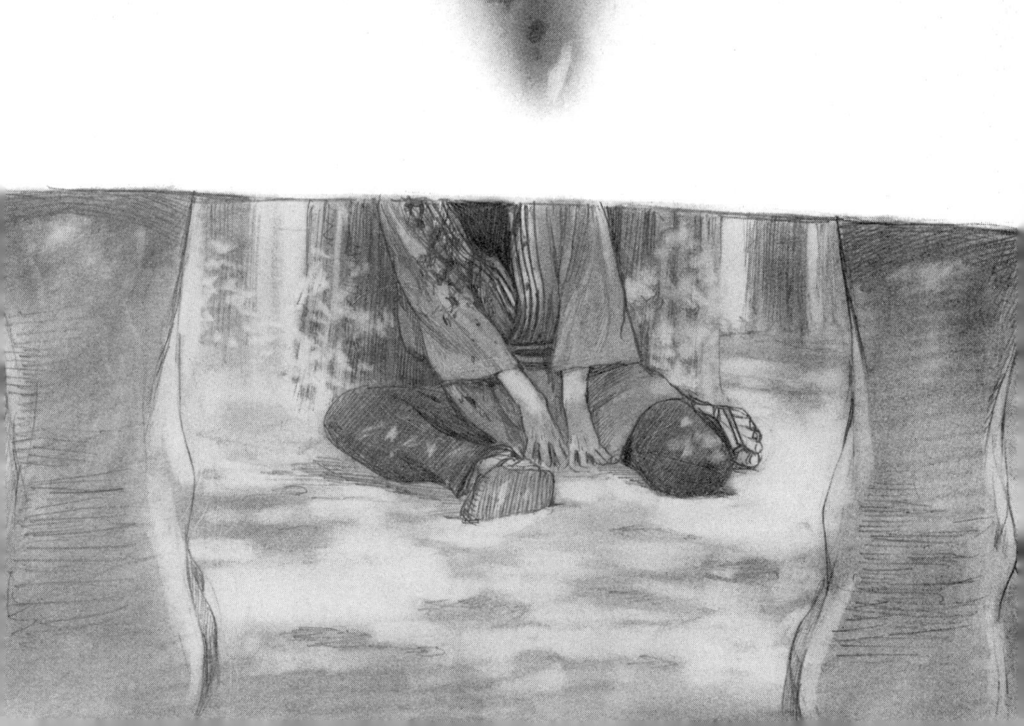

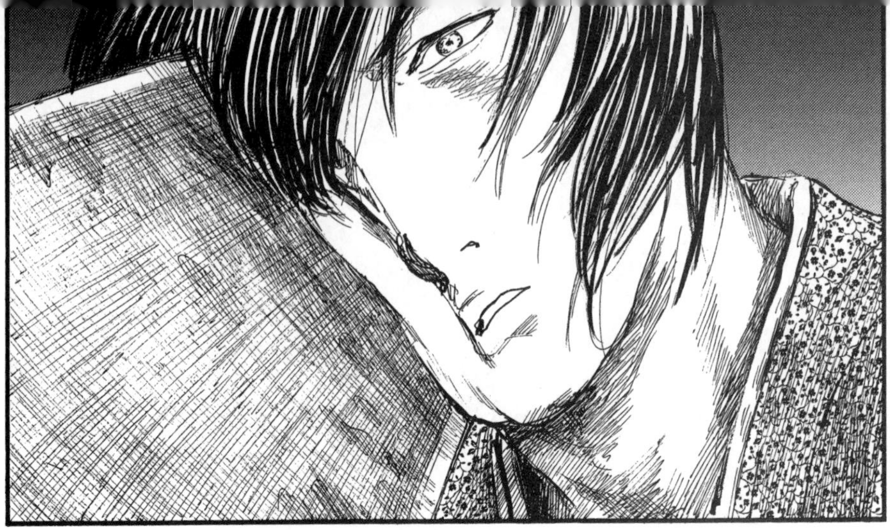

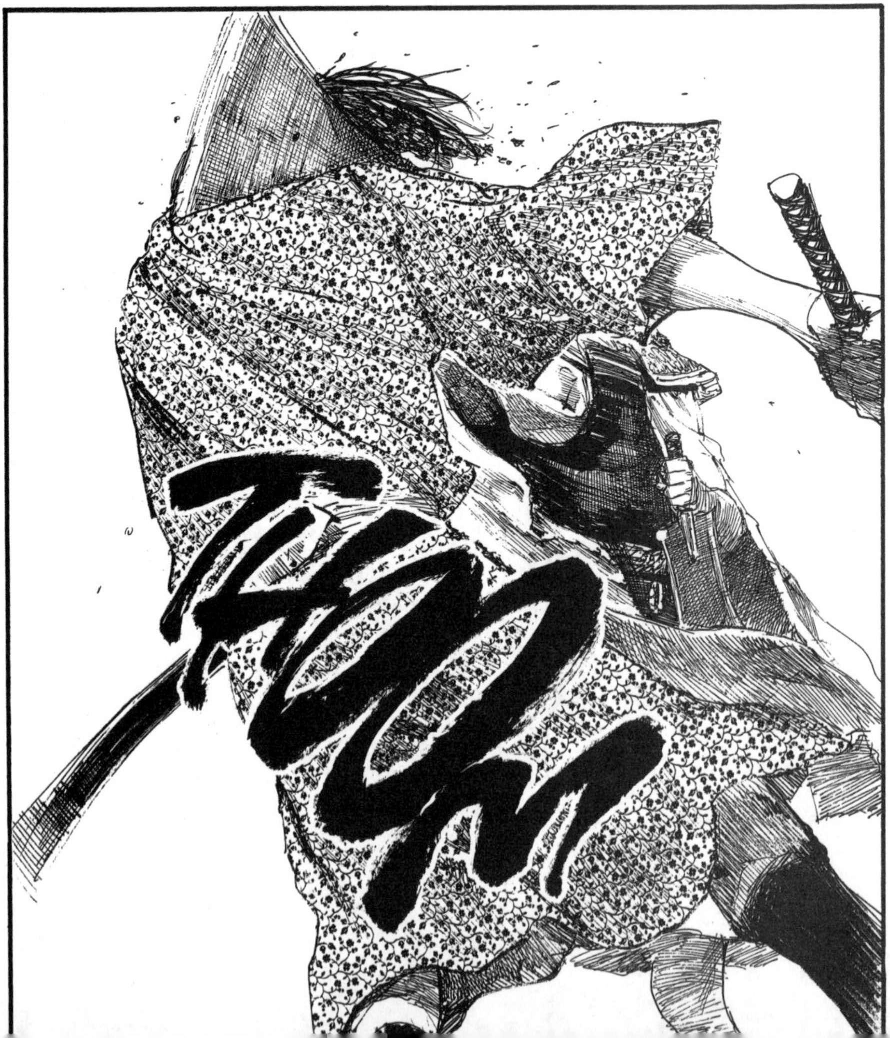

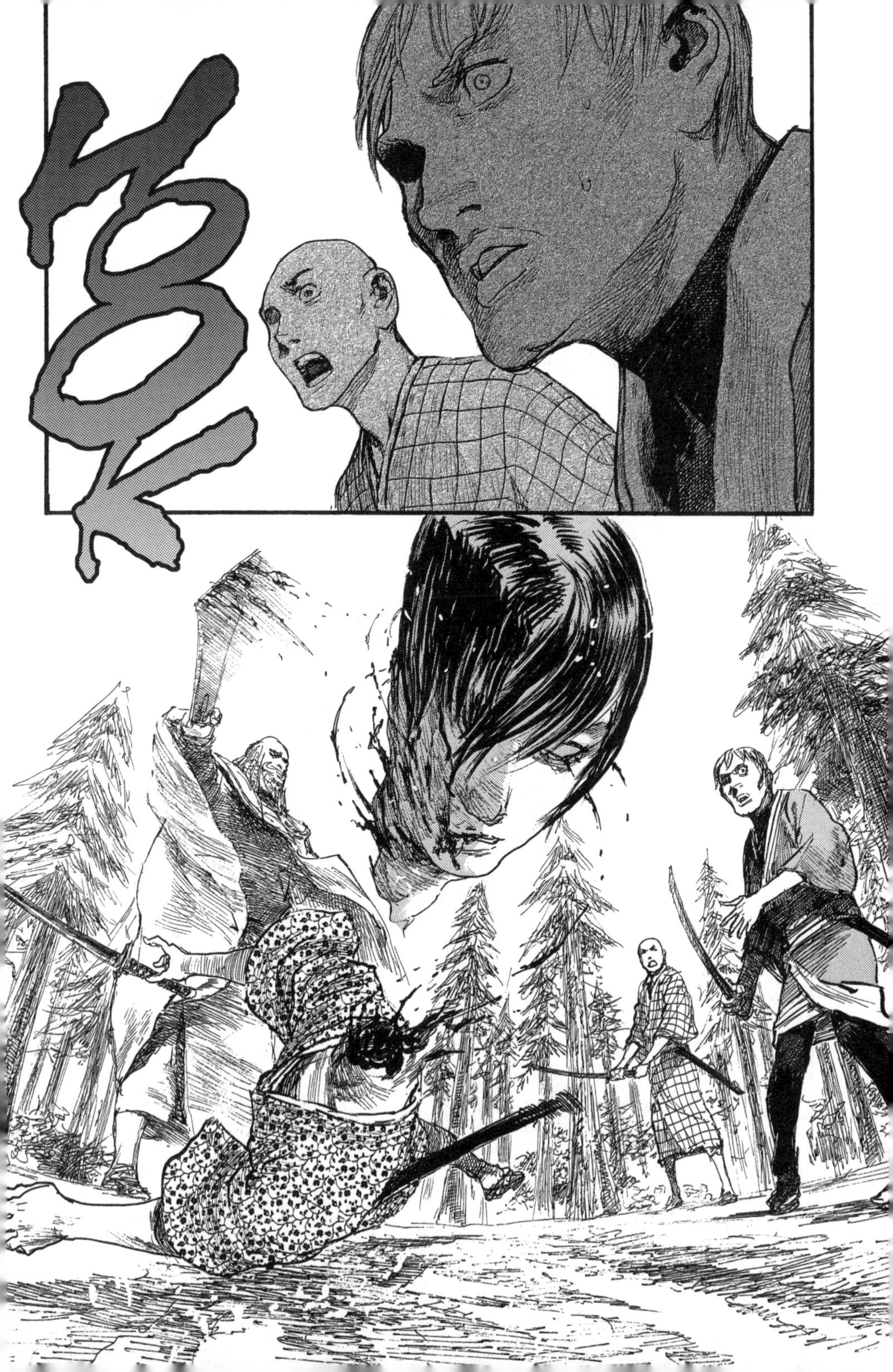

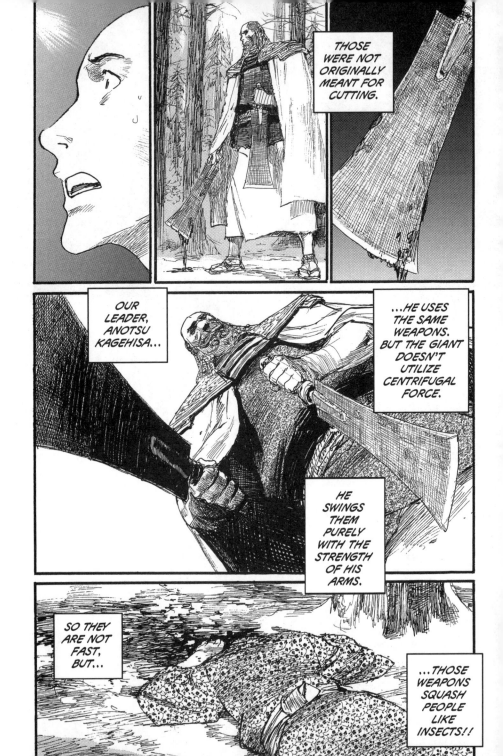

THOSE WERE NOT ORIGINALLY MEANT FOR CUTTING.

OUR LEADER, ANOTSU KAGEHISA...

...HE USES THE SAME WEAPONS. BUT THE GIANT DOESN'T UTILIZE CENTRIFUGAL FORCE.

HE SWINGS THEM PURELY WITH THE STRENGTH OF HIS ARMS.

SO THEY ARE NOT FAST, BUT...

...THOSE WEAPONS SQUASH PEOPLE LIKE INSECTS!!

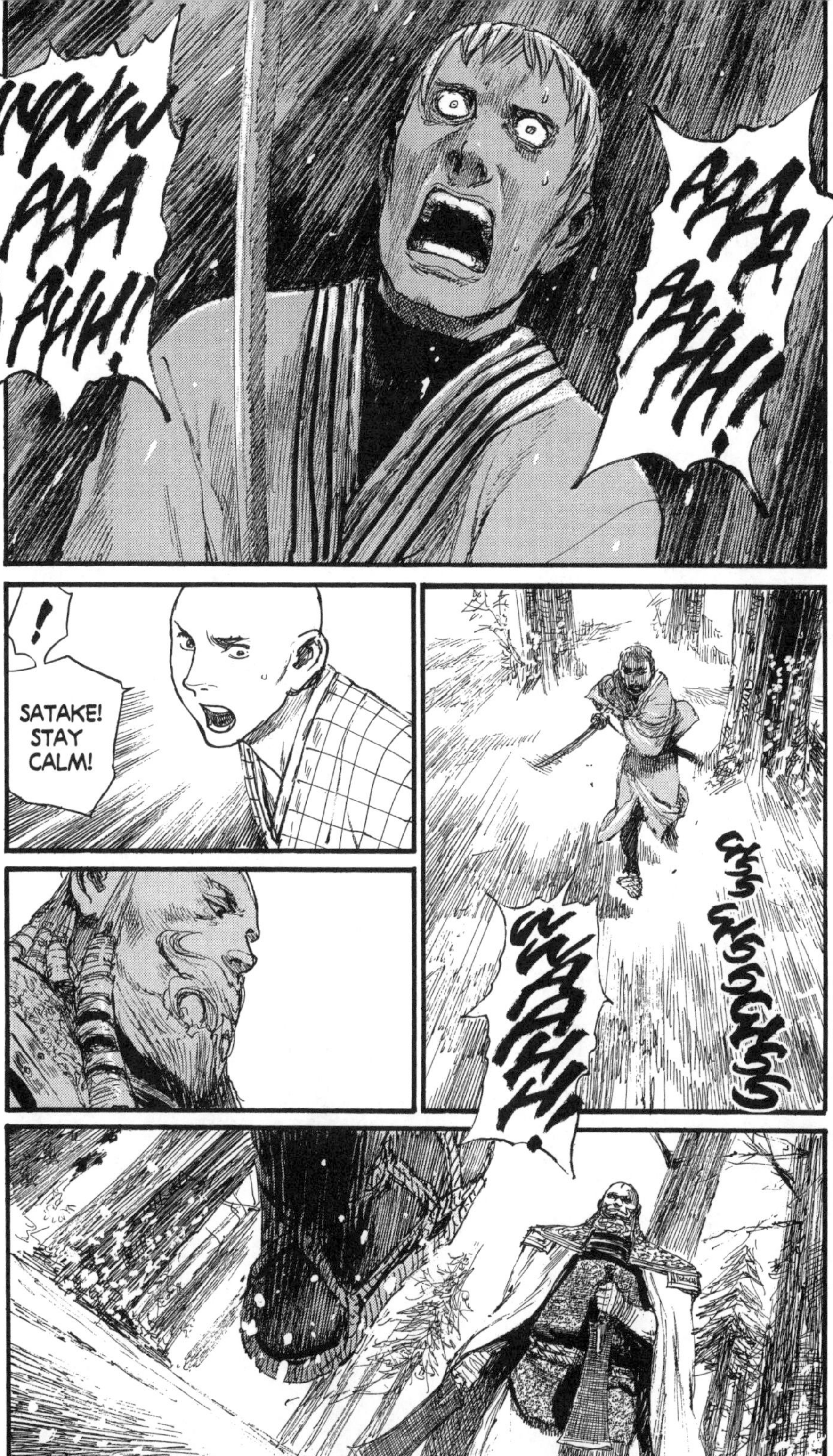
!
SATAKE! STAY CALM!

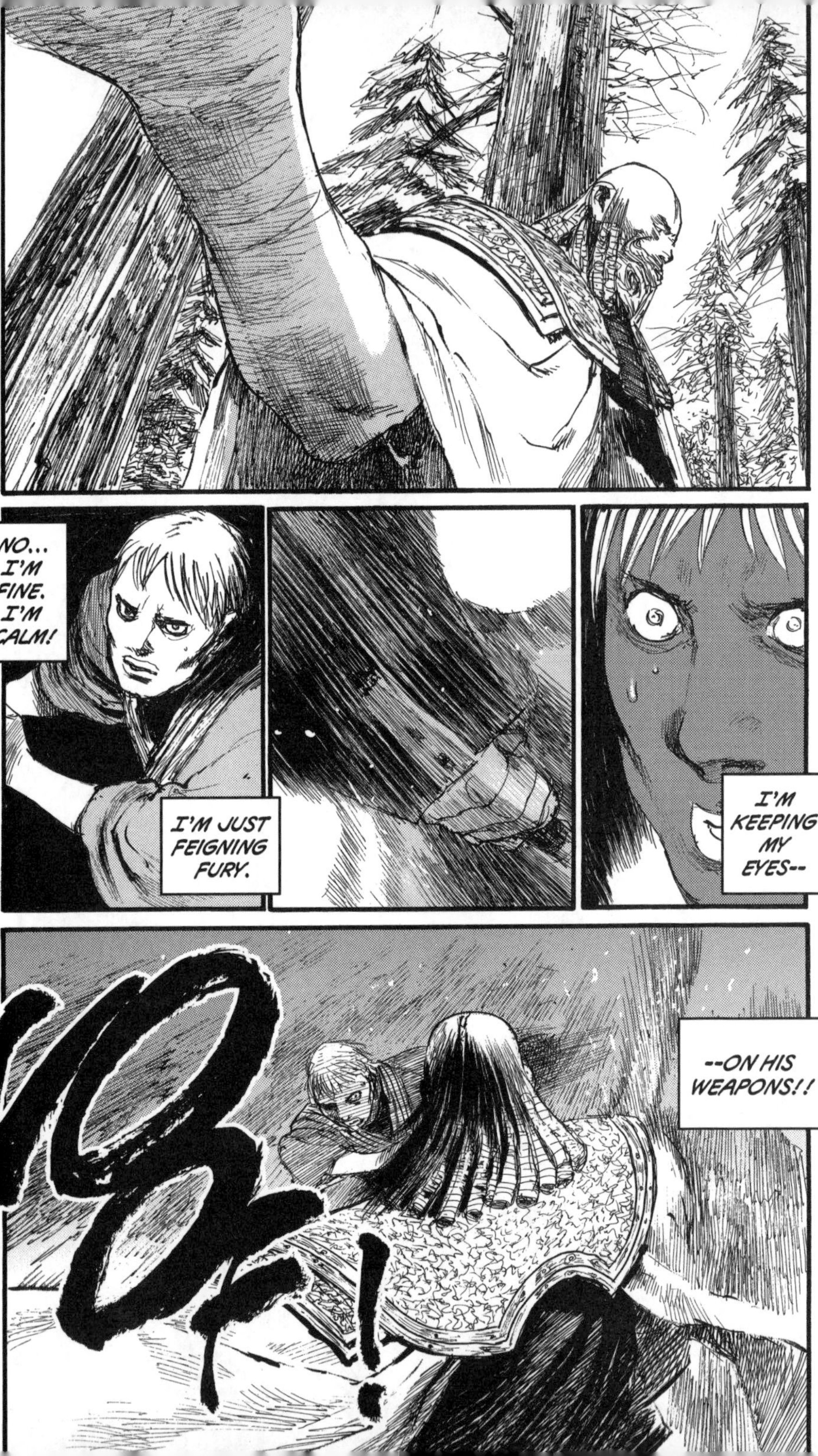
NO... I'M FINE. I'M CALM!
I'M JUST FEIGNING FURY.
I'M KEEPING MY EYES--
--ON HIS WEAPONS!!

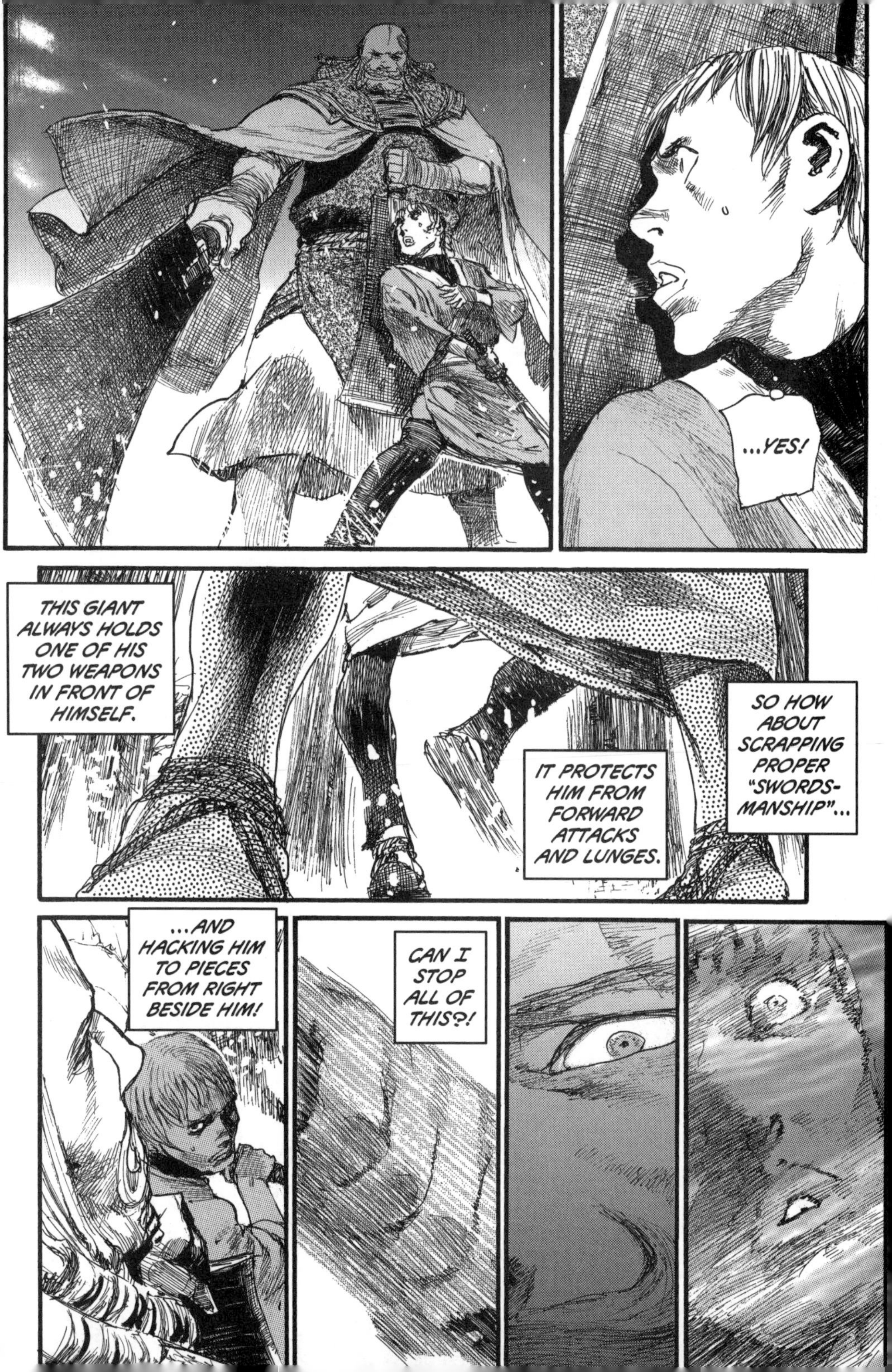
...YES!
THIS GIANT ALWAYS HOLDS ONE OF HIS TWO WEAPONS IN FRONT OF HIMSELF.
IT PROTECTS HIM FROM FORWARD ATTACKS AND LUNGES.
SO HOW ABOUT SCRAPPING PROPER "SWORDS-MANSHIP"...
...AND HACKING HIM TO PIECES FROM RIGHT BESIDE HIM!
CAN I STOP ALL OF THIS?!

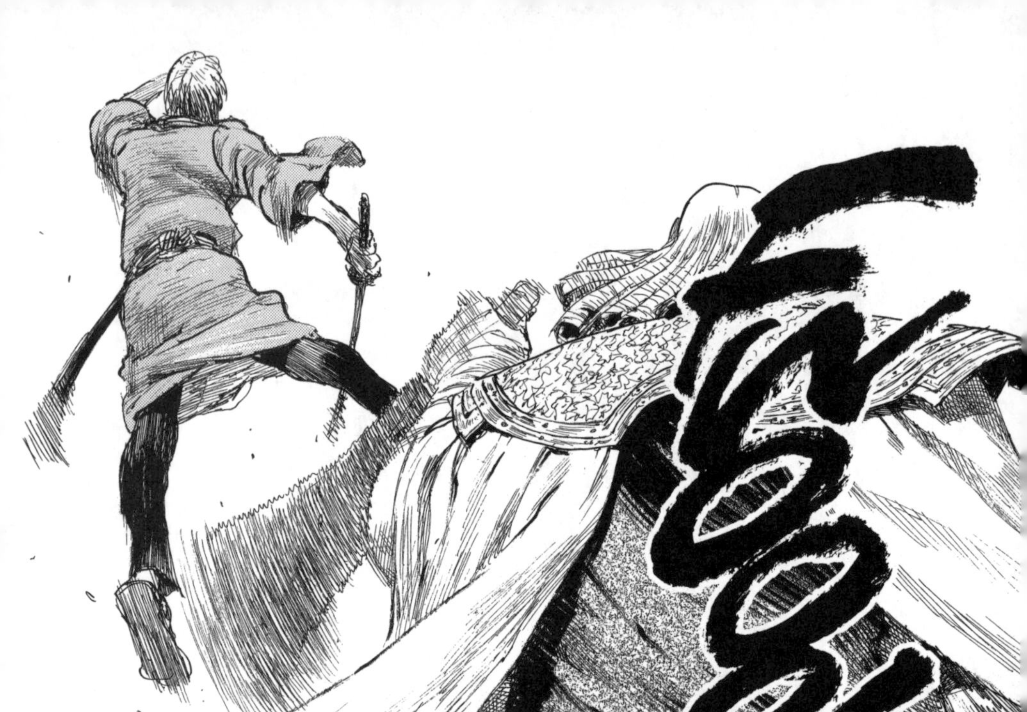
FWOOO!
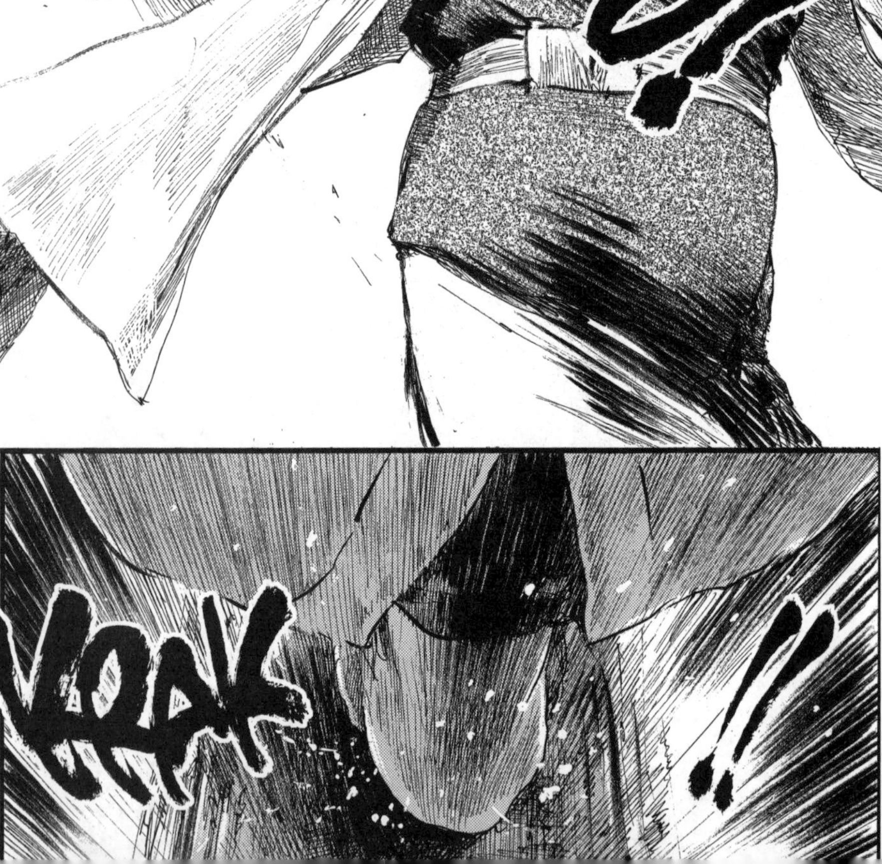
KRAK!!

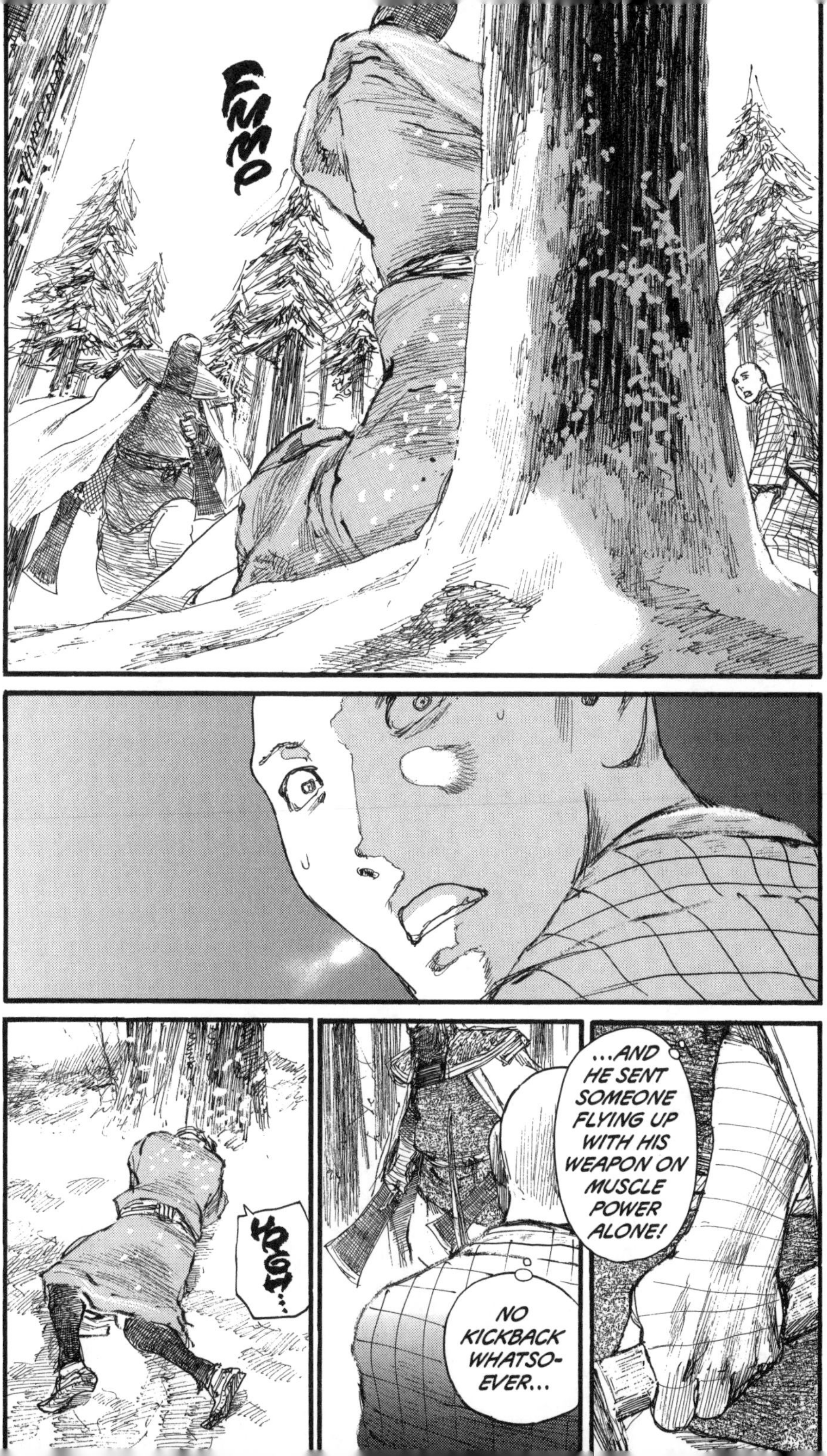
FMMP
NO KICKBACK WHATSO-EVER...
...AND HE SENT SOMEONE FLYING UP WITH HIS WEAPON ON MUSCLE POWER ALONE!
UGH...

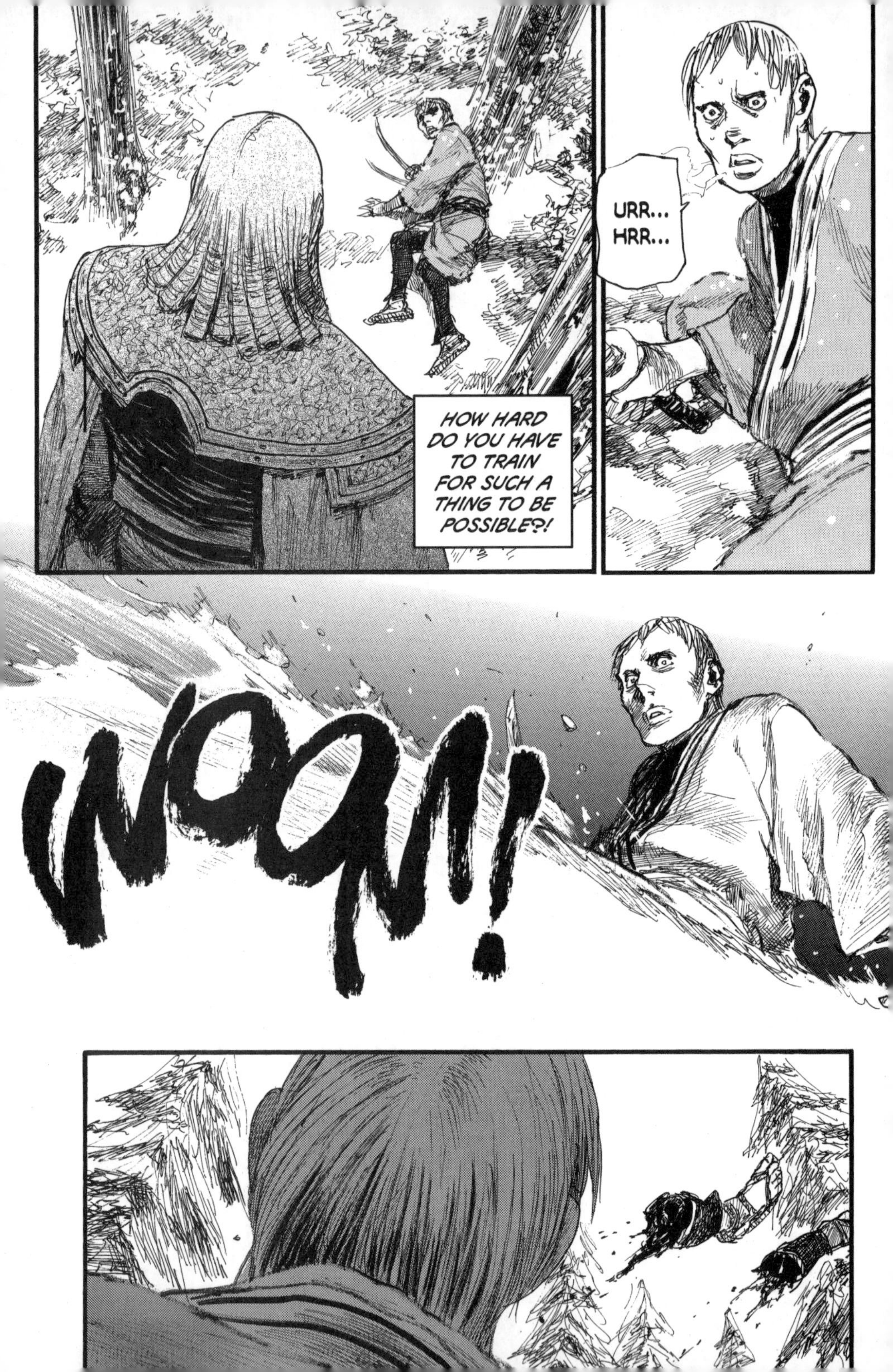
URR... HRR...
HOW HARD DO YOU HAVE TO TRAIN FOR SUCH A THING TO BE POSSIBLE?!

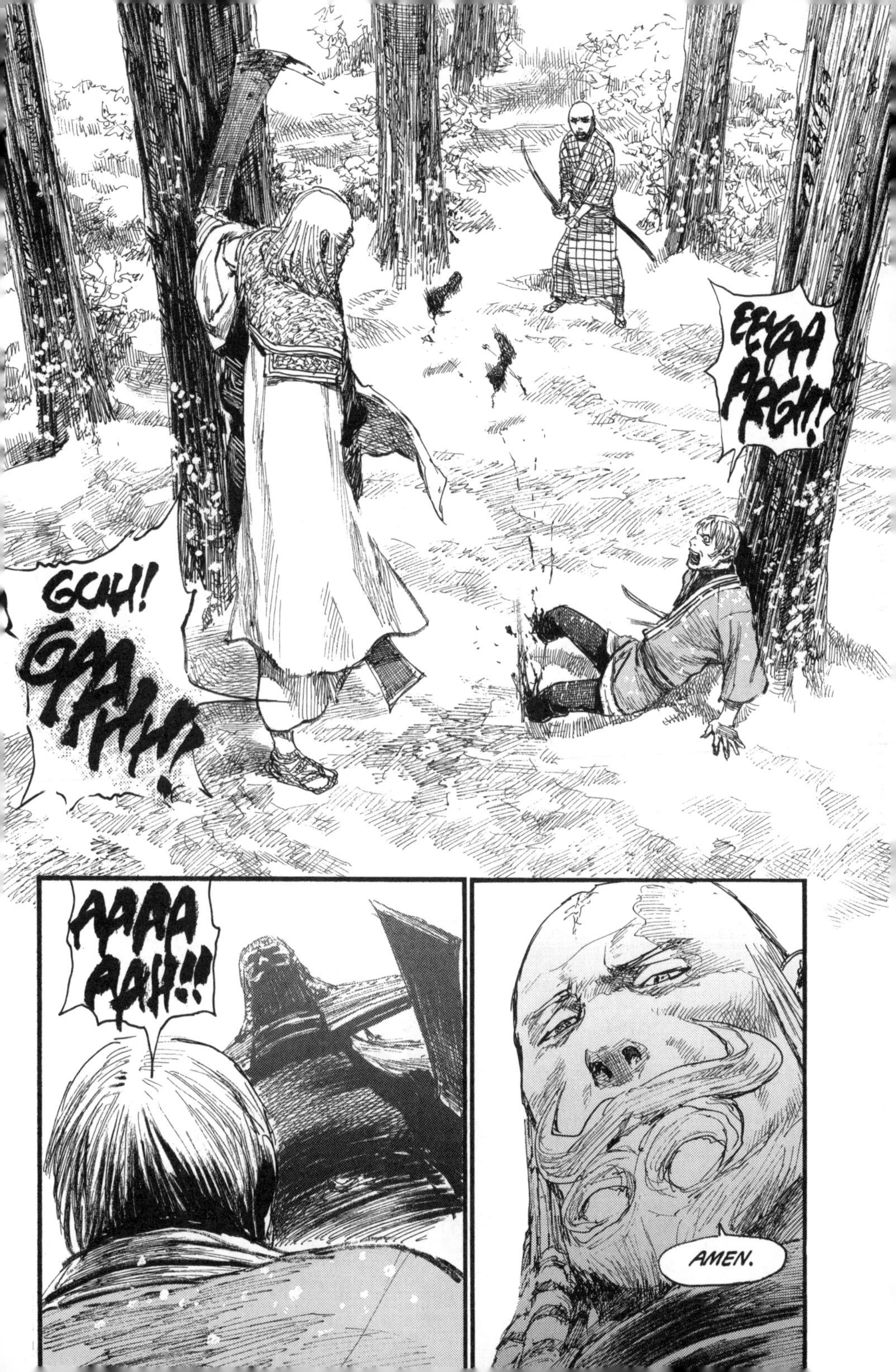
EEYAA ARGH!
GUH! GAAHH!
AMEN.
AAAA AAH!!

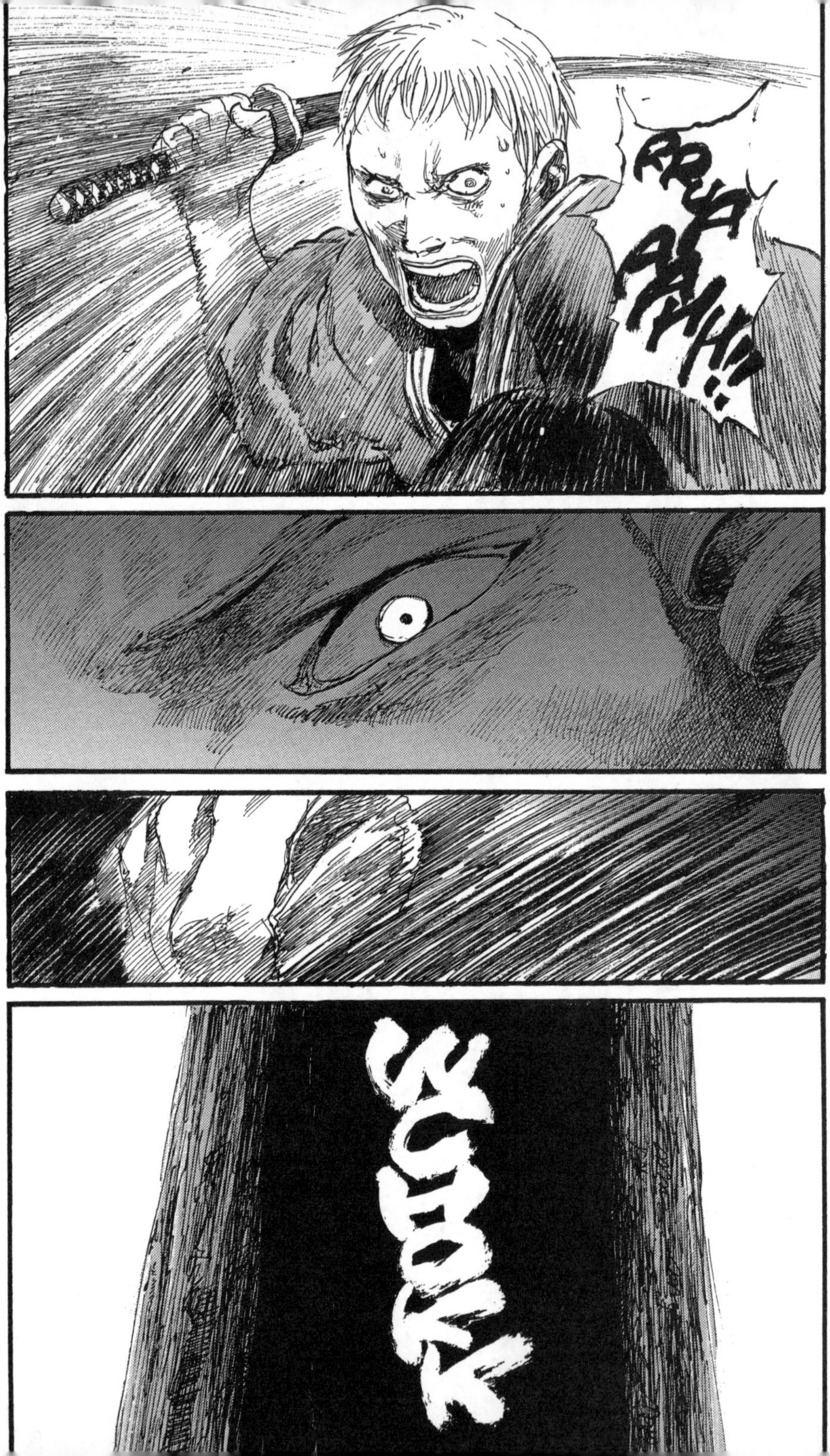
RRAAAHH!!
SCHOK

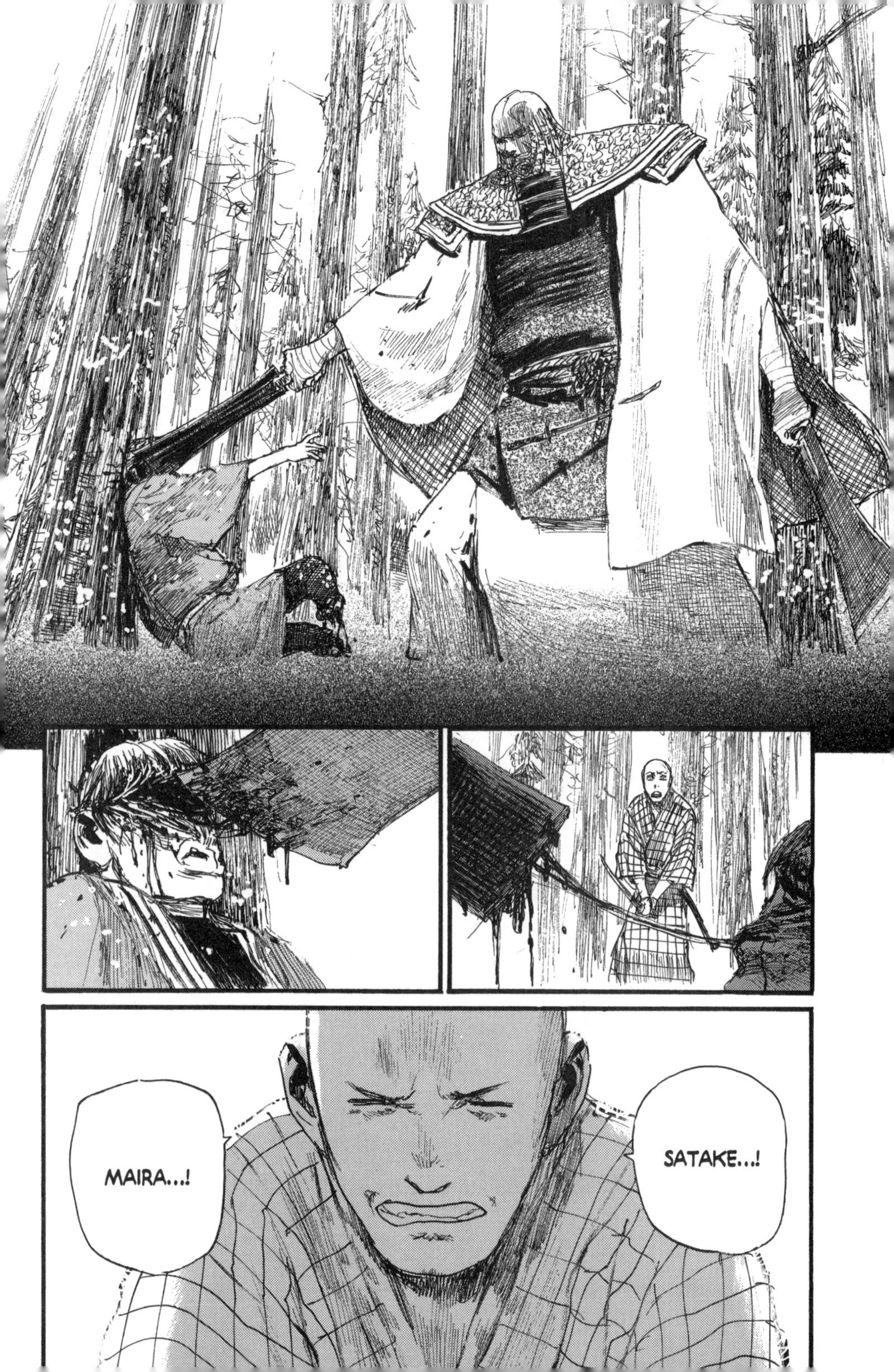
SATAKE...!
MAIRA...!

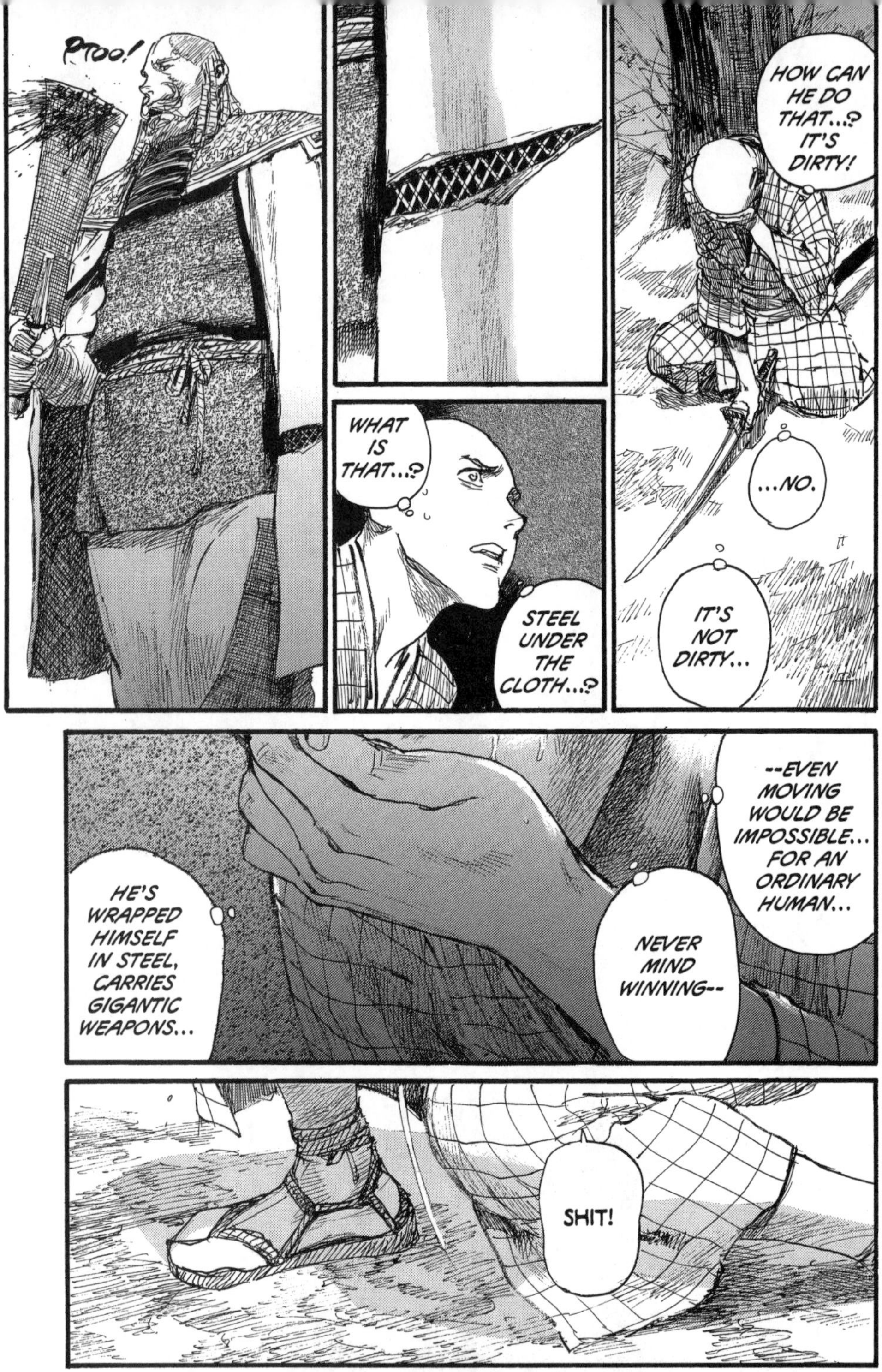
HOW CAN HE DO THAT...? IT'S DIRTY!
...NO.
IT'S NOT DIRTY...
WHAT IS THAT...?
STEEL UNDER THE CLOTH...?
PTOO!
--EVEN MOVING WOULD BE IMPOSSIBLE... FOR AN ORDINARY HUMAN...
NEVER MIND WINNING--
HE'S WRAPPED HIMSELF IN STEEL, CARRIES GIGANTIC WEAPONS...
SHIT!

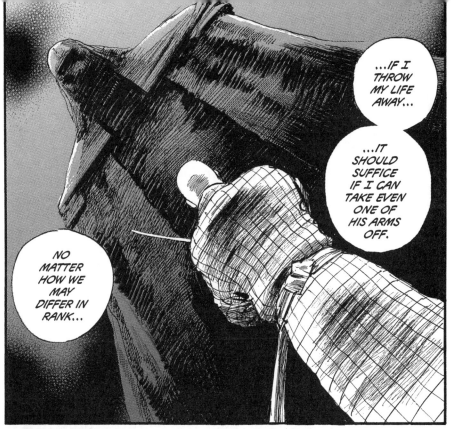

...IF I THROW MY LIFE AWAY...

...IT SHOULD SUFFICE IF I CAN TAKE EVEN ONE OF HIS ARMS OFF.

NO MATTER HOW WE MAY DIFFER IN RANK...

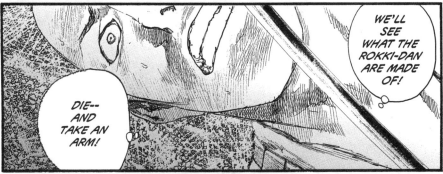

WE'LL SEE WHAT THE ROKKI-DAN ARE MADE OF!

DIE-- AND TAKE AN ARM!

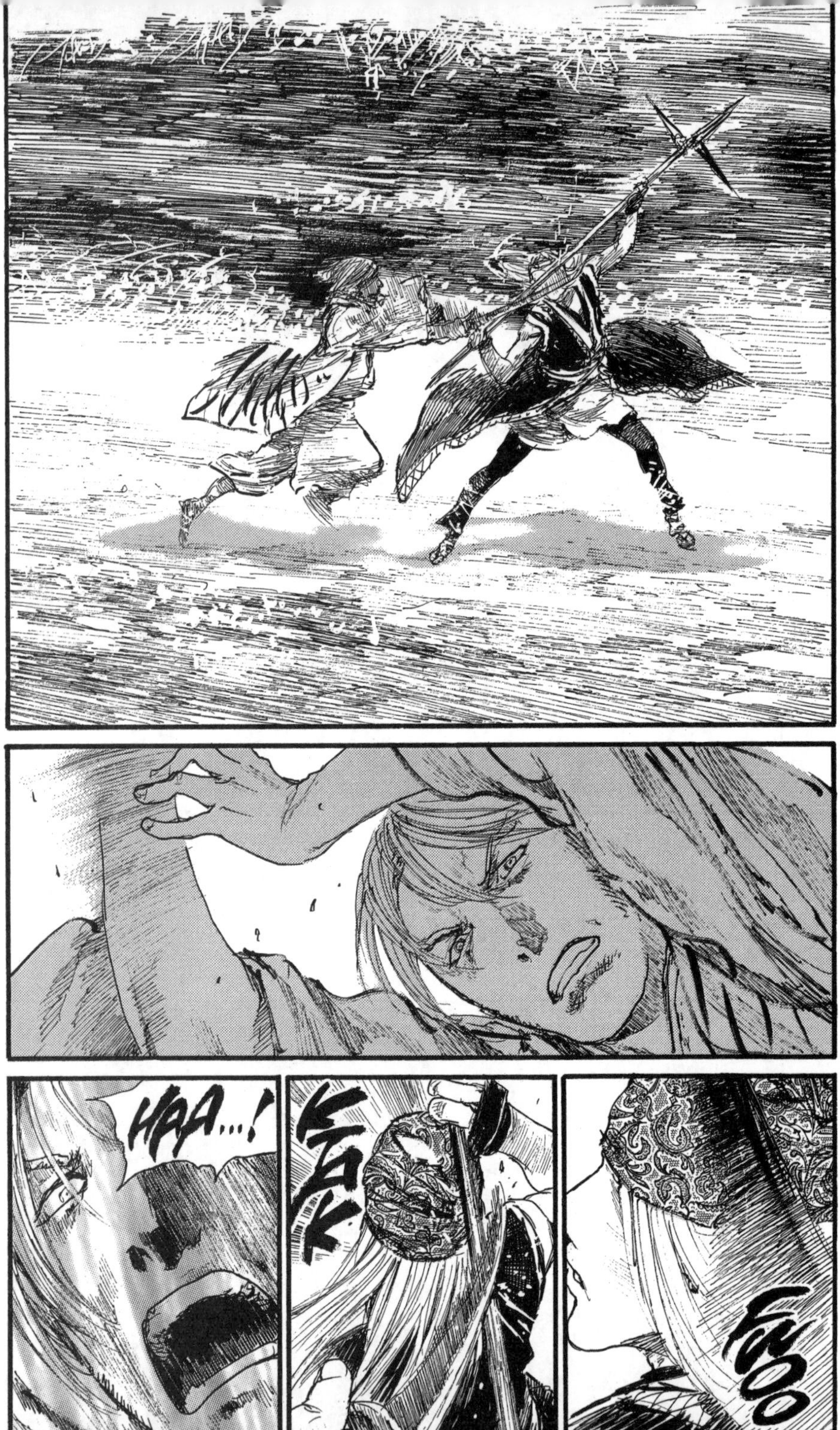
FWOO
KLAK
HAA...!

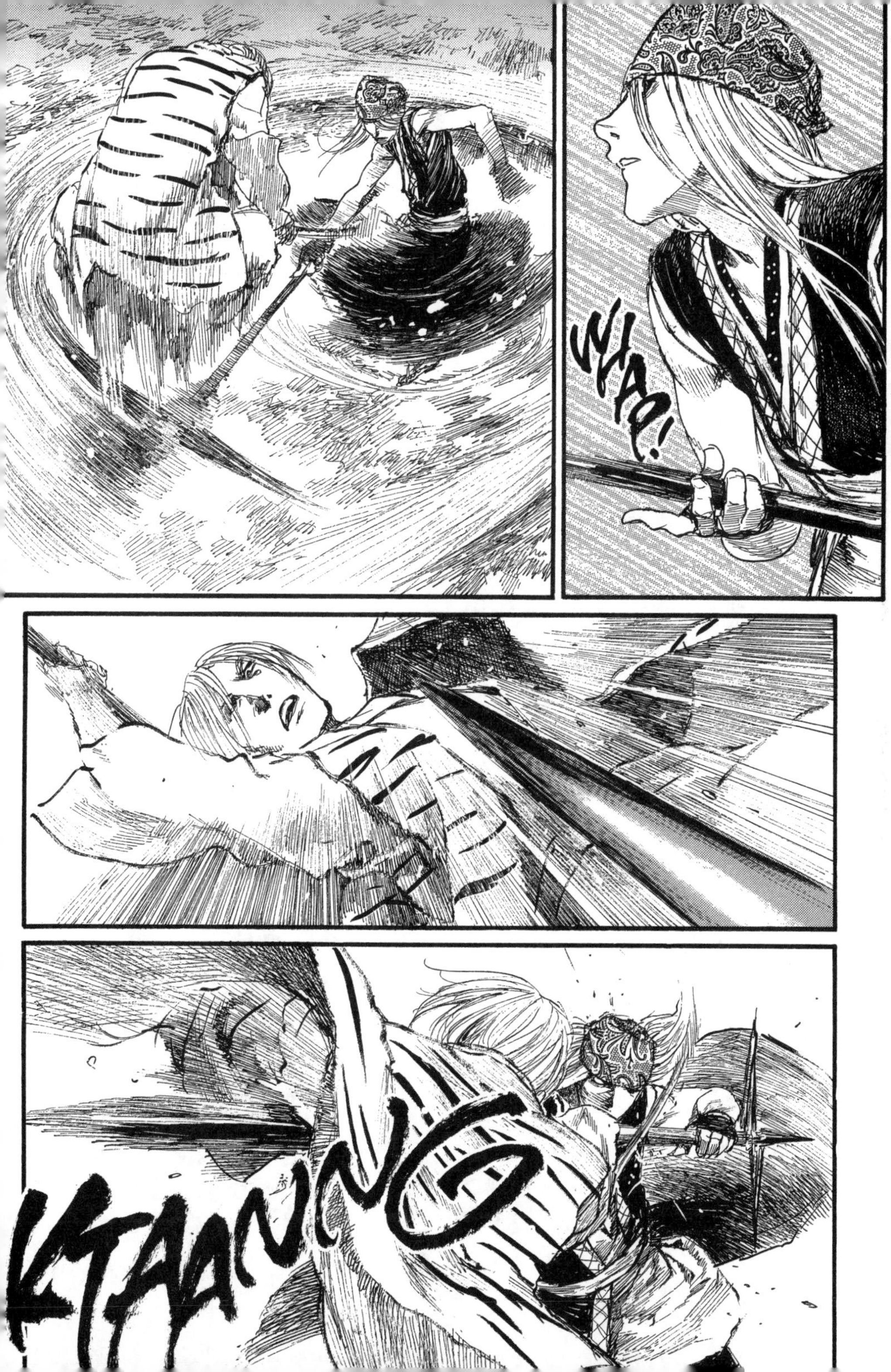
WHAO!
KLAANNG

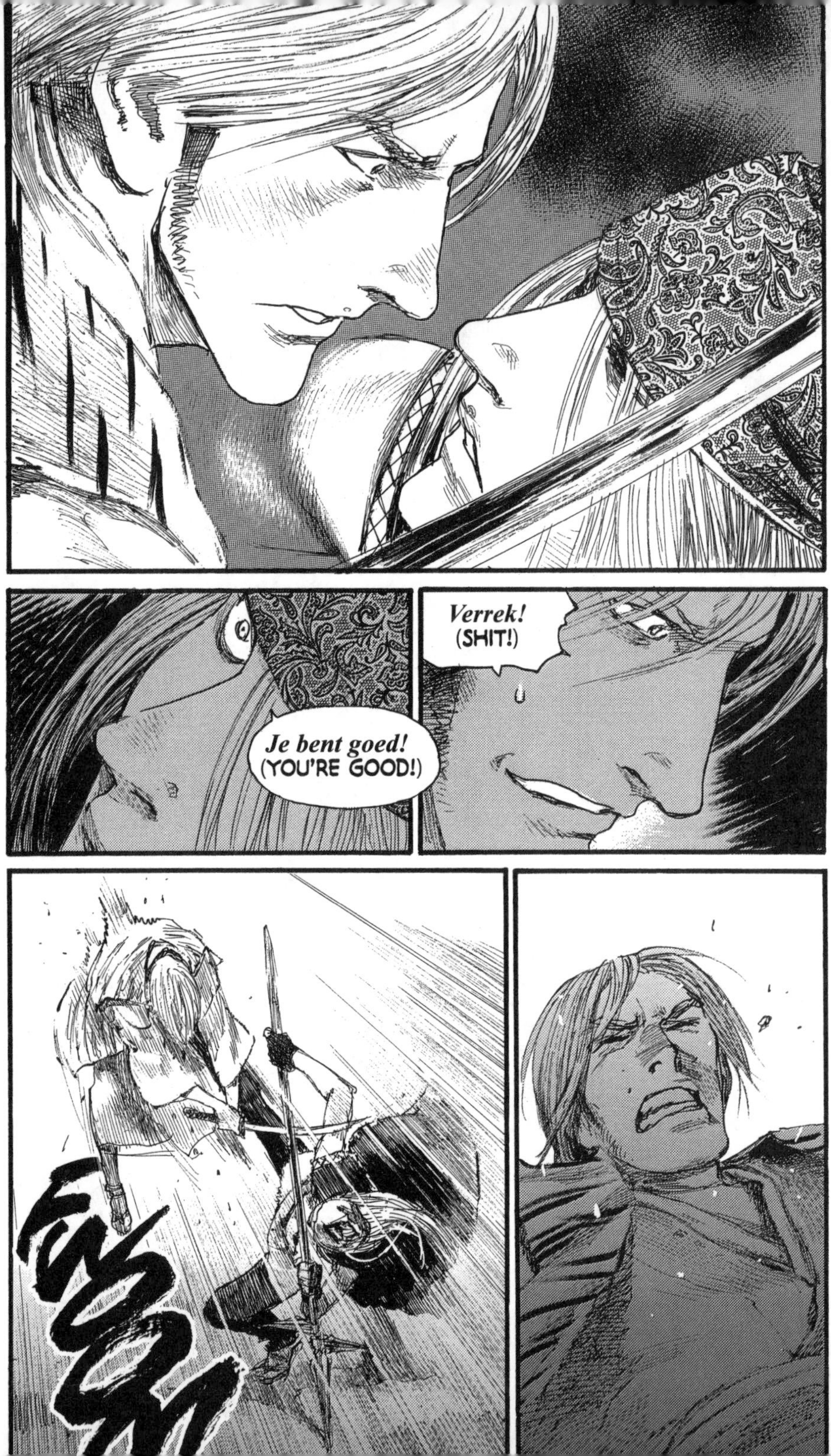
Verrek! (SHIT!)
Je bent goed! (YOU'RE GOOD!)

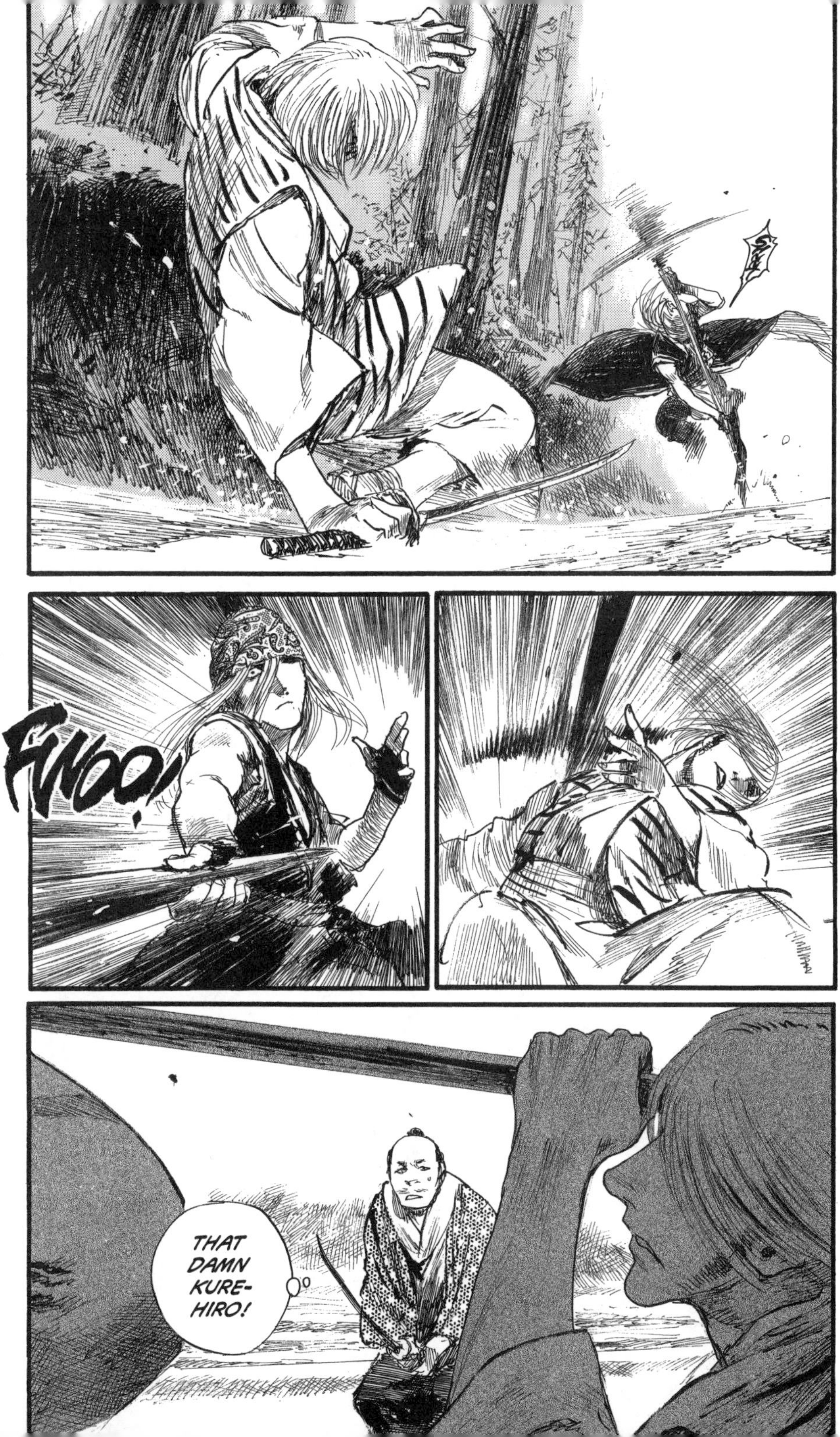
FWOO!
THAT DAMN KURE-HIRO!

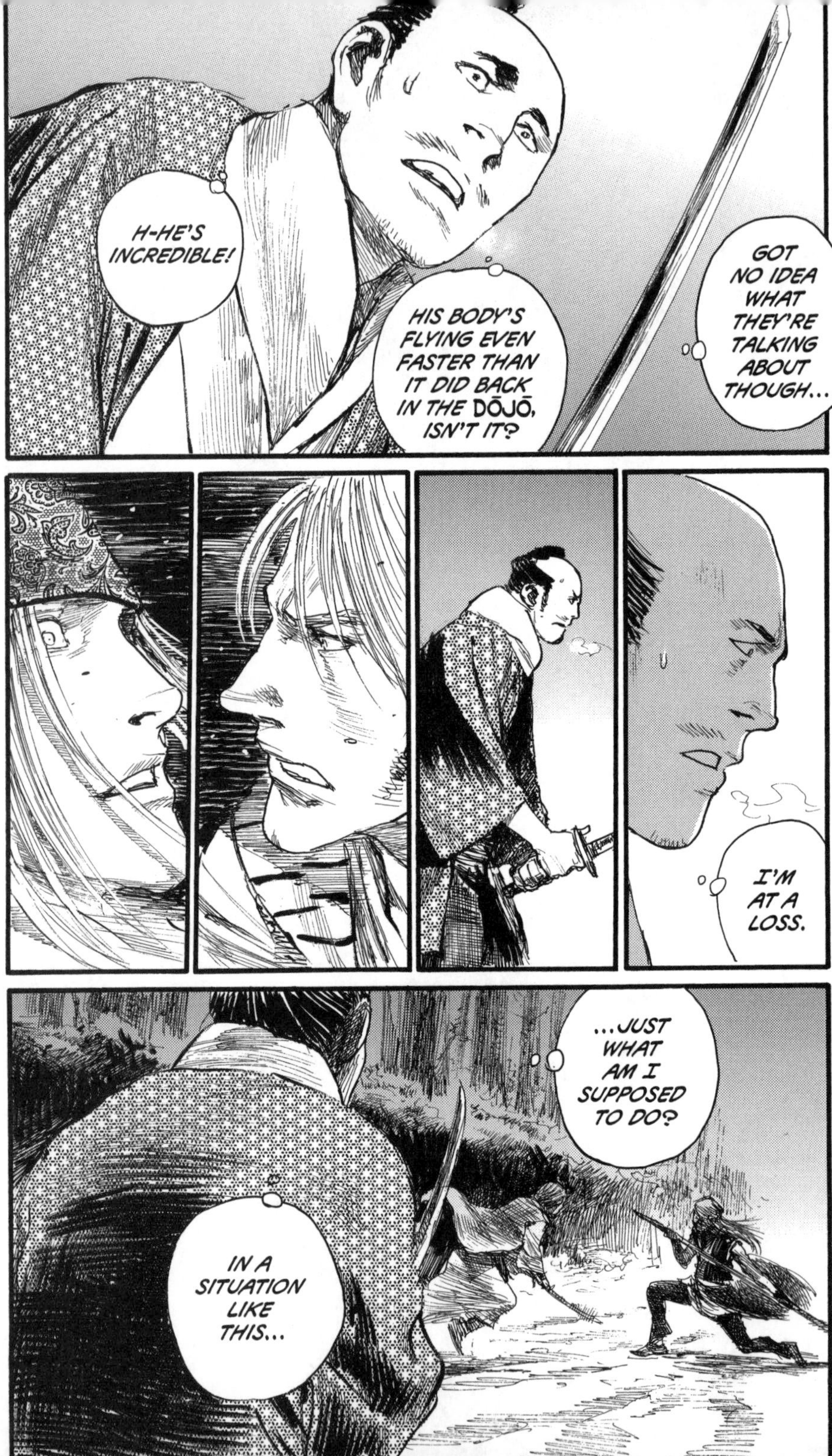
H-HE'S INCREDIBLE!
HIS BODY'S FLYING EVEN FASTER THAN IT DID BACK IN THE DŌJŌ, ISN'T IT?
GOT NO IDEA WHAT THEY'RE TALKING ABOUT THOUGH...
I'M AT A LOSS.
...JUST WHAT AM I SUPPOSED TO DO?
IN A SITUATION LIKE THIS...

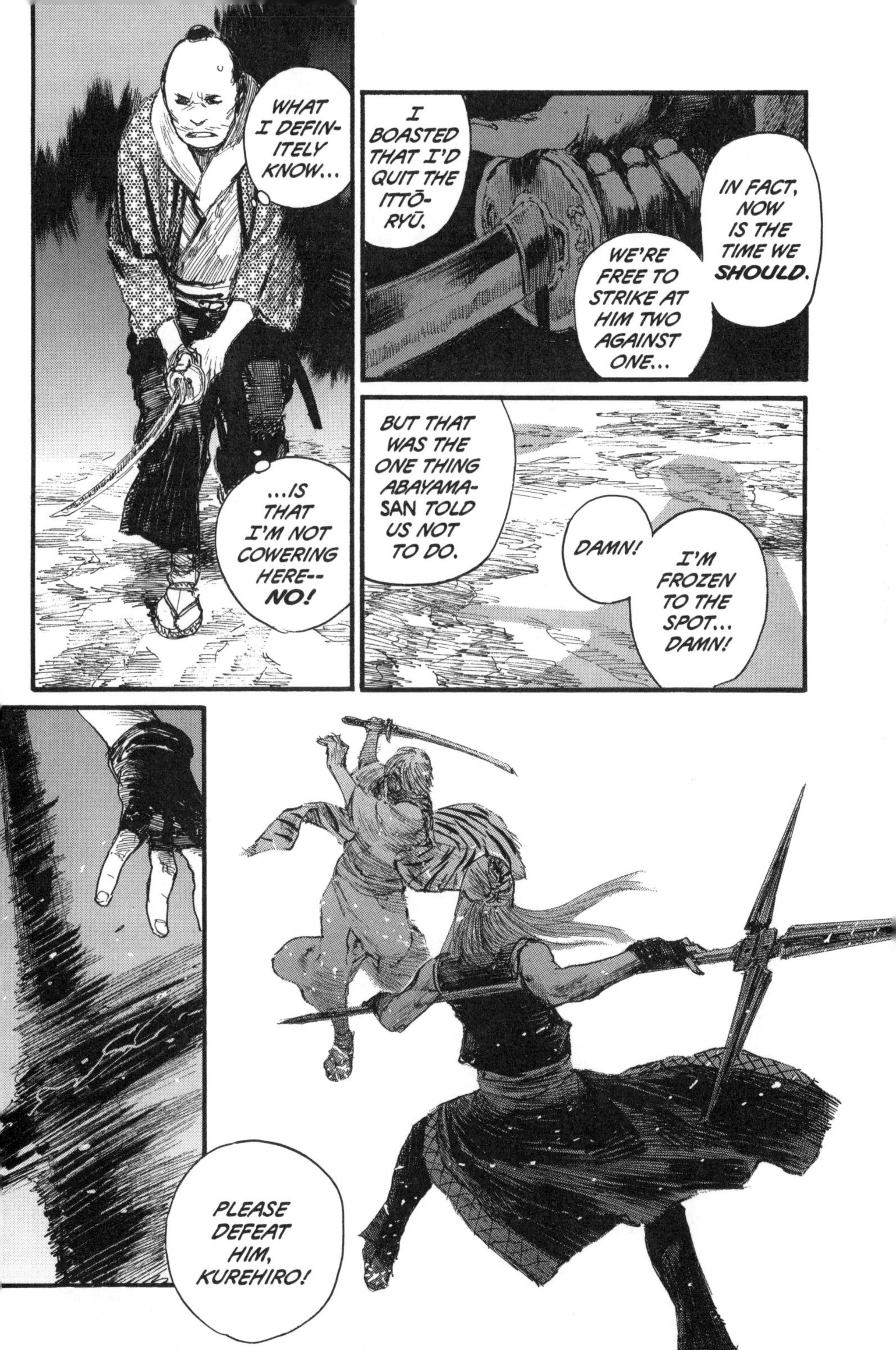
I BOASTED THAT I'D QUIT THE ITTŌ-RYŪ.
WE'RE FREE TO STRIKE AT HIM TWO AGAINST ONE...
IN FACT, NOW IS THE TIME WE **SHOULD**.
BUT THAT WAS THE ONE THING ABAYAMA-SAN TOLD US NOT TO DO.
DAMN!
I'M FROZEN TO THE SPOT... DAMN!
WHAT I DEFINITELY KNOW...
...IS THAT I'M NOT COWERING HERE-- **NO!**
PLEASE DEFEAT HIM, KUREHIRO!

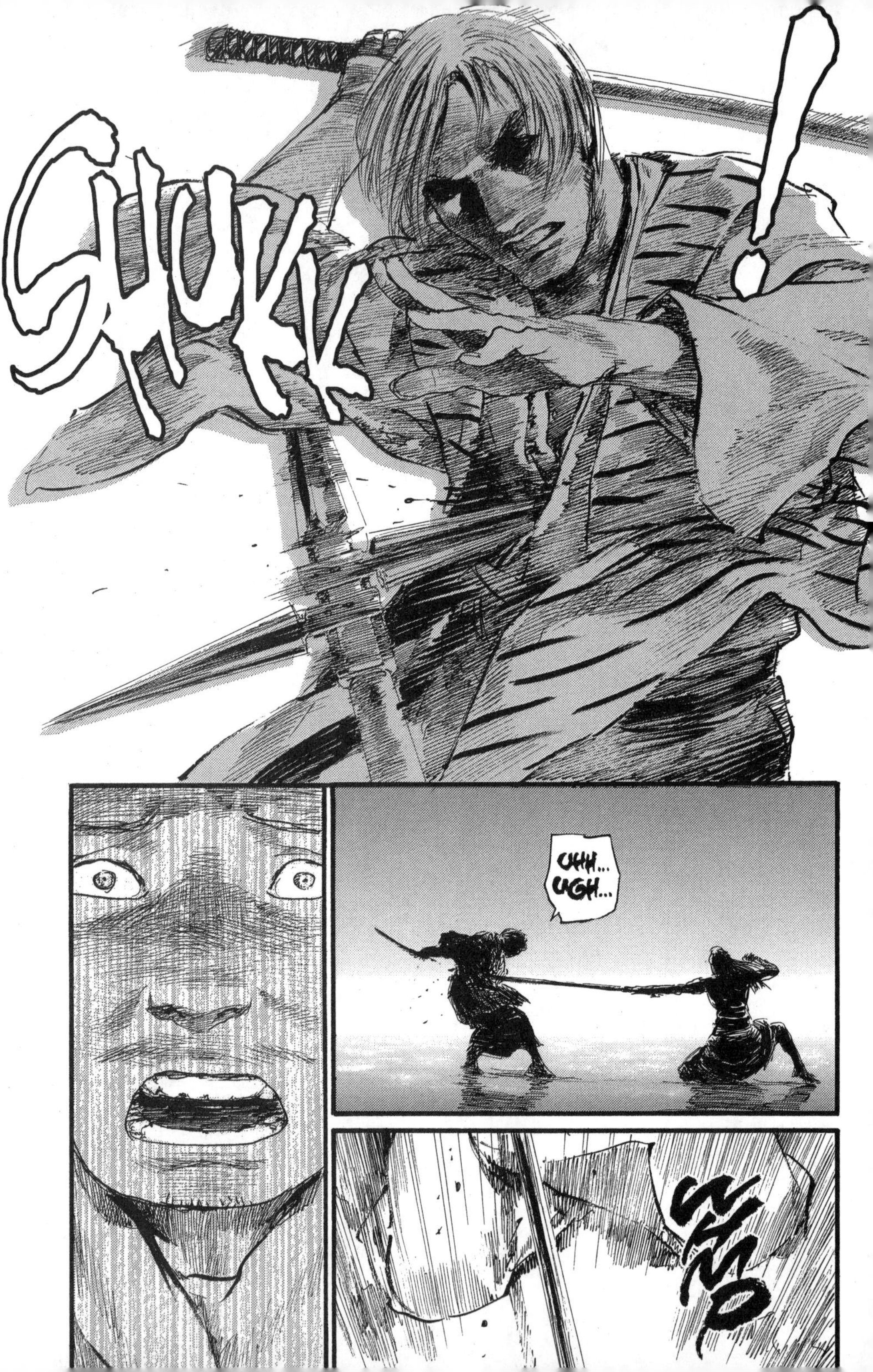
SHUKK!
UHH...
UGH...

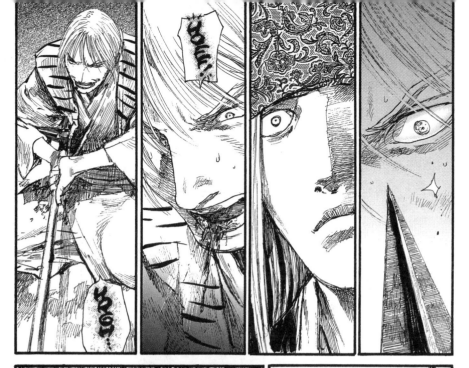

<...FIVE YEARS AGO...>

<...THE SHIP I WAS ON MET WITH A STORM OFF THE COAST OF SURUGA...>

<I WAS TOSSED INTO THE OCEAN.>

<I WASHED ASHORE AT ODAWARA.>

<WHEN I FINALLY DID SEE AN OFFICIAL FACE TO FACE...>

<...I HAD STOLEN MANY, MANY TIMES TO SURVIVE AND HAD BEEN BEATEN BADLY BY SOME FARMERS, WHO THEN HANDED ME OVER. IT WAS THE WORST POSSIBLE CIRCUMSTANCE TO BE IN.>

<AND THEN I MET ARASHINO SHISHIYA.>

<HE SPOKE FLUENT JAPAN-ESE, AND IF IT WEREN'T FOR HIS DEFENSE...>

<...MY EXECUTION WOULD HAVE BEEN CARRIED OUT A FEW DAYS LATER...>

<IN TRADE, ARASHINO'S SHIP WAS EMBARGOED FROM BUSINESS DEALINGS THAT YEAR.>

<...BUT TO LET THIS NUISANCE ON BOARD AND TURN BACK FOR HOME.>

<HIS LONG VOYAGE HAD ALL COME TO NAUGHT, AND HE HAD NO CHOICE...>

<AS YOU CAN GUESS, ON THIS JOURNEY...>

<...HE AND I WERE STRUNG UP BY THE ENTIRE SHIP'S CREW AND CAST OVER-BOARD INTO THE SEA.>

<THEY CRACKED MY HEAD OPEN... GOUGED MY EYEBALL OUT.>

<I THOUGHT I WAS SURELY DEAD, THEN.>

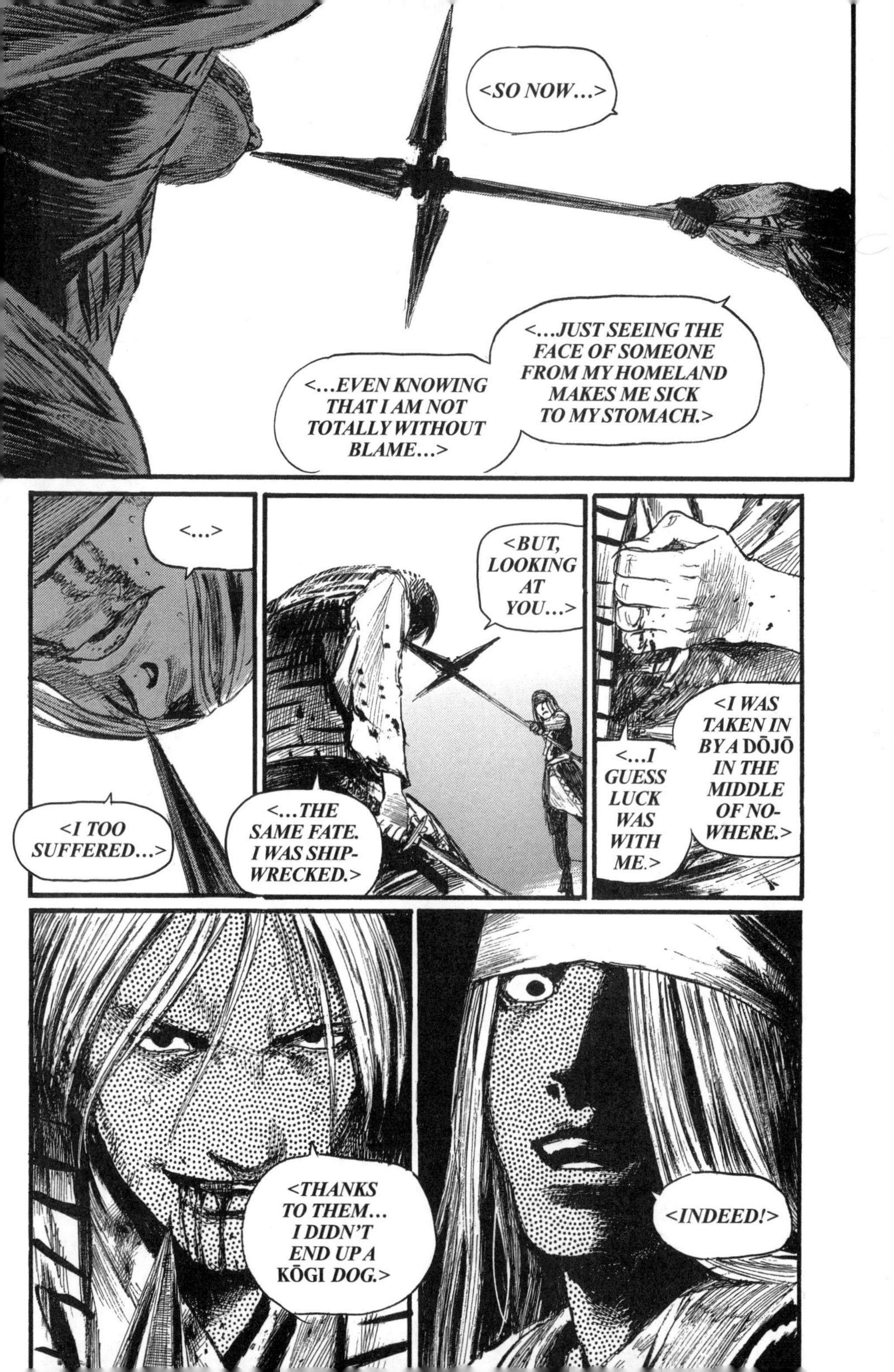
<SO NOW...>
<...EVEN KNOWING THAT I AM NOT TOTALLY WITHOUT BLAME...>
<...JUST SEEING THE FACE OF SOMEONE FROM MY HOMELAND MAKES ME SICK TO MY STOMACH.>
<...>
<I TOO SUFFERED...>
<...THE SAME FATE. I WAS SHIP-WRECKED.>
<BUT, LOOKING AT YOU...>
<...I GUESS LUCK WAS WITH ME.>
<I WAS TAKEN IN BY A DŌJŌ IN THE MIDDLE OF NO-WHERE.>
<THANKS TO THEM... I DIDN'T END UP A KŌGI *DOG.*>
<INDEED!>

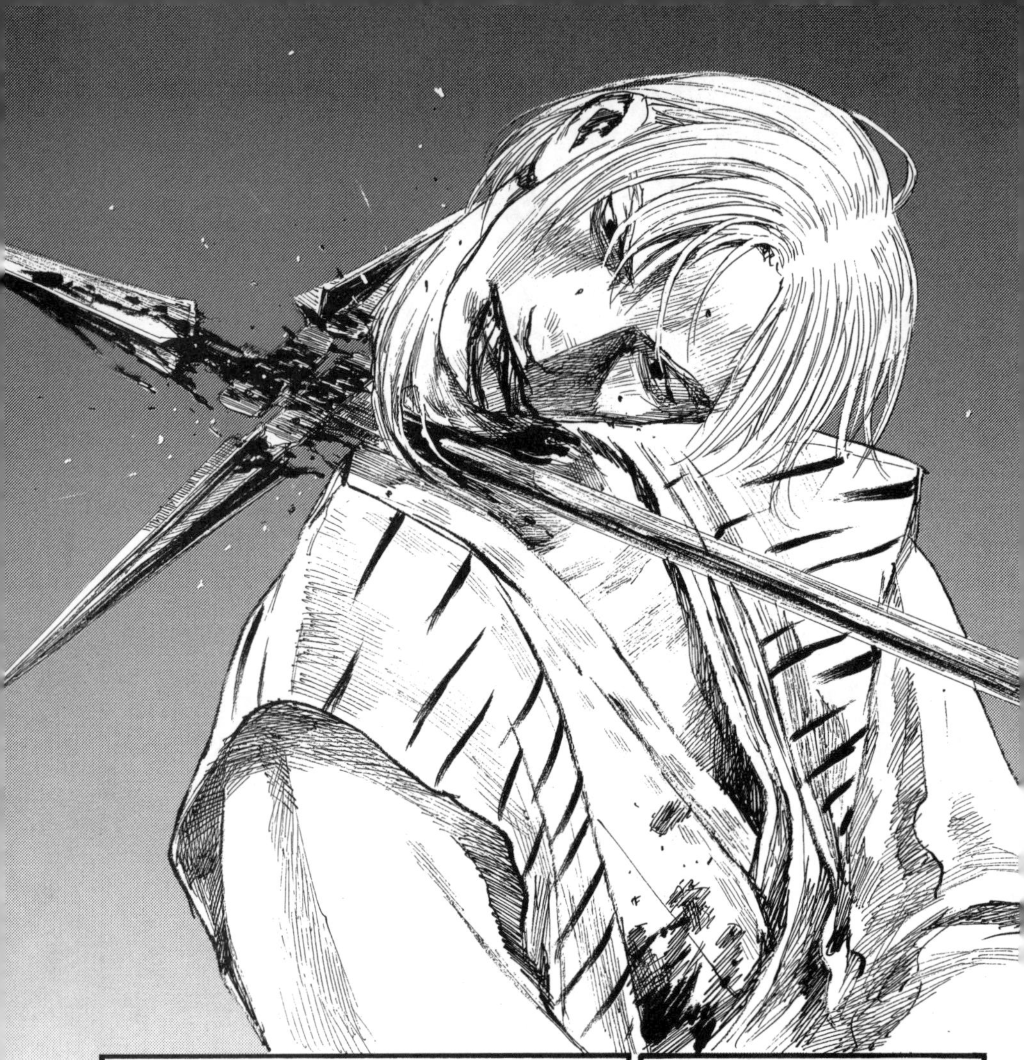

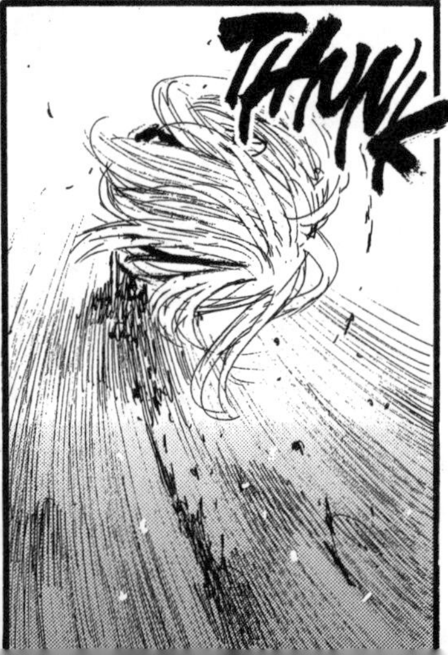
THUNK

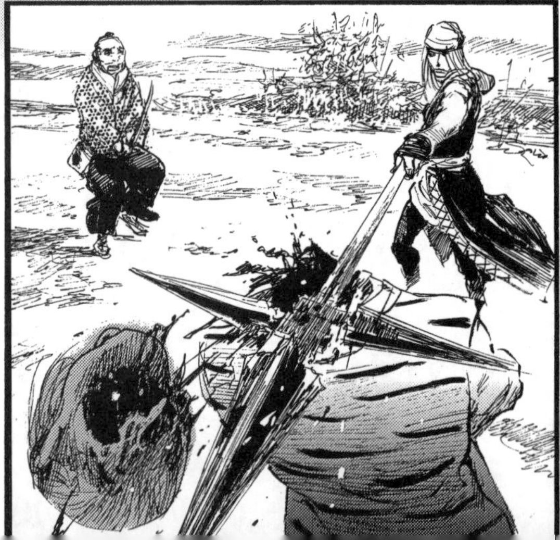

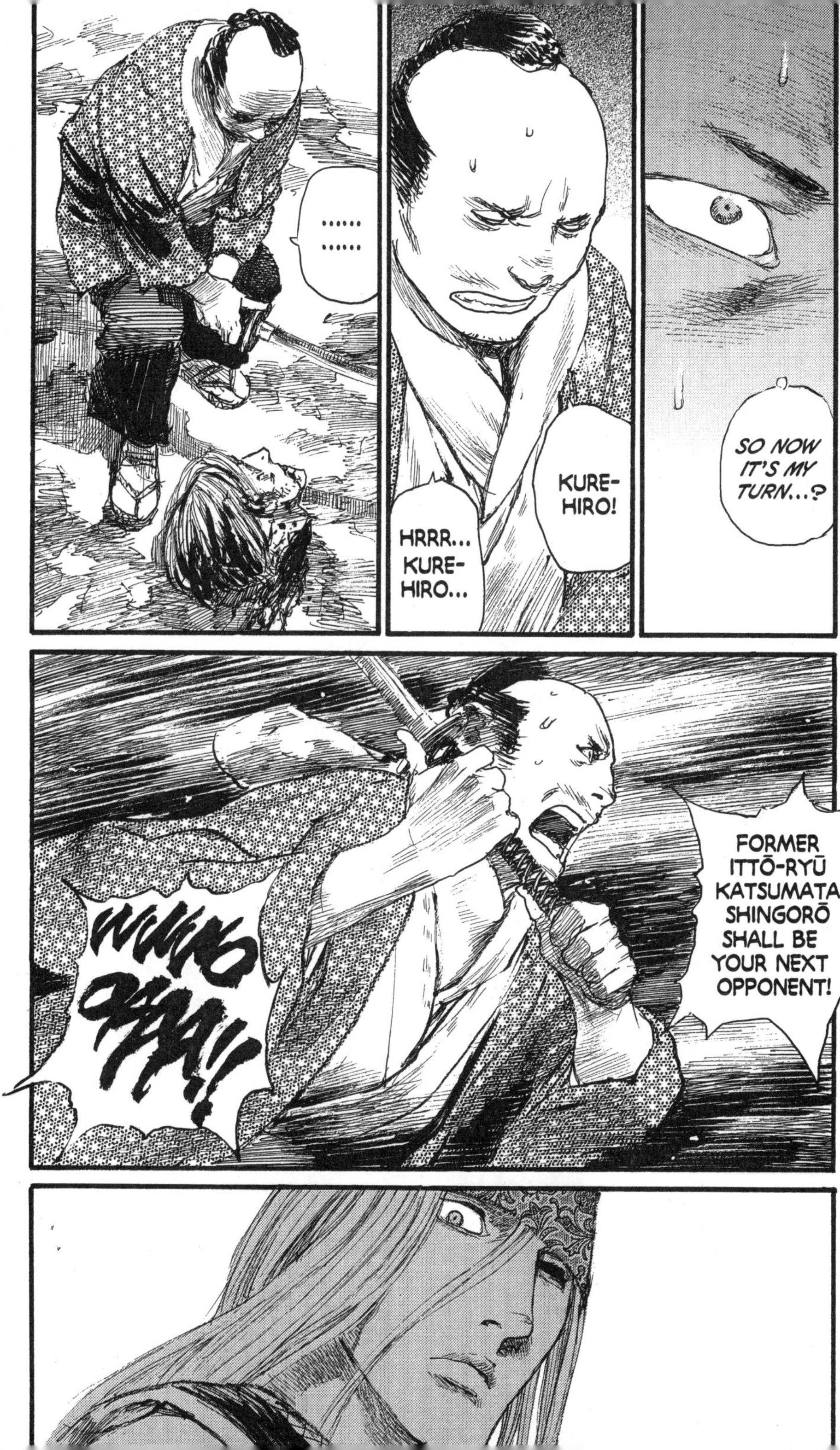
SO NOW IT'S MY TURN...?
KURE-HIRO!
HRRR... KURE-HIRO...
......
......
FORMER ITTŌ-RYŪ KATSUMATA SHINGORŌ SHALL BE YOUR NEXT OPPONENT!

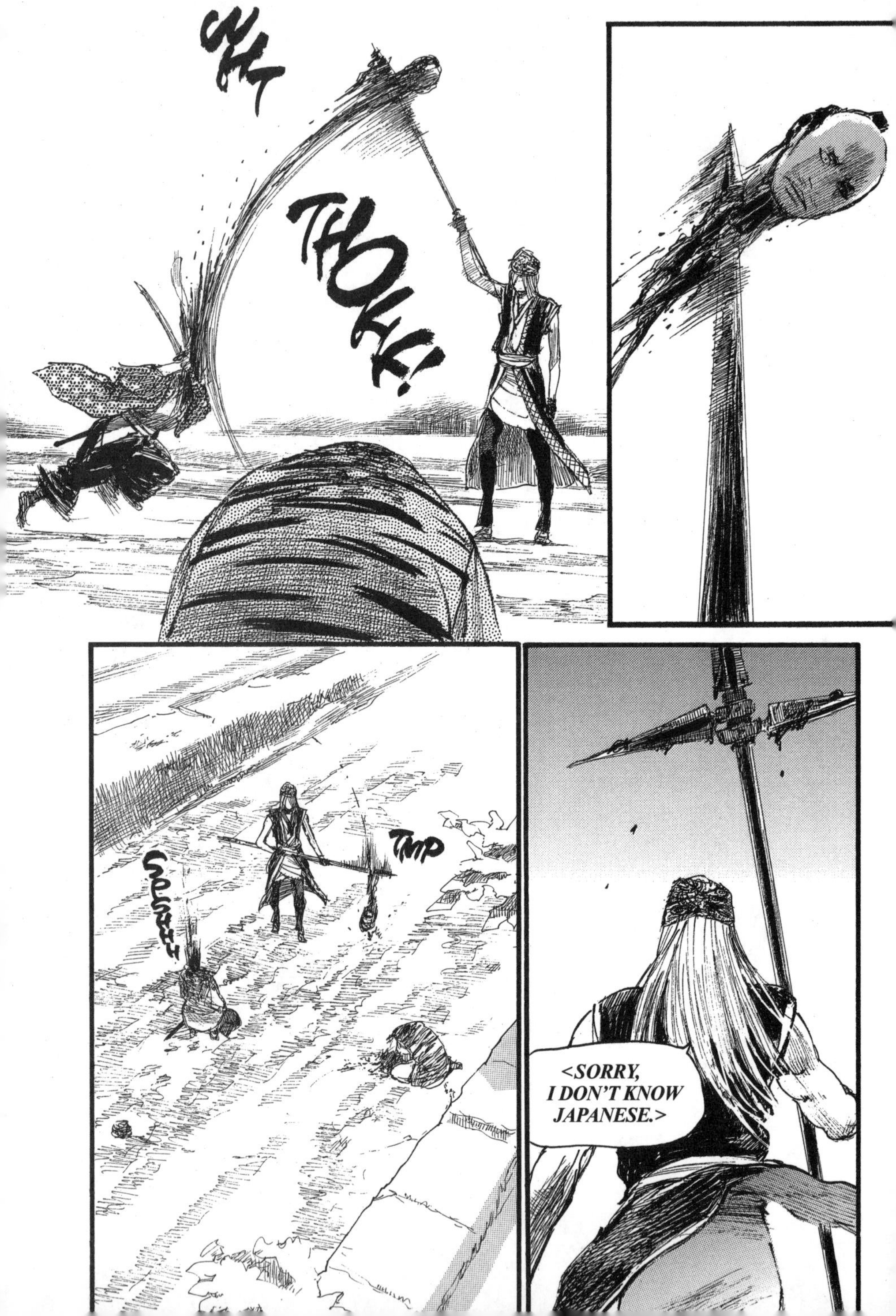
THOKK!
<SORRY, I DON'T KNOW JAPANESE.>
TMP
SPLSHHH

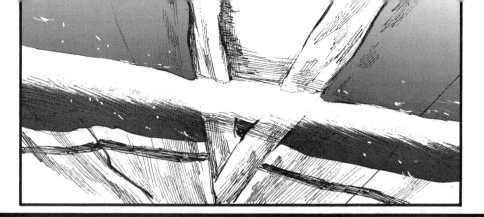

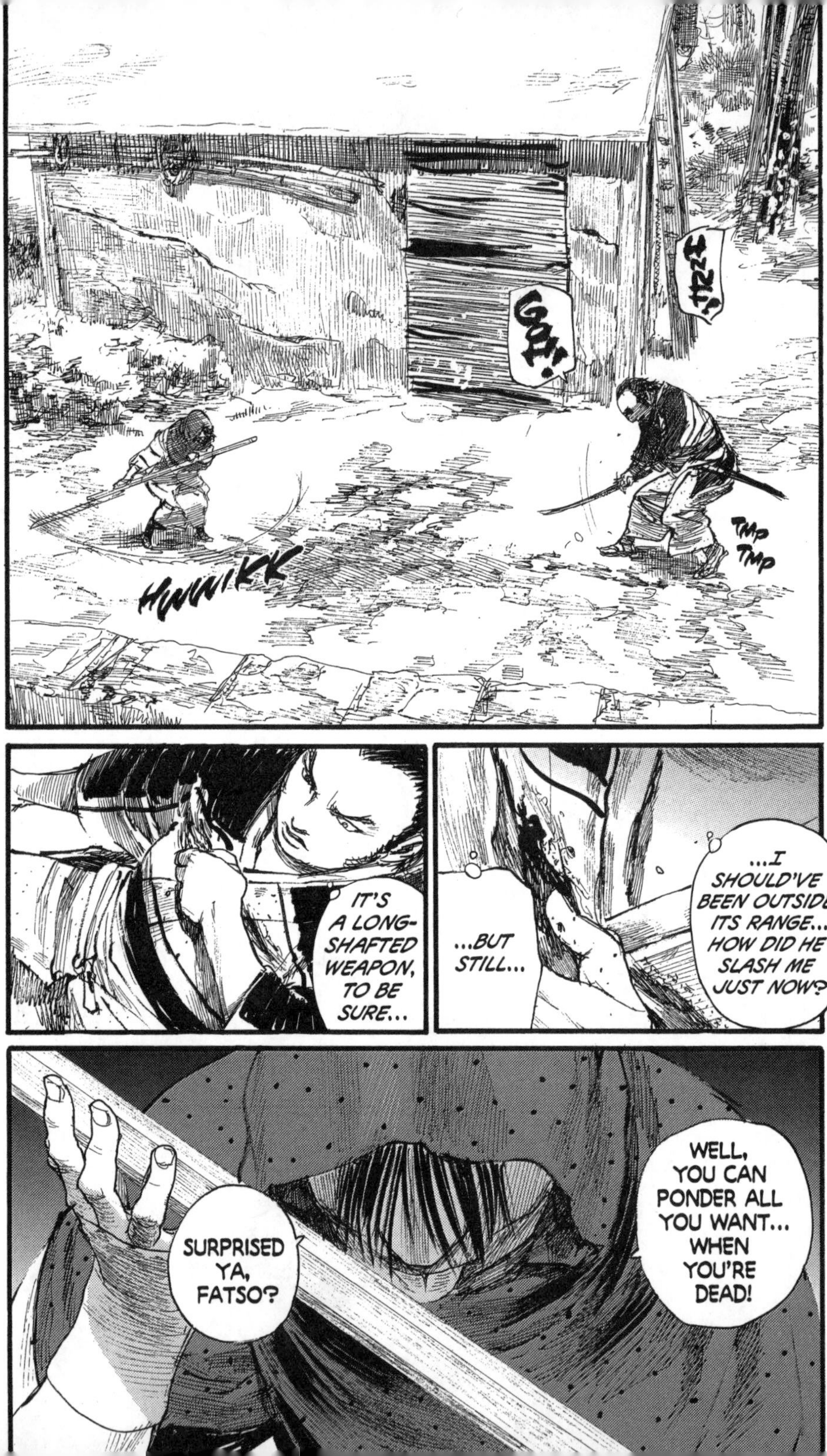
HNNF!
GOH!
TMP TMP
HWWIKK
...I SHOULD'VE BEEN OUTSIDE ITS RANGE... HOW DID HE SLASH ME JUST NOW?
...BUT STILL...
IT'S A LONG-SHAFTED WEAPON, TO BE SURE...
SURPRISED YA, FATSO?
WELL, YOU CAN PONDER ALL YOU WANT... WHEN YOU'RE DEAD!

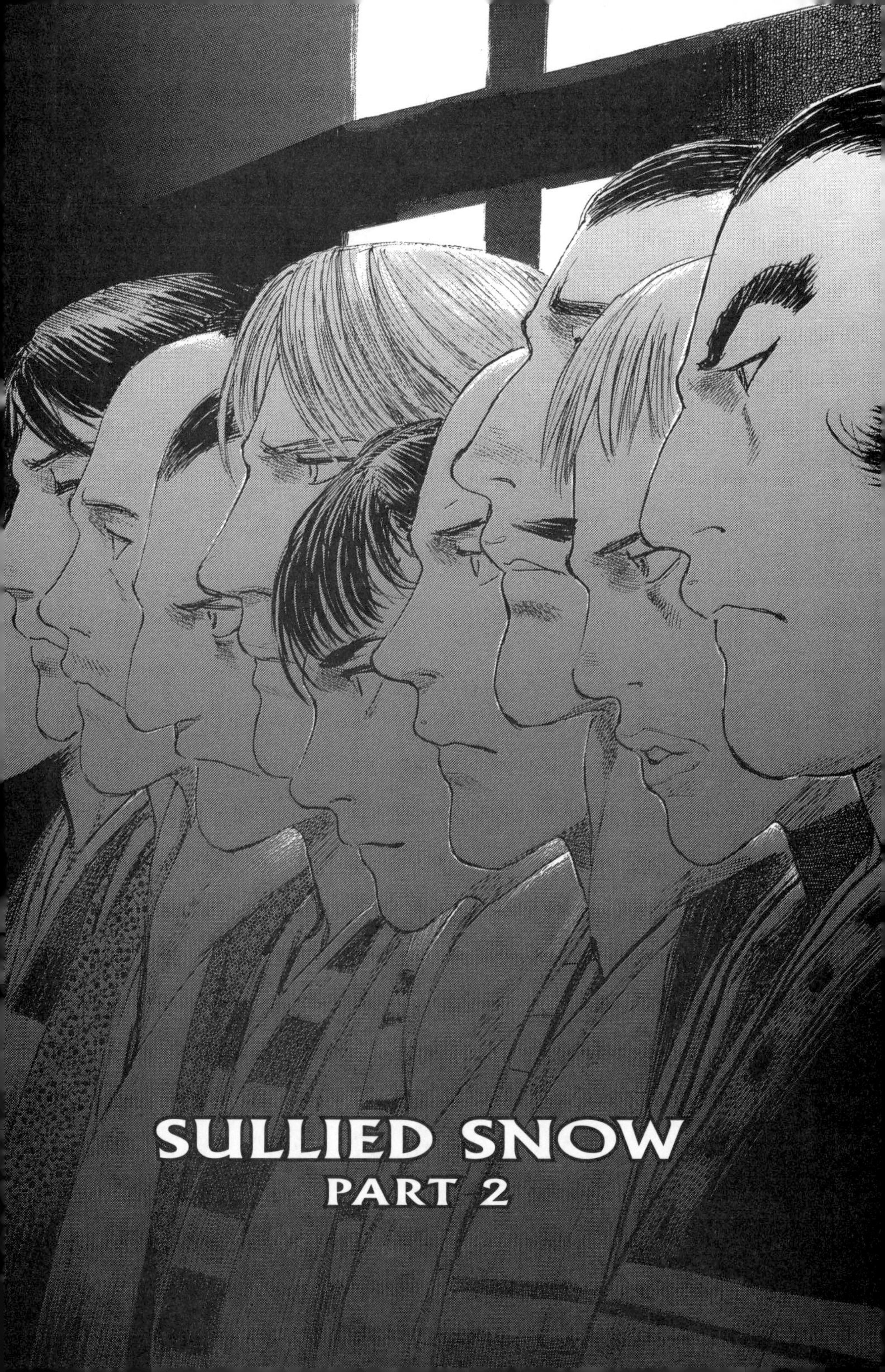
SULLIED SNOW
PART 2

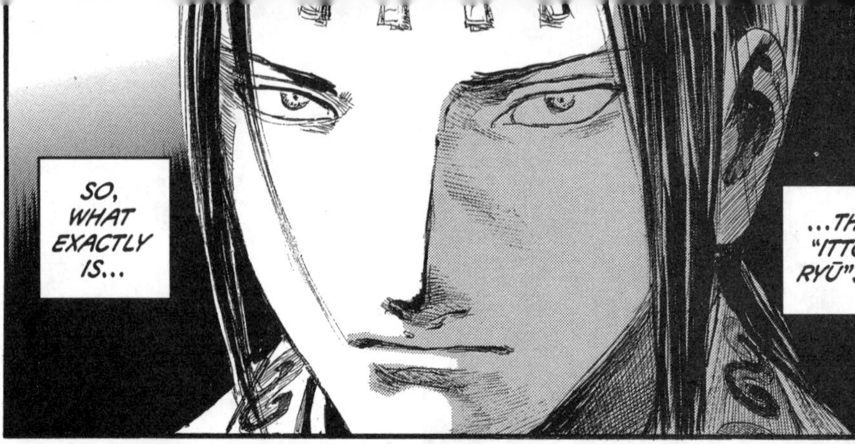
SO, WHAT EXACTLY IS...
...THE "ITTŌ-RYŪ"...?
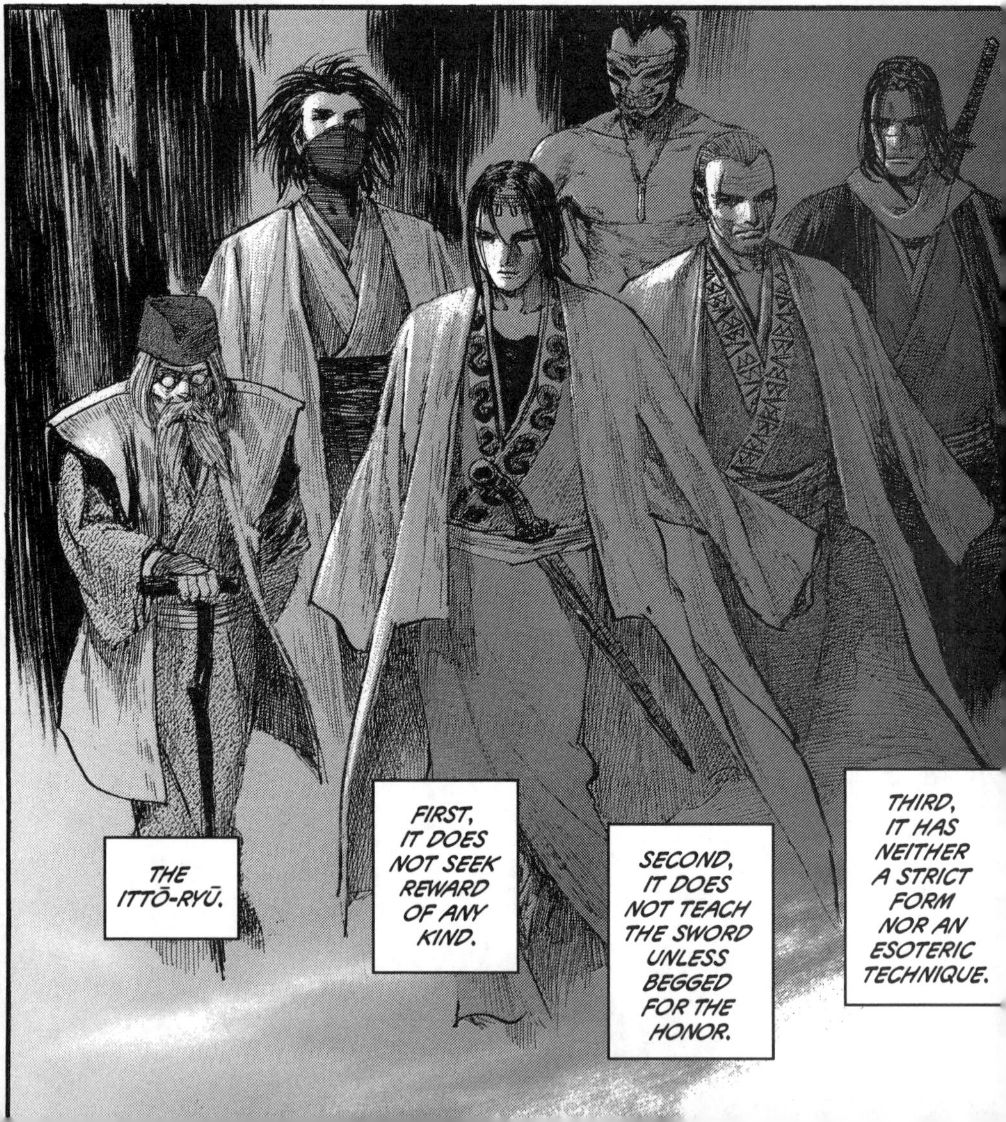
THE ITTŌ-RYŪ.
FIRST, IT DOES NOT SEEK REWARD OF ANY KIND.
SECOND, IT DOES NOT TEACH THE SWORD UNLESS BEGGED FOR THE HONOR.
THIRD, IT HAS NEITHER A STRICT FORM NOR AN ESOTERIC TECHNIQUE.

OKAY, THEN...

...SO IF ONE FREQUENTS THE DŌJŌ, DOES THAT MAKE HIM ITTŌ-RYŪ?

IF ONE FIGHTS ALWAYS ONE AGAINST ONE, DOES THAT MAKE HIM ITTŌ-RYŪ?

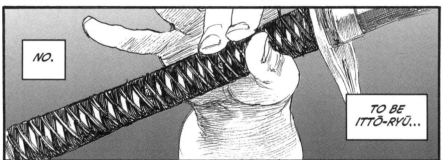

NO.

TO BE ITTŌ-RYŪ...

...ONE MUST WIN A MULTITUDE OF CONTESTS, AGAIN AND AGAIN, BY NO ONE'S TEACHING-- BY INSTINCT ALONE.

THE NAME IS THE ACCOMPLISH-MENT OF THESE.

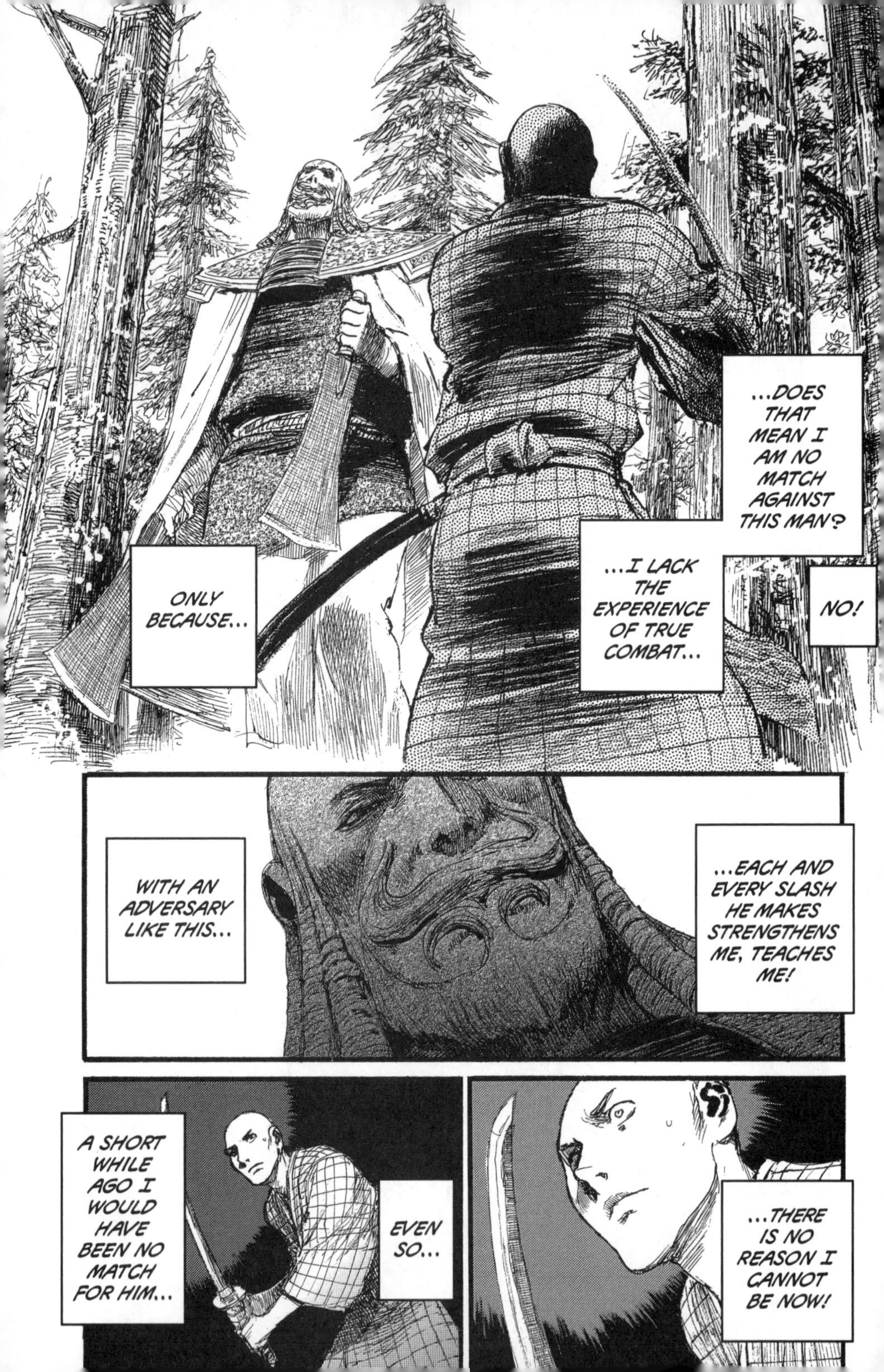

ONLY BECAUSE...
...I LACK THE EXPERIENCE OF TRUE COMBAT...
...DOES THAT MEAN I AM NO MATCH AGAINST THIS MAN?
NO!
WITH AN ADVERSARY LIKE THIS...
...EACH AND EVERY SLASH HE MAKES STRENGTHENS ME, TEACHES ME!
A SHORT WHILE AGO I WOULD HAVE BEEN NO MATCH FOR HIM...
EVEN SO...
...THERE IS NO REASON I CANNOT BE NOW!

COUNTING FROM THE TIME WE MET...

...HE HAS SWUNG THOSE GREAT BLADES SEVEN TIMES.

I HAVE WITNESSED HIS SWORDS-MANSHIP SEVEN TIMES NOW.

IF I DO NOT TURN THIS KNOWLEDGE INTO FLESH AND BLOOD, HOW CAN I MAKE AMENDS TO MY TWO DEAD COMRADES?!

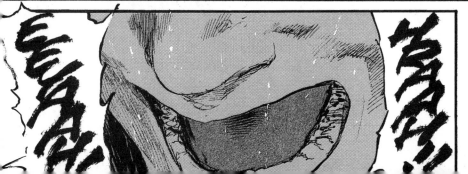

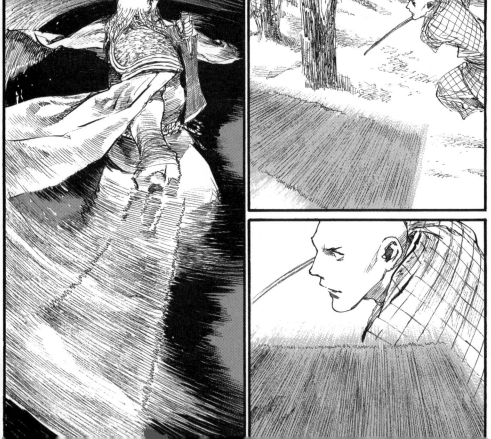

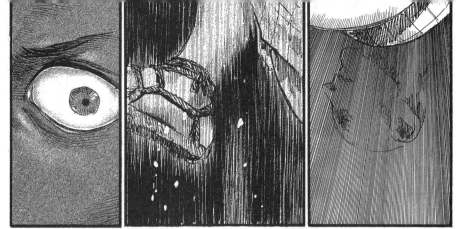

I'M CALMER THAN I'VE EVER BEEN.

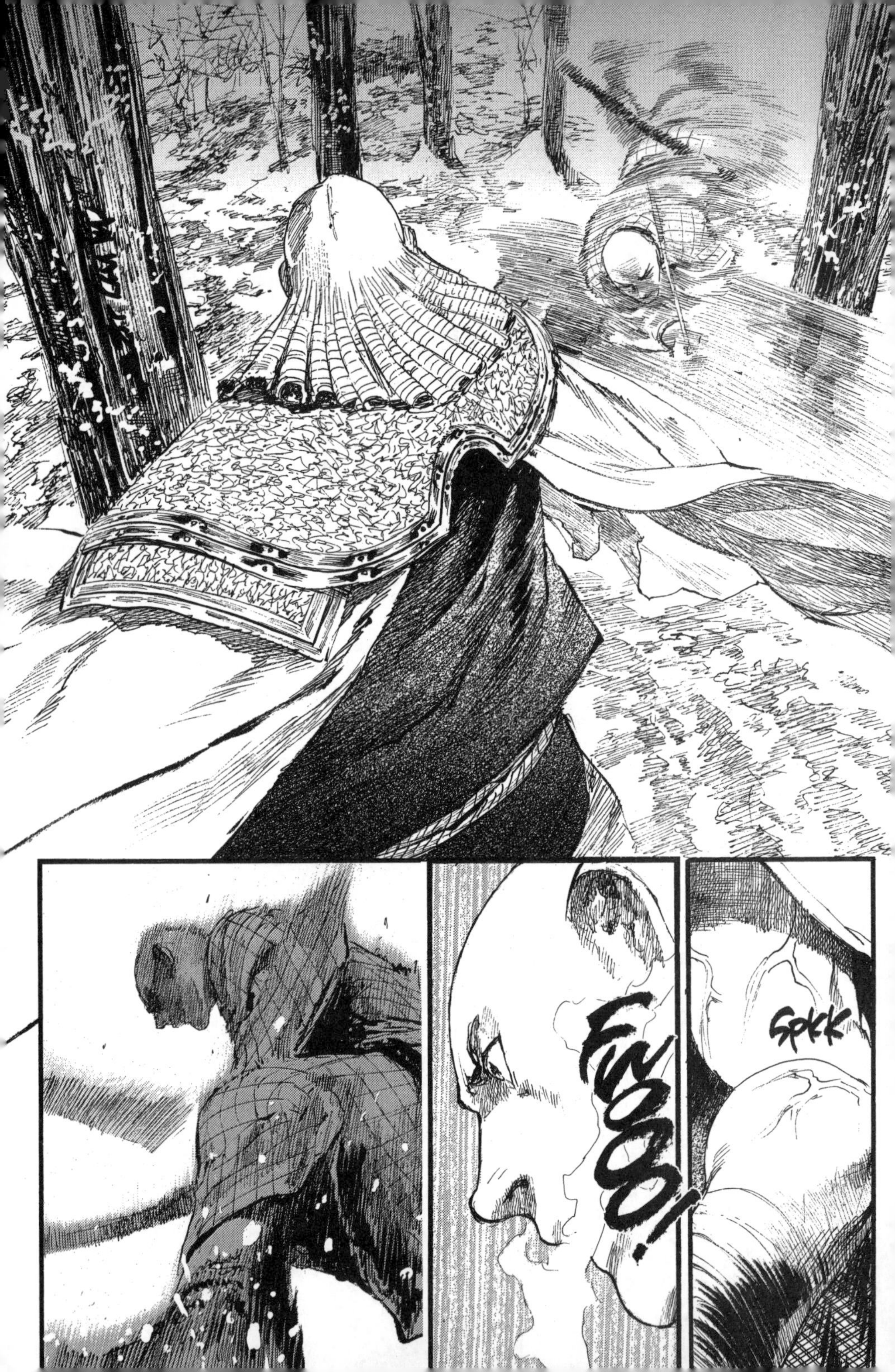
SPKK
FWOOO!

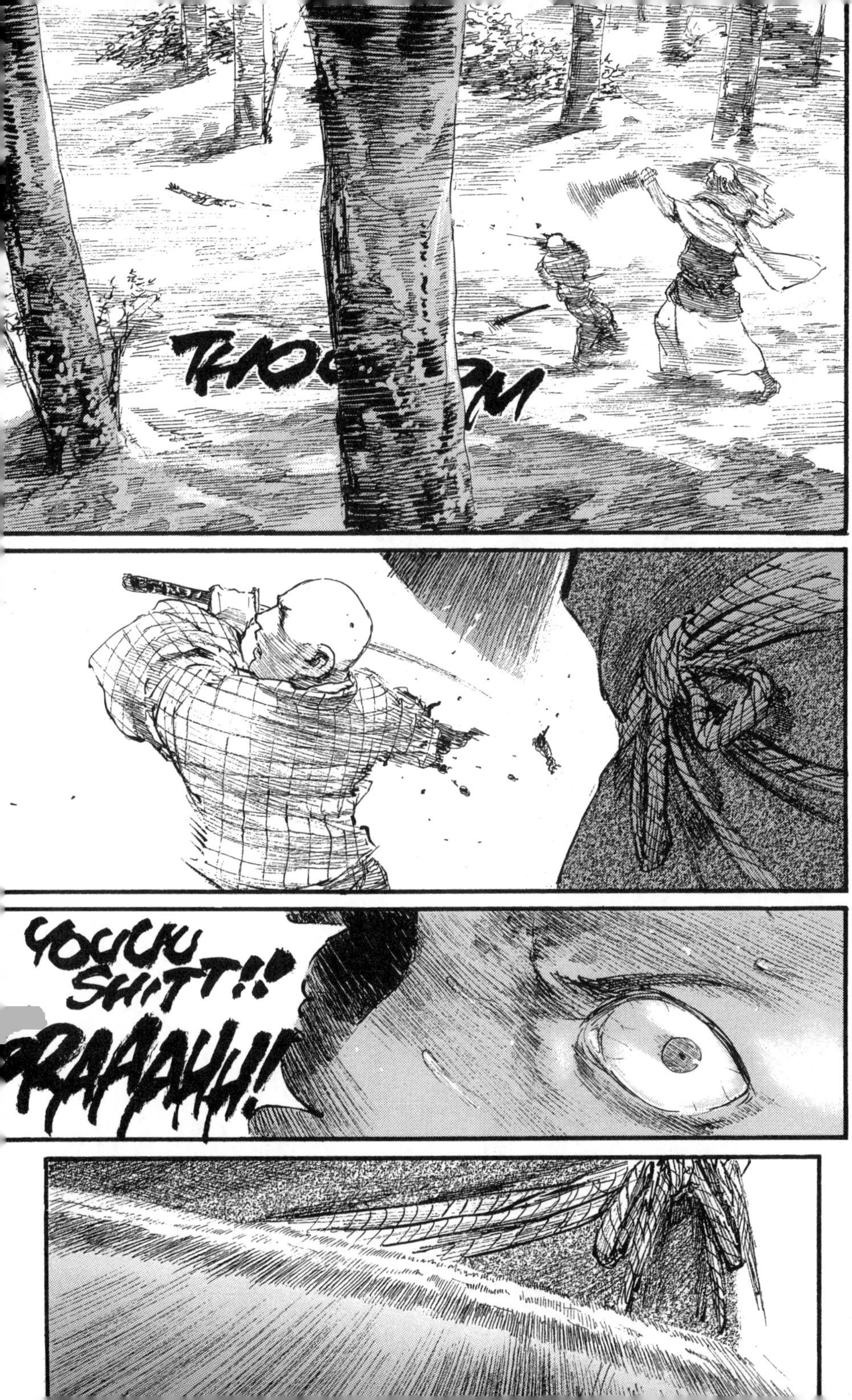
THOOOOOM
YOUUU SHIT!!
RAAAHH!

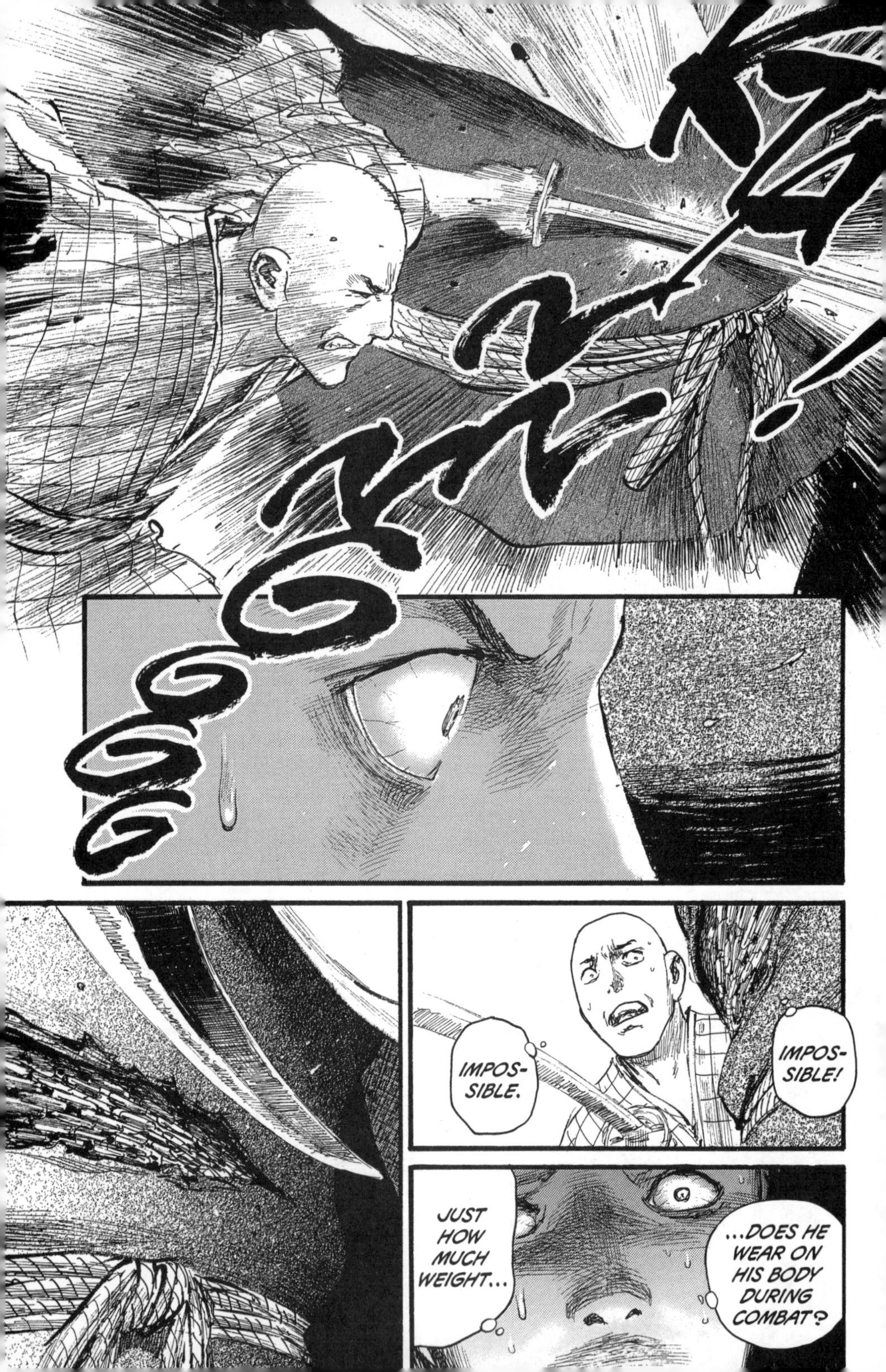
IMPOS-SIBLE!
IMPOS-SIBLE.
...DOES HE WEAR ON HIS BODY DURING COMBAT?
JUST HOW MUCH WEIGHT...

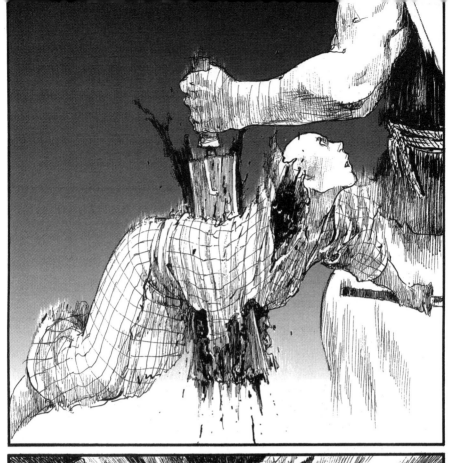

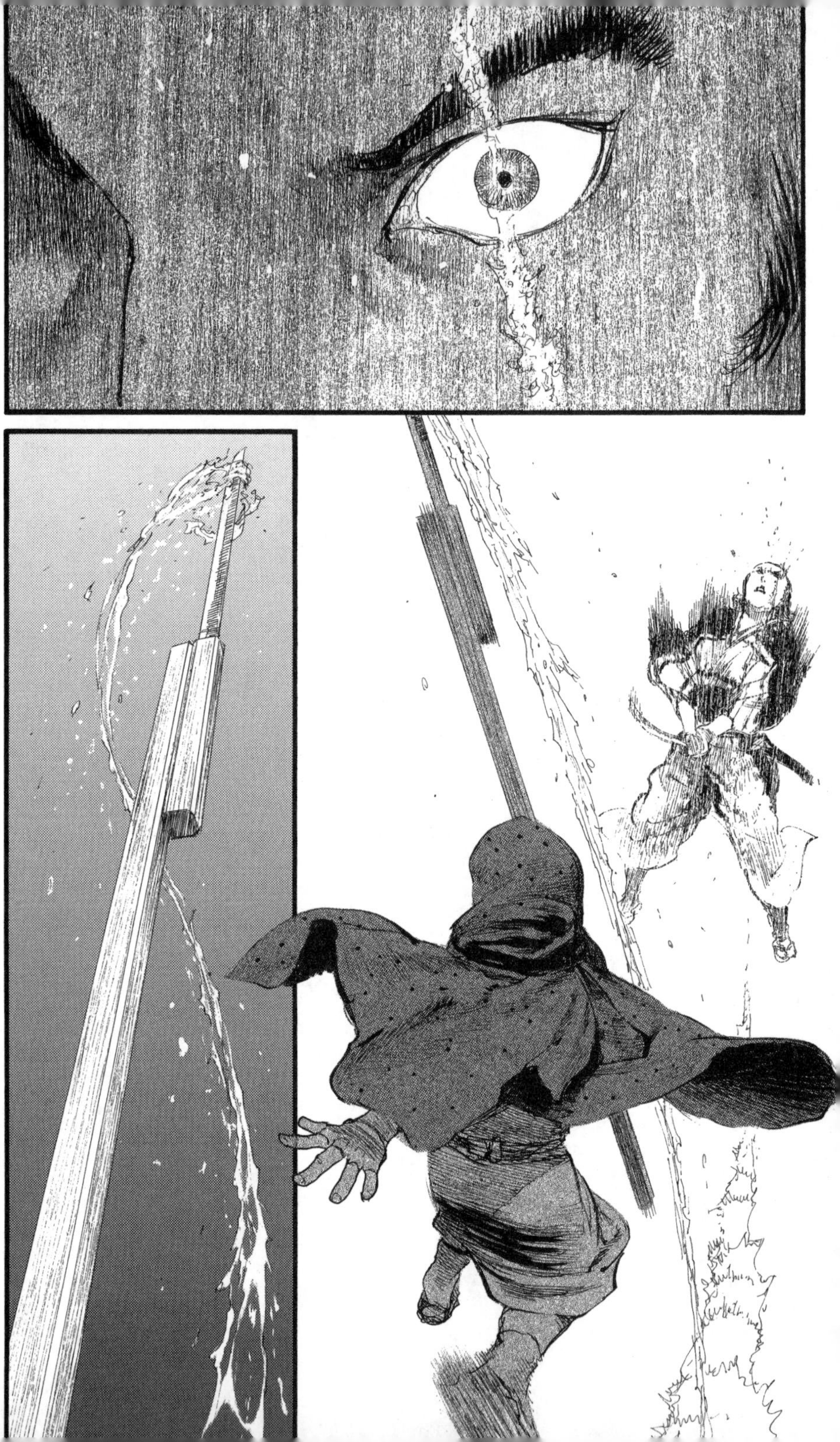

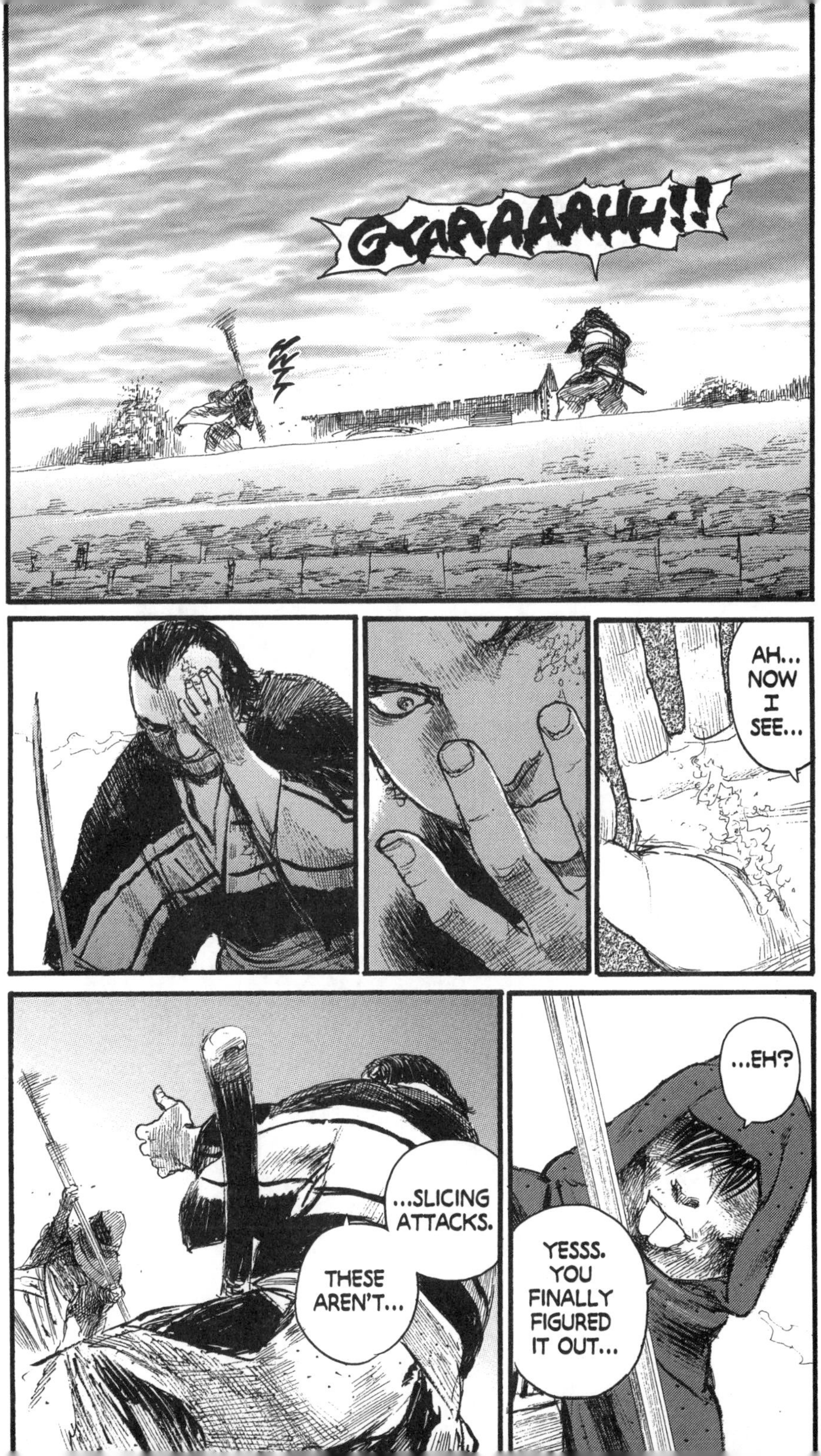
GYAAAAAHH!!
AH... NOW I SEE...
THESE AREN'T...
...SLICING ATTACKS.
...EH?
YESSS. YOU FINALLY FIGURED IT OUT...

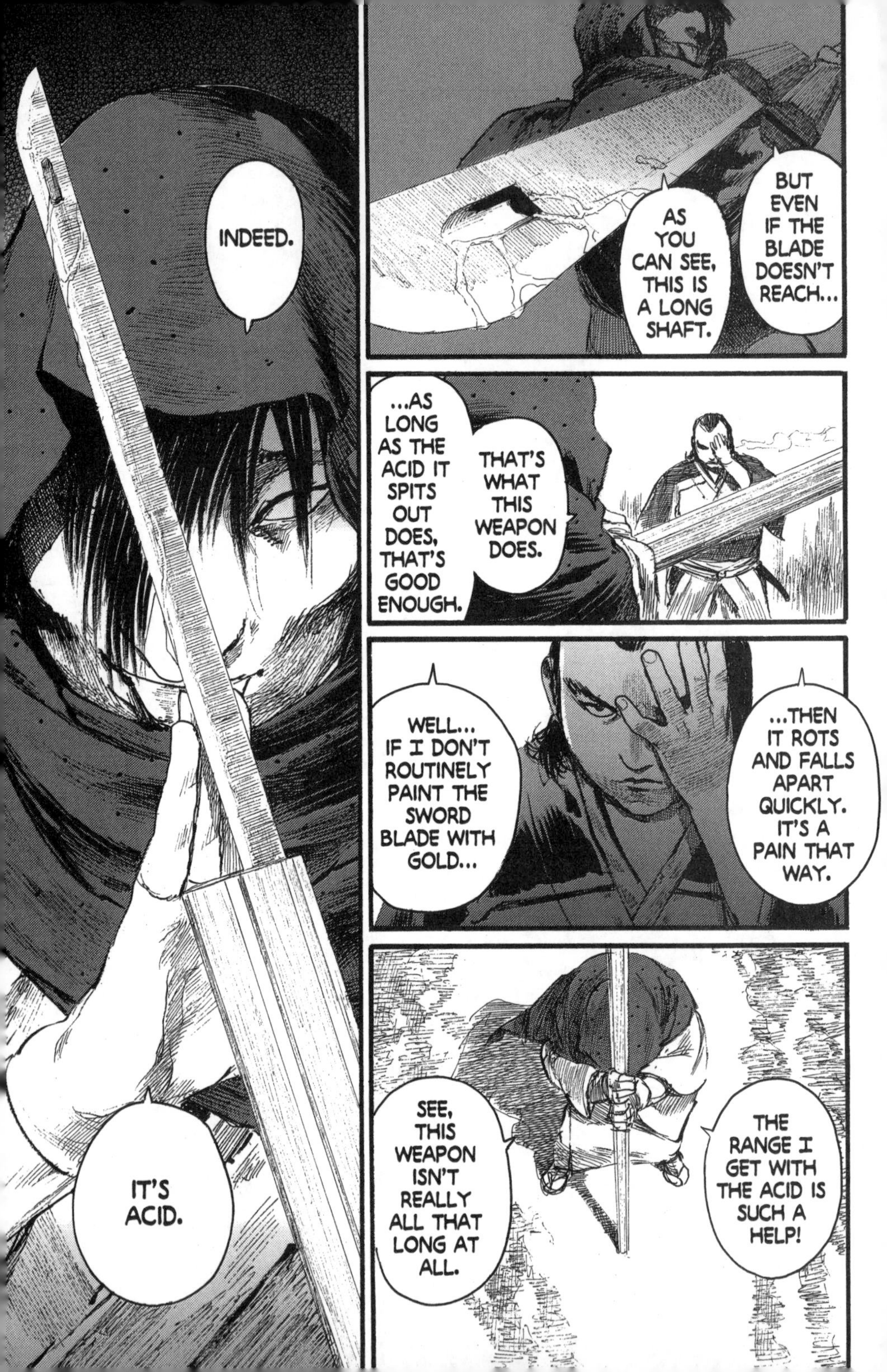
INDEED.
IT'S ACID.
AS YOU CAN SEE, THIS IS A LONG SHAFT.
BUT EVEN IF THE BLADE DOESN'T REACH...
...AS LONG AS THE ACID IT SPITS OUT DOES, THAT'S GOOD ENOUGH.
THAT'S WHAT THIS WEAPON DOES.
WELL... IF I DON'T ROUTINELY PAINT THE SWORD BLADE WITH GOLD...
...THEN IT ROTS AND FALLS APART QUICKLY. IT'S A PAIN THAT WAY.
SEE, THIS WEAPON ISN'T REALLY ALL THAT LONG AT ALL.
THE RANGE I GET WITH THE ACID IS SUCH A HELP!

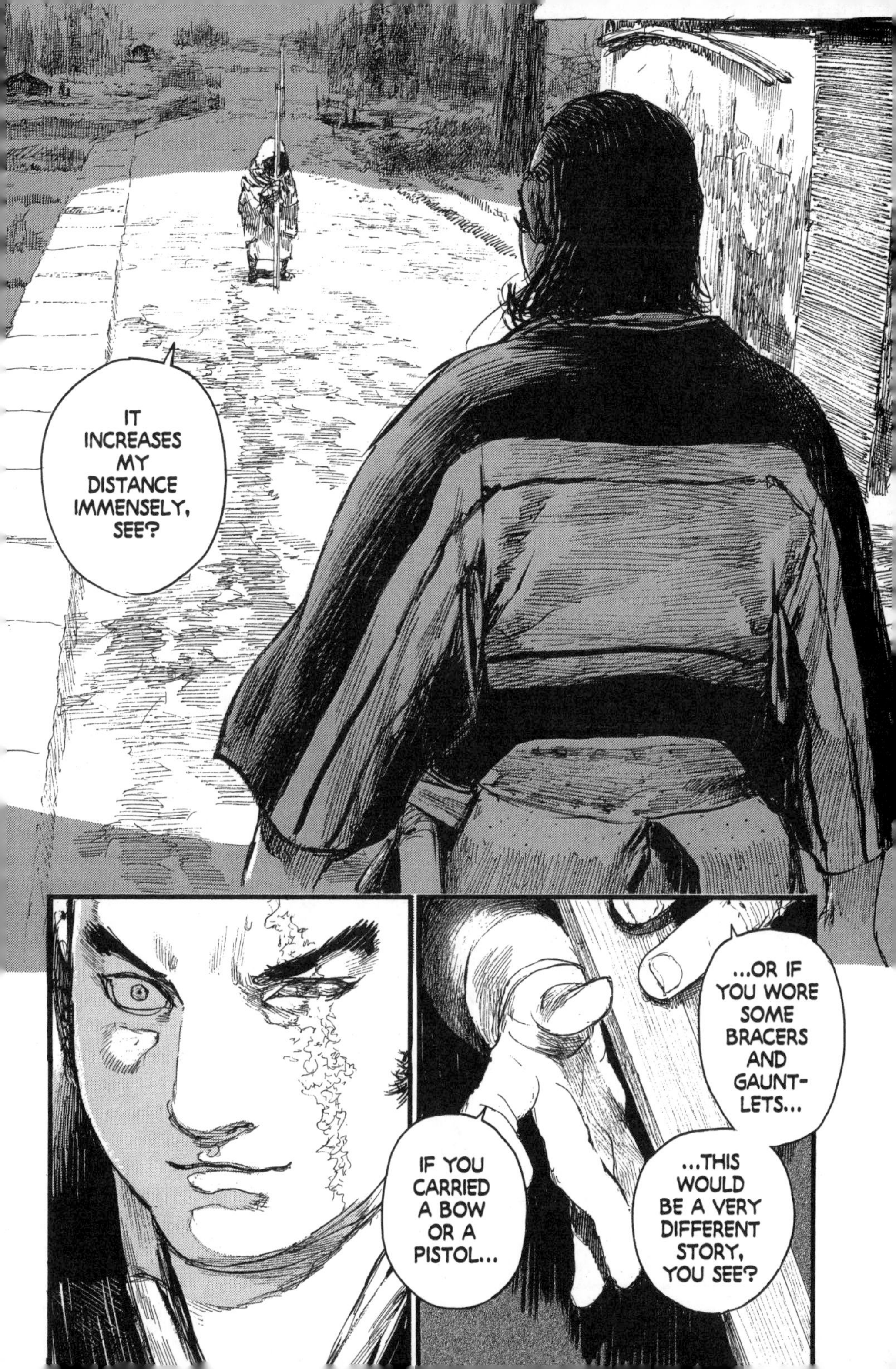
IT INCREASES MY DISTANCE IMMENSELY, SEE?
IF YOU CARRIED A BOW OR A PISTOL...
...OR IF YOU WORE SOME BRACERS AND GAUNT-LETS...
...THIS WOULD BE A VERY DIFFERENT STORY, YOU SEE?

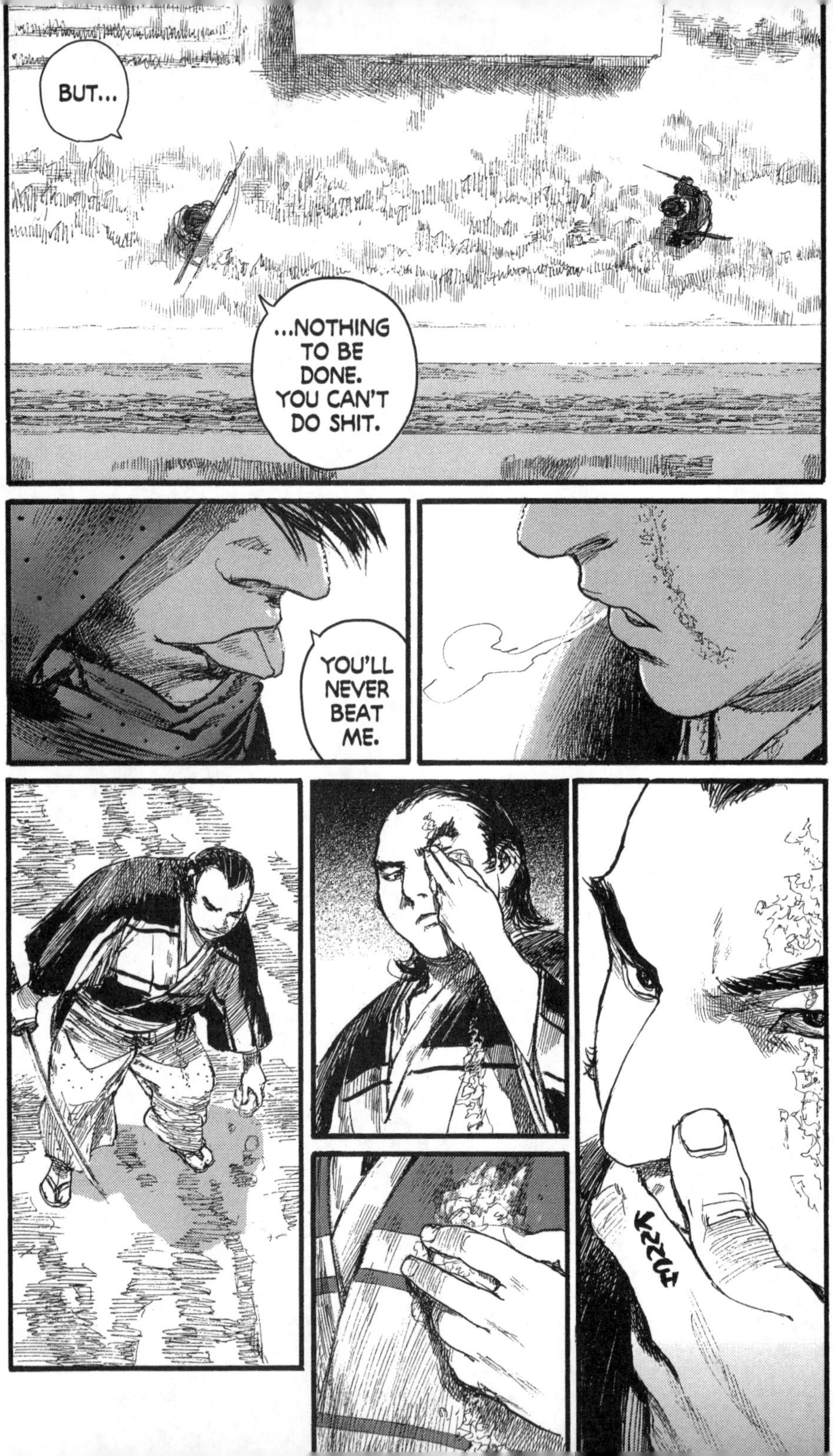
BUT...
...NOTHING TO BE DONE. YOU CAN'T DO SHIT.
YOU'LL NEVER BEAT ME.
KZZCH

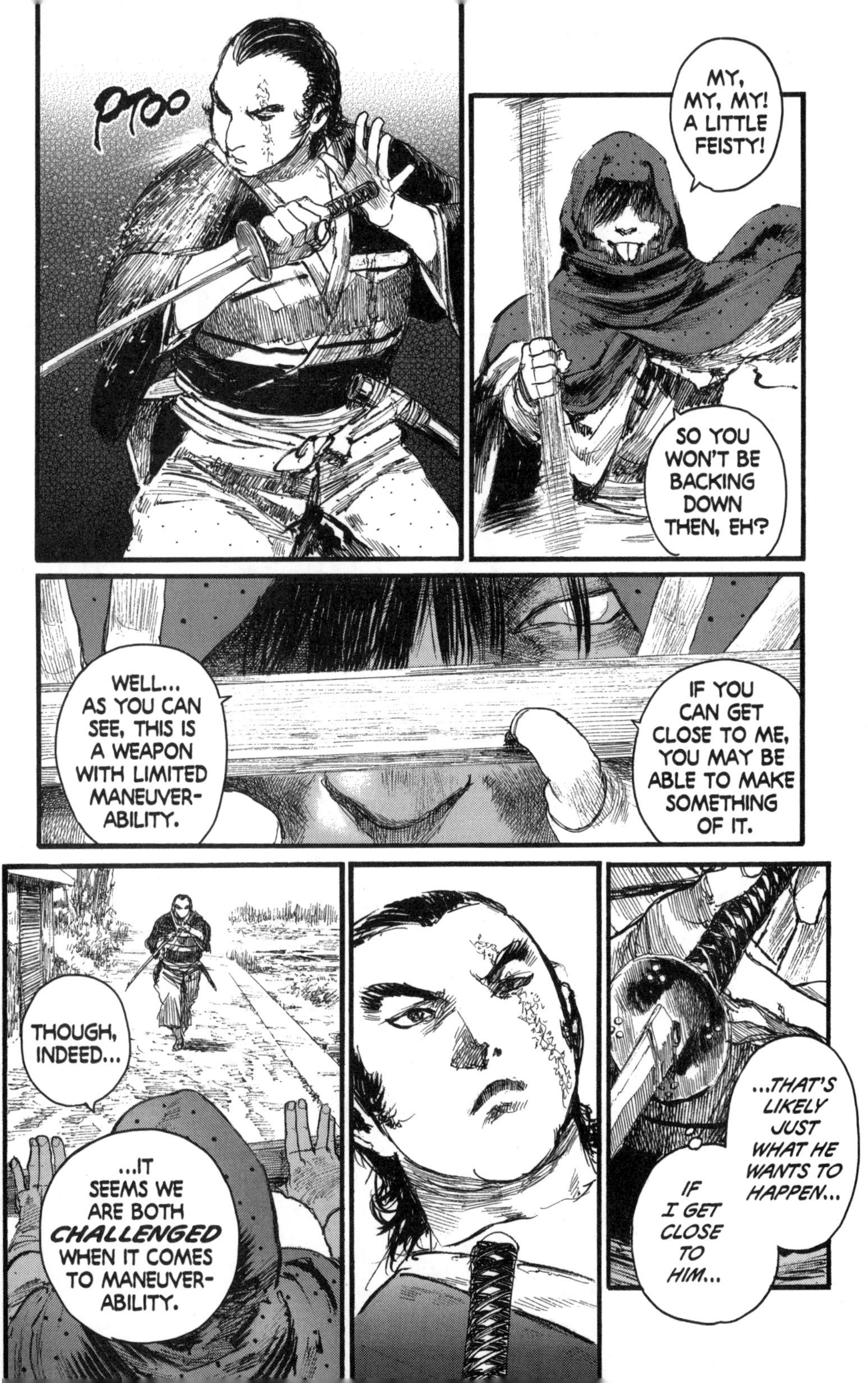
PTOO
MY, MY, MY! A LITTLE FEISTY!
SO YOU WON'T BE BACKING DOWN THEN, EH?
WELL... AS YOU CAN SEE, THIS IS A WEAPON WITH LIMITED MANEUVER-ABILITY.
IF YOU CAN GET CLOSE TO ME, YOU MAY BE ABLE TO MAKE SOMETHING OF IT.
THOUGH, INDEED...
...IT SEEMS WE ARE BOTH ***CHALLENGED*** WHEN IT COMES TO MANEUVER-ABILITY.
IF I GET CLOSE TO HIM...
...THAT'S LIKELY JUST WHAT HE WANTS TO HAPPEN...

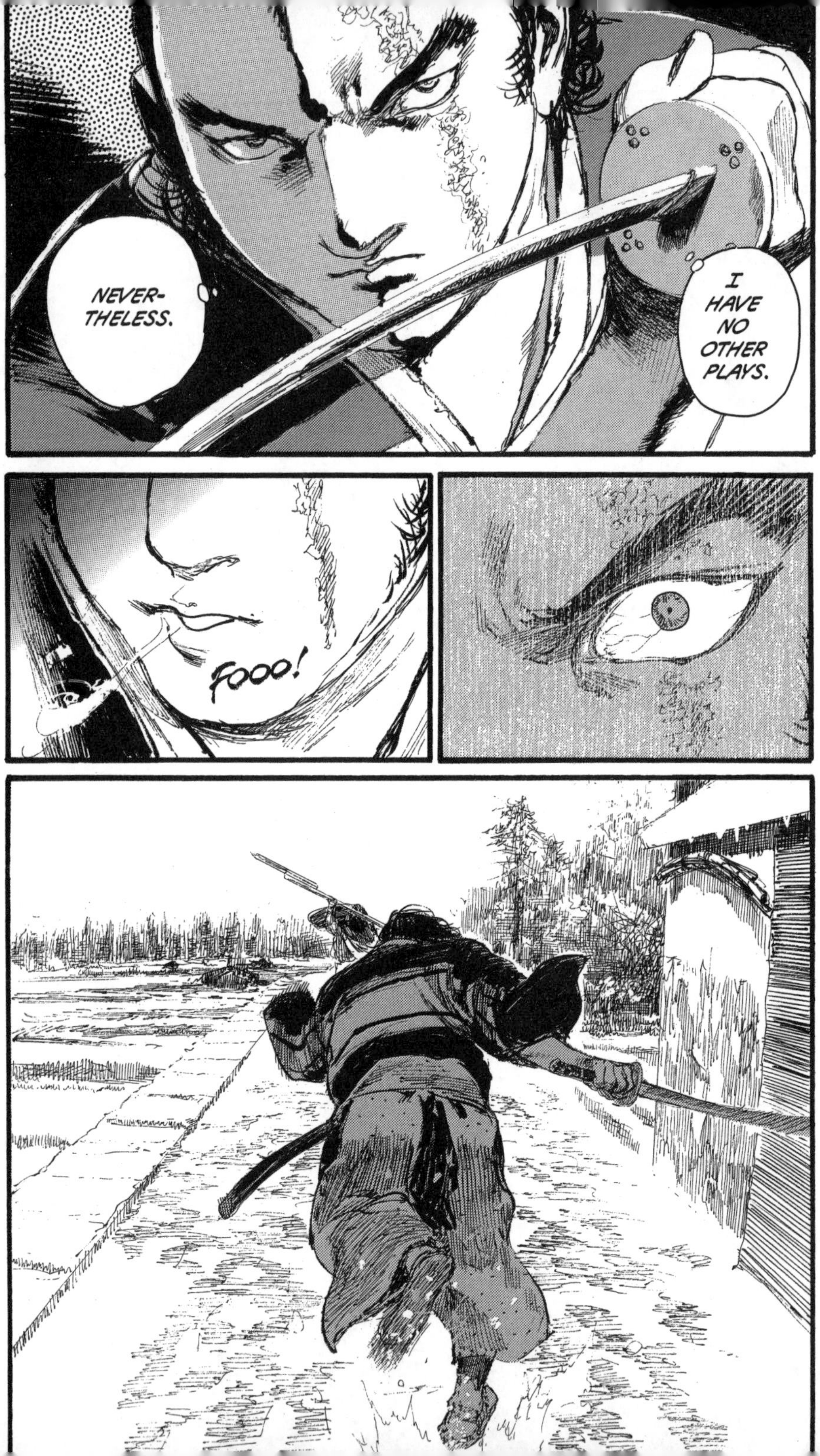
I HAVE NO OTHER PLAYS.
NEVER-THELESS.
FOOO!

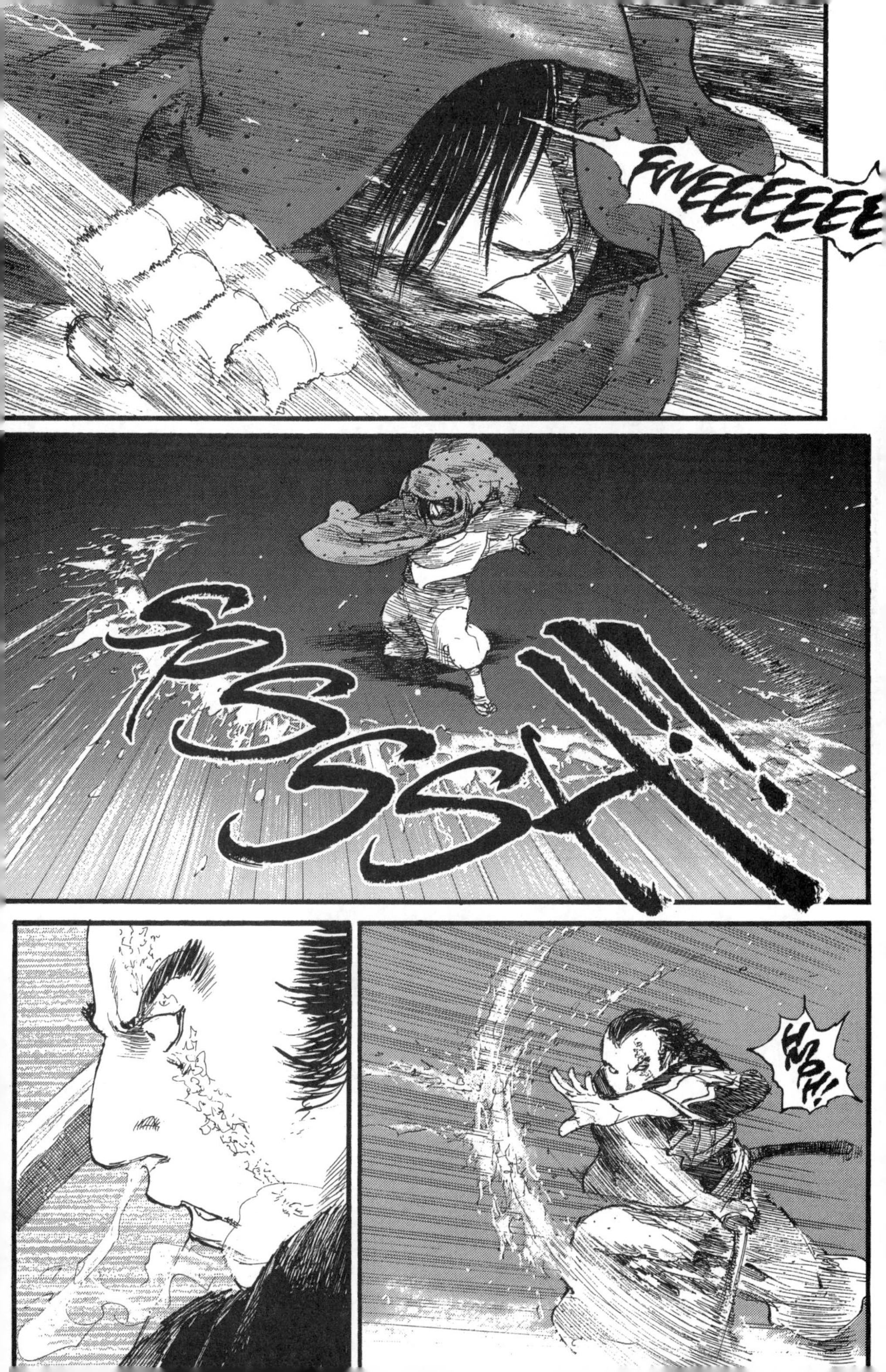
FWEEEEEEEE
SPSSSH!!
HSAH!!

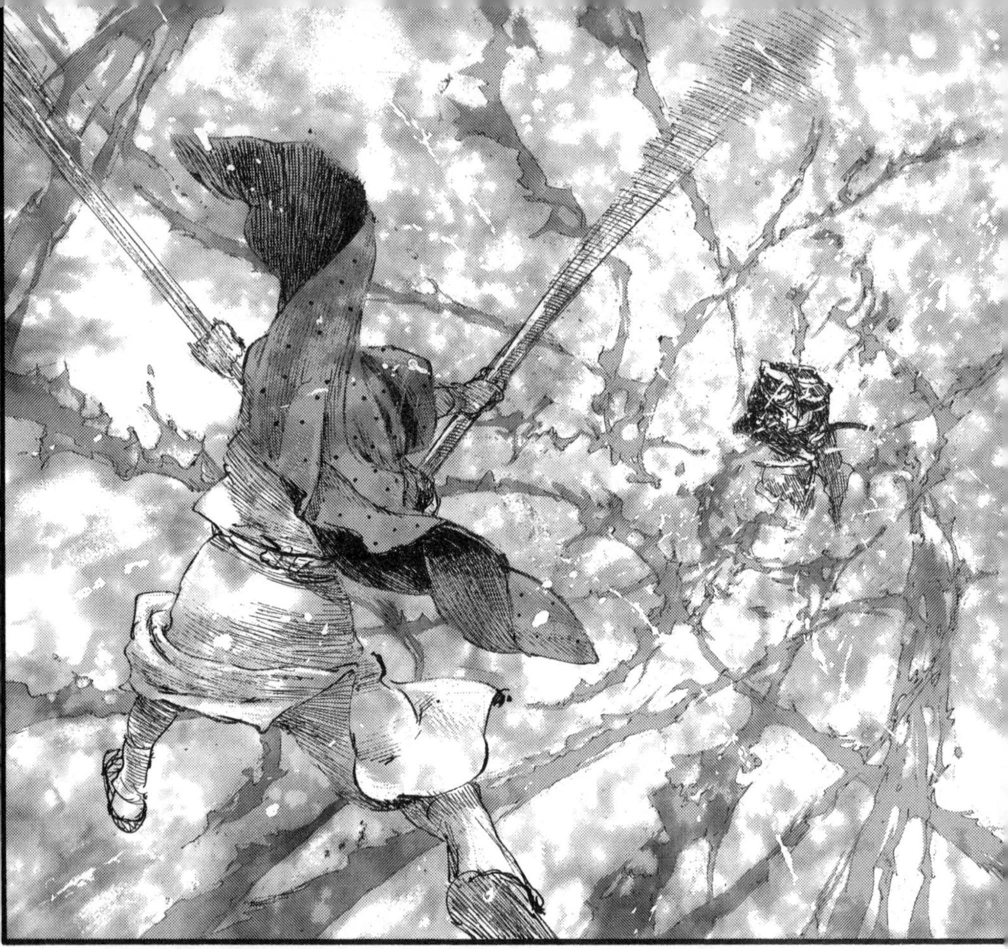
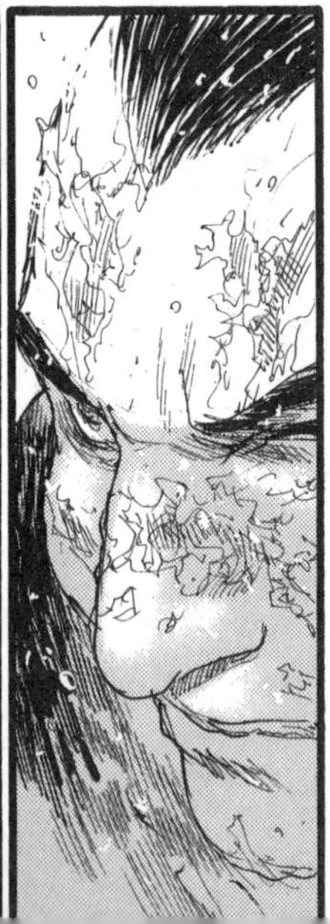
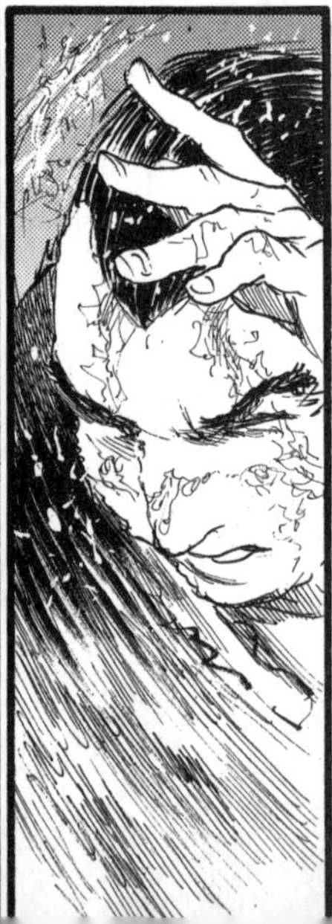
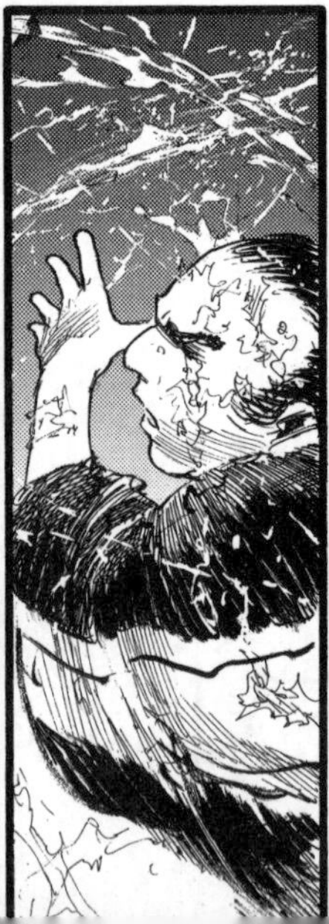
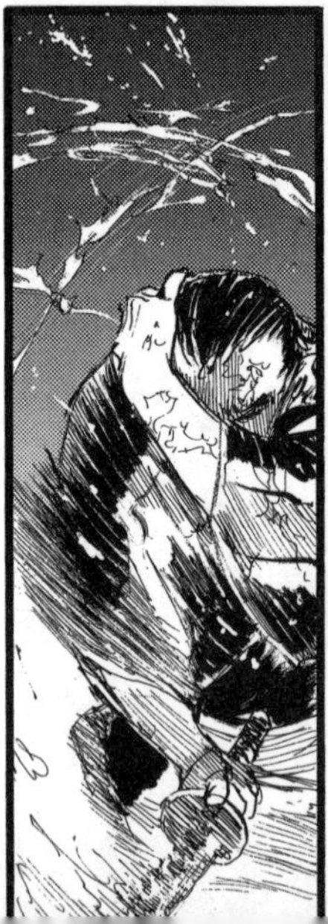

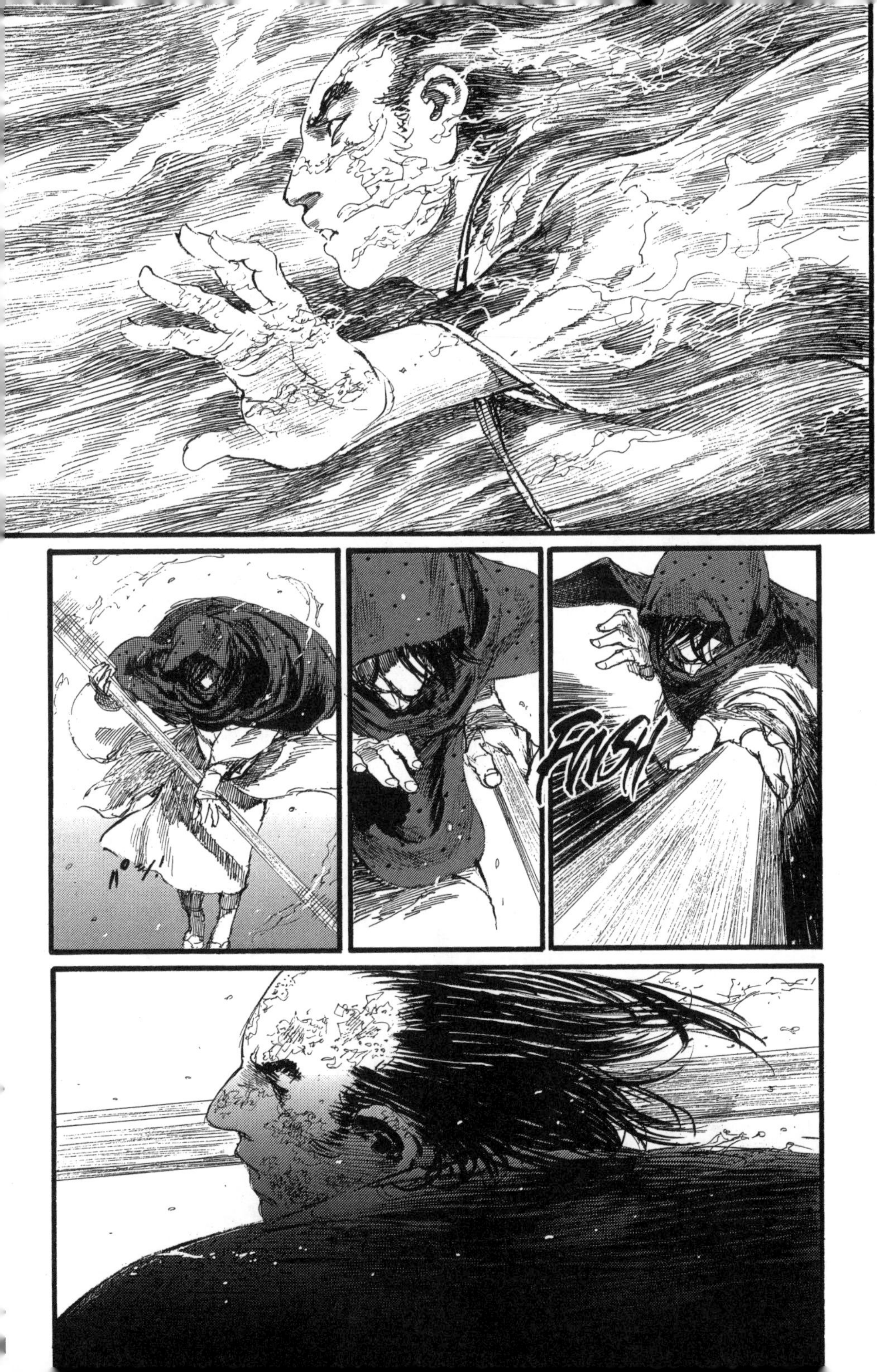
FINSH

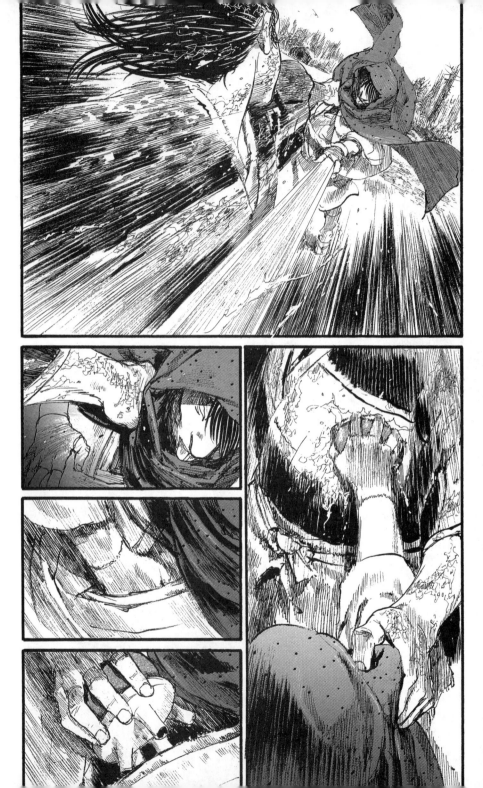

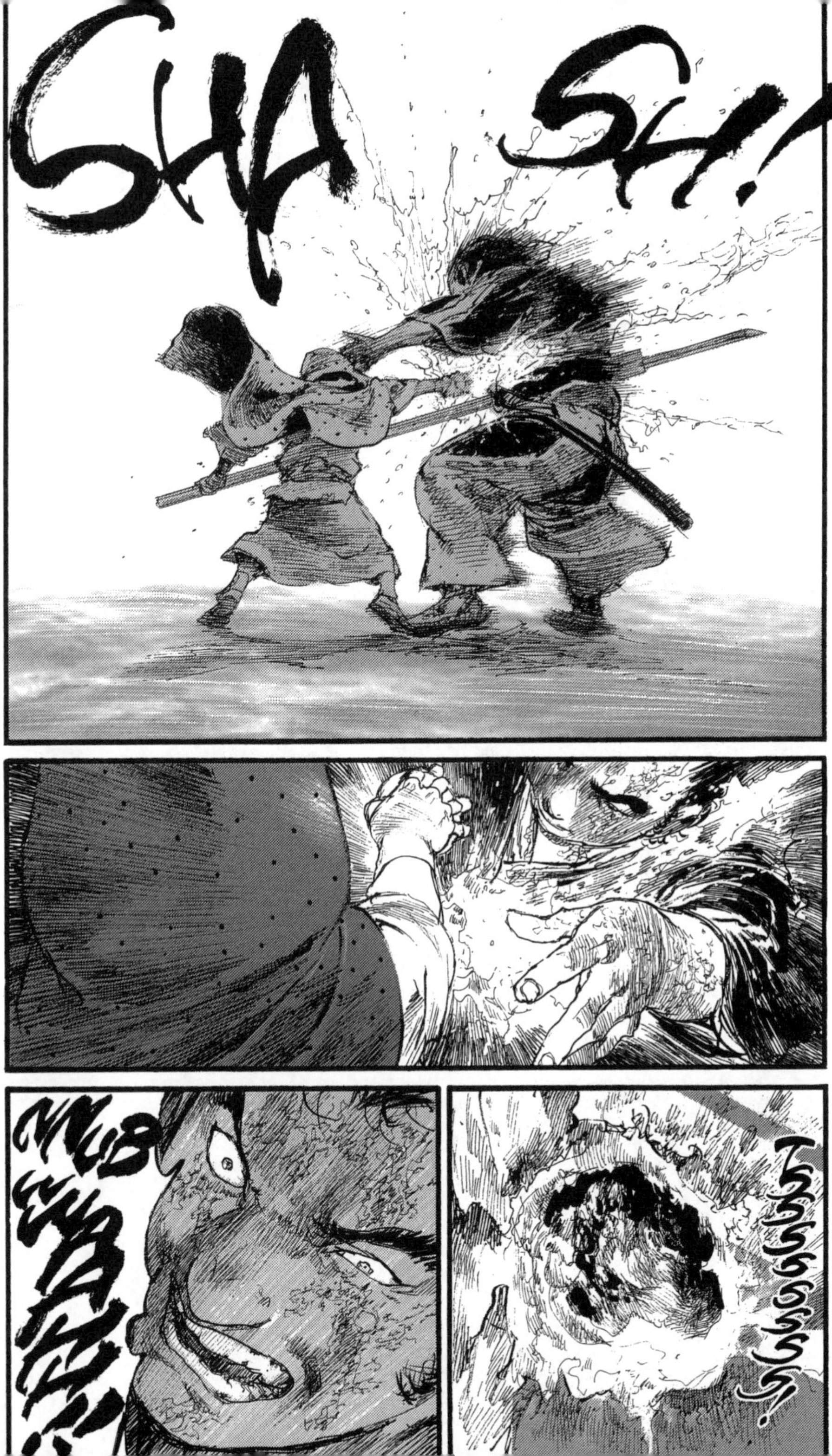
SHA SH!
TSSSSSSSS!
BWWSHHH!!

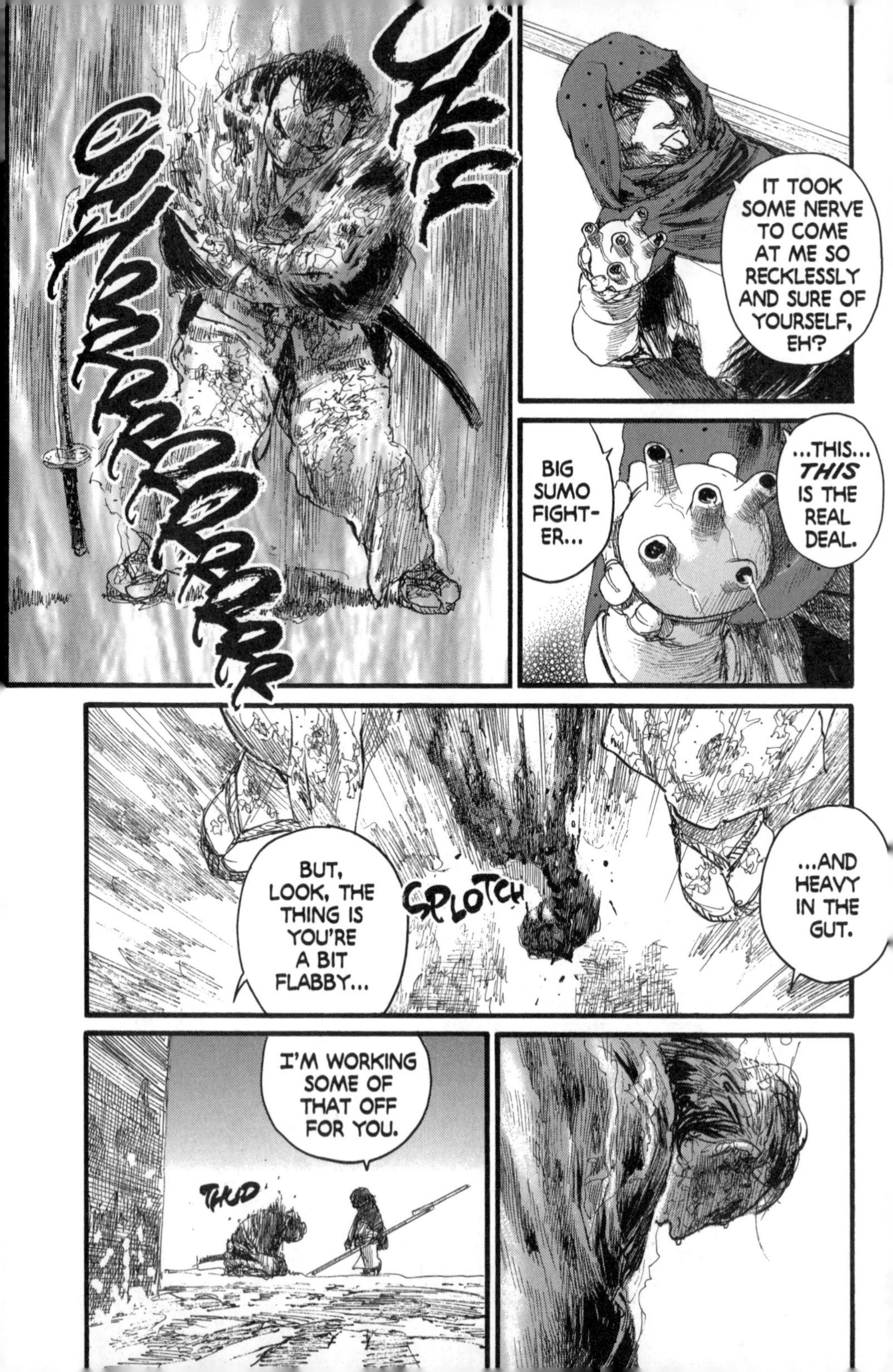
IT TOOK SOME NERVE TO COME AT ME SO RECKLESSLY AND SURE OF YOURSELF, EH?
BIG SUMO FIGHTER...
...THIS... *THIS* IS THE REAL DEAL.
BUT, LOOK, THE THING IS YOU'RE A BIT FLABBY...
SPLOTCH
...AND HEAVY IN THE GUT.
I'M WORKING SOME OF THAT OFF FOR YOU.
THUD

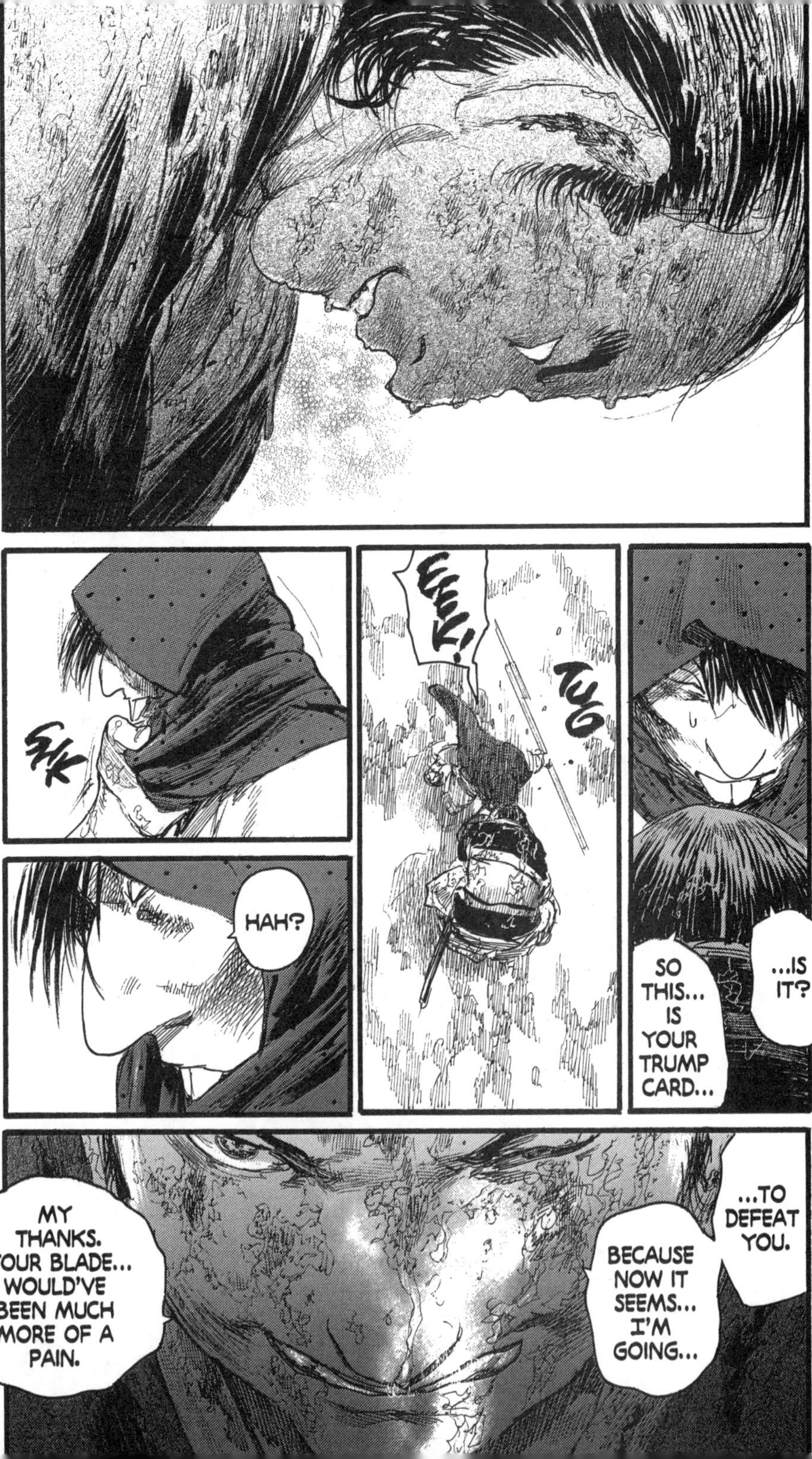
SO THIS... IS YOUR TRUMP CARD...
...IS IT?
EEEK!
TUG
GAK
HAH?
BECAUSE NOW IT SEEMS... I'M GOING...
...TO DEFEAT YOU.
MY THANKS. YOUR BLADE... WOULD'VE BEEN MUCH MORE OF A PAIN.

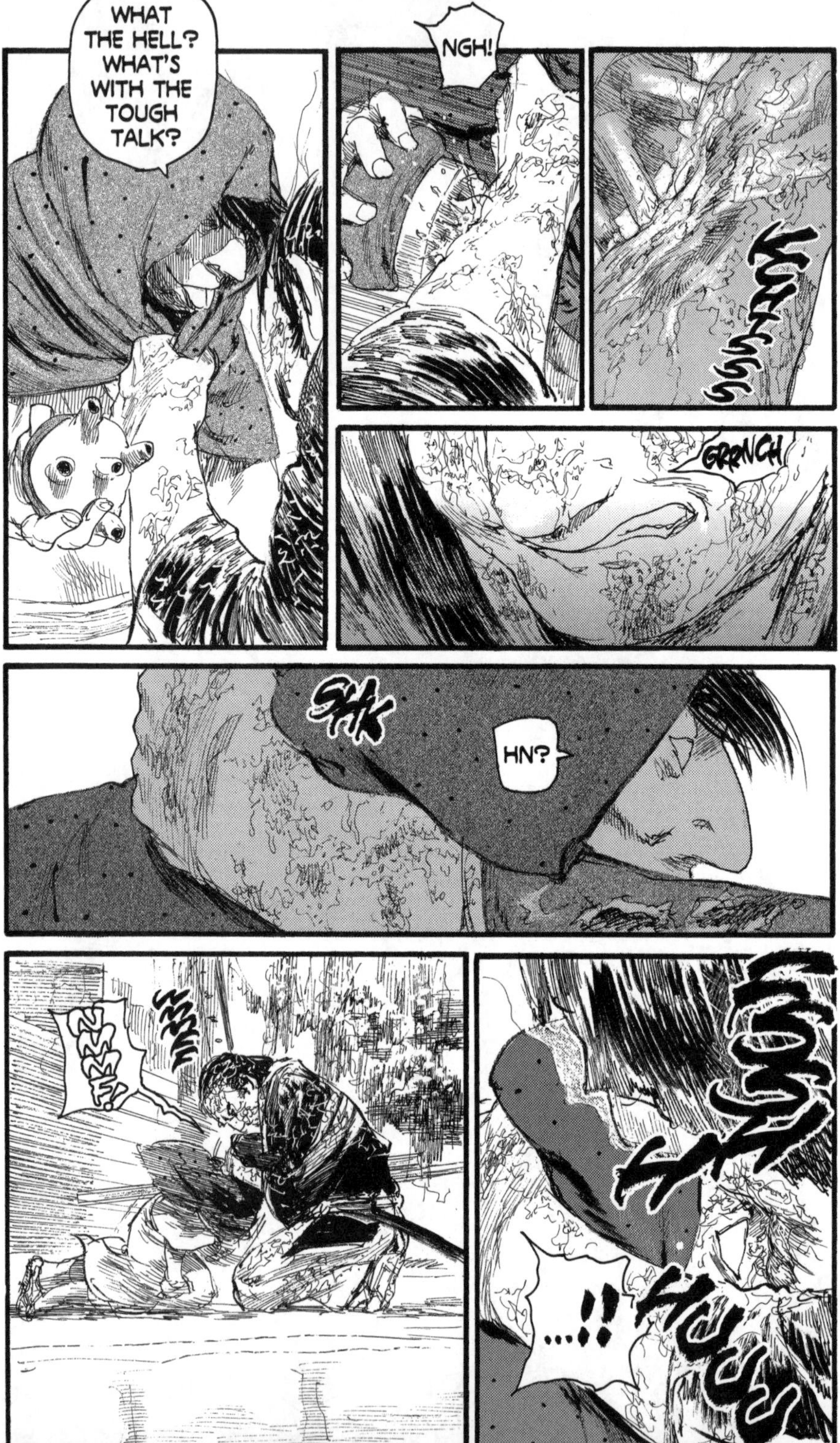
KUH-SSSS
NGH!
GRRNCH
WHAT THE HELL? WHAT'S WITH THE TOUGH TALK?
SHAK
HN?
...!!
ZUMF!

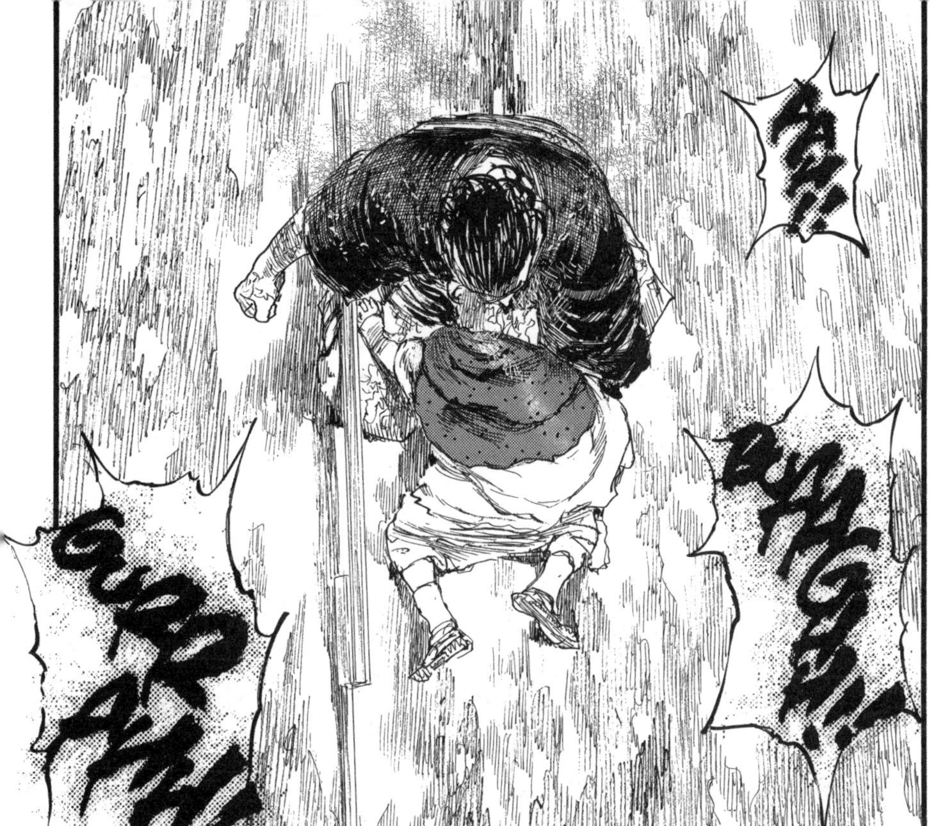
AAH!!
BWAGAH!!
GURRAH!!
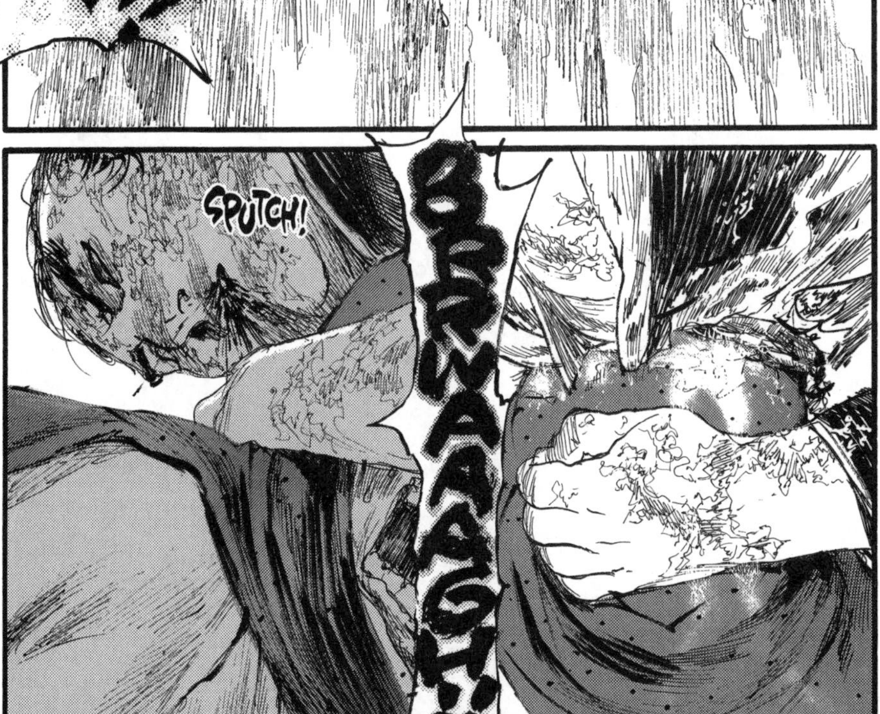
BERWAAAGH!!
SPUTCH!

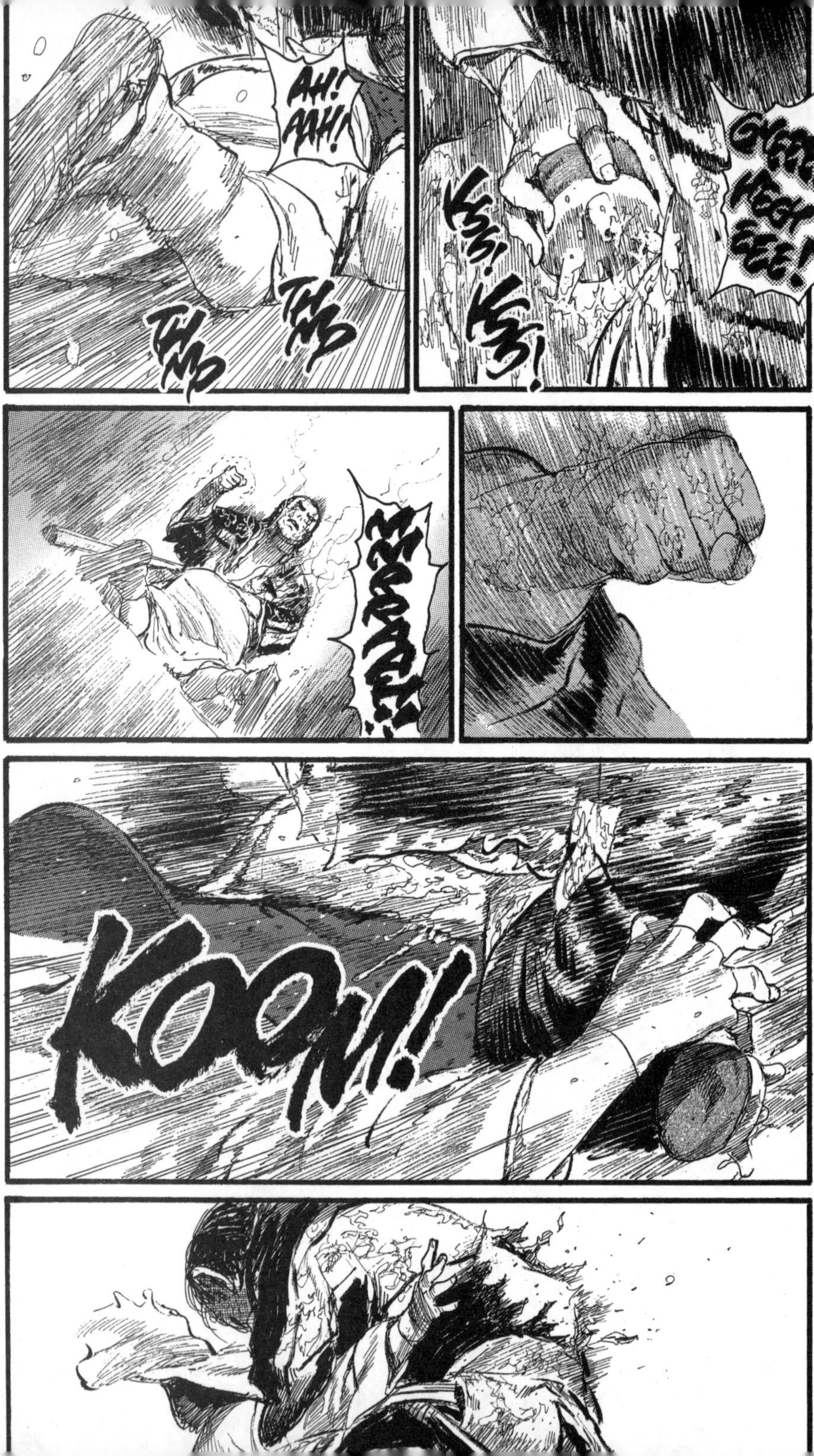
GYEEE! HEGH EEE!
KSS! KSS!
AH! AAH!
THMP
THMP
MMRRRGH!!
KOOM!

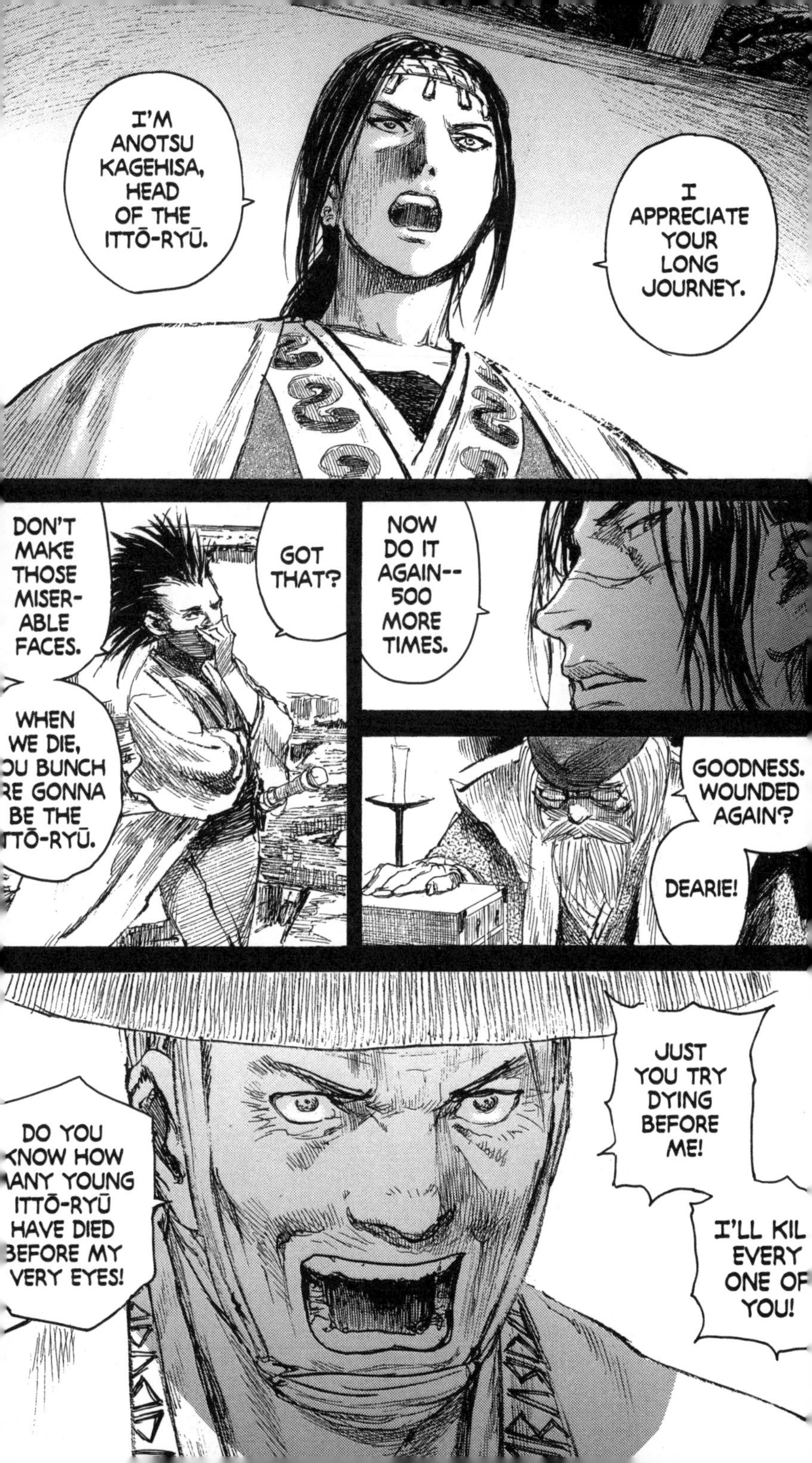

I'M ANOTSU KAGEHISA, HEAD OF THE ITTŌ-RYŪ.
I APPRECIATE YOUR LONG JOURNEY.
DON'T MAKE THOSE MISER-ABLE FACES.
GOT THAT?
WHEN WE DIE, OU BUNCH RE GONNA BE THE TTŌ-RYŪ.
NOW DO IT AGAIN-- 500 MORE TIMES.
GOODNESS. WOUNDED AGAIN?
DEARIE!
DO YOU KNOW HOW ANY YOUNG ITTŌ-RYŪ HAVE DIED BEFORE MY VERY EYES!
JUST YOU TRY DYING BEFORE ME!
I'LL KIL EVERY ONE OF YOU!

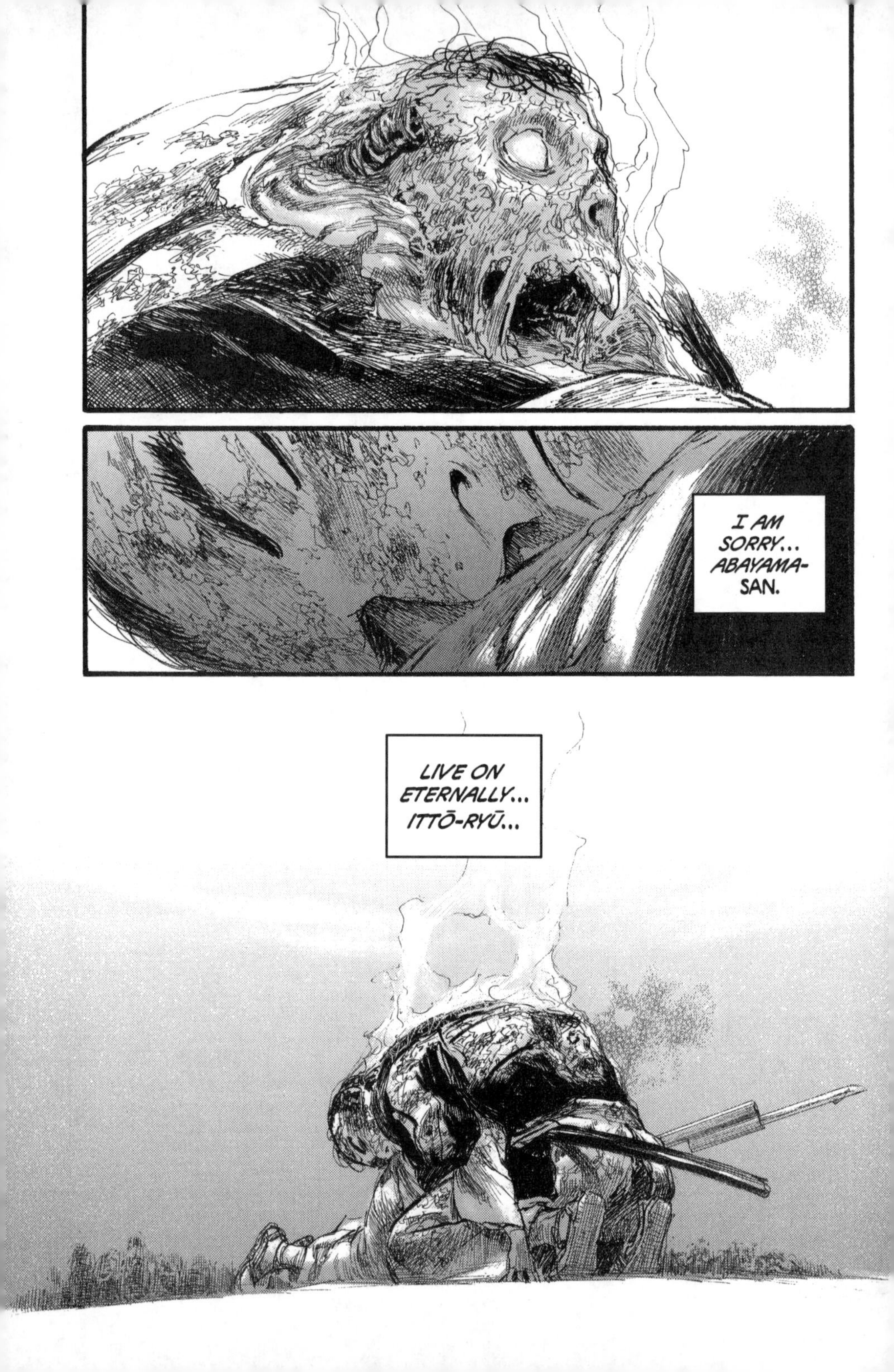
I AM SORRY... ABAYAMA-SAN.
LIVE ON ETERNALLY... ITTŌ-RYŪ...

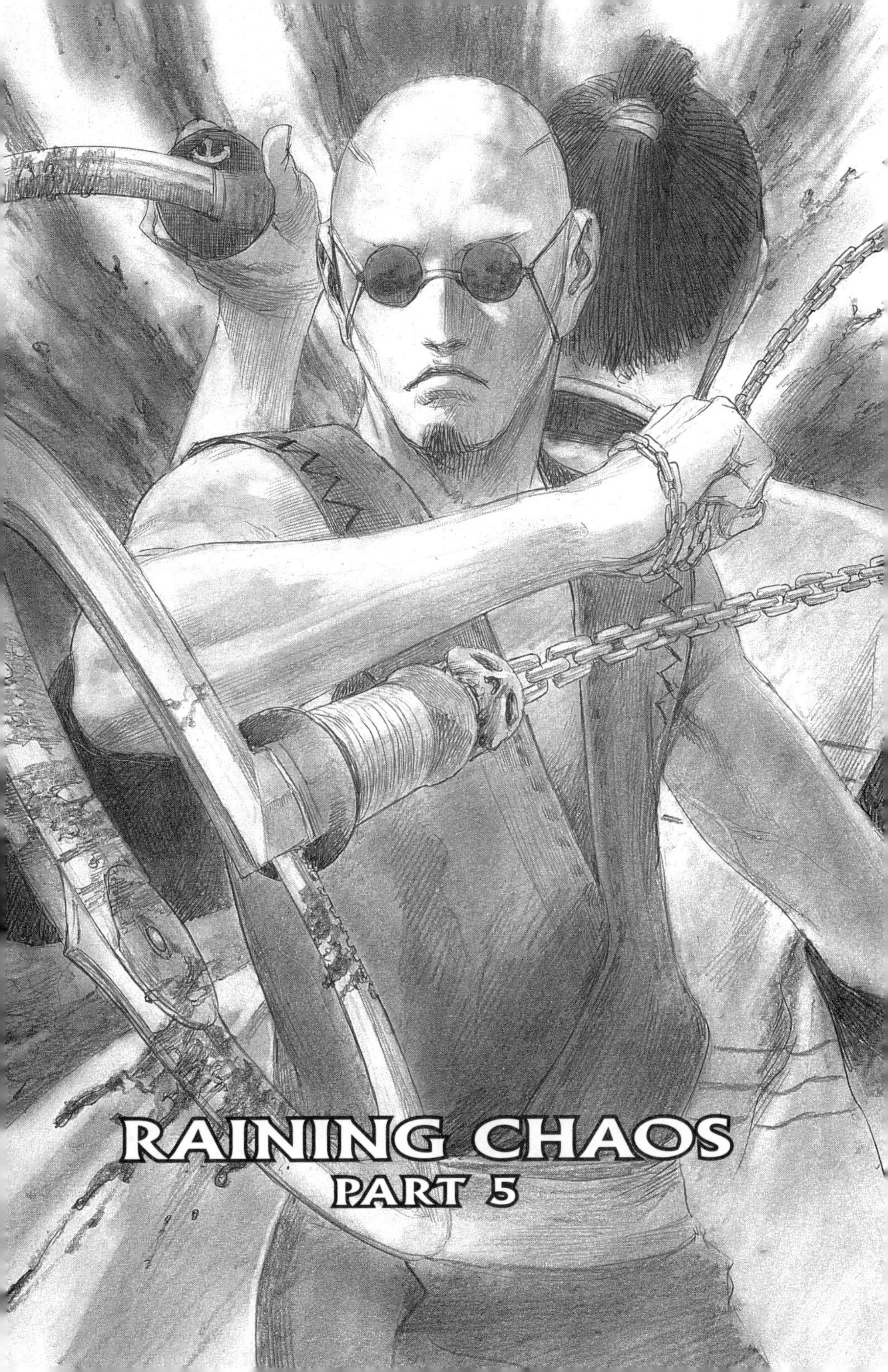
RAINING CHAOS
PART 5

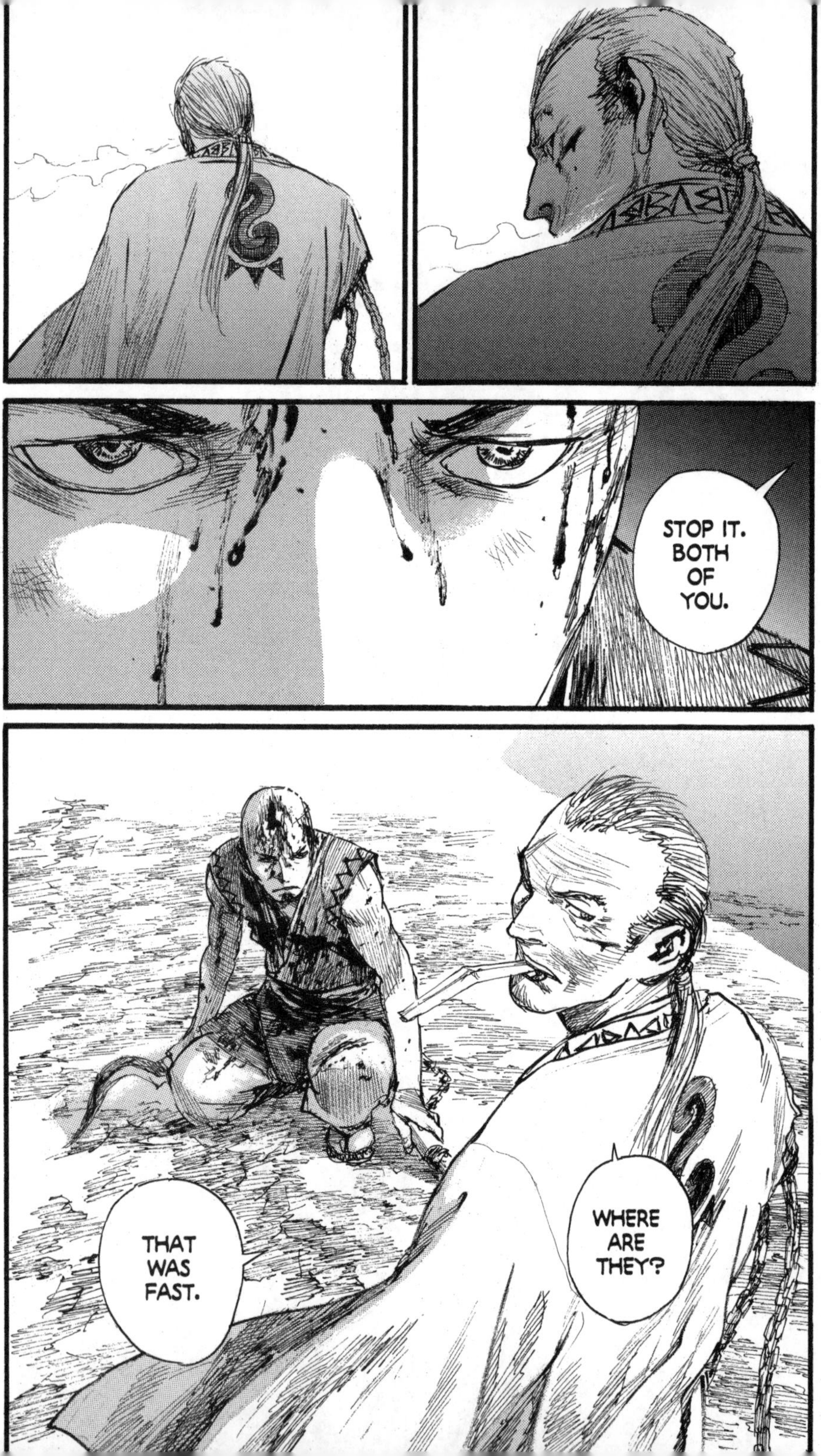
STOP IT. BOTH OF YOU.
WHERE ARE THEY?
THAT WAS FAST.

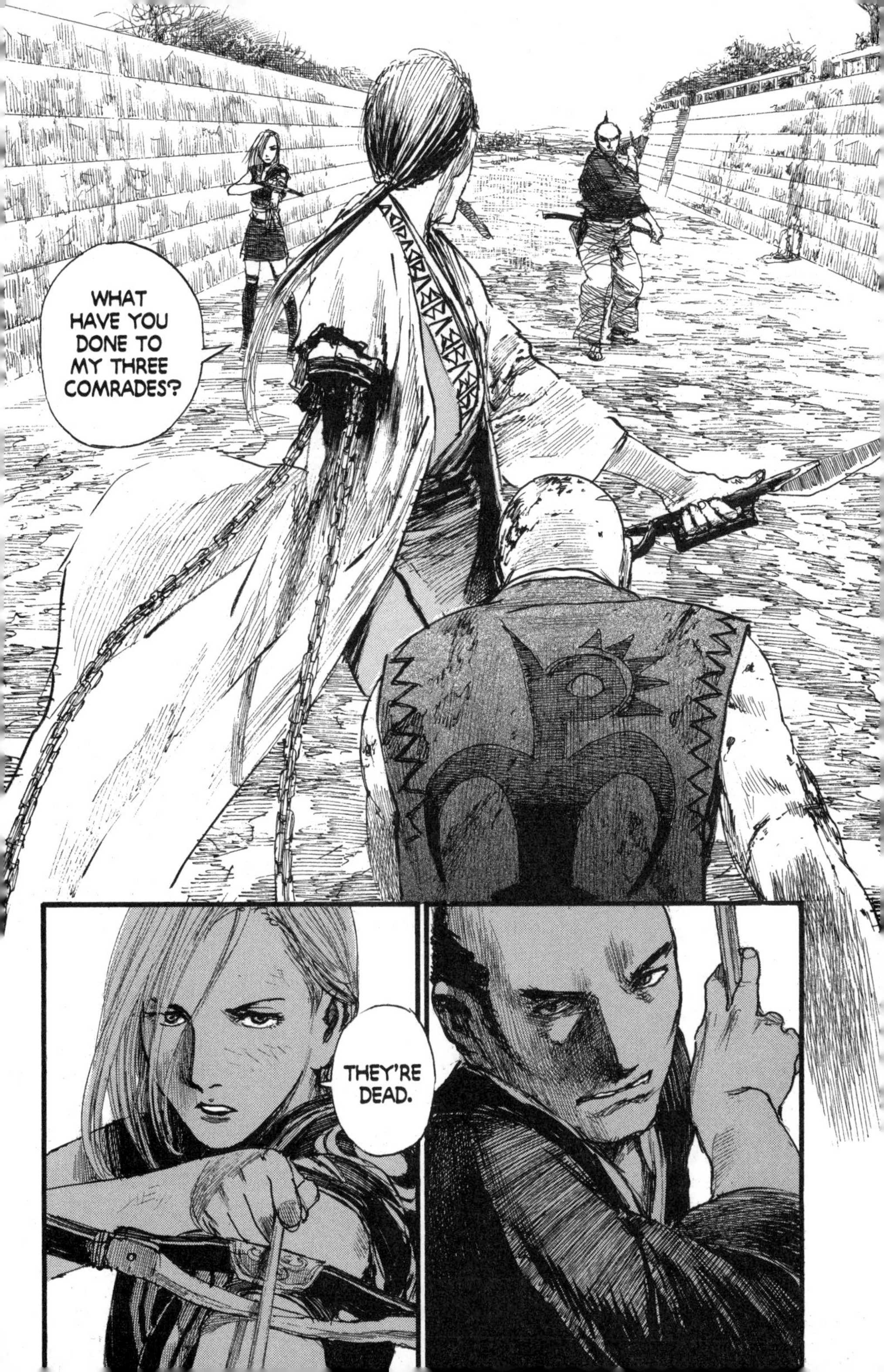
WHAT HAVE YOU DONE TO MY THREE COMRADES?
THEY'RE DEAD.

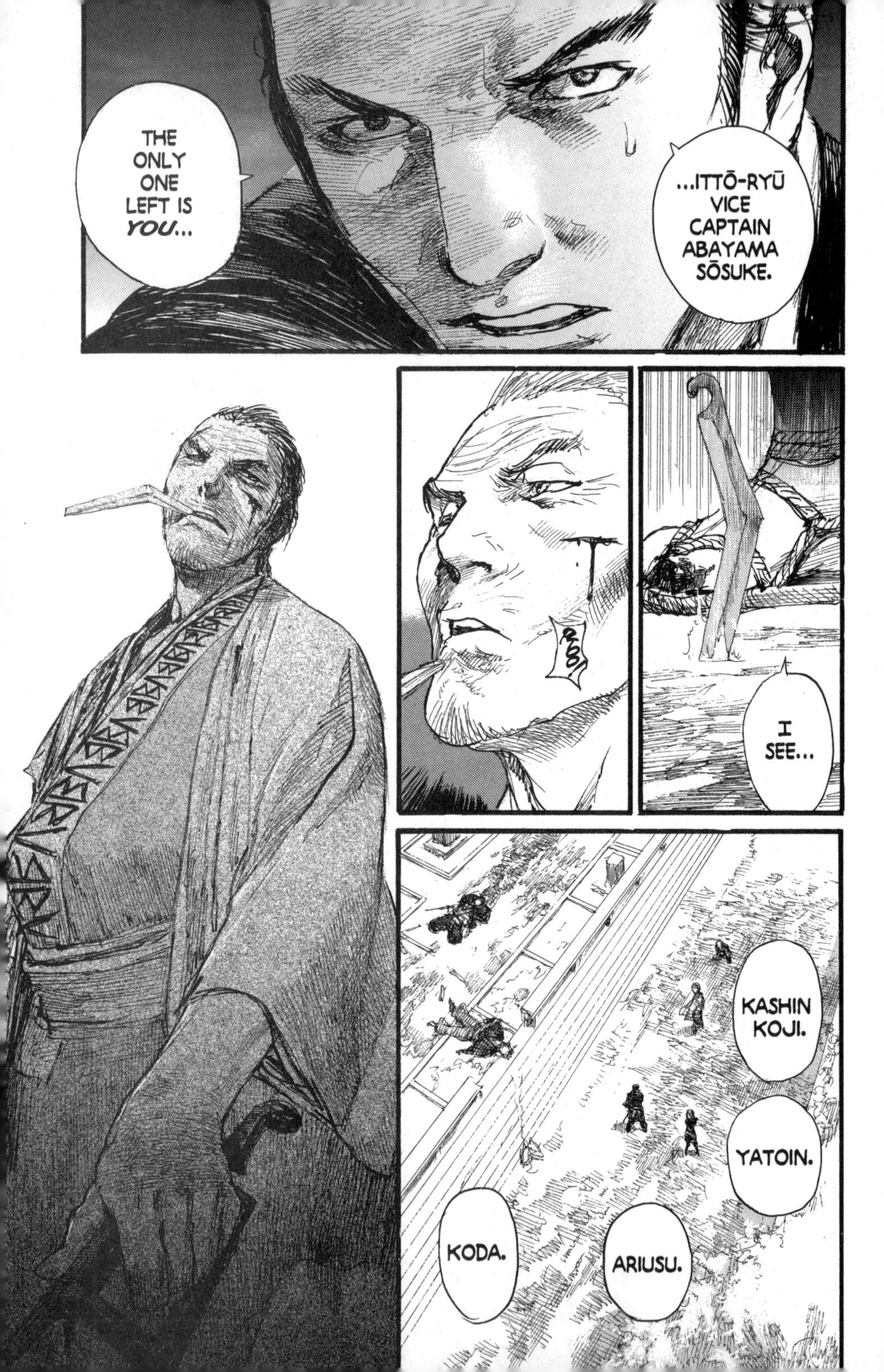
...ITTŌ-RYŪ VICE CAPTAIN ABAYAMA SŌSUKE.
THE ONLY ONE LEFT IS *YOU*...
I SEE...
ROO!
KASHIN KOJI.
YATOIN.
ARIUSU.
KODA.

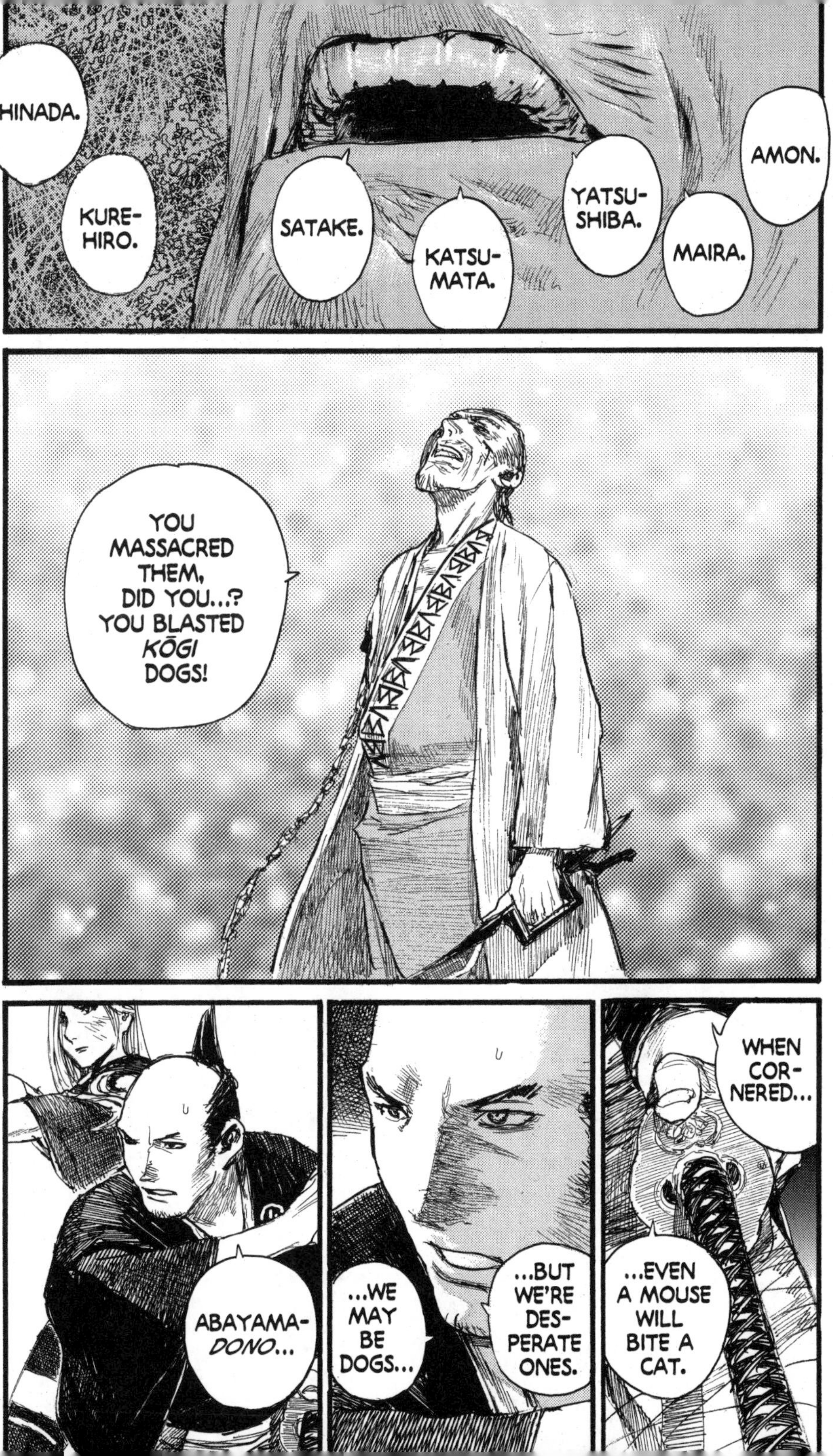
SHINADA.
KURE-HIRO.
SATAKE.
KATSU-MATA.
YATSU-SHIBA.
MAIRA.
AMON.
YOU MASSACRED THEM, DID YOU...? YOU BLASTED *KŌGI* DOGS!
ABAYAMA-*DONO*...
...WE MAY BE DOGS...
...BUT WE'RE DESPERATE ONES.
WHEN CORNERED...
...EVEN A MOUSE WILL BITE A CAT.

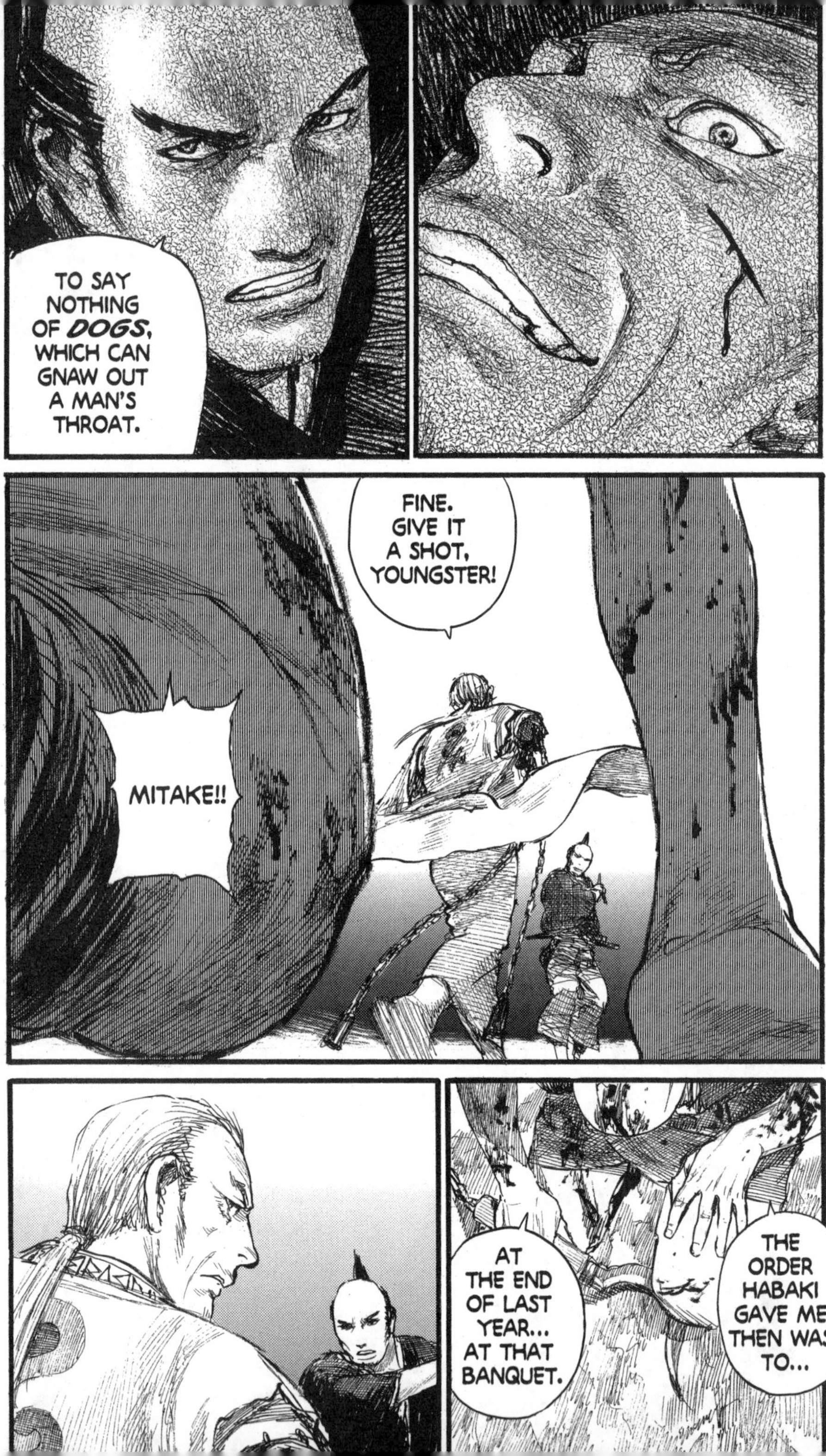
TO SAY NOTHING OF *DOGS*, WHICH CAN GNAW OUT A MAN'S THROAT.
FINE. GIVE IT A SHOT, YOUNGSTER!
MITAKE!!
AT THE END OF LAST YEAR... AT THAT BANQUET.
THE ORDER HABAKI GAVE ME THEN WAS TO...

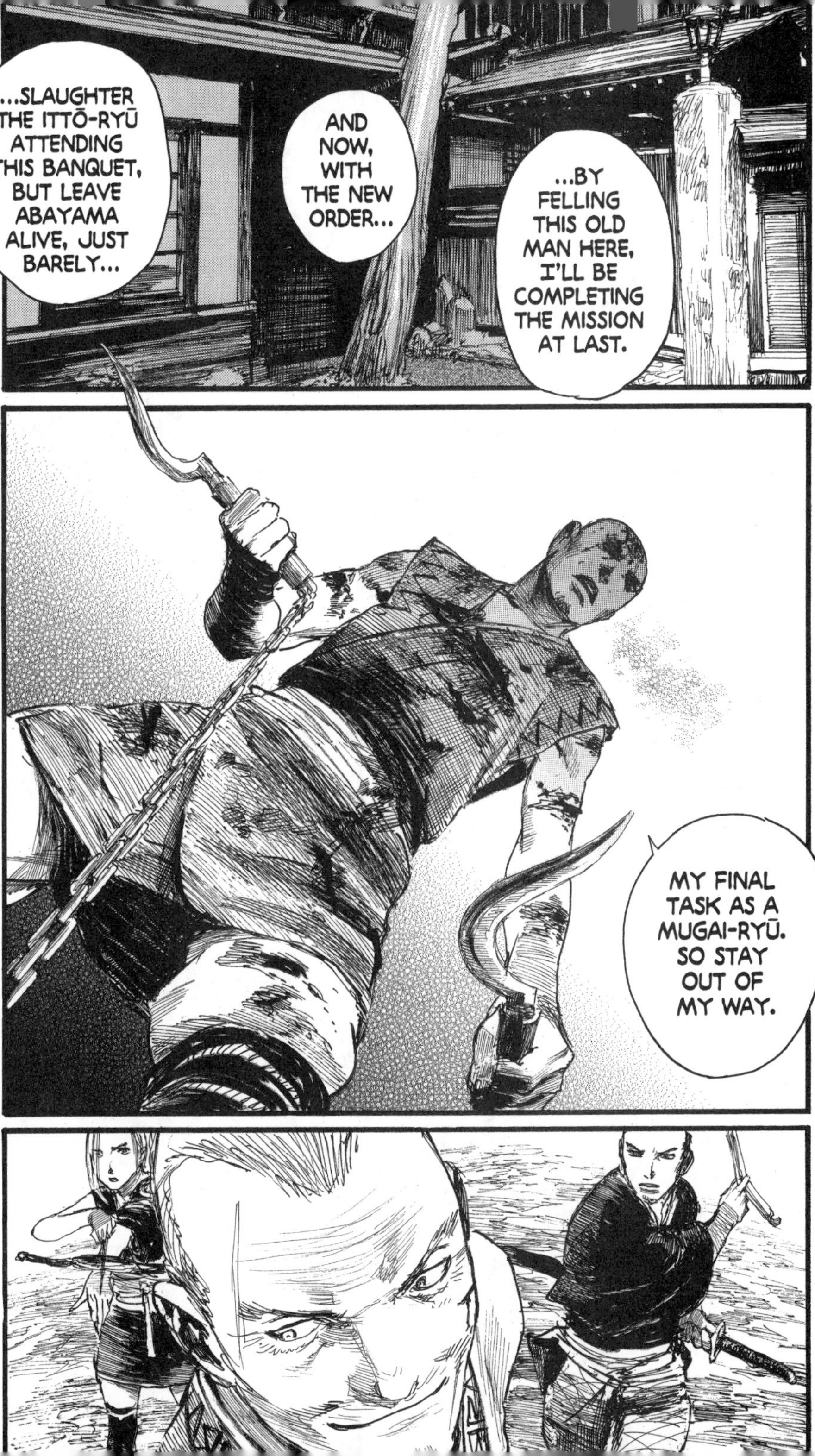
...SLAUGHTER THE ITTŌ-RYŪ ATTENDING THIS BANQUET, BUT LEAVE ABAYAMA ALIVE, JUST BARELY...
AND NOW, WITH THE NEW ORDER...
...BY FELLING THIS OLD MAN HERE, I'LL BE COMPLETING THE MISSION AT LAST.
MY FINAL TASK AS A MUGAI-RYŪ. SO STAY OUT OF MY WAY.

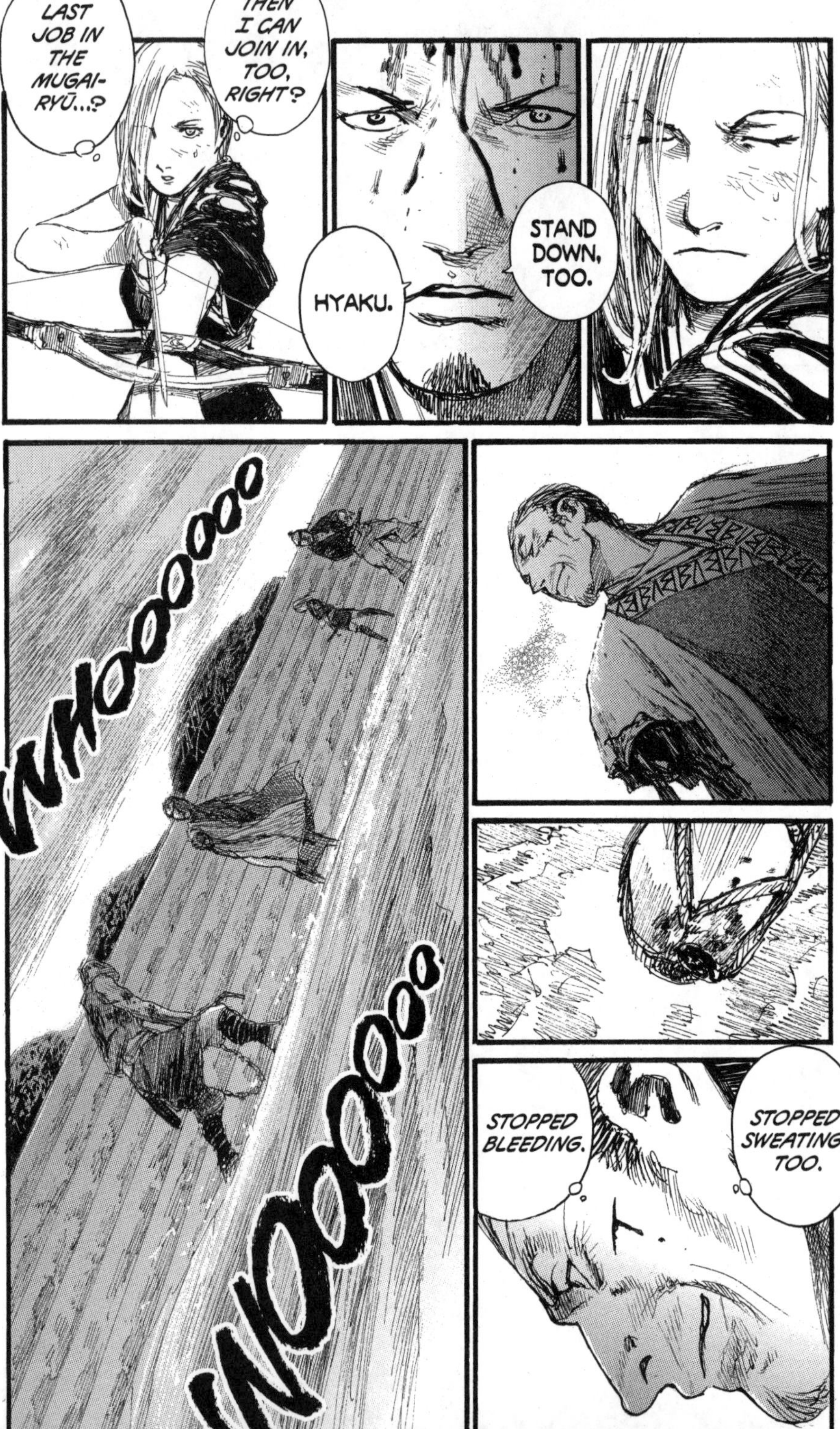
LAST JOB IN THE MUGAI-RYŪ...?
THEN I CAN JOIN IN, TOO, RIGHT?
HYAKU.
STAND DOWN, TOO.
WHOOOOOOO
WHOOOOOOO
STOPPED BLEEDING.
STOPPED SWEATING, TOO.

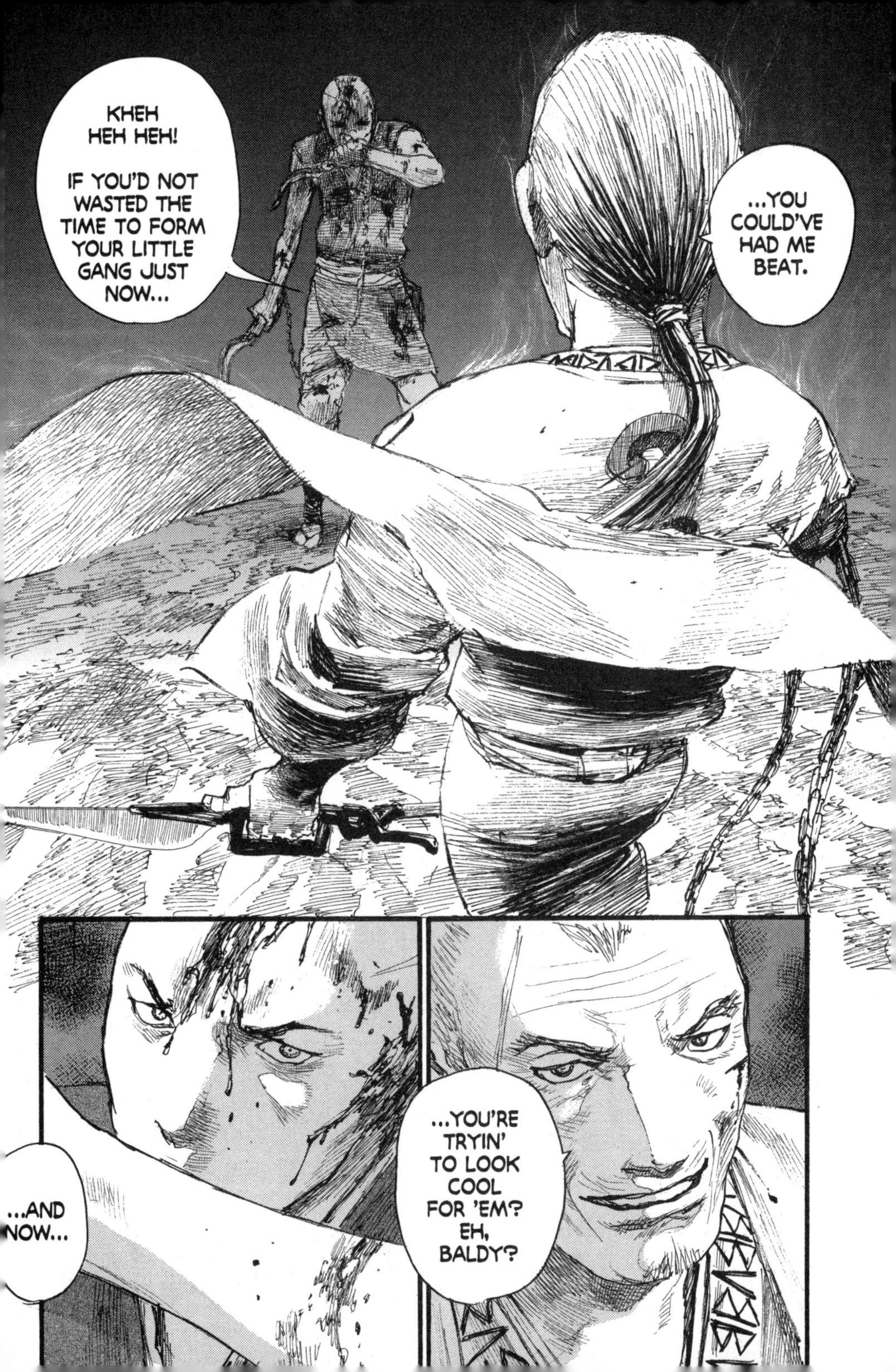
KHEH HEH HEH!
IF YOU'D NOT WASTED THE TIME TO FORM YOUR LITTLE GANG JUST NOW...
...YOU COULD'VE HAD ME BEAT.
...AND NOW...
...YOU'RE TRYIN' TO LOOK COOL FOR 'EM? EH, BALDY?

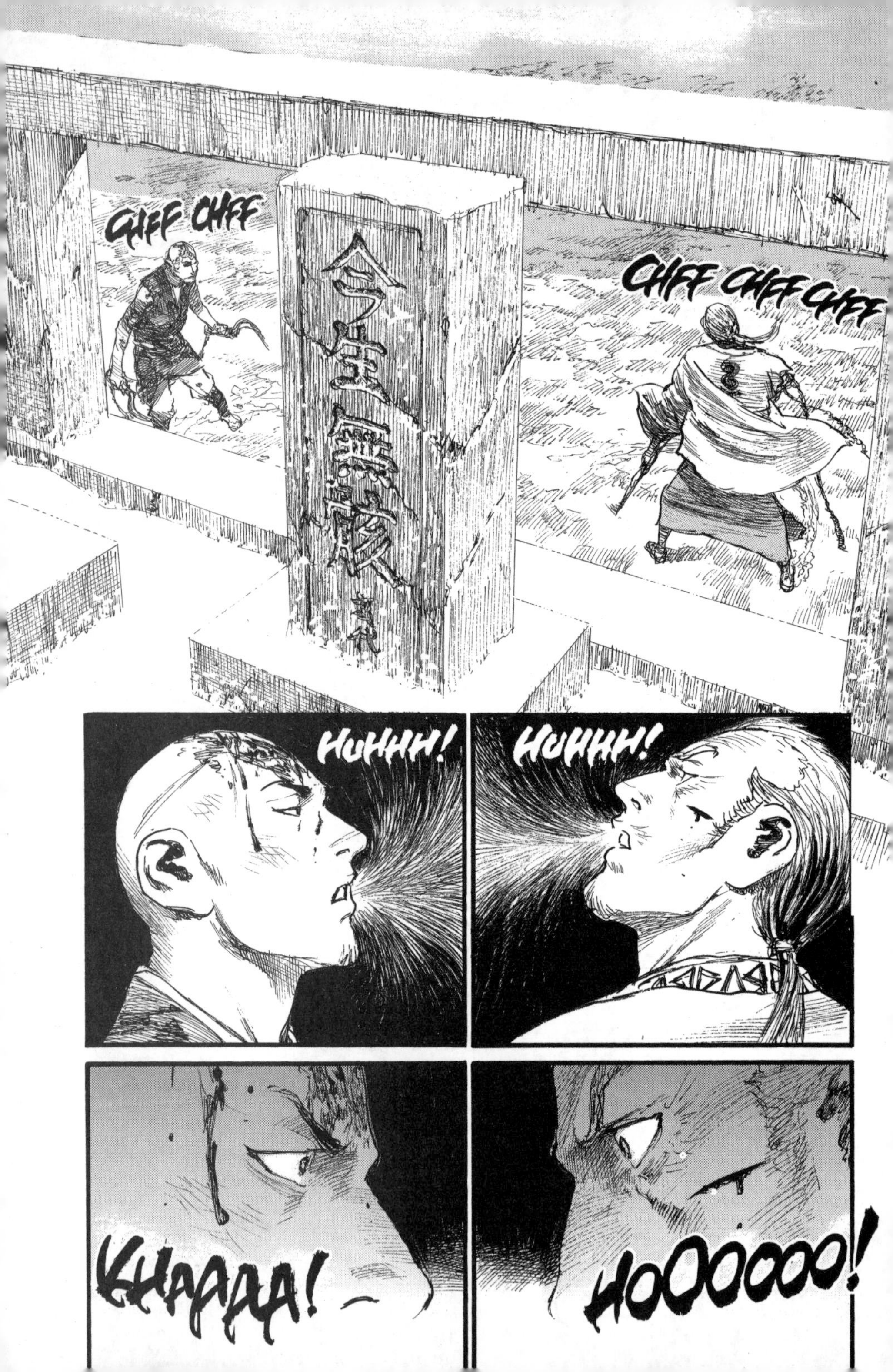
CHFF CHFF
CHFF CHFF CHFF
HUHHH!
HUHHH!
HOOOOOO!
KHAAAA!

GI--

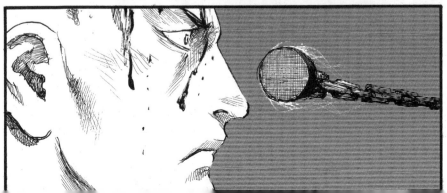

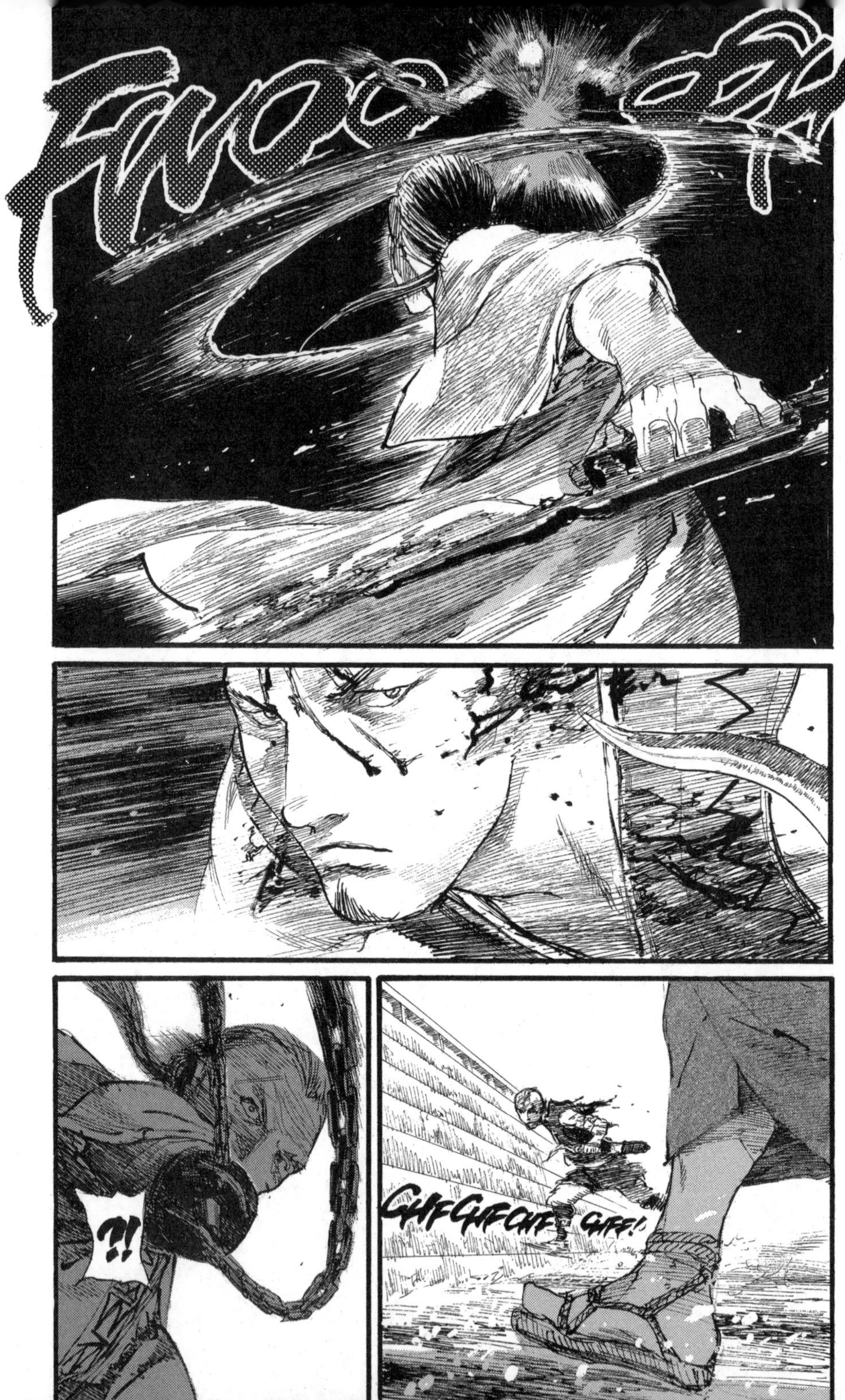
FWOOSH
?!
GHF GHF GHF GHF!

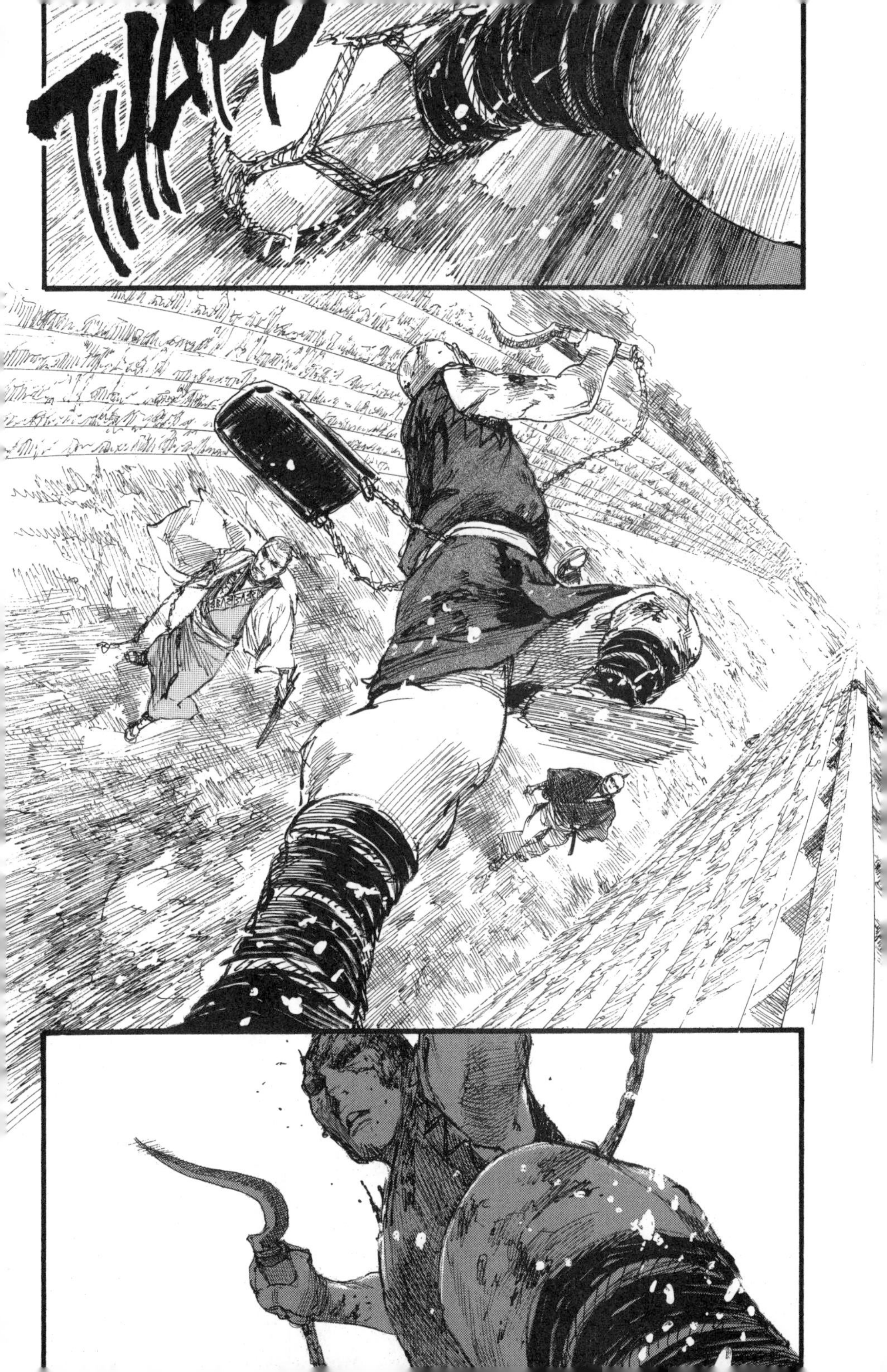
THAPP

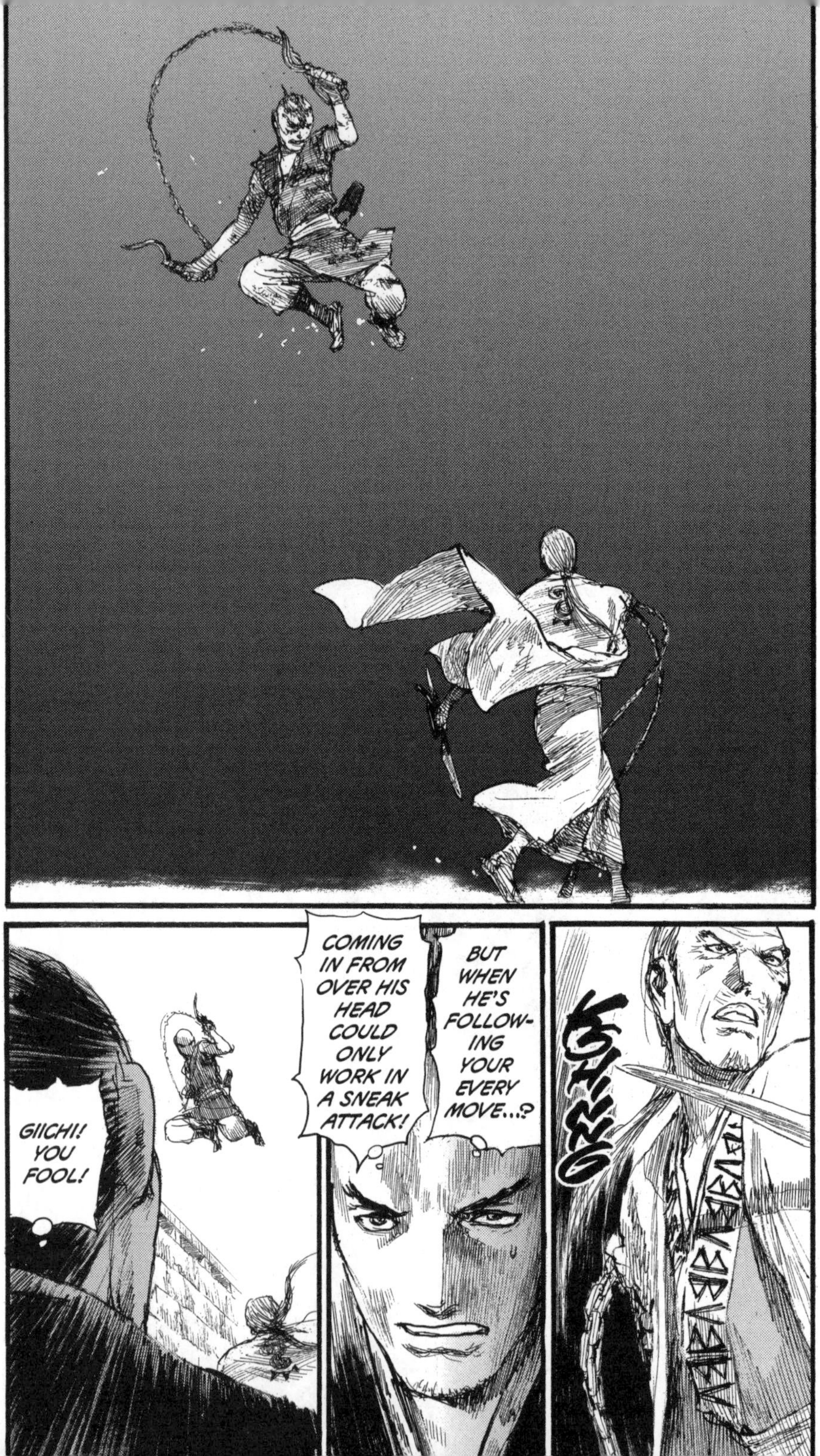
KSHING
COMING IN FROM OVER HIS HEAD COULD ONLY WORK IN A SNEAK ATTACK!
BUT WHEN HE'S FOLLOWING YOUR EVERY MOVE...?
GIICHI! YOU FOOL!

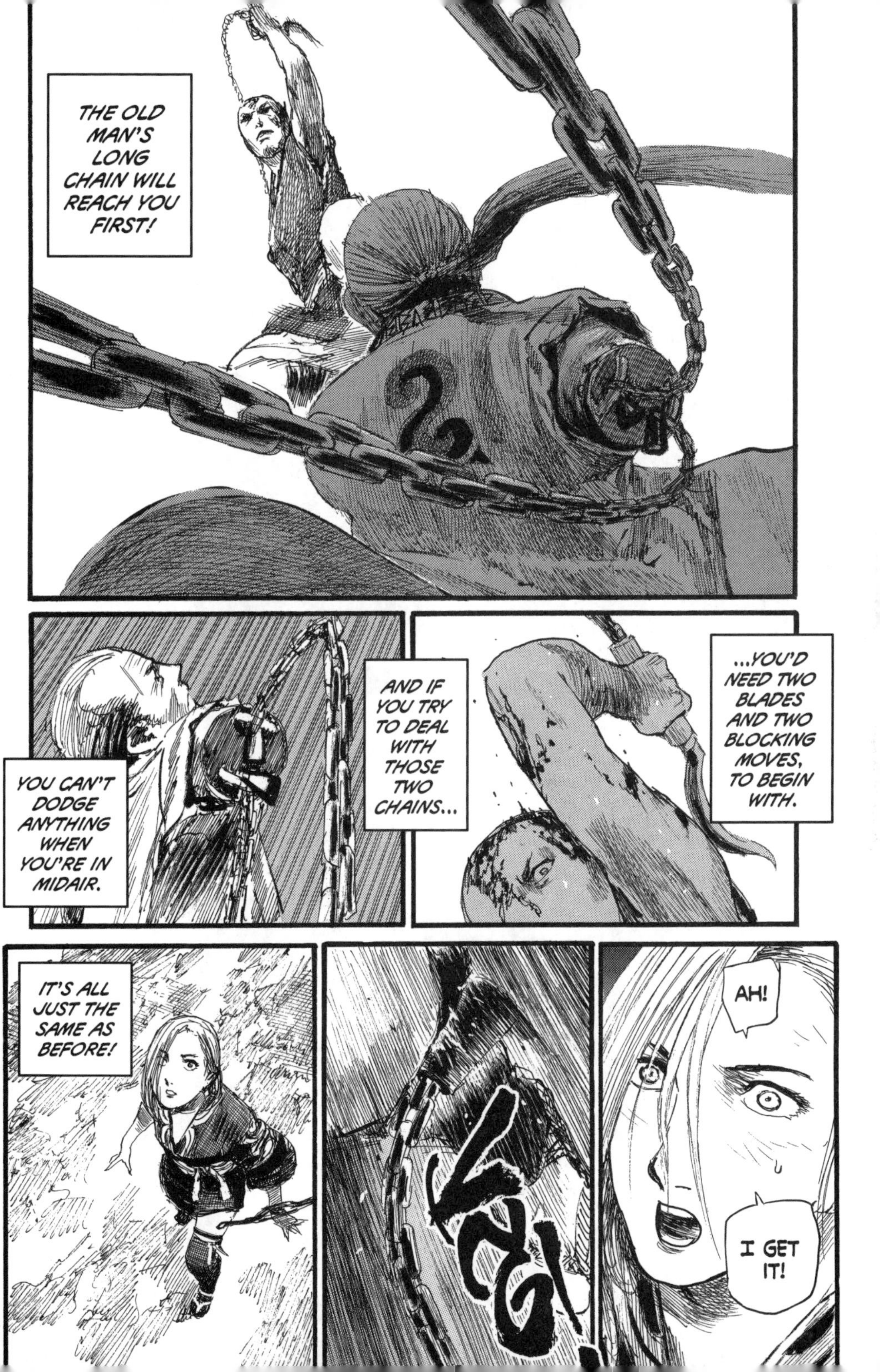
THE OLD MAN'S LONG CHAIN WILL REACH YOU FIRST!
YOU CAN'T DODGE ANYTHING WHEN YOU'RE IN MIDAIR.
AND IF YOU TRY TO DEAL WITH THOSE TWO CHAINS...
...YOU'D NEED TWO BLADES AND TWO BLOCKING MOVES, TO BEGIN WITH.
IT'S ALL JUST THE SAME AS BEFORE!
AH!
I GET IT!

THOSE CHAINS ARE WEAPONS THAT STRIKE AT THE ENEMY DIRECTLY AT HIS SIDE IN TWO HORIZONTAL ROWS.

BUT... IF THEY'RE SWUNG VERTICALLY TO CATCH AN ENEMY OVERHEAD...

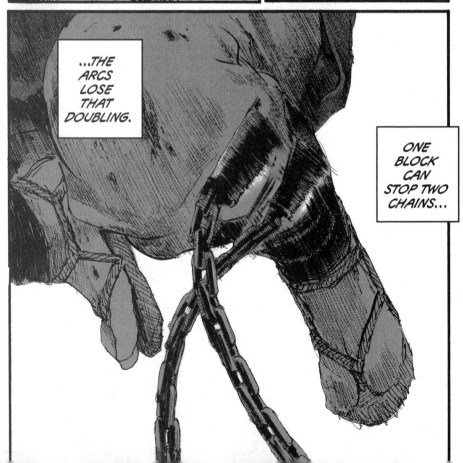

...THE ARCS LOSE THAT DOUBLING.

ONE BLOCK CAN STOP TWO CHAINS...

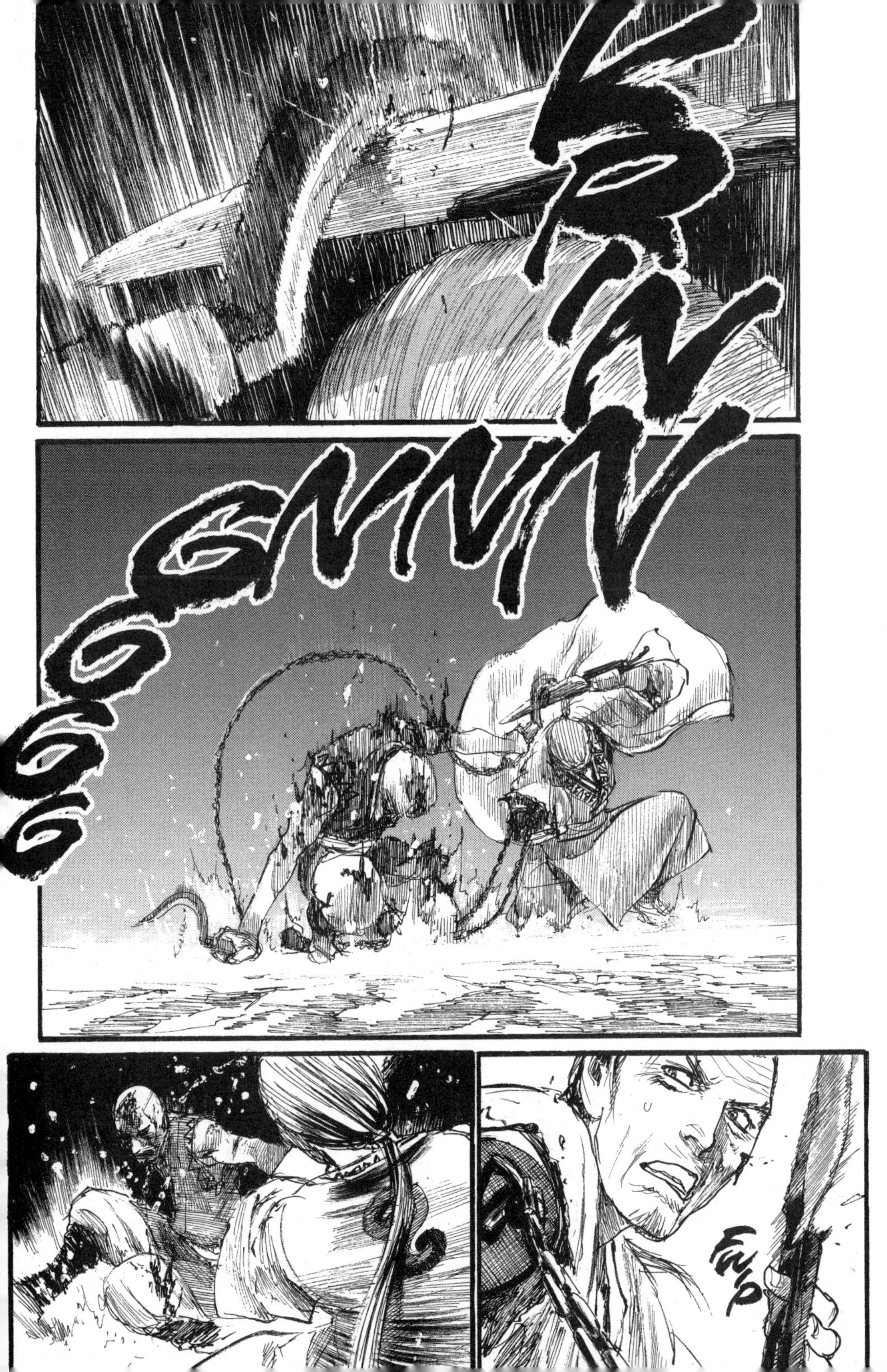
KRANNNNGGGG
FWIP

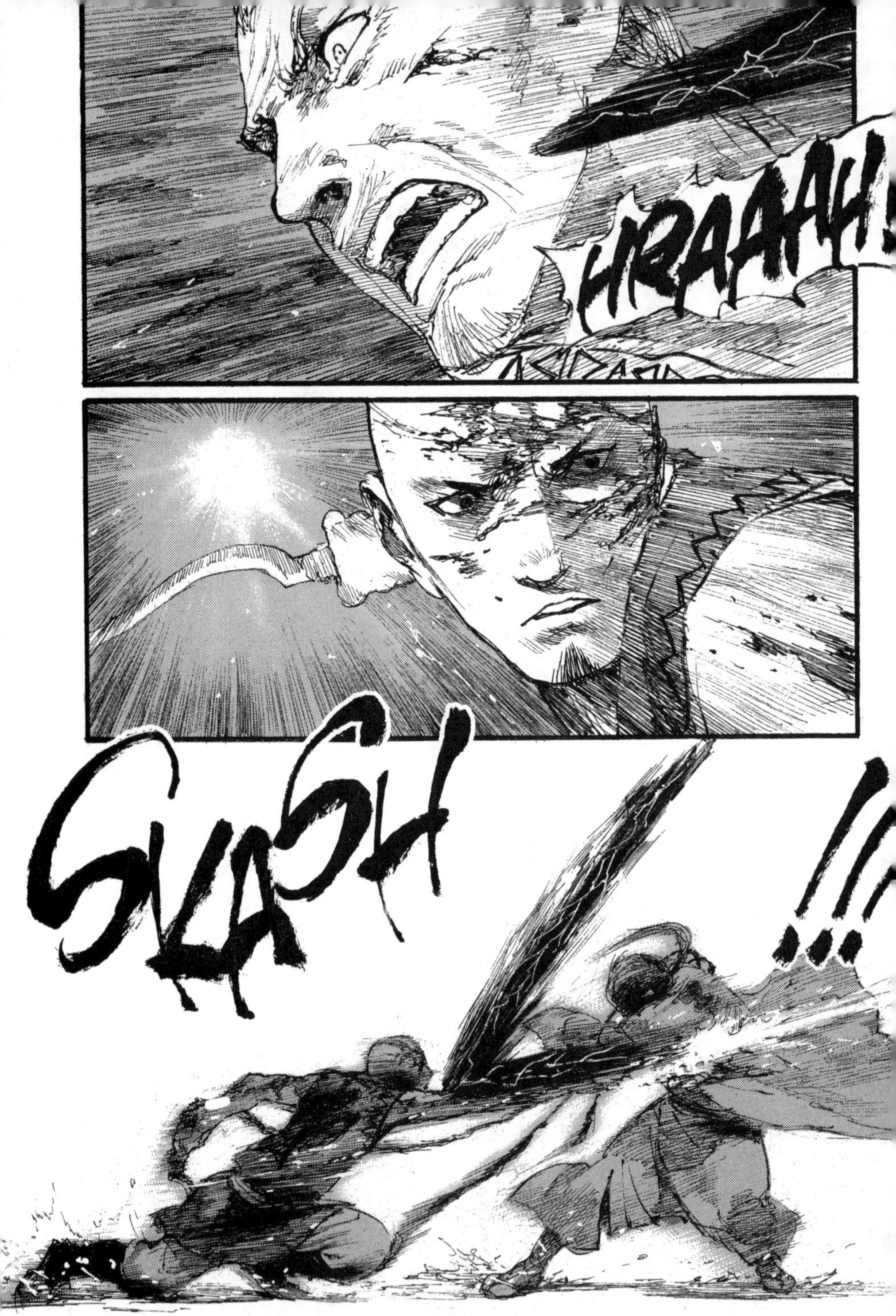
HRAAAH!
SLASH!!!

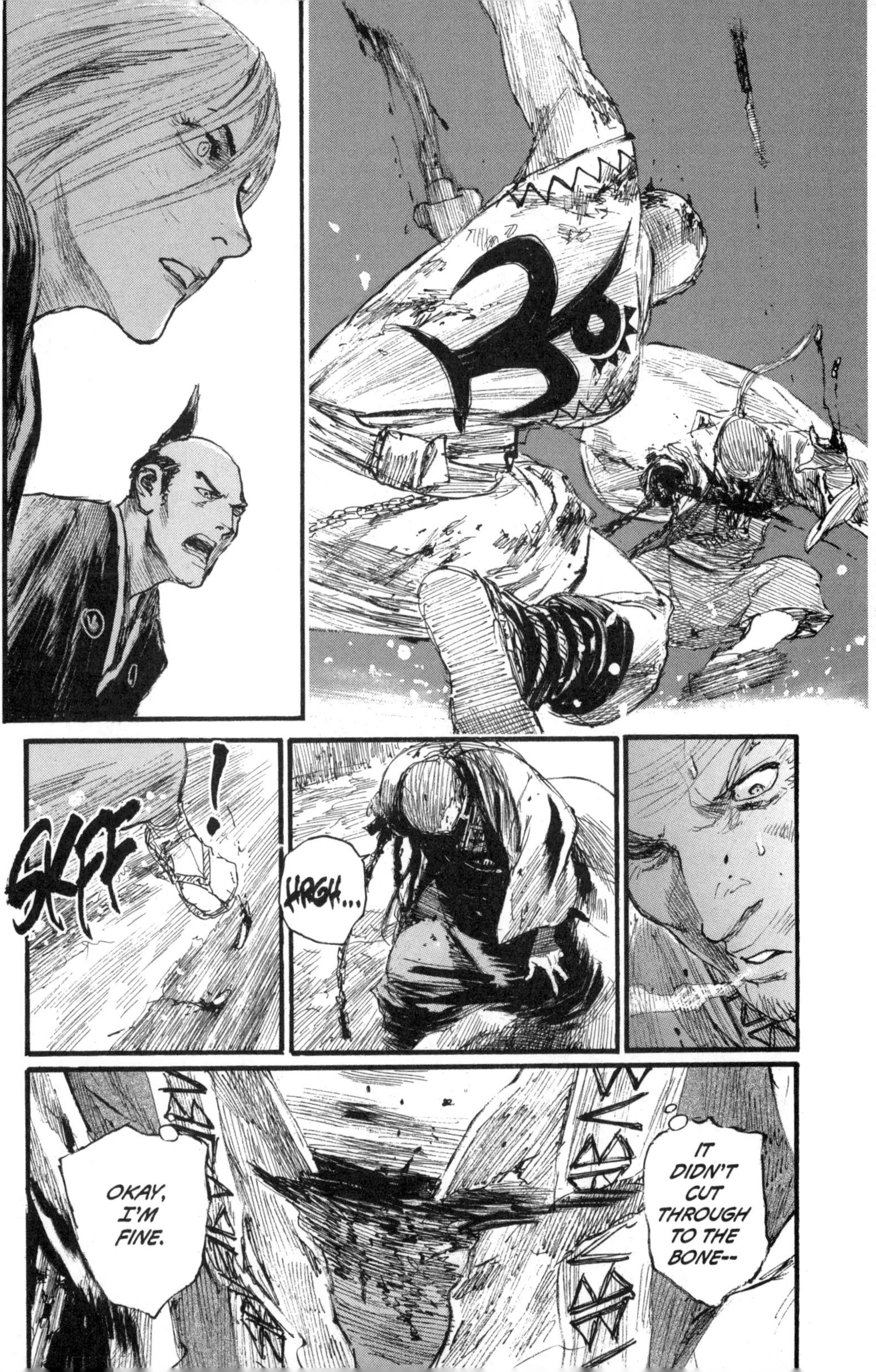
SKFF
!
URGH...
IT DIDN'T CUT THROUGH TO THE BONE--
OKAY, I'M FINE.

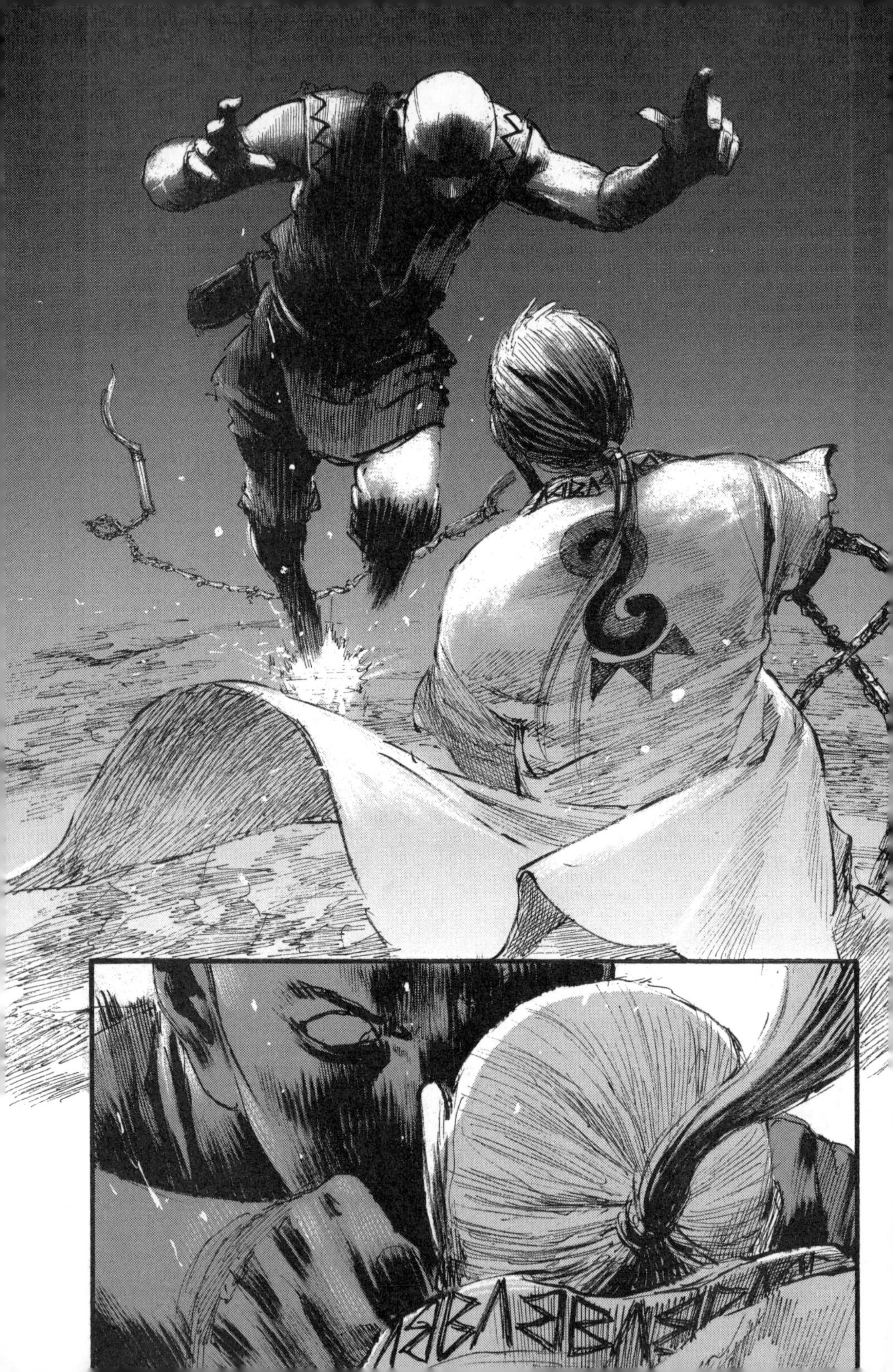

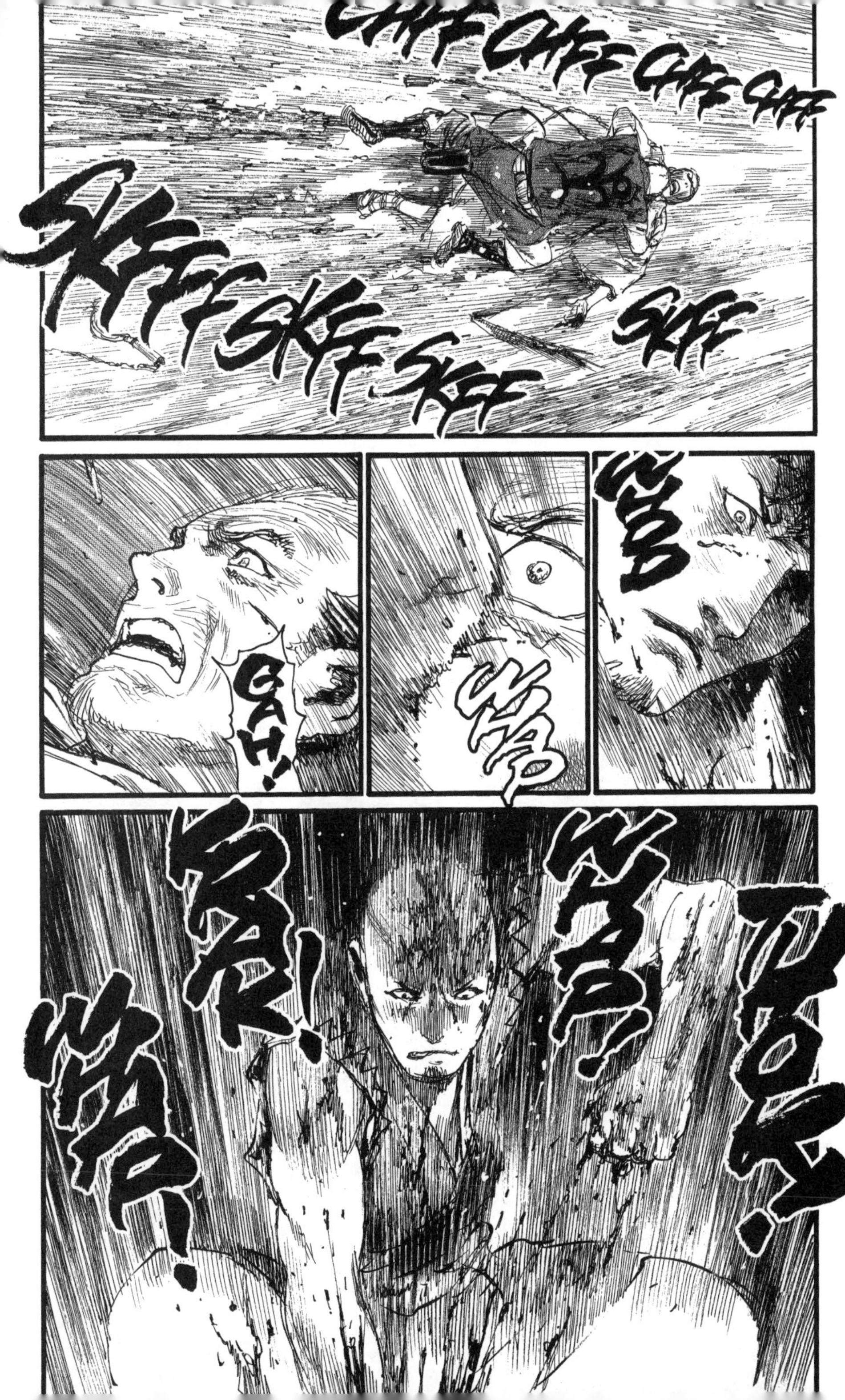
CHFF CHFF CHFF CHFF
SKFF SKFF SKFF SKFF
WHAP
GAH!
THOK!
WHAP!
WHAP!

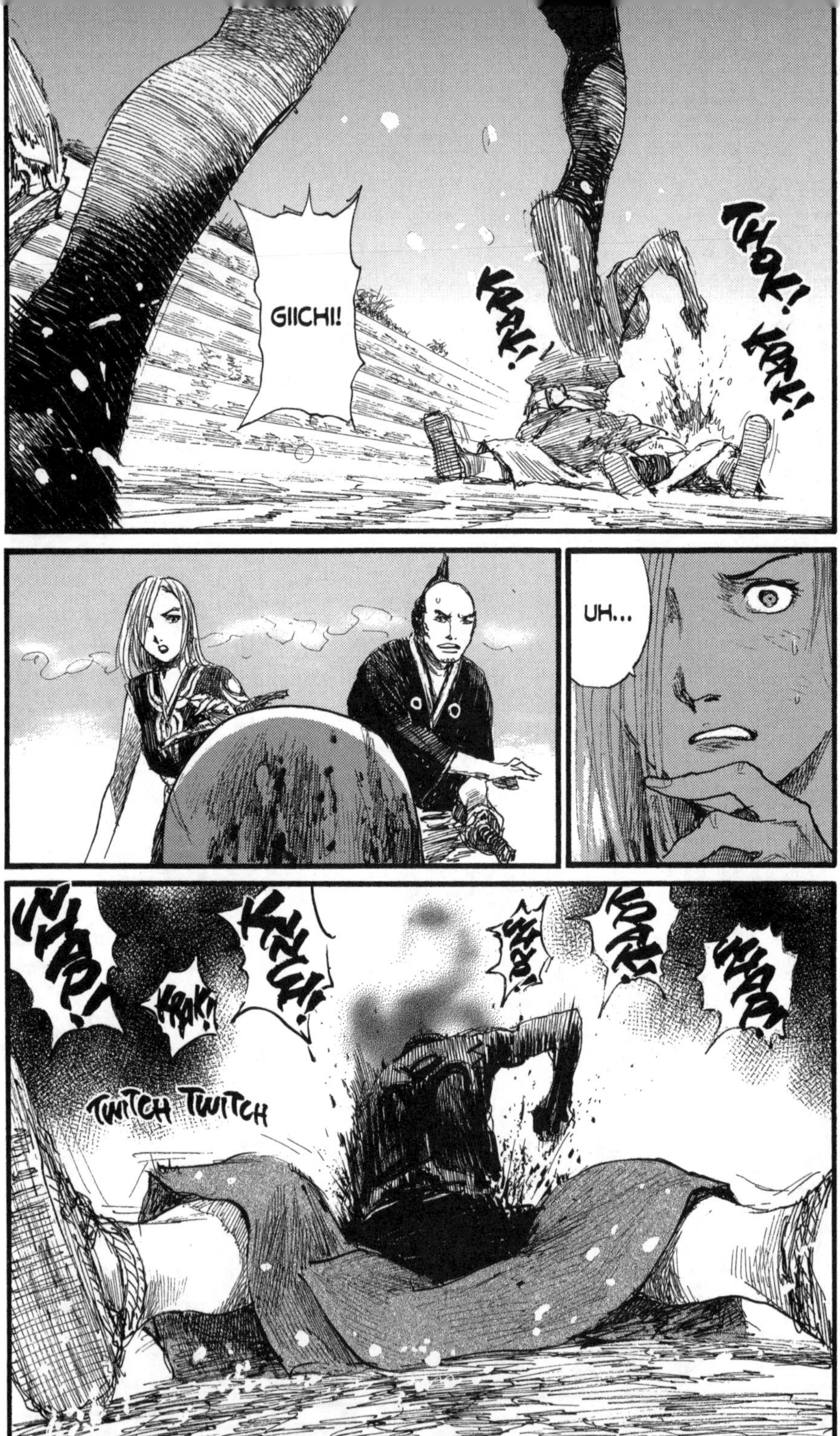
THOK!
KRAK!
KRAK!
GIICHI!
UH...
KRUNCH!
KRAK!
SNAP!
TWITCH TWITCH

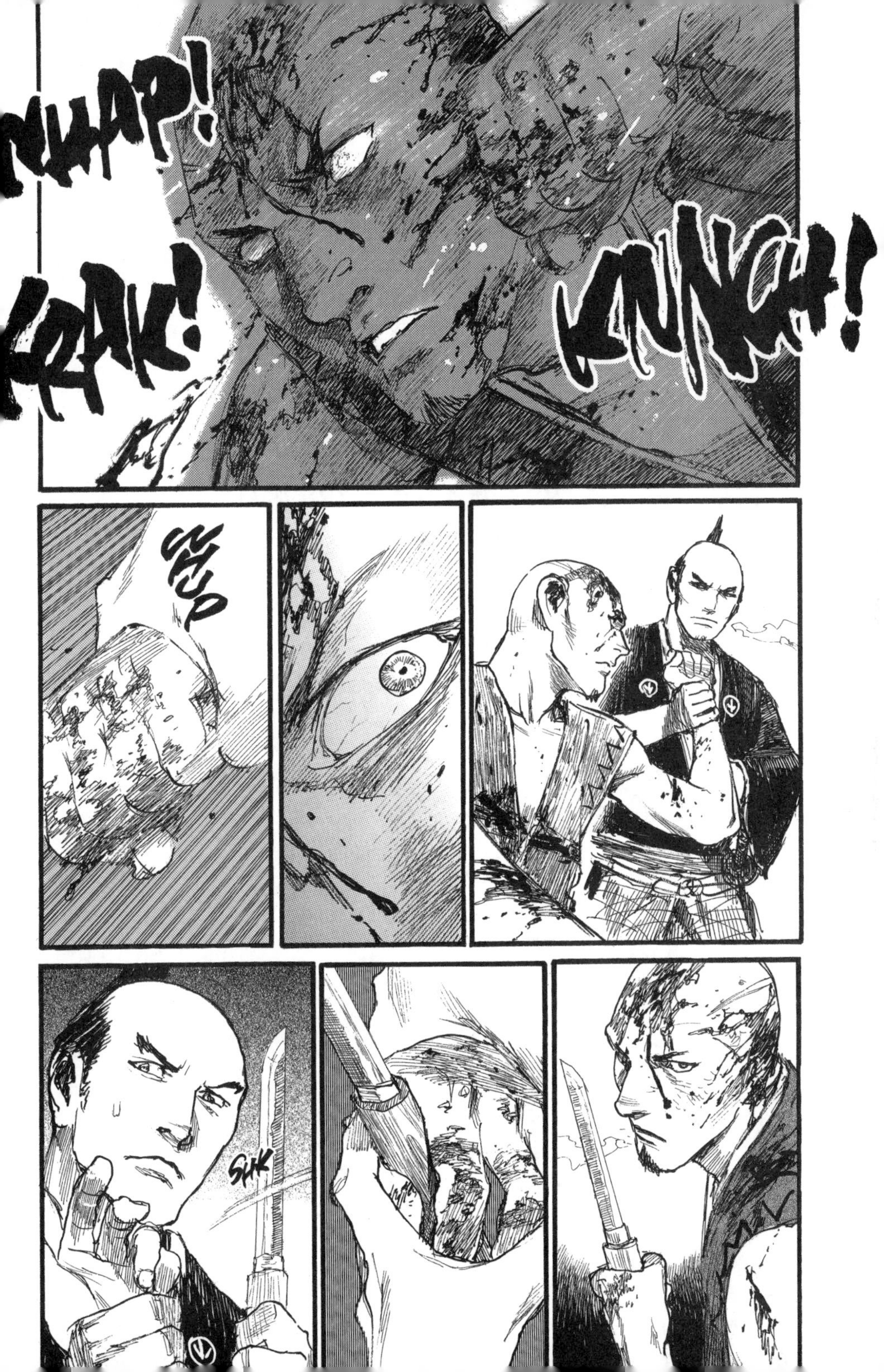
KRUNCH!
WHAP!
KRAK!
SHUP
SLIK

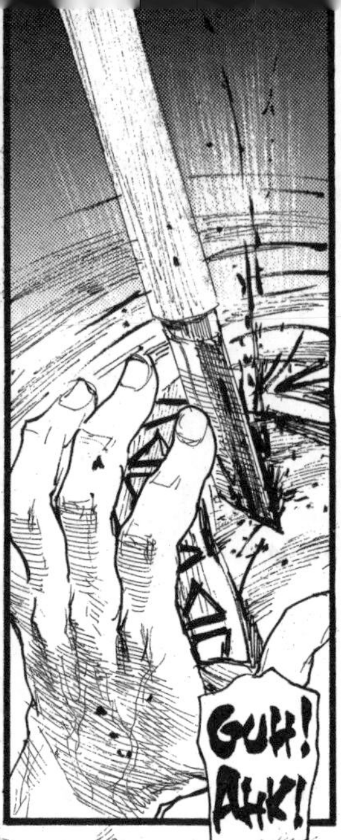
GUH! AHK!
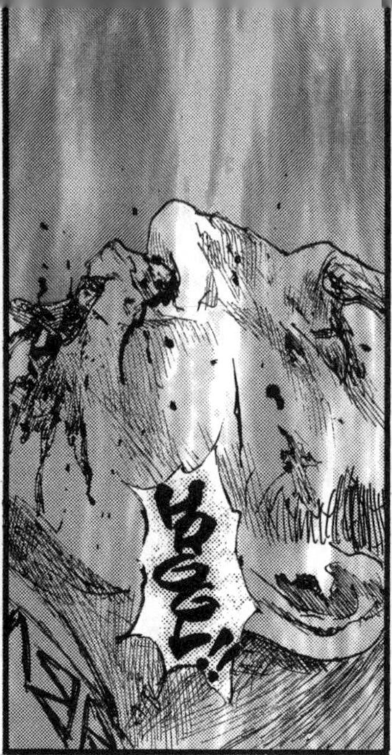
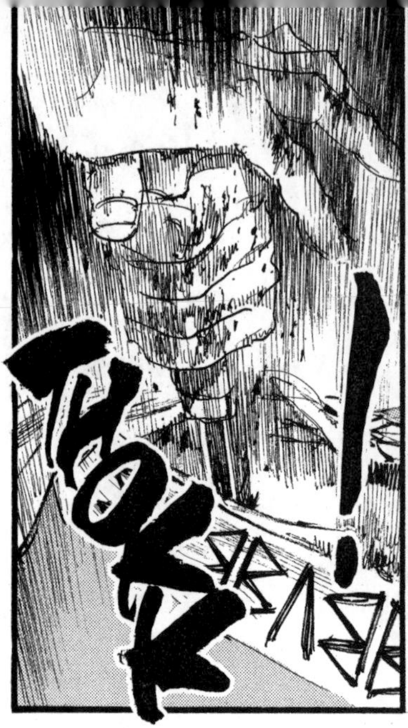
TOK!
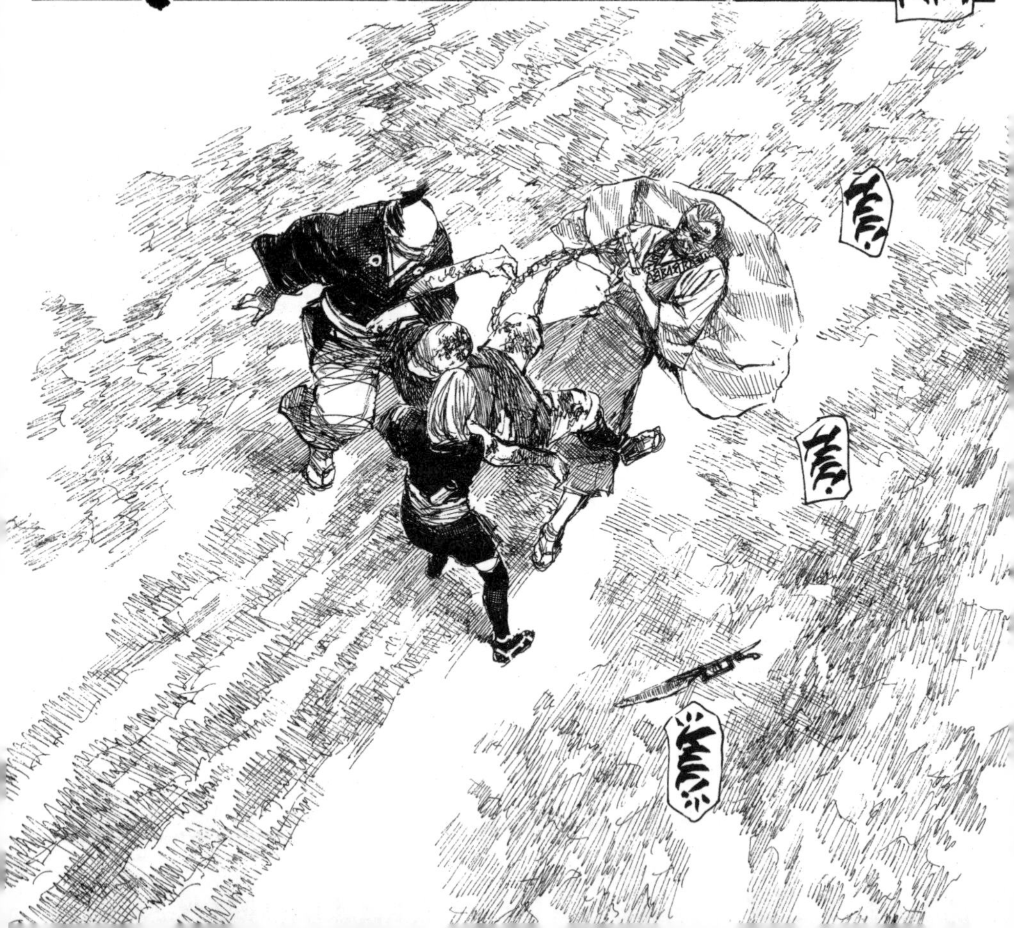
HEF!
HEF!

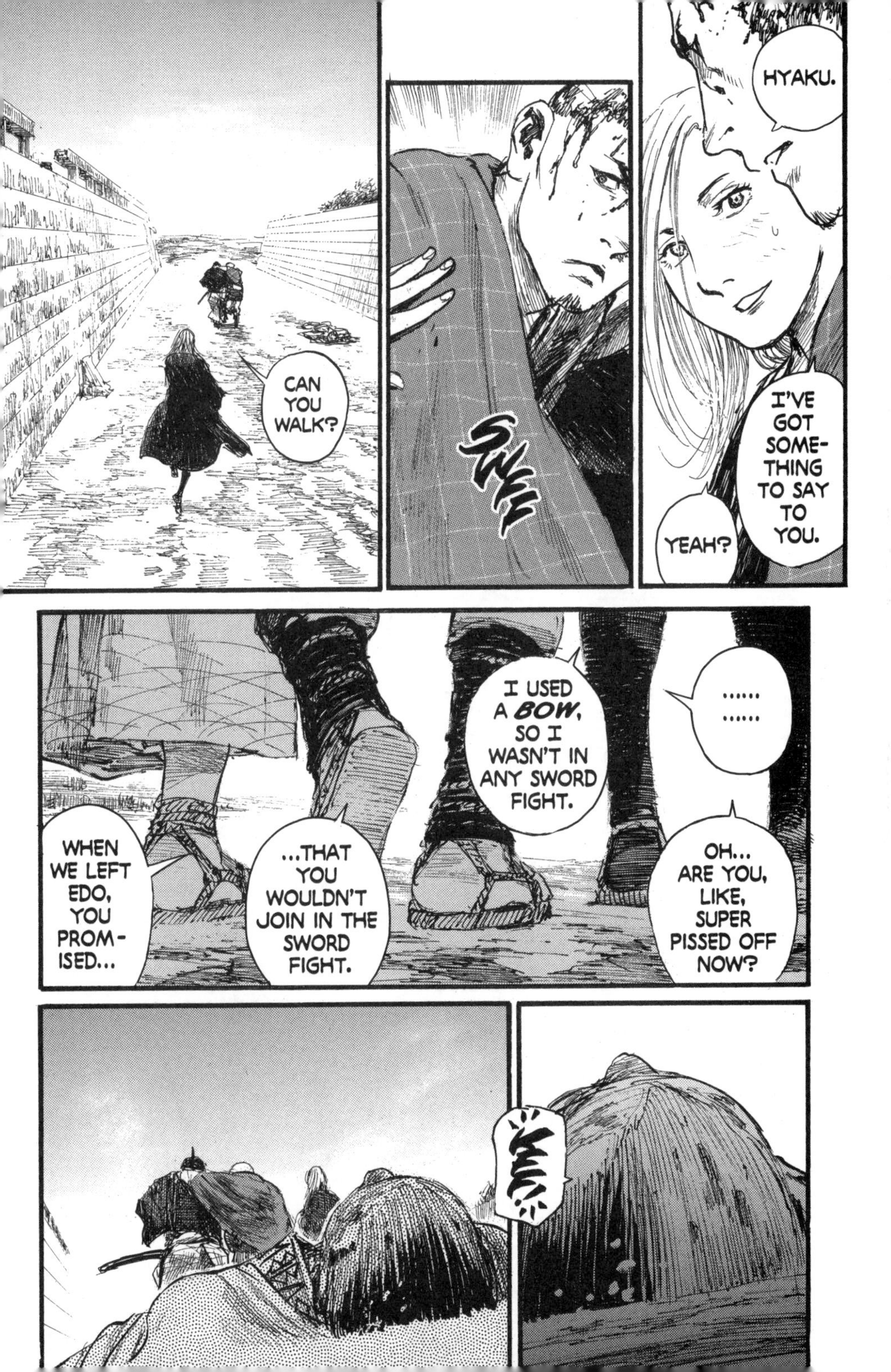
CAN YOU WALK?
HYAKU.
YEAH?
I'VE GOT SOMETHING TO SAY TO YOU.
WHEN WE LEFT EDO, YOU PROMISED...
...THAT YOU WOULDN'T JOIN IN THE SWORD FIGHT.
I USED A *BOW*, SO I WASN'T IN ANY SWORD FIGHT.
......
......
OH... ARE YOU, LIKE, SUPER PISSED OFF NOW?

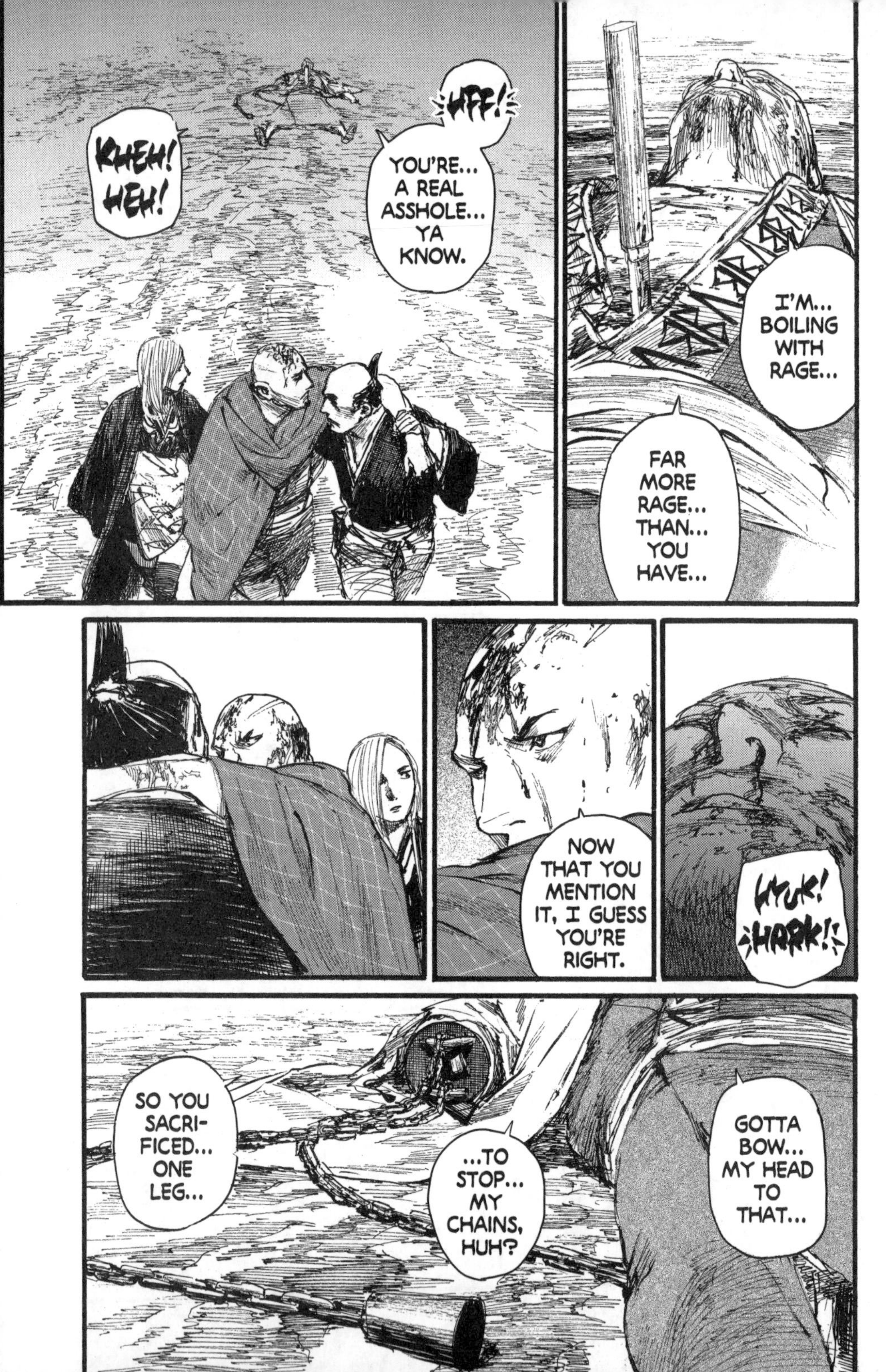
I'M... BOILING WITH RAGE...
FAR MORE RAGE... THAN... YOU HAVE...
HFF!
YOU'RE... A REAL ASSHOLE... YA KNOW.
KHEH! HEH!
HYUK! HARK!
NOW THAT YOU MENTION IT, I GUESS YOU'RE RIGHT.
SO YOU SACRIFICED... ONE LEG...
...TO STOP... MY CHAINS, HUH?
GOTTA BOW... MY HEAD TO THAT...

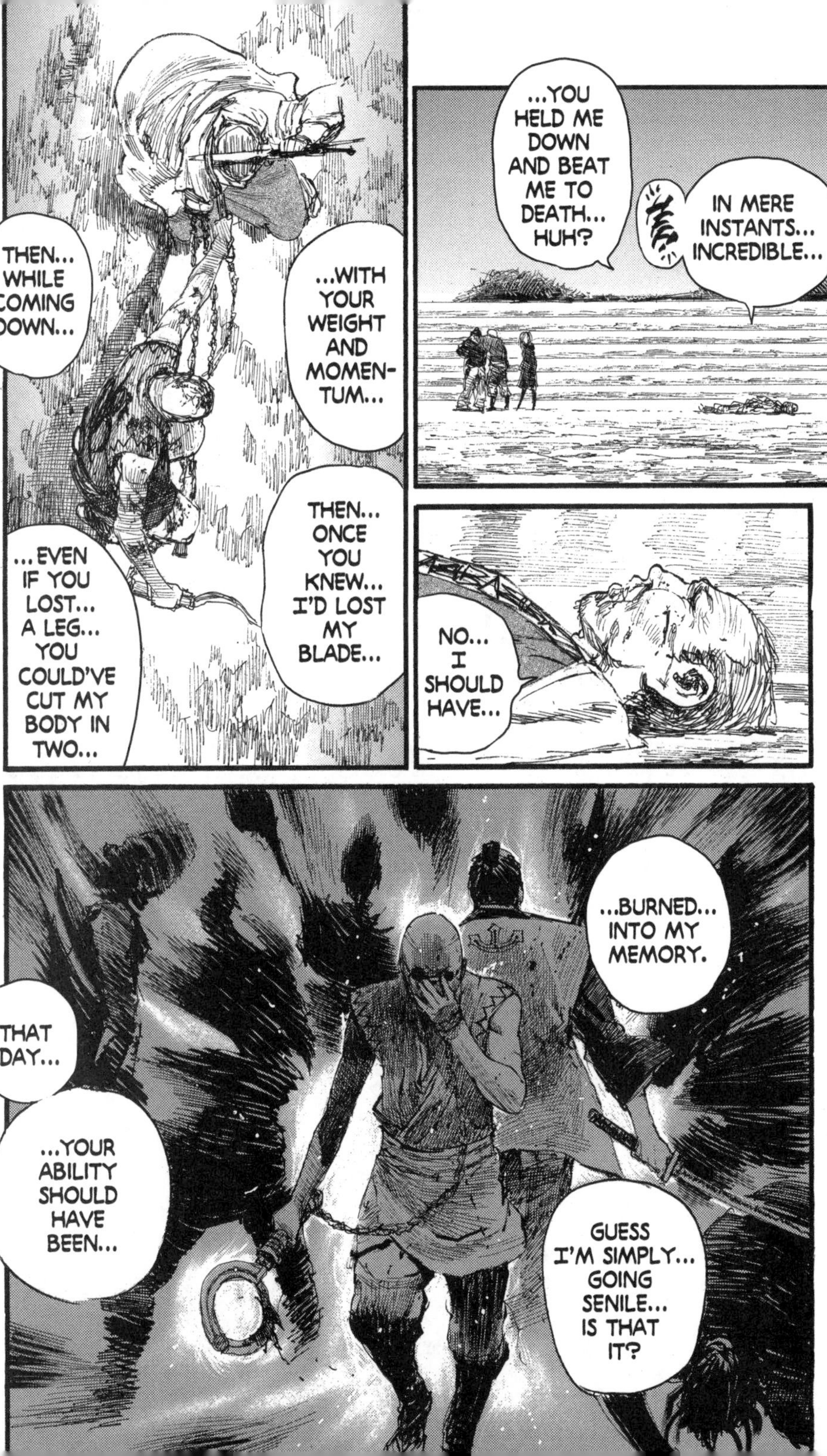
IN MERE INSTANTS... INCREDIBLE...
...YOU HELD ME DOWN AND BEAT ME TO DEATH... HUH?
NO... I SHOULD HAVE...
THEN... WHILE COMING DOWN...
...WITH YOUR WEIGHT AND MOMENTUM...
THEN... ONCE YOU KNEW... I'D LOST MY BLADE...
...EVEN IF YOU LOST... A LEG... YOU COULD'VE CUT MY BODY IN TWO...
THAT DAY...
...YOUR ABILITY SHOULD HAVE BEEN...
...BURNED... INTO MY MEMORY.
GUESS I'M SIMPLY... GOING SENILE... IS THAT IT?

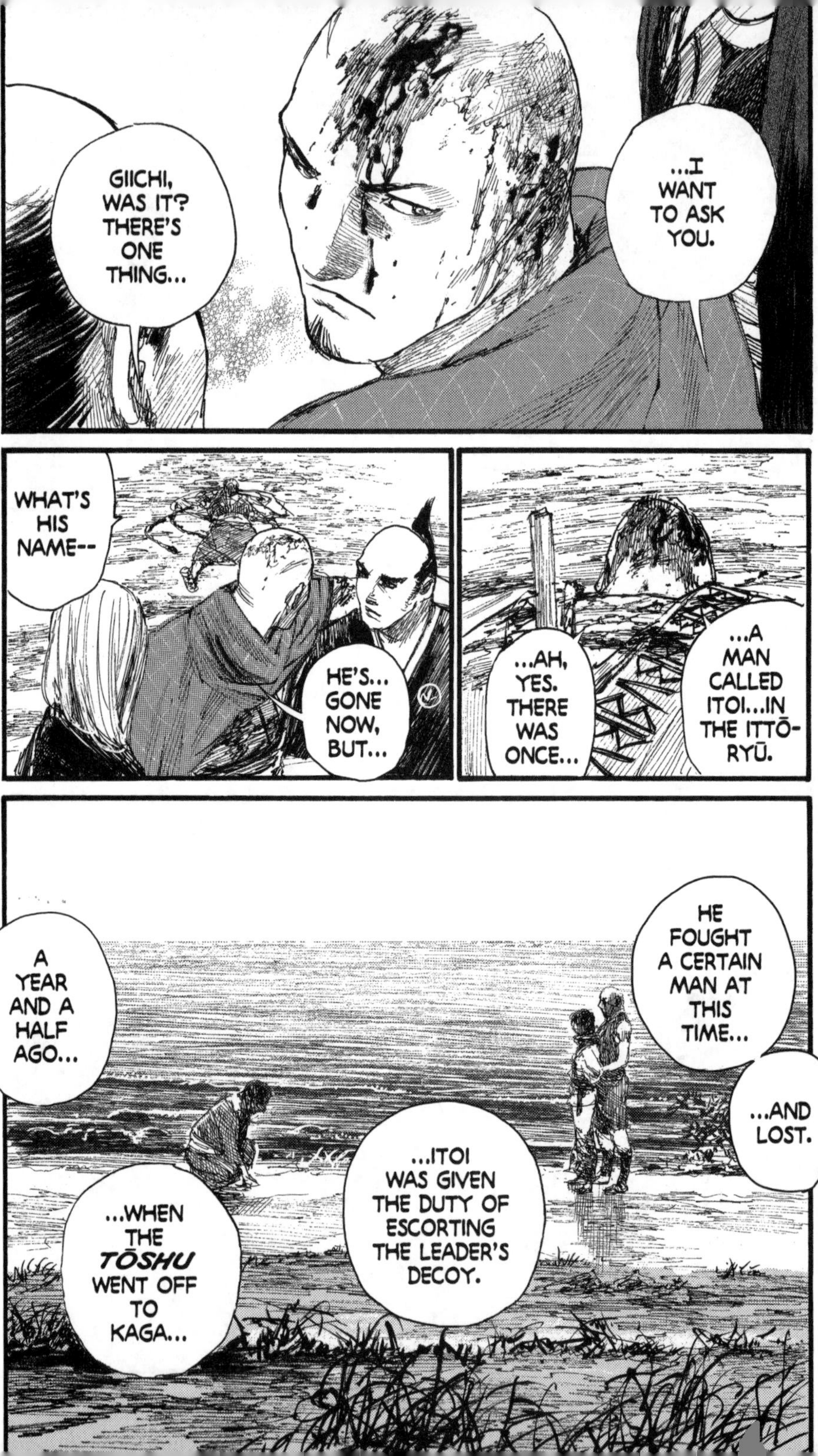
GIICHI, WAS IT? THERE'S ONE THING...
...I WANT TO ASK YOU.
WHAT'S HIS NAME--
HE'S... GONE NOW, BUT...
...A MAN CALLED ITOI...IN THE ITTŌ-RYŪ.
...AH, YES. THERE WAS ONCE...
A YEAR AND A HALF AGO...
...WHEN THE *TŌSHU* WENT OFF TO KAGA...
...ITOI WAS GIVEN THE DUTY OF ESCORTING THE LEADER'S DECOY.
HE FOUGHT A CERTAIN MAN AT THIS TIME...
...AND LOST.

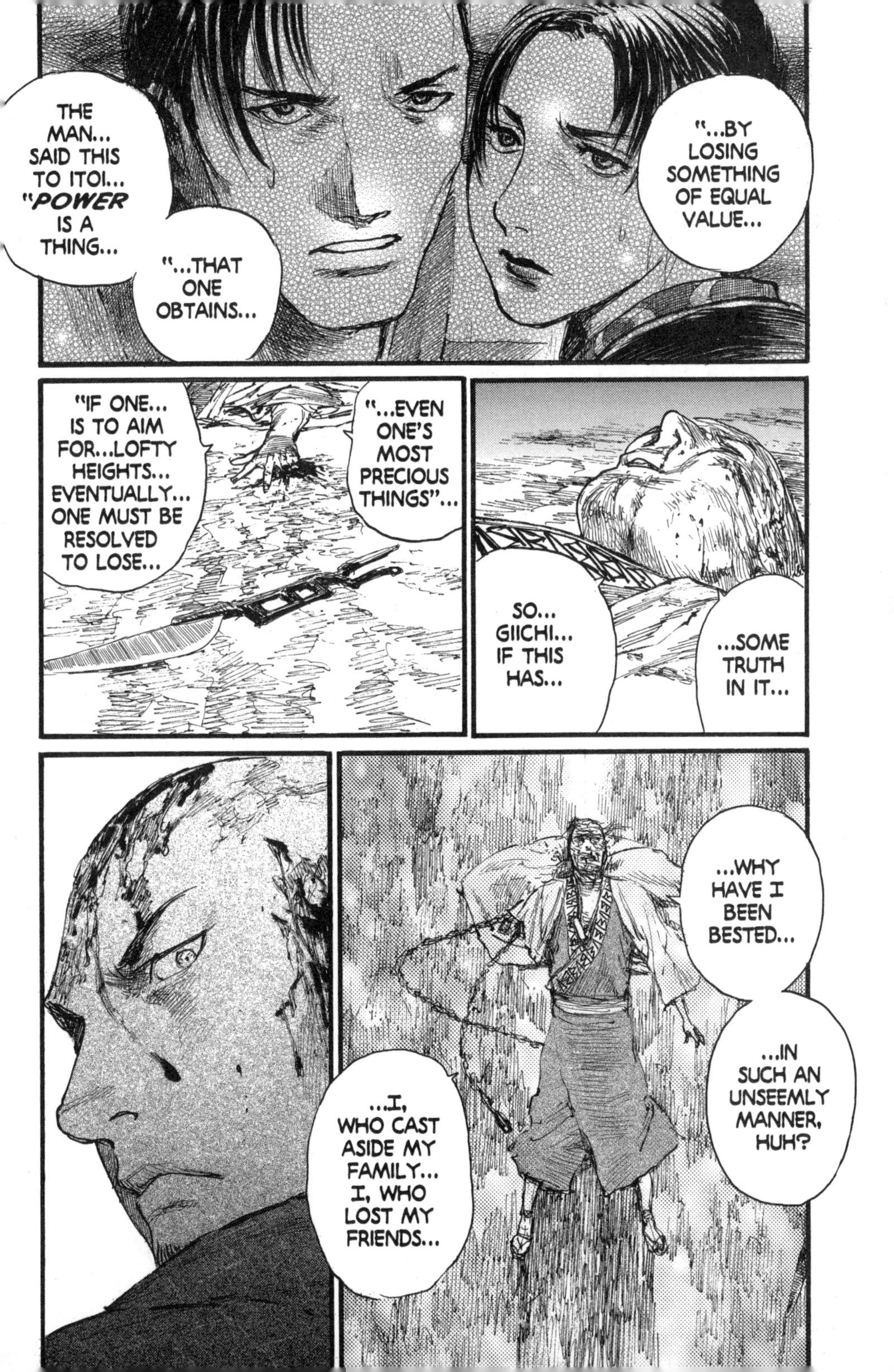
THE MAN... SAID THIS TO ITOI... "*POWER* IS A THING...
"...THAT ONE OBTAINS...
"...BY LOSING SOMETHING OF EQUAL VALUE...
"IF ONE... IS TO AIM FOR...LOFTY HEIGHTS... EVENTUALLY... ONE MUST BE RESOLVED TO LOSE...
"...EVEN ONE'S MOST PRECIOUS THINGS"...
SO... GIICHI... IF THIS HAS...
...SOME TRUTH IN IT...
...I, WHO CAST ASIDE MY FAMILY... I, WHO LOST MY FRIENDS...
...WHY HAVE I BEEN BESTED...
...IN SUCH AN UNSEEMLY MANNER, HUH?

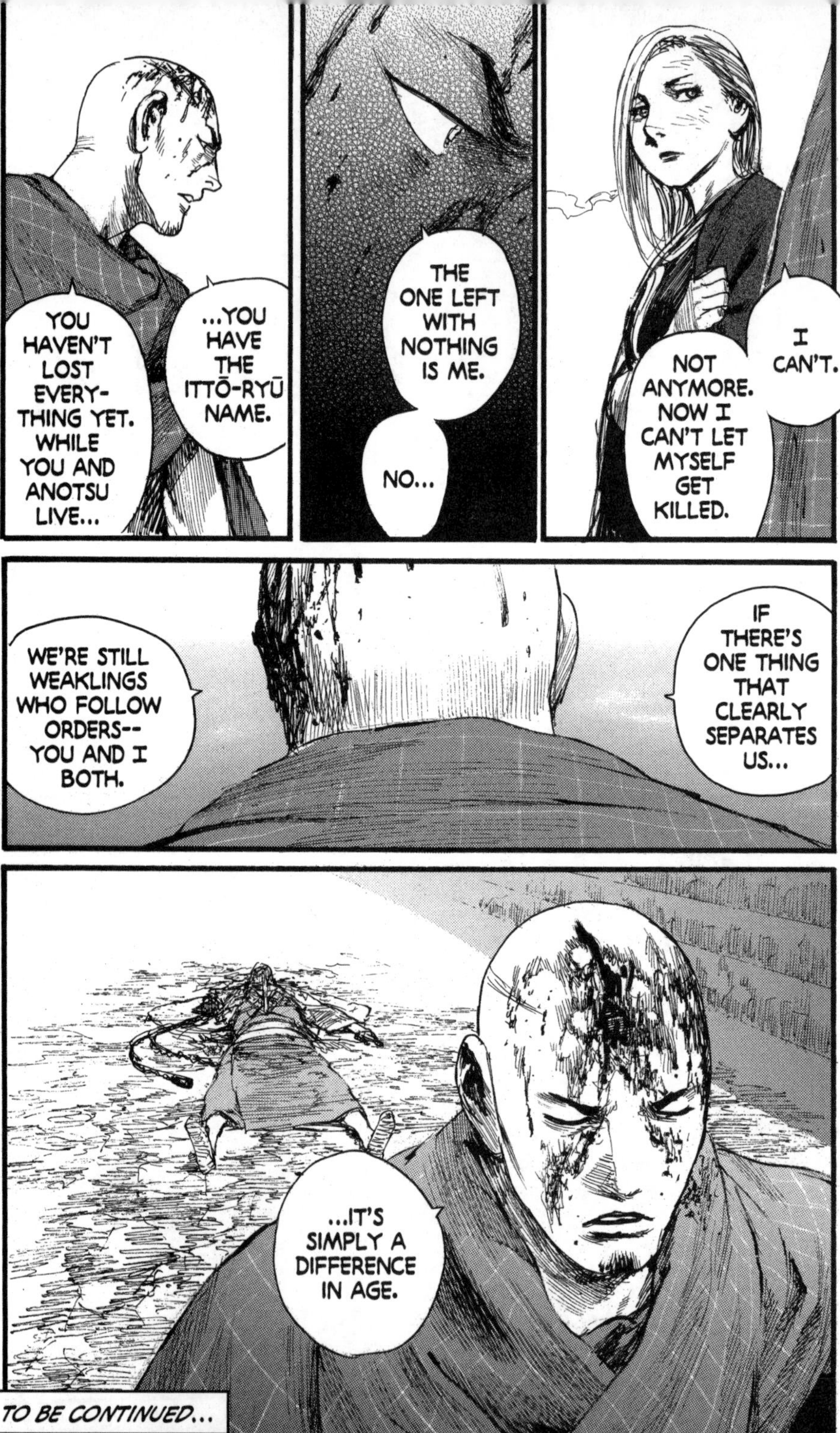
I CAN'T.
NOT ANYMORE. NOW I CAN'T LET MYSELF GET KILLED.
THE ONE LEFT WITH NOTHING IS ME.
NO...
...YOU HAVE THE ITTŌ-RYŪ NAME.
YOU HAVEN'T LOST EVERY-THING YET. WHILE YOU AND ANOTSU LIVE...
WE'RE STILL WEAKLINGS WHO FOLLOW ORDERS-- YOU AND I BOTH.
IF THERE'S ONE THING THAT CLEARLY SEPARATES US...
...IT'S SIMPLY A DIFFERENCE IN AGE.
TO BE CONTINUED...

—— BONUS SECTION ——

TAKEN FROM ACT 178: "ABAYAMA'S CASSANDRA"

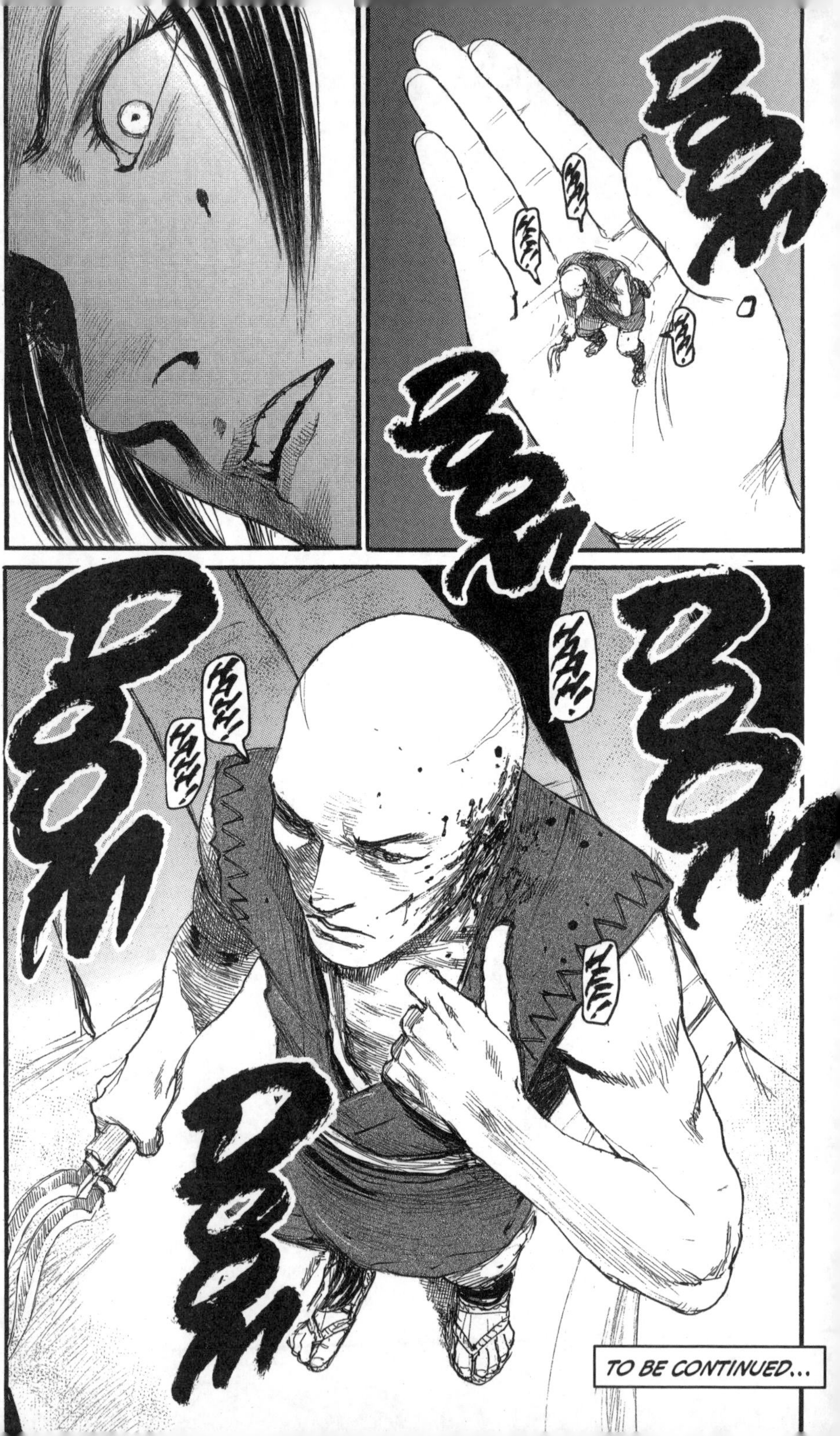
DOOM
DOOM
DOOM
DOOM
DOOM
TO BE CONTINUED...

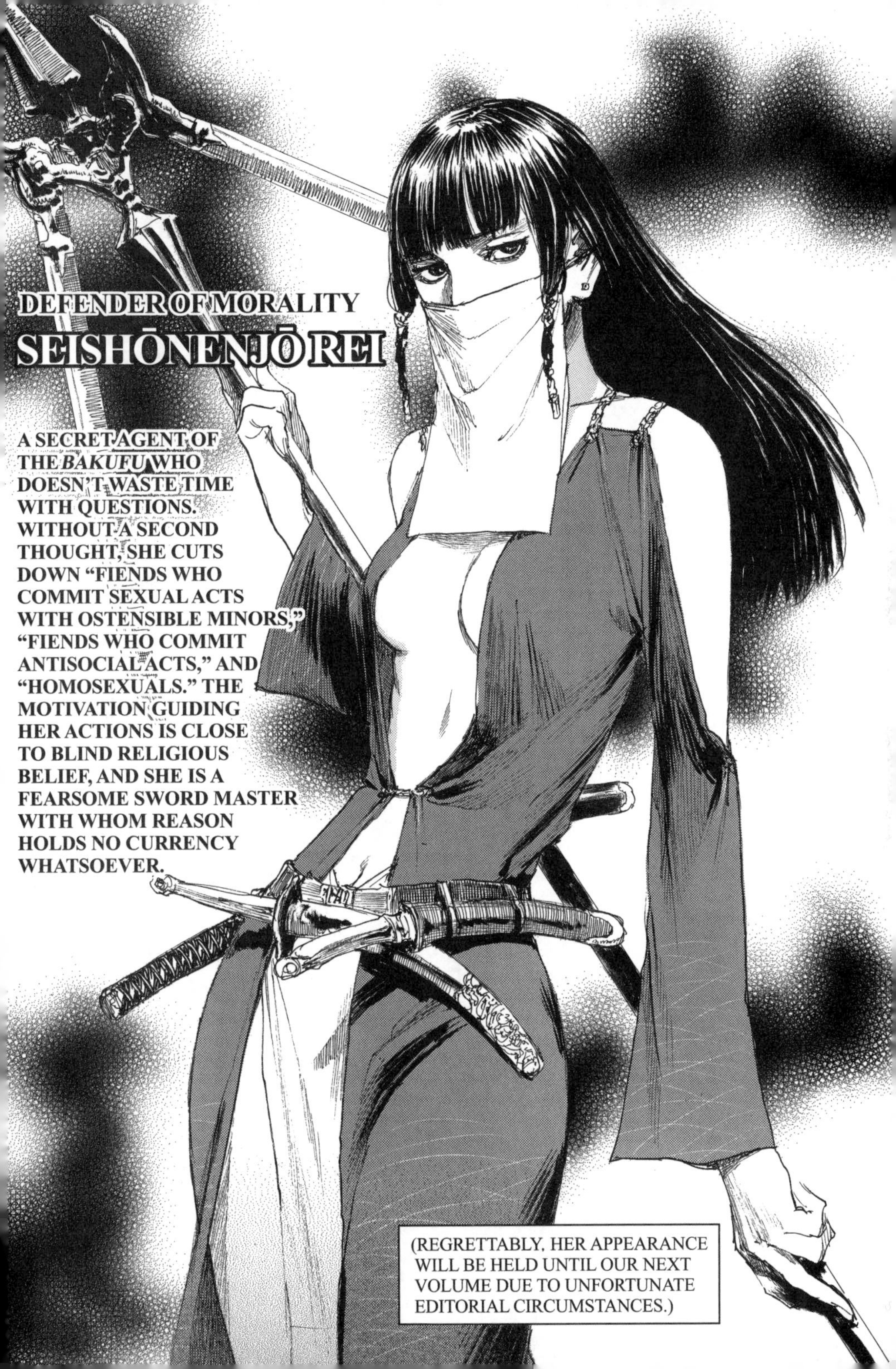
DEFENDER OF MORALITY
SEISHŌNENJŌ REI
A SECRET AGENT OF THE *BAKUFU* WHO DOESN'T WASTE TIME WITH QUESTIONS. WITHOUT A SECOND THOUGHT, SHE CUTS DOWN "FIENDS WHO COMMIT SEXUAL ACTS WITH OSTENSIBLE MINORS," "FIENDS WHO COMMIT ANTISOCIAL ACTS," AND "HOMOSEXUALS." THE MOTIVATION GUIDING HER ACTIONS IS CLOSE TO BLIND RELIGIOUS BELIEF, AND SHE IS A FEARSOME SWORD MASTER WITH WHOM REASON HOLDS NO CURRENCY WHATSOEVER.
(REGRETTABLY, HER APPEARANCE WILL BE HELD UNTIL OUR NEXT VOLUME DUE TO UNFORTUNATE EDITORIAL CIRCUMSTANCES.)

GLOSSARY

bakufu: (1) The central government originally established in Edo (today's Tokyo) by the warlord Tokugawa Ieyasu. (2) The bureaucracy that grew up around the Tokugawa shoguns.

chan: Honorific used to show affection, most often toward young people and sometimes between close friends.

daimyō: Ruler of a *han*, or feudal fiefdom. By the late Edo period of *Blade of the Immortal*, the shogunate had evolved into a de facto central government, with only a few unruly *han* resisting assimilation.

dōjō: A school for combat and self-defense training in martial arts; here, a training center for swordsmanship.

dono: Archaic honorific used to show respect, usually for someone of higher rank.

Edo: Capital of premodern Japan, later renamed Tokyo.

han: A feudal estate or fiefdom.

hana-gumi: The "flower group" or "flower team" that Habaki Kagimura has put together to help him kill off the Ittō-ryū—these are the more elite fighters.

hara-kiri: Ritual suicide by disembowelment.

hebi-gumi: The "snake group" or "snake team" that Habaki Kagimura has put together to help defeat the Ittō-ryū—these are the less-skilled fighters in Kagimura's small army.

Ittō-ryū: The radical sword school of Anotsu Kagehisa.

kenshi: A swordsman or swordswoman, not necessarily born into the samurai caste.

kessen-chū: The "sacred bloodworms." A person infected by them cannot die but feels pain like a mortal.

kōgi: The Tokugawa shogunate, which is also referred to as the Tokugawa *bakufu* and the Edo *bakufu*.

Mugai-ryū: Sword school of the Akagi assassins; literally, "without form." Created and then disbanded by Habaki Kagimura, the Mugai-ryū included Giichi, Hyakurin, the evil Shira, and the deceased Shinriji.

Mutenichi-ryū: The sword school led by Rin's father (now deceased), destroyed by Anotsu Kagehisa.

palanquin: An enclosed travelers' litter carried on poles on the shoulders of bearers.

Rokki-dan: *Rokki* means "six demons," and *Rokki-dan* means "band of six demons." They are Habaki Kagimura's new group of warriors— a small army set to take down Anotsu Kagehisa and the Ittō-ryū.

ryū: A sword school.

sama: Honorific used to show respect, mainly referring to people who are much higher in rank and sincerely admired.

san: Honorific used to show respect, usually when addressing equals.

shinobi: Ninja.

shogun: Title for the former military dictator of Japan.

tōshu: Leader; master.

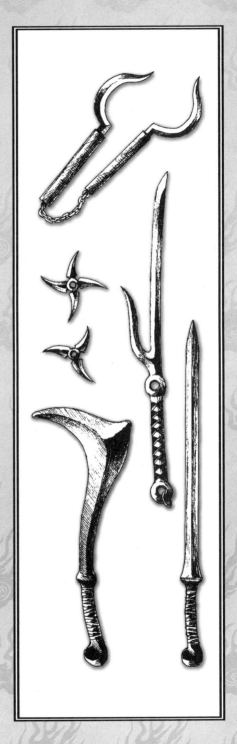

ALSO BY HIROAKI SAMURA
SAMURA'S FIRST SHORT STORY COLLECTION!
NOW AVAILABLE FROM DARK HORSE MANGA!
(ISBN 978-1-59307-622-1)

Hiroaki Samura's Eisner Award–winning manga epic

BLADE OF THE IMMORTAL

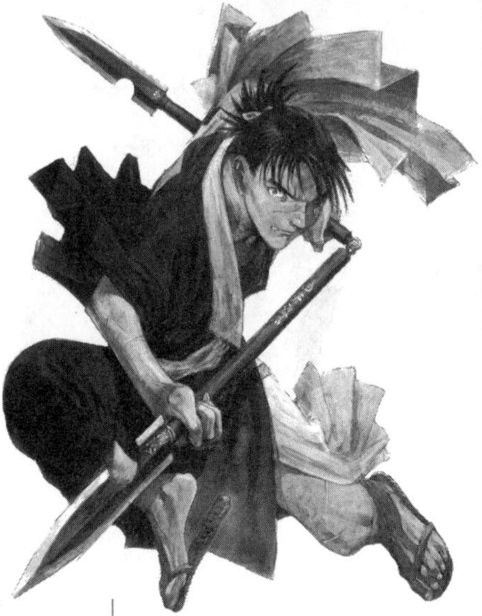

Volume 1: Blood of a Thousand
ISBN 978-1-56971-239-9
$14.99

Volume 2: Cry of the Worm
ISBN 978-1-56971-300-6
$14.99

Volume 3: Dreamsong
ISBN 978-1-56971-357-0
$14.99

Volume 4: On Silent Wings
ISBN 978-1-56971-412-6
$14.99

Volume 5: On Silent Wings II
ISBN 978-1-56971-444-7
$14.99

Volume 6: Dark Shadows
ISBN 978-1-56971-469-0
$14.99

Volume 7: Heart of Darkness
ISBN 978-1-56971-531-4
$16.99

Volume 8: The Gathering
ISBN 978-1-56971-546-8
$15.99

Volume 9: The Gathering II
ISBN 978-1-56971-560-4
$15.99

Volume 10: Secrets
ISBN 978-1-56971-746-2
$16.99

Volume 11: Beasts
ISBN 978-1-56971-741-7
$14.99

Volume 12: Autumn Frost
ISBN 978-1-56971-991-6
$16.99

Volume 13: Mirror of the Soul
ISBN 978-1-59307-218-6
$17.99

Volume 14: Last Blood
ISBN 978-1-59307-321-3
$17.99

Volume 15: Trickster
ISBN 978-1-59307-468-5
$16.99

Volume 16: Shortcut
ISBN 978-1-59307-723-5
$16.99

Volume 17: On the Perfection of Anatomy
ISBN 978-1-59307-782-2
$16.99

Volume 18: The Sparrow Net
ISBN 978-1-59307-871-3
$19.99

Volume 19: Badger Hole
ISBN 978-1-59307-969-7
$17.99

Volume 20: Demon Lair
ISBN 978-1-59582-199-7
$19.99

Volume 21: Demon Lair II
ISBN 978-1-59582-323-6
$19.99

Volume 22: Footsteps
ISBN 978-1-59582-443-1
$19.99

Volume 23: Scarlet Swords
ISBN 978-1-59582-671-8
$19.99

Volume 24: Massacre
ISBN 978-1-59582-751-7
$19.99

Volume 25: Snowfall at Dawn
ISBN 978-1-59582-883-5
$19.99

Volume 26: Blizzard
ISBN 978-1-61655-098-1
$19.99

Volume 27: Mist on the Spider's Web
ISBN 978-1-61655-215-2
$19.99

Volume 28: Raining Chaos
ISBN 978-1-61655-321-0
$19.99

Also by Hiroaki Samura:

Hiroaki Samura's Emerald and Other Stories
ISBN 978-1-61655-065-3
$12.99

Ohikkoshi
ISBN 978-1-59307-622-1
$12.99

The Art of Blade of the Immortal
ISBN 978-1-59582-512-4
$29.99

AVAILABLE AT YOUR LOCAL COMICS SHOP OR BOOKSTORE • To find a comics shop in your area, call 1-888-266-4226
For more information or to order direct visit DarkHorse.com or call 1-800-862-0052 Mon.–Fri. 9 AM to 5 PM Pacific Time.
*Prices and availability subject to change without notice

DARK HORSE MANGA
DarkHorse.com

EDEN

It's an Endless World!

Volume 1
ISBN 978-1-59307-406-7

Volume 2
ISBN 978-1-59307-454-8

Volume 3
ISBN 978-1-59307-529-3

Volume 4
ISBN 978-1-59307-544-6

Volume 5
ISBN 978-1-59307-634-4

Volume 6
ISBN 978-1-59307-702-0

Volume 7
ISBN 978-1-59307-765-5

Volume 8
ISBN 978-1-59307-787-7

Volume 9
ISBN 978-1-59307-851-5

Volume 10
ISBN 978-1-59307-957-4

Volume 11
ISBN 978-1-59582-244-4

Volume 12
ISBN 978-1-59582-296-3

Volume 13
ISBN 978-1-59582-763-0

Volume 14
ISBN 978-1-61655-288-6

$12.99 each

AVAILABLE AT YOUR LOCAL COMICS SHOP OR BOOKSTORE!

To find a comics shop in your area, call 1-888-266-4226.
For more information or to order direct visit
DarkHorse.com or call 1-800-862-0052, Mon.–
Fri. 9 A.M. to 5 P.M. Pacific Time. *Prices and
availability subject to change without notice.

Eden © Hiroki Endo. First published
in Japan by Kodansha Ltd.,
Tokyo. Publication rights for these
English editions arranged through
Kodansha Ltd. (BL 7041)

DARK HORSE MANGA

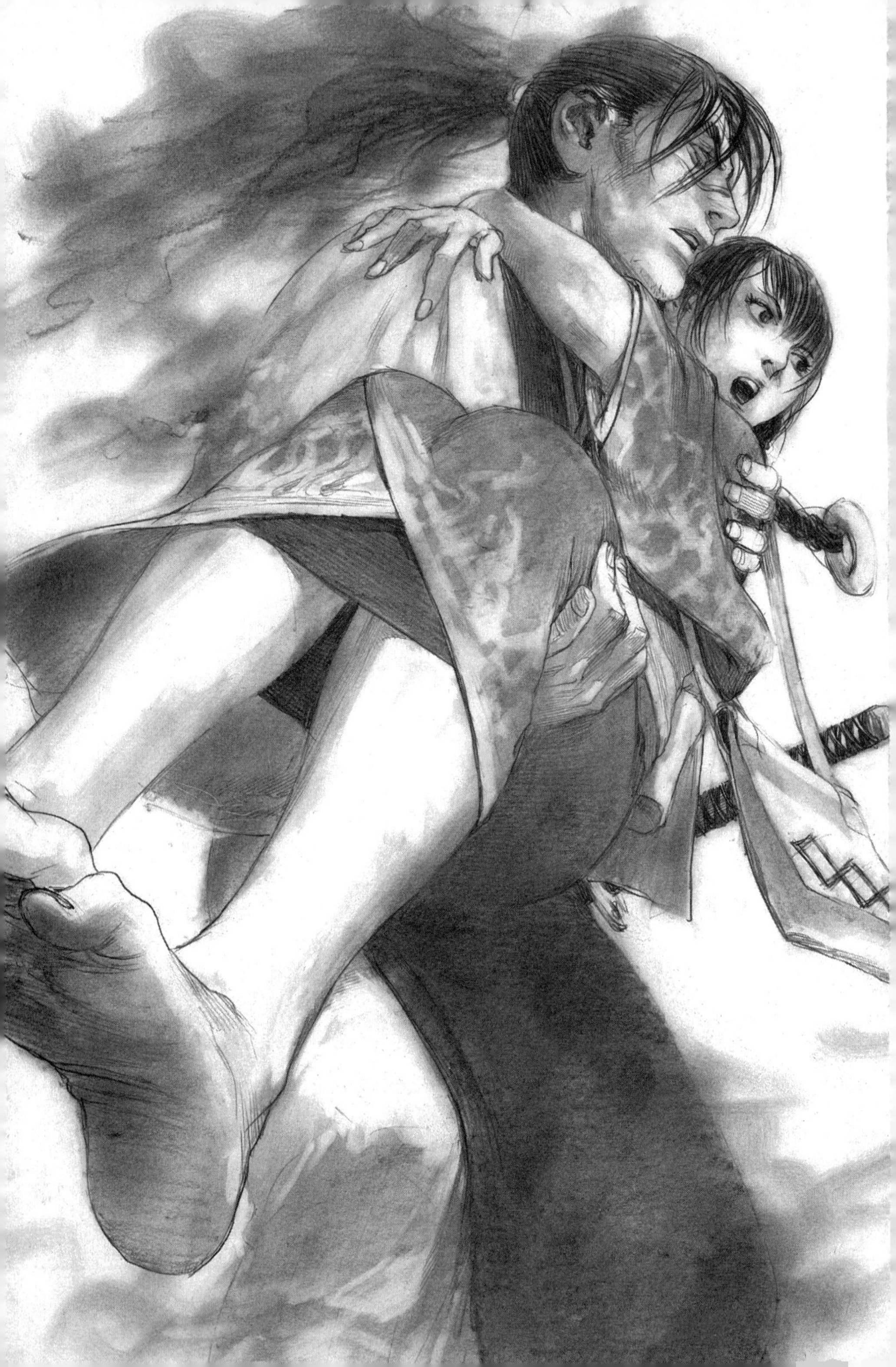

art and story
HIROAKI SAMURA

translation
Kumar Sivasubramanian

English adaptation
Tomoko Saito and Philip R. Simon

lettering and retouch
Tomoko Saito

Raining Chaos

DARK HORSE MANGA™

ABOUT THE TRANSLATION

The Swastika

The main character in *Blade of the Immortal*, Manji, has taken the "crux gammata" as both his name and his personal symbol. This symbol is also known as the *swastika*, a name derived from the Sanskrit *svastika* (meaning "welfare," from *su* — "well" + *asti* — "he is"). As a symbol of prosperity and good fortune, the swastika was widely used throughout the ancient world (for example, appearing often on Mesopotamian coinage), including North and South America, and has been used in Japan as a symbol of Buddhism since ancient times. To be precise, the symbol generally used by Japanese Buddhists is the *sauvastika*, which moves in a counterclockwise direction, and is called the *manji* in Japanese. The sauvastika generally stands for night, and often for magical practices. The swastika, whose arms point in a clockwise direction, is generally considered a solar symbol. It was this version (the *hakenkreuz*) that was perverted by the Nazis. It is important that readers understand that the *swastika* has ancient and honorable origins, and it is those that apply to this story, which takes place in the eighteenth century (ca. 1782–83). *There is no anti-Semitic or pro-Nazi meaning behind the use of the symbol in this story. Those meanings did not exist until after 1910.*

The Artwork

The author of *Blade of the Immortal* requested that we make an effort to avoid mirror imaging his artwork. Some manga are first copied in a mirror image in order to facilitate the left-to-right reading of the pages. However, Mr. Samura decided that he would rather see his pages reversed via the technique of cutting up the panels and repasting them in reverse order. While we feel that this often leads to problems in panel-to-panel continuity, we place primary importance on the wishes of the creator. Therefore, most of *Blade of the Immortal* has been produced using the "cut and paste" technique. There are, of course, some sequences where it was impossible to do this, and mirror-imaged panels or pages were used instead.

The Sound Effects & Dialogue

Since some of Mr. Samura's sound effects are integral parts of the artwork, the decision was made to leave those in their original Japanese. When it was crucial to the understanding of the panel that the sound effect be in English, however, Mr. Samura chose to redraw the panel. We hope readers will view the unretouched sound effects as essential portions of Mr. Samura's extraordinary artwork. In addition, Mr. Samura's treatment of dialogue is quite different from that featured in average samurai manga and is considered to be one of the things that has made *Blade of the Immortal* such a huge hit in Japan. Mr. Samura has mixed a variety of linguistic styles in this fantasy story, where some characters speak in the mannered style of old Japan, while others speak as if they were street-corner punks from a bad area of modern-day Tokyo. The anachronistic slang used by some of the characters in the English translation reflects the unusual mix of speech patterns from the original Japanese text.